HARVARD STUDIES
IN BUSINESS HISTORY

HARVARD STUDIES IN BUSINESS HISTORY
VIII

Edited by N. S. B. Gras

STRAUS PROFESSOR OF BUSINESS HISTORY

GRADUATE SCHOOL OF BUSINESS ADMINISTRATION

GEORGE F. BAKER FOUNDATION

HARVARD UNIVERSITY

LONDON : GEOFFREY CUMBERLEGE

OXFORD UNIVERSITY PRESS

A Whitesmith at Work

THE WHITESMITHS OF TAUNTON

A History of Reed & Barton 1824–1943

BY

GEORGE SWEET GIBB, M.B.A.

RESEARCH ASSISTANT IN BUSINESS HISTORY
GRADUATE SCHOOL OF BUSINESS ADMINISTRATION
GEORGE F. BAKER FOUNDATION
HARVARD UNIVERSITY

CAMBRIDGE, MASSACHUSETTS
HARVARD UNIVERSITY PRESS
1946

Second Printing

To

MY WIFE

CONTENTS

PART I

THE EARLY STRUGGLE FOR EXISTENCE, 1824–1836

PART II

GROWTH AND INDUSTRIAL LEADERSHIP OF THE FIRM UNDER HENRY G. REED, 1837–1860

PART III

GEORGE BRABROOK AND THE SHIFT TO A MARKETING EMPHASIS, 1860–1900

PART IV

FINANCIAL CONSOLIDATION UNDER
WILLIAM B. H. DOWSE, 1901–1923

PART V

THE RECENT PERIOD, 1923–1943

ILLUSTRATIONS

TABLES

CHARTS

EDITOR'S INTRODUCTION

SOME YEARS AGO a colleague suggested that a history of Reed & Barton, a firm with a long experience as silversmiths, would be decidedly worth while. On inquiry, I found that Mr. Sinclair Weeks, president of the company, was favorably inclined to the idea if there were satisfactory records. On visiting the factory in Taunton, I was informed there were probably no records, for they had been discarded when repairs were being made to the roof of the building in which they had been stored — repairs necessitated by the great hurricane. On a second visit many accounts, letter books, catalogues, and miscellanea were found in the attic and especially in one of the vaults. Returning home that night I was caught in the big blizzard (1940). But the documents had been unearthed, and afterwards they were deposited in the Baker Library. Research on the history actually began late in January, 1941.

Deciding upon a man to undertake the study and writing was easy, for I remembered the quiet, promising student, Mr. George S. Gibb, who had already taken a position as an accountant. Mr. Gibb had completed two years of study of business administration, including a course in business history. Moreover, he had spent two years in the study of design, and, coming from the Taunton district, he had jewelry and silverware in his blood. Everything went propitiously till the War came along. Faithful in all things, Mr. Gibb worked hard to finish his manuscript. As Ensign Gibb, he was graduated from the Navy Supply School at the Harvard School of Business Administration and assigned to duty on the high seas. Besides competence and loyalty, Ensign Gibb displays great modesty in all his work. In the present book, we can rarely see the great amount of study that lies in a single statement of generalization or even of fact.

The materials available for this history are the Reed & Barton Collection at the Baker Library, the firm's records in the Boston office and in the Taunton plant, correspondence between the author and various former employees and others, and conversations with executives and workmen. The records in the Old Colony Historical Society provided background and invaluable direct information for the early period.

The story that Mr. Gibb unfolds is one of metals and men. The firm got its start in supplanting pewter by Britannia ware, then progressed in plated silverware, and reached its present distinction in sterling silverware.

The men who created Reed & Barton have been a cross section of America. They have worked hard, devised new methods, and contrived new procedures. But like their compatriots, they have borrowed much from abroad — ideas, ideals, and skill. Such borrowing has been the substance, though not the heart, of America. The frontier influence was but a temporary throw-back in American up-building. What has counted in our mature growth has been the infiltration of Anglo-Saxon and Latin-Teutonic culture. Every nation has its Nordic weakness, which, however, need not be an obsession. A feeling of political independence has continued to reject a recognition of our indebtedness to a foreign country, particularly England, although much of two-thirds of our history has lain in political, commercial, and financial revolutions away from dependence upon England. The cultural revolution has not yet come. At any rate, this history throws light on some of the essentials of both our creative work and our borrowing.

The history of Reed & Barton exemplifies the business systems that have come and gone. The first partners in the firm were clearly petty capitalists who operated in a local and coastal market. Through hard work and ingenuity, they pioneered in their part of the American industrial revolution. There was little or no mercantile capitalism in the history of the firm. The merchants of Boston and Providence did not buy up the product for sale in distant parts. And also no such persons stood ready to contribute capital and administrative ability to an industry which in early days sorely needed them both. The great development came when the workshop of the petty capitalists became the factory of industrial capitalism (the 1830's to about 1900). The usual development occurred in this industrial capitalistic stage. The hold-over of petty capitalistic influence was strong, especially in Henry Reed, who for much of his 73 years of service was a dominant figure in the firm. He was essentially a production man who lingered long at the bench and who would have probably wrecked the firm in the downtrend in prices and profits (1866–97), if someone else had not been available to counteract his emphasis on production and neglect of marketing. The necessary leader was found in George Brabrook, who increasingly from the 1870's till 1907 was the savior of the company through his able management of marketing. Brabrook's weakness was finance, of which he was also in charge. The needed financial competence was supplied first by Dowse and then by Mr. Weeks from 1901 to the present. By them, many of the aspects of financial capitalism were introduced into the firm. Neither had inside experience in the company. Both continued to live elsewhere and to be occupied with other matters as well as the administration of Reed & Barton. Both concentrated on policy-formulation, leaving management to trusted aids, largely introduced from the outside.

Beyond all else, both Dowse and Mr. Weeks have emphasized finance, that is, the over-all result of the business. Dowse had a reservoir of financial strength which could be used to aid and support Reed & Barton in time of need. Without selling securities to the public, as an investment banker would have done in order to raise more capital, he stood ready to provide funds through the use of his personal and family fortune. Since the days of Dowse there has been no occasion to endorse the notes of Reed & Barton and no need for borrowing funds, other than from time to time to provide temporary working capital.

The latest stage in the history of Reed & Barton is national capitalism. This has not entered by the door of the New Deal, which apparently had little effect upon the firm, but through the War which has gripped the company as in a vise. Through the control of raw material, the government shut off civilian production. Through its own necessities, the government reached out for the production of instruments of war. The firm was patriotic and willing to coöperate in war work. What permanent effect there will be remains to be seen.

The story of Reed & Barton is the history of continuous co-operation of men and women, executives and workmen, to turn out a high-class product which the American public will like and will buy. The life history of such a business gives us the greater reality — the real inside story of what happened and how it happened, how some men put pressure on others, and how these yielded or resisted but worked on in informal co-operation. Such is the stuff of social evolution. Such is the life that men live.

Reed & Barton is over a century old but it is up to the minute in its war work. Its walls are heavy with solid brick but its machinery is working with brisk nimbleness. Many of its workers are old or aging but its products are fresh and shiny. A stream divides the plant but there is no breach in the goodwill of workers and management. There is no cafeteria for the workers but that's because so many walk home to lunch. There is emphasis on machine production but there's no neglect of human factors. There's no formal pension system but no employee is cast off because of old age or sickness. New men are brought in from the outside but there's a strong preference for the men who grow up in the plant. Every effort is made to lead in design but there is no joy in creations which fly by night and are gone. The owners of the plant are no longer close at hand but their hearts are not absent. There is no soft sentimentalism on the part of management but there is a deep respect for the worth of every grimy hand. Leadership is expected from the experts but it is found burning brightly at the bench as well. There is no strife except the struggle for creative production and each man plays his part and is honored for his work.

The men who have worked in Reed & Barton have been chiefly local people who have learned the trade through apprenticeship and proudly watched their firm, their family, and their town grow around them. Mr. J. H. Martin, vice-president in charge of sales, is a good illustration of this. There has been a continuous infiltration from the outside commonly through general migration from foreign countries, especially Great Britain, but sometimes through migration specially for work in Reed & Barton's. But whichever the stream, there has been complete merging in the community of Taunton. The outside has made its contributions of able men almost by way of loans. Three of the chief executives today came from the outside and still live outside. Of course, their loyalty and ability to serve suffer in no way from this fact. The rise of specialized schools has had some but not great influence on Reed & Barton. Practical engineers and designers have entered to play their parts. The author of this book seems to be the first graduate of a school of business administration to be a factor, however slight, in the company's history. I believe he has played his part well.

Reed & Barton has made this history possible. The officials have given records, information, and criticism. They have left the author free to formulate his own generalizations and state his own opinions. They have financed both research and publication but in an admirably detached fashion, which bodes well for business if generally adopted. Without the coöperation of

Mr. Sinclair Weeks the work could not have been undertaken, and without the help of company officials and workers it would have been a failure.

N. S. B. GRAS

June, 1943

AUTHOR'S PREFACE

THE ASSISTANCE of many people has gone into the preparation of this book, and the interest and encouragement encountered in every quarter has made the author's experience pleasant throughout.

Without exception, the coöperation extended to the author by the Reed & Barton management and employees has been hearty. Mr. Weeks has met every request promptly, and has spared no effort to see that all data were made available for study. At the factory, Mr. Arthur Ashworth laid open sources of information and extended every courtesy. Mr. C. A. Rivard and Mr. Russell G. Scott contributed much in the way of material aid and encouragement. Mr. William T. Hurley, Jr., placed the facilities of the advertising department at the author's disposal; his work resulted in the jacket of the book and a large number of the illustrations for the last six chapters. Mr. J. H. Martin contributed much material to the history, and his great interest in the company's past proved an indispensable aid in the preparation of the book. The personal reminiscences which he recorded have preserved a significant and perishable segment of Reed & Barton's history. Retired company employees in Taunton have also been unstinting in their aid, without which certain sections of the history could not have been written. Every visit with them has been profitable, and a great personal pleasure to the author. The assistance of Mr. N. A. Cushman, Mr. David Howe, Mr. Mark Anthony, and Mr. Percy B. Minchew is sincerely appreciated. The late Frank W. Knox had preserved, both in the form of personal reminiscence and in documentary material, information of a highly essential nature. His death in 1942 terminated a devoted career with the company and a friendship which the author recalls with pleasant memory.

Mr. Frank Walcott Hutt, of the Old Colony Historical Society, rendered innumerable favors and placed a large store of material at the author's disposal. Greatest credit is due Mr. Hutt and the Society for preserving so fine a collection of data on Taunton history, and for making the material so readily accessible. The International Silver Company and Mr. W. G. Snow, company historian, placed at the disposal of the author the finest collection of published and manuscript trade material. Mr. Snow, in addition, read, corrected, and augmented those sections of the history which touched on the Connecticut factories.

Mr. Ledlie Irwin Laughlin, of Princeton, New Jersey, gave much valuable information about early Britannia workers and lent photographs which would not otherwise have been obtainable. His study *Pewter in America* was frequently referred to in the preparation of the first chapters of the Reed & Barton history. Mr. Charles Vanderveer of Freehold, New Jersey, kindly extended permission for the use of two plates from J. B. Kerfoot's *American Pewter*.

In addition the author is indebted to Miss Helen Ballou, of Attleboro, Massachusetts, for her fine reconstructive drawings of early company buildings and factory scenes; to Mr. Richmond F. Bingham, of the Harvard Graduate School of Business Administration, for his careful preparation of the charts; to Mrs. Lewis H. Benton, of Taunton, for the photograph upon which the reconstruction of the Fayette Street shop was based; to Mrs. Farrell, of Reed & Barton, for the many hours she spent in preparation of illustrations; to Mr. Jack Fisher, of Reed & Barton, for several fine photographs taken in the factory; to Mr. George A. Rich, of Attleboro, for reading certain sections of the manuscript; to Miss Maydell Murphy of the Taunton Public Library; to Mr. C. E. Almy for much valuable information about William Dowse; to Miss Margaret Dowse of Newton, Massachusetts; to Mr. Roger Hallowell, of Reed & Barton; and to many others whose kindness and aid is remembered with appreciation.

Professor N. S. B. Gras of the Department of Business History, Harvard Graduate School of Business Administration, has stood ready on every occasion to advise and assist. His direction of the project has been clear, farsighted, and at all times stimulating. To work under his guidance has been a very real privilege.

Dr. Henrietta M. Larson and Dr. Ralph M. Hower in the Business History Department proved most willing to assist when the occasion presented. Mrs. Elsie Hight Bishop's editing has been constructive, her proofreading expert, and the reader will find the index which she prepared pertinent and usable. Miss Josepha M. Perry's assistance in research and consolidation of findings has been patient, thorough, and indispensable. Her interest in the work at hand has been responsible for uncovering some of the most valuable details of early company operations, and her response to the demands made upon her has contributed much to every phase of the study.

Most of the manuscript was typewritten by the author's wife, Ruth W. Gibb. This task in itself was no small one, but an even greater contribution was her constructive criticism of the work in progress and her unfailing support and encouragement throughout.

GEORGE SWEET GIBB

July, 1943

PART I

THE EARLY STRUGGLE
FOR EXISTENCE
1824–1836

CHAPTER I

MEN AND METAL

THE STORY of Reed & Barton follows the efforts of men and women in a century-old firm to secure a comfortable living by providing America with the appointments of luxurious living. It is a story which starts on a fertile plain of southeastern Massachusetts where Yankee farmers, traders, and fledgling industrialists had gathered together to form the town of Taunton. It takes us first on the decks of coasting schooners down Taunton Great River to Narragansett Bay, and later it leads east and south and west to markets of the world. It follows the vicissitudes of business through spectacular failures and great triumphs, and it tells of sweat, determination, and talent. It is a story of balance sheets and dividends, but far more than this it is a human story of everyday people.

PIONEER FIRM AND BRITANNIA WARE

The firm of Reed & Barton owes its birth and continued existence to the demands of American people for something finer than their fathers had possessed. This process of betterment characterizes all phases of civilization, but has never been better demonstrated than in the centuries-old drive for a more comfortable home and a maximum of luxury. Wooden platters and bowls surrendered their place of honor on the tables of the wealthy to the new and fashionable pewter. Wooden ware left by way of the servants' quarters, and ended its career in the hovels of the poor. Pewter enjoyed a brief triumph; then it, too, began to be relegated to dusty top shelves as porcelain and china made their bow to fame.[1] Metal workers fought the spreading popularity of glass with a new British alloy called Britannia ware, and this is where the story of Reed & Barton begins. The origins of the firm reach back to a group of little-known men and a company that bore a different name.

Two village mechanics, Isaac Babbitt and William Crossman, founded their partnership in 1824. From these men and this event evolved the Reed & Barton organization. A continuity of management and, to a lesser degree, a continuity of ownership, characterized this evolutionary process. True, the partnership of Babbitt & Crossman was itself short-lived, but in its brief existence a product was created, techniques were devised, and a working force built up which were later to form the nucleus of Reed & Barton. The developmental period saw a succession of companies — Babbitt & Crossman; Babbitt, Crossman & Company; Crossman, West & Leonard; Taunton Britannia Manufacturing Company; Leonard, Reed & Barton; and, since 1840, Reed & Barton. Titles changed, but in tradition and in fact each company was but an enlarged edition of its predecessor, and the history of Babbitt & Crossman is the history of Reed & Barton.

While it is often difficult to designate exact starting points with perfect historical accuracy, and to say, "It happened here; these men were present, did this, and said that," yet certain rare personal reminiscences have preserved for us some such information about how Isaac Babbitt neglected his jewelry shop to conduct an experiment and found an industry in Taunton.[2]

The firm of Babbitt & Crossman was as yet unplanned when Isaac Babbitt opened his jewelry store at Number 3 Merchants' Row, Taunton, in 1822.[3] In this venture the young man sustained family tradition, and followed in the footsteps of uncle Ebenezer Babbitt, cousin Seth, and older brother Charles.[4] It was behind the watch-hung, ornament-littered window of the latter that Isaac Babbitt, and probably William Crossman as well, served apprenticeship.[5] The Babbitts were the gadget-makers of Taunton — a family which consistently bequeathed

ISAAC BABBITT, 1799–1862

to each new generation some degree of mechanical ingenuity and manual skill.[6] These talents were usually employed in, though not confined to, the jewelers' trade, for in these early days the village jeweler manufactured many of the products which he sold, and serviced the minor mechanical needs of the community.

Isaac Babbitt's store did not differ greatly from the other small shops upon which the dust of Main Street settled. It, too, was an insignificant venture by which an independent craftsman received a modest living. But, as in many other such tiny establishments throughout the nation, a new spirit stirred behind the shop window — a spirit which historians were later to call Industrial Revolution, but which Taunton in 1822 labeled youthful impatience. For Babbitt was not content to sit behind his counter and listen for customers' footsteps on the board walk of Merchants' Row. Selling trinkets and repairing watches did not hold the young man's attention nor satisfy his urge to experiment; accordingly, he fitted out a small shed at the rear of the store for a workshop. There he employed his leisure turning out pewter lather-boxes, looking-glass frames, and other small articles which could be cast in his rough molds and finished on a foot lathe.[7] As time went on, Babbitt's preoccupation with metal-working grew, and his interest came to center more in the back-alley workshop than in the main-street store. Throughout 1823 he was often to be found engrossed in discussion of pewter and other alloys with William W. Porter, whose experience in the pewter-button shop of his father provided a bond of mutual interest and assistance.

It was Babbitt's connection with the retail jewelry trade, however, which brought forcibly to his attention the fact that more and more people were asking for the shiny new Britannia metal tableware from English factories. The jeweler and his friend, Porter, speculated often upon the nature of this new alloy, which was so superior in appearance and working qualities to old-

fashioned pewter, and the store saw less and less of Babbitt as
the germ of an idea took root.

Antimony, copper, tin, lead, zinc — all went into the melting
pot in countless different combinations as Babbitt labored to discover the constituents of Britannia metal. Melt after melt was
discarded, but the experiments went on. In the absence of exact
metallurgical knowledge, self-taught skill and rare native in-
ventiveness were brought to bear on the problem. Yankee stubbornness conceded no defeat. And through all disappointments
the thought that Britannia ware could be manufactured in
Taunton persisted in Babbitt's mind.

One day early in 1824, William Porter pushed open the workshop door, and stepped into the midst of the founding of an
enterprise. Babbitt looked up from a piece of metal which he
was examining. "Well, Porter, I believe I have got it at last, and
if you will help turn the rolls we will see if it will prove good
metal." [8]

What happened next is told by William Porter's son, Edmund: [9]

As a singular coincidence, William A. West, another of the coterie of
young metal men (and who was to be heard from later) happened in at
that time, and taking hold of the rolls (a set of jeweler's hand rolls) with
Porter with Babbitt to guide the plate, the first sheet of Britannia . . .
was soon before them. This was carefully tried and tested and pronounced a success.

Babbitt returned to his store elated with the results of his experiment, but Taunton might well have waited longer for its
first Britannia ware if an experiment in Castleton, Vermont,
had not been abandoned.

William W. Crossman, born into a prominent Taunton family in 1794,[10] elected to enter the jewelers' trade, and completed
his apprenticeship just as young Isaac Babbitt was being initiated
into the mysteries of the profession.[11] The Crossmans were retailers, but for some reason William scorned the family's retail

clothing business and departed from Taunton to seek his fortune in a jewelry store in Castleton. Of this venture, little is
known, but evidently it did not measure up to the young man's
expectations. Perhaps the northern farmers frowned on the
frivolities of life, or it may have been that he saw greater possibilities elsewhere. Whatever the reason, the retailing experiment was abandoned, and in 1823 the jeweler returned to
Taunton.[12]

Once back in his native environment, William Crossman
naturally sought out his old-time acquaintances in the Taunton
jewelry trade, and he probably followed with interest the
metal-mixing which was going on in the Babbitt workshop.
If any disappointment over the result of the Castleton venture
remained in Crossman's mind, it was speedily dispelled in early
1824 by the excitement attending Isaac Babbitt's discovery, and
in May the two men formed the partnership of Babbitt &
Crossman.

The immediate object of the partnership was to merge the experience and resources of the two men in ownership and management of the store at Number 3 Merchants' Row. On May 7,
1824, a newspaper notice informed the public of the alliance.[13]

There is no indication that Babbitt & Crossman ever engaged
in the "Gold and Silversmith business" in any other than a retailing capacity, and the only evidence of the success of the store
lies in its continued existence. In the summer of 1824 the partners were advertising briskly in the local newspaper, and the
activities which went on in the modest little shop became more
diversified with the growing abilities of its proprietors.[14]

Partnership in the retail venture, however, was only a prelude
to more ambitious plans, and the jewelry store may have been
kept in operation in order to finance those plans. Carefully,
throughout the summer, the results of Babbitt's experiment
were weighed, and at last the partners decided to venture into
the manufacture of Britannia ware.

No protracted planning period followed this decision, nor was an elaborate organization devised to put it into effect. With unstudied versatility and the typical petty capitalist faculty for getting things done, the partners proceeded at once to raise cap-

Copartnership Formed.

THE Subscribers would inform their friends and the public, that they have formed a connection in the Gold and Silversmith business, under the firm of *BABBITT & CROSSMAN*, and will continue the business in all its various branches, at the Store No. 3, Merchants Row, formerly occupied by Isaac Babbitt—where they intend also to keep on hand a general assortment of Jewelry, &c.

ISAAC BABBITT,
WILLIAM W. CROSSMAN.

Notice of the Formation of the Babbitt & Crossman Partnership
Taunton *Free Press*, May 14, 1824

ital, select a factory site, design, build, and install machinery, and train workmen.

Of these diverse necessities, that of financing the start of the enterprise seems to have provided the least difficulty. Both Babbitt and Crossman had inherited small family competences, and the initial financial requirements of the Britannia venture were modest. The partnership was fortunate, moreover, in securing an accessible and inexpensive room in which to commence operations. In September, 1824, Roswell Ballard was advertising floor space for rent in his cloth-dressing mill on

Spring Street. Such a location offered to Babbitt & Crossman room and water power sufficient to serve the enterprise in its early experimental stage without tying up large amounts of capital in real estate. The site, moreover, was a convenient one, pleasantly situated on the banks of the Mill River just down

SHELL, HORN, AND IVORY COMBS.

Babbitt & Crossman,
NO. 3, *MERCHANTS'-ROW*,
RESPECTFULLY inform their friends and the publick generally, that they have on hand and keep constantly for sale,
Clocks, Watches, Time-pieces, Silver and Silver plated Ware, Jewelry,

of all descriptions,
WARRANTED
GOLD BEADS,
Gold, Silver, Steel and Gilt Watch Trimmings,
HARDWARE, &c.
TOGETHER WITH A LARGE AND HANDSOME ASSORTMENT OF
Shell, Horn, and Ivory
COMBS.
——ALSO——
☞The original and genuine *MACASSAR OIL;* first quality ANTIQUE OIL; French POMATUM; PERFUMERY; Naples, Transparent, and *Winsor* SHAVING SOAP.
** All the above articles will be sold on the most accommodating terms for *CASH.*
N. B. *Clocks, Watches and Jewelry,* cleaned and repaired at the shortest notice, at the old stand
No. 3, Merchants'-Row.
Taunton, June 9, 1824.   [67]

BABBITT & CROSSMAN ADVERTISEMENT
Columbian Reporter, and Old Colony Journal

the hill from Main Street [15] and within easy carting distance of Taunton River, the main artery of trade. Ballard's offer appeared to attract the partners, and the space was hired. Shrewdness thus tempered optimism, and, so far as shop commitments were concerned, the way was judiciously left clear for an inexpensive retreat.

Taunton and Its District

The choice of location, though inevitable, perhaps, and conditioned by lack of capital and experience, was a fortunate one. The swift and narrow Mill River was good manufacturing water, but more important still, Taunton was a good manufacturing town.

Like many other Massachusetts communities of 1824, Taunton was too prosperous to be attractive. Main Street was a straggling line of board walks, hitching posts, and obtrusive brick and wooden buildings spreading out in a curving line eastward from the Green toward Taunton River. White colonial mansions and stately elms graced the fringes of town, but colonial charm never hung heavy over the plateau between the Mill and Taunton Rivers, and life there had seldom pursued a quiet, leisurely pace.

Even prehistoric days witnessed active commerce as the hordes of Narragansett Indians migrated north each spring to settle in noisy cantonments along the banks of Mill River and scoop their year's supply of alewives from the shallows.[16] Early English settlers, however, found other uses for the abundant water supply. Saw and grist mills rose on camp sites of the Narragansetts, and Indian dugouts yielded place to river sloops.

Mercantile interests developed early in the town's history, and assumed a prominent place in the life of the community. Taunton itself was available from the coast entirely by water routes, and the Taunton River provided a deep, seventeen-mile-long water highway to the head of Mount Hope Bay.[17] By 1700 small shallops were plying a vigorous trade between Taunton and coastal towns, and in 1800, sixteen schooners and sloops were owned by Taunton merchants alone,[18] while other vessels which were regularly stopping there must have been considerably in excess of this number. With the growth of manufacturing enterprise, the Taunton River transportation system was to become increasingly vital and to provide an economical means of importing bulky raw material and of shipping out finished products.

Within a radius of forty miles there were markets in New Bedford, Providence, Pawtucket, Boston, and many smaller communities more than adequate to provide a flourishing trade for one small town. Transportation facilities, though leaving much to be desired, were about as good as those serving other sections of the country and provided an outlet to markets all the way down the Atlantic seaboard. In 1824 a stage line ran regularly from Taunton to Boston,[19] while boat and wagon communication was maintained with Providence, Newport, and New Bedford, all prominent shipping centers for the coasting and transatlantic trade.

Taunton in 1824 also furnished a wealth of industrial precedent in the metal trades. The abundance of bog iron, water power, and wood proved so attractive to manufacturing interests that Taunton developed a thriving industry at a time when most Massachusetts communities were concerned only with agriculture and trade. As early as 1652 it had entered into an agreement with Henry and James Leonard and Ralph Russell of Braintree, Massachusetts, to set up a "Bloomery Work" on the Two Mile River,[20] and, from this time on, the growth of Taunton's iron industries parallels the growth of Taunton's commerce. Other industries also sprang up in rapid succession, and in 1820 the little town of 4,500 inhabitants boasted nail works, rolling and slitting mills, a foundry, a pottery works, an iron hollow ware manufactory, cotton mills, a calico print works, and many small home industries.[21] Banking facilities were provided by the Taunton Bank, incorporated in 1812 with a capitalization of $100,000, and in 1821 a weekly newspaper was established.[22]

Taunton, then, had an accumulation of broad experience to offer Babbitt & Crossman. Workmen who had grown up in

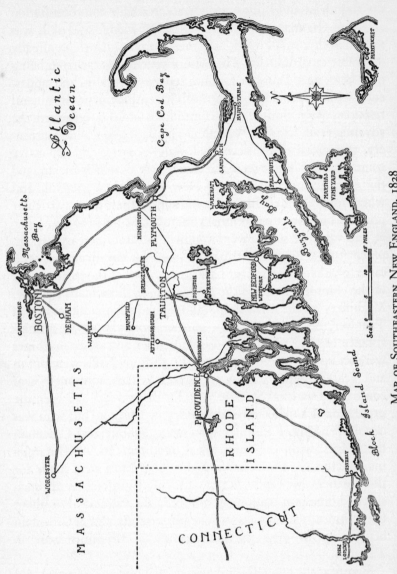

MAP OF SOUTHEASTERN NEW ENGLAND, 1828

the foundries and rolling mills were available for consultation and hire. In 1824 such a backlog of knowledge and skill was rare in such a small town, and contributed much to an already favorable environment. The factory system was far from being new here, and Taunton families looked naturally, and apparently without prejudice, to the mills for employment. If mineral resources were limited, the community at least possessed the advantages of "close settlement, a population apt with machinery, numerous easily developed water-powers, and an active commerce." [23] These were the characteristics which encouraged the early industrialization of New England in general, and when found united in one community, they gave particular promise of more than ordinary manufacturing progress.

The value of such an environment became increasingly apparent to Babbitt & Crossman as plans for the Britannia shop came to be executed, for the background both of the partners and of the community made the realization of those plans possible. Machinery for the small shop was designed and manufactured in Taunton and installed by the partners with the advice and assistance of local mechanics. Several lathes and other machines were set up and a pair of 4″ x 12″ English steel rolls were put in and geared to the mill water wheel.[24] This equipment was constructed by Elias Strange, who for many years had been the proprietor of a tool shop and foundry in Taunton, but who was certainly no more familiar than were Babbitt and Crossman themselves with the mechanical requirements of Britannia manufacturing. Dies, molds, and smaller tools were made for the partners by Caleb Porter, also of Taunton. With such simple homespun equipment and only the vaguest ideas about the technical requirements of the business, Babbitt & Crossman began, late in 1824, the manufacture of Britannia ware in Taunton.

Significantly enough, and wisely, Babbitt & Crossman did not abandon the jewelry store at once. However boldly the little

Spring Street shop breathed defiance at venerable English competitors, its owners realized the great propriety of retaining the Merchants' Row meal ticket. Visions of success in the Britannia trade at this time could not but be clouded by doubt and uncertainty as to what the future might hold. The times presented to new American industries, sharing their uncertain infancy with Babbitt & Crossman, an environment charged with hope for spectacular success, but complicated also by destructive influences, particularly inherent in the background of the Britannia industry at home and abroad.

CHAPTER II

BABBITT & CROSSMAN FACES THE WORLD, 1824

A POTENT DANGER which Babbitt & Crossman faced in 1824 was competition with several English companies long and well established in the trade, for in the early years of the nineteenth century Britannia ware was new only to American manufacturers. The story of Britannia metal in England is interesting, the more so for its very illusiveness, not only for the mystery which surrounds the origin of the metal, but also for the direct influence it exerted on the early history of Reed & Barton.

In order to establish even the approximate period in which English pewterers commenced the manufacture of Britannia ware, we must clearly distinguish between the old alloy, pewter, and the new alloy, Britannia. Of such a definition, Kerfoot says: [1]

> Actually then . . . the tin-copper-antimony alloys that are indubitably fine, and to be called "pewter," merge into those that are progressively less fine, until they come to coincide with our later-day notions of "britannia," so gradually that no hard-and-fast line of differentiation exists between them.

Kerfoot also gives the following "characteristic formulae": [2]

	Parts Tin	Parts Copper	Parts Antimony
Plate pewter	150	3.33	11
Good britannia metal ..	150	3.00	10

These formulae should not be regarded as typical of all pewter or of all Britannia metal. The different combinations which come within the definitions of these two metals are probably as numerous as the makers themselves. Confusion between the two classes of alloys arises from the fact that, although most pewter differs in composition and appearance from Britannia metal, at one point the two metals tend toward identity. Kerfoot, starting with this point, says:[3] ". . . as from a continental divide, *the country runs downhill both ways.* On the pewter slope it declines toward 'leadiness.' On the britannia side it falls off toward 'tinpanishness.'"

In view of these difficulties of definition and classification, the most that can be said is that some time in the middle of the eighteenth century high-content tin alloys were probably first used in the manufacture of tableware, and that such alloys (or the terminology used in referring to such alloys) gradually made the transition from pewter to Britannia.[4]

THE ENGLISH BRITANNIA INDUSTRY

The discovery of Britannia metal may have been the result of fortuitous circumstances, but its widespread adoption and commercialization by English pewterers in the latter part of the eighteenth century and the opening decades of the nineteenth appears to have been a measure consciously designed and adopted to offset disturbing developments in the pewter market. Widespread as was the use of pewter in England at the beginning of the eighteenth century, the competitive influence of pottery and china was already beginning to exert itself and to make inroads on the domestic market which pewter had virtually monopolized for a century.[5] English pewter began to degenerate from its high position as the universally fashionable ware in direct proportion to the increasing popularity of imported and domestic pottery and china. After 1760 the rate of decline accelerated as the great potteries of Wedgwood and Lowestoft came into vigorous existence, and china, porcelain, and pottery began to flow in ever increasing volume from the Chelsea, Bristol, Worcester, and Derby works.

English pewterers also encountered serious competition from

within the metal trade. The discovery of fusion plating in Sheffield in 1743 and widespread commercialization of the process several decades later made ownership of silver tableware and ornament possible for a great many more families than ever before. Not only did pewter suffer from the direct competition with Sheffield plate which existed as a result of partially overlapping price ranges, but the increased quantity of silverware on the market inevitably cheapened pewter and made the possession of ware from the baser metal far less desirable than before. In these unfavorable circumstances pewterers began to seek means of improving their competitive standing, and enlisted the aid of new metals, or old metals with new names. It has been said that the name "Britannia metal" was coined in this era of nationalism to publicize and popularize the alloy, and dignify a "superior grade of pewter with the patriotic and high sounding trade-name." [6]

However potent this advertising scheme may have been as a means of increasing sales, the metal itself had much to offer in tangible values to the purchaser, and represented a distinct improvement over its pewter ancestors in many respects. The new Britannia ware was more durable than pewter — harder, lighter, and more resistant to heat. Its sheen was almost that of silver, and the ware appears to have been more attractive to the silver-conscious market of the time than were its duller pewter counterparts. Most significant of all, the metal lent itself far more readily than did pewter to large-scale production. Because Britannia could be rolled in the sheet and spun into thin-walled vessels over inexpensive wooden molds,[7] production costs were lower, and a much less expensive product could be placed on the market. While Sheffield plate was to make silver available to more and more households of moderate means, Britannia ware was to push the market for shiny, durable, metal table utensils even into the homes of the poor.

However early in the century Britannia ware may have orig-

inated, there is little evidence of its widespread adoption until
after 1780. Unquestionably, many eighteenth-century craftsmen were using alloys which might come under the heading of
Britannia or its first cousin, "white metal," even though not so
designated at the time. It is not, however, the individual craftsman substituting the manufacture of this new alloy for that of
pewter in his home workshop who was responsible for the
great surge of popularity which Britannia ware enjoyed in the
early nineteenth century. For an explanation of this phenome-
non we must turn to Sheffield. Here transpired, for the first
time in the Britannia industry, widespread commercial exploitation of the metal. Frederick Bradbury presents the following
account of the founding of the white-metal or Britannia trade
in Sheffield: [8]

> I have heard it said that Mr. Nathaniel Gower was the first person who
> began this trade. . . . Mr. Gower was an early manufacturer and a very
> respectable one for the trade in its infancy; but Mr. James Vickers, late
> of Garden Street, was the first person who began manufacturing articles
> in the white-metal trade in Sheffield.
>
> About the year 1769 a person was very ill and James visited him. This
> man was in the possession of the receipt how to make white-metal. James
> told him he would give him 5s. for the receipt, and he accepted the offer.
> James tried the receipt and found the metal was a very good colour. He
> then got some spoon moulds and began casting spoons, and getting them
> finished well he had a tolerable sale for them as far as his trade extended.
> He then got moulds for vegetable forks, and these made a variety for the
> market.

The 1787 Sheffield directory mentions James Vickers as utilizing white metal for measures, teapots, castor frames, salts,
spoons, and similar articles, while at the same time a dozen or
more firms were entered as "makers of White-Metal and metal-
framed knives." [9] In 1804 James Dixon established the company which was soon to become the most famous of the English
Britannia manufacturers.

The appearance of these names in the trade directories of

the day publicized a vital new change in the industry — a development with which English textile and iron men had not long since begun to experiment, and the results of which must have been forcibly impressed, by proximity if by nothing else, on Vickers, Gower, Dixon, and the rest. Utilizing the tools which mechanical ingenuity had placed at their disposal, English manufacturers began to operate on a more pretentious scale than ever before. The course of industrialization began to lead the Sheffield Britannia men from workshop to factory — a change made familiar, and possibly less painful, by contemporaneous examples in other lines of enterprise.[10] These early owners were capable craftsmen in their own right, but unlike most of their pewter-making forebears, and on a scale quite unprecedented, they were employers. By 1810 the workbench had progressed far along the path toward becoming the production line, and the multiple operations which the hand craftsmen of earlier days had been forced to master became separated and were made in each instance the specialized function of one or more employees in the factory. Management became as tangible and distinct a task as soldering, and fewer owners were to be found working side by side with their employees in the shop.

BRITANNIA WARE IN AMERICA

As technical progress and growth in textiles and iron in eighteenth-century England had preceded such progress and growth in America, so did the English Britannia industry establish itself and begin to mature even before American craftsmen had emerged from the stage of hand-wrought manufacture. In 1789, when James Vickers was making teapots, measures, castor frames, and spoons and when a dozen other English manufacturers were listed as white-metal workers, American pewterers were apparently unconcerned about the new developments. The metal certainly must have been familiar to them, through imports from England if not from personal experimentation, but the manufacture of Britannia ware on this side of the Atlantic seems to have waited upon the turn of the century. While we know that for many years American pewterers had been using alloys which closely resembled Kerfoot's "good britannia metal," available evidence points to the fact that it was not until the first decade of the nineteenth century that the term Britannia began to be applied to American products, and that pewterers began to differentiate in terminology as well as in formula between the new alloy and fine pewter.[11]

One of the earliest accounts of Britannia manufacturing in this country was written in a diary on February 25, 1814, by the Reverend William Bentley of Salem, Massachusetts.[12]

Capt. Bowditch living in Turner St. below Derby st. informed me this day that he had begun the work of the Britania Ware, which had been carried on for several months with success in Beverly. The manufacture is of zinc & tin, & is rolled out. The articles to which the manufacture is at present confined are teapots & cream cups, & the present demand makes it profitable. From this notice I passed to Beverly & visited Mr. Trask who introduced the manufacture into that place. He was a goldsmith & jeweller, & employs about a dozen hands & sells his work in Boston. Just above his works a Mr. Smith, formerly a cabinet maker, who has gone to the same extent of the same business & the persons he employs are seamen & fishermen. They seem to be pleased with the present success & both of them sell to the same dealers in Boston. . . . At the Brit[ania] ware factory the engraving was done with great facility by tools which Mr. Traske made.

Even as late as 1824, when Babbitt & Crossman commenced operations in the Spring Street mill, the manufacture of Britannia and pewter ware in America seems to have been on a very limited scale and to have been confined, with a few exceptions, to small shops employing only one or two men.[13]

THE CONDITIONS OF TRADE

While these early American craftsmen and industries benefited as a result of temporary immunity from English competition during the years of embargo and the War of 1812, the effects of that competition became increasingly difficult to cope with upon resumption of normal trade relations in 1815, and the decade immediately preceding the founding of Babbitt & Crossman was a difficult one for the metal trades.

A flood of English goods descended on American markets in 1816, the net imports being nearly double those of any preceding year in the country's history. In July of that year a new tariff law went into effect, meeting the country's need for greater revenues with rates higher than any previous peacetime measures. This tariff provided the Britannia and pewter manufacturers with a measure of protection against English competition and allowed the principal raw materials to be imported free of duty, but still it did not seem to put an end to the large inflow of foreign goods. Poor harvest, unemployment, and over-production in England between 1815 and 1819 created a situation in which manufacturers in that country were compelled to sacrifice large stocks of material and finished goods, and American industries suffered in consequence from greatly increased competition.

Unfortunately, statistics for the period are so incomplete that it is virtually impossible to discover how much Britannia and pewter ware was being imported, or to relate such imports to domestic production. Investigations made in connection with the census of 1820, however, furnish some pertinent comments on the general state of trade in industries closely related to the Britannia makers and indicate that the business of most of the reporting companies was severely depressed.[14] That such conditions were entirely attributable to foreign competition is a matter of some doubt. Generally declining prices, a currency inflation crisis in 1819, and local depressions also contributed to the unstable conditions.

To whatever causes the position of American manufacturers in 1820 may be attributed, one result of depression and uncertainty was a growing demand for more tariff protection. Between 1816 and 1824, protectionists eloquently attacked the foreign policy of the government, and demands were loudly made for a "genuine American system" of encouragement to industry. A great organization movement swept the country, resulting in scores of trade associations devoted to the protection and advancement of industrial groups and areas. Finally protectionist efforts were climaxed by passage of the Tariff Act of 1824, which gave American Britannia manufacturers 5 per cent higher duties than before. According to the terms of this law, foreign manufactures of brass, iron, steel, pewter, lead, and tin, and all plated and japanned wares were taxed 25 per cent ad valorem.[15] While this represented a relatively small increase in rates, the effect of the 1824 legislation upon the Britannia-pewter industry should not be underestimated. The final passage of the bill, almost irrespective of the rates provided by it, was, if not a material stimulus, at least a psychological one.[16] The accumulating pressure of years of agitation and complaint had suddenly been released, and though that release was to be only temporary, the immediate effect of the 1824 tariff was to instill new hope into industrial areas of the country. Babbitt & Crossman could start its lathes turning with confidence. The government had committed itself anew to the protection of American manufacturers.

There was another trend in American thinking which provided a spur to manufacturing effort in 1824. Growing national consciousness and pride in the progress of the country gave substance and strength to patriotic buying motives. Tariff discussions between 1816 and 1824 constantly emphasized the merits of American products, and these claims were excellent advertising copy. Throughout the period the public was urged by editors, congressmen, governors, presidents, and, of course, by manufacturers themselves to "Buy American." [17] Unfortunately, however, tangible results from this movement were somewhat vitiated by the reputation which imported products had built up in America during the years when agriculture and commerce, rather than manufacturing, had been the primary interests of the country. American consumers paid enthusiastic lip tribute to American manufactures, and continued, also with enthusiasm, to buy English goods. This contradiction was disturbing, but the very fact that locally produced articles were beginning to achieve vocal preference provided hope that perhaps material preference and success might soon follow.

The undertaking which Isaac Babbitt and William Crossman launched in 1824 was well supplied with precedent in other industries, and the example of many manufacturing establishments already in successful operation could hardly have escaped notice. This was an era of industrial promotion and expanding markets. Like Babbitt & Crossman, a majority of the newly formed companies were small, "with resources hardly exceeding those needed to run a farm." [18] Like the founders of Babbitt & Crossman, petty capitalists were often both capitalists and laborers and found their efforts attended with a high degree of speculative risk. The Taunton Britannia men could therefore justify their enterprise by pointing to the great number of small companies which were springing into existence, and at the same time could draw for ideas and inspiration on the relatively large, well-founded, and impressive mills in operation throughout New England. Notwithstanding the discouragement of frequent failures, fluctuating prices, crises at home and abroad, and the generally unstable economic conditions, the lure of high profits remained and stimulated American manufacturers to action.[19]

THE CHANGING TECHNIQUE OF MANUFACTURE

The period in which Babbitt & Crossman began the manufacture of Britannia ware might aptly be termed the crisis in craftsmanship. The close of the eighteenth century witnessed a profound change taking place in America — a broad, far-reaching movement which was to alter the whole basis of the country's economy — the change from a mercantile to an industrial system of capitalism.[20] Developments which occurred between 1820 and 1840 in the Britannia industry were, in a sense, simply small-scale counterparts of the larger movement, reflecting, and to some extent caused by, industrialization in larger, more important trades. Industrial revolution, with its increased production and growing wealth, created new purchasing power; at the same time it taught the Britannia men how to manufacture their wares more economically, sell more cheaply, and enlarge existing markets by their own efforts. The demand for utilitarian and ornamental metal ware was clearly expanding, and hand craftsmanship was inadequately adapted to supply a rapidly growing market.[21]

Handicrafts, and methods of production that follow the precedent of handicrafts, serve best an aristocracy of consumers, while factories serve best the consumption of a democracy. The secret of the prosperity of metal manufacturing in New England lies in its adaptation to this popular market, which during these years was growing more rapidly than any other or than at any previous period in history.

In terms of the years through which individual hand craftsmanship had been virtually the only method of production, the changes which occurred in the second, third, and fourth decades of the nineteenth century were dazzling in their speed.[22] To the craftsman himself, looking back over years of relatively stable tradition, the changes must have been appalling in their effects. Almost overnight, comparatively speaking, factory techniques had come into being which threatened the existence of the whole system of hand production which had prevailed before. The growth of the Britannia industry and the decline of pewter typified the change. During the 1820–1825 period the manufacture of pewter plates for tableware virtually ceased,[23] but those same years saw new Britannia makers established in business, output of the hard-metal wares increasing, and new operating principles beginning to be applied. The transition from hand craftsmanship to machine methods of production had begun.

Mechanization of the industry destroyed many establishments of the old, hand-wrought order in the years following 1825, but the crisis in craftsmanship was not necessarily fatal. There were three avenues of escape. The craftsman could become a new-style manufacturer — casting aside old techniques and adopting new ones, employing labor, enlarging his facilities, and changing his product with the market to lighter, cheaper wares. Such a change required boldness, vision, capital, and versatility of a high degree, but it was accomplished by several men. Ashbil Griswold in Connecticut, Rufus Dunham in Maine, and Roswell Gleason in Massachusetts all started on a small scale as pewterers of the old school, later expanding their home workbenches into modest shops, employing the new methods and manufacturing Britannia utensils.

A second alternative was for the hand craftsman to subordinate himself to the new manufacturers, to give up his shop and enter the factory. This change was a difficult one, for it usually meant abandoning many functions and specializing in one or two operations. No longer could individual pride and care be lavished on one piece of ware from unworked beginning to polished end. Such a move involved, moreover, the loss of personal liberty which went with ownership.

The third alternative was for the hand craftsman to persist in his traditional techniques, meeting competition as best he could. The Boardmans, of Hartford, were the outstanding advocates of such a course, retaining, as they did, many of their old methods and continuing the manufacture of pewter. Such cases, where unusual ability and great efficiency prolonged the existence of outmoded procedures, were the exception, and this alternative doomed most of its adherents to eventual failure.

Babbitt & Crossman had no such problems of adjustment. Without personal precedent or tradition the firm was free to engage in machine manufacture unfettered by the vestiges of hand production. Their problems lay in what was to come, not in what had been.

The crisis in craftsmanship manifested itself in other than industrial circles. The whole social fabric of the nation was in a transitional state, the outcome of which was to be influenced by, as well as to influence, the course of manufacturing history. The fate of the Britannia industry was more closely allied than most to the progress of social custom, style, and taste; and it was vital to Babbitt & Crossman's existence to know in 1824 what the aesthetic temper of the people was to be.

THE PROMISE OF GREAT TRADITIONS

Early nineteenth-century America was heir to a magnificent artistic inheritance. Great names in American arts and crafts were still personal memories, and masterpieces of the hand-wrought school were in constant evidence. The 1820's may have marked the beginning of the end for hand craftsmanship, but, as in all transitional periods, examples of the old order and of the new were found side by side. In the early 1800's only the most astute and progressive had sensed the change which was soon to come. Artistic life for the majority of Americans pursued its even, eighteenth-century tenor.

Much work of outstanding individual merit was performed between 1800 and 1824, and a truly fine tradition of craftsmanship was upheld. Samuel McIntyre, of Salem, and his followers were making valuable additions to the colonial architectural beauty of New England towns; Duncan Phyfe was making his best furniture; the Boardmans were producing superb pewter; the work of the clockmakers of Connecticut still exhibited the results of personal care and craftsmanship. The forms in which artistic feeling expressed itself in the early part of the century were logical continuations of ages of development; and the fact that such continuity had persisted through so many social upheavals was the grounds for hoping that the tradition of craftsmanship would survive another crisis.

England was idling through the period of the Regency, and much of her art was displaying a refined simplicity, expressing the "atmosphere of logic, of hope, and of modesty which characterized early-nineteenth-century English life." [24] Great promise for continued development and cultural advance in England was inherent in the state of the arts, and this promise was expressed by a comparable situation in America. Cultural development here was also idling at the end of an old period — waiting to see what the coming years held in store. After 1815 the delicacy and attenuated detail of Adamesque styles began to appear effete and inappropriate to a young, bold, and vigorous nation. More and more the classic influence of Jefferson and the Roman-Greek revival began to appeal to America as a fitting medium for expression of the national personality.

The year 1824, then, was a time of great hope and promise. Classicism had provided an instrument of expression, and the tradition of individualism and pride in personal performance, stretching back through the colonial period in America, had provided the activating force by which a great national culture could be made to arise. The intrusion of industrialization upon the stage presented a problem — reconciliation of individualism and careful craftsmanship with rapid and large-scale machine techniques — but problems of adjustment had been solved before. Once the initial dislocations invariably attending a great social and economic change had been overcome, industrial revolution might assist in building up a great national culture by rapidly producing and distributing the products of the new era. Clearly the stage was set for drama on a tremendous scale. The traditions, spirit, and means were at hand for developing one of the most talented, artistic, and cultured civilizations in history. That such great promise faded, even temporarily, with the passing years will always be a source of regret.

CHAPTER III

BEGINNING OF THE ENTERPRISE

THE SMALL SCALE upon which Babbitt & Crossman commenced operations detracts little from the achievement of its organizers in mastering diverse and unfamiliar details of management. While certain of the beginning problems were resolved by application of common rules of small-scale trading, in many cases a complete dearth of precedent called for decisions involving the keenest foresight and, perhaps, more than usual good luck.

The only contemporary account we have of the start of the business indicates that even in an era of great entrepreneurial courage and intense speculative confidence, the Taunton venture was regarded with doubt, surprise, and unstinted admiration.[1]

There is one fact highly honorable to the perseverance and ingenuity of the proprietors, of the correctness of which we have the assurance of one of the company, or we should almost doubt its accuracy. When this establishment was first put into operation, not an individual employed in it, from the principals down to the lowest laborer, had ever seen any thing of the kind, or witnessed the process of its manufacture. The requisite machinery and the method by which the several parts were formed and combined, were wholly new to them. Yet under these discouraging circumstances, the compound was formed, the dies or moulds cast and polished, and the whole machinery made and put into successful operation by the unaided ingenuity of native Yankees. It, therefore, has almost the merit of an original invention.

The beginning of the enterprise and the adoption of machine methods of manufacture were dependent on the elimination of certain basic technical obstacles which, for the most part, were characteristic only of the 1824 era. The discovery of lathe spinning and adoption of the technique in America were essential to the rapidly unfolding program of mechanization in the Britannia industry.[2] Mechanization also waited upon the discovery of a metal capable of being rolled and spun, fuller comprehension of the technique and potentialities of mechanical rolling, and more complete realization of the advantages of such a method over the old process of hammering out flat sheets by hand.

The solution of these and other mechanical problems in the early nineteenth century was a distinct triumph, but a triumph which brought Babbitt & Crossman and other workers of this transitional period face to face with a more subtle difficulty. Preoccupation with the mechanics of production could assure large output and low costs; but without the painstaking super-vision, artistic individualism, and manual skill of the old-time craftsman, low costs might degenerate to commonplaceness and large output bear insistent testimony to uninspired design. This very real danger apparently was not a conscious concern of the early manufacturers. In the spring of 1824, Babbitt and Crossman were less aware of the aesthetic obligations of their contract with the machine age than they were of the necessity for decisive action on many fronts.

Early Operations, 1824–1828

Such scanty information as exists about early operations at the Spring Street shop serves more to arouse than to satisfy curiosity.[3] Of techniques and methods we know only that the first wares of the company were cast in metal molds rather than stamped out with drop press and dies, which was the procedure later employed. In many respects the shop of Babbitt & Crossman was closer akin to the pewter-making establishments of the old era than to the factories of the rapidly developing machine age. Isaac Babbitt and William Crossman, typical of a period in industrial history when ownership was synonymous with active

management, worked at their own lathes and rolls, experimenting with unfamiliar problems and guiding the efforts of the five
or six men whom they employed during 1824 and 1825. The
products of the Spring Street shop were at first limited, and
indicate the acumen with which the partners formulated their
early policies. We are told that Britannia inkstands, shaving
boxes, looking-glass frames, and cups were manufactured in the
new shop.[4] Babbitt & Crossman continued, however, to turn
out and strenuously promote the line of pewter ware which
Babbitt had made in the Merchants' Row store. Until such
time as the company's ability to manufacture and sell Britannia
ware should be clearly demonstrated, the partners seemed un-
willing to risk complete dependence upon it. Certainly the
maintenance of a line of ware of proven marketability, in the
manufacture of which the partners were experienced, was a
wise and conservative policy.

The uncertainty which attended initial operations at the
Spring Street shop was speedily dispelled, and the partners met
with immediate and positive encouragement in their new line.
Operations rapidly outgrew the capacity of the shop, and the
water power available at Spring Street proved inadequate to
roll the increasingly large amounts of metal required in the
business. In 1826 the partners decided to expand the business,
abandon the uncertain water power of the Mill River, and con-
struct a factory specifically designed to meet the requirements
of Britannia manufacturing. A move so important in those
years of inexperience and risk must certainly have been preceded
by earnest consideration and anxious discussion. Alternatives
which we by hindsight know held much promise of success
presented themselves to Babbitt and Crossman only as risky
potentialities. It is easy to visualize the two young men poring
over vital, though modest, financial statements, or walking side
by side over the dirt lanes of Taunton, examining, discussing,
rejecting first one site and then another. Misgivings surely

attended the decision of the partners to abandon seasonally unreliable water power for the promising but almost as unreliable steam engine! Late in 1826 a location on Fayette Street [5] close to the center of town was chosen, and a two-story brick shop erected. A James rotary-valve steam engine was installed to provide power, and a new set of rolls to augment the old machinery was made for the partners by Nathaniel Leonard of Taunton. By the end of the year the new Britannia works were in operation with fifteen men employed. Isaac Babbitt assumed the direction of the works in the capacity of superintendent, and installed as foreman and overseer William W. Porter, who had taken an active interest in Babbitt's earlier experiments and had been present when the first Britannia sheet was rolled. William Crossman's duties at this time are not clear and his name is not connected with any function in the works. Possibly he assumed the task of managing the Merchants' Row store and of directing the sale of the company's wares.

After a period of readjustment and experimentation with improved machinery and methods of work, the company late in 1827 turned at last to the manufacture of Britannia teaware. A sample teapot was turned out and exhibited in the show window of the store, where it created a satisfying stir among the townsfolk—"people visiting in crowds to look upon the wonderful triumph of American ingenuity and skill." [6] Following this first teapot, a batch of eighteen was completed and sold—which lot, Edmund Porter assures us,[7] was the first order on this continent for wares of this kind and marked a notable era in national manufacture. This claim, however, does not agree with known facts, for other manufacturers elsewhere had been engaged in similar work for several years.

The only information which has survived concerning the technique employed by Babbitt & Crossman in manufacturing this first teaware is that "The pots were stamped in lead dies under a screw press [not cast, as the earlier wares had been] and

the bodies fluted like the English style," and that "The soldering
was done at this time with a hot air blast blown through a pipe
from a charcoal stove, a rude invention that made it a warm
place for a man to work throughout the day." [8]

While the claim that these first Taunton teapots constituted
a "notable era" in the history of American manufactures appears to be somewhat inflated by local pride and loyalty, they
did at least mark a significant point in the affairs of Babbitt &
Crossman. In the early 1800's the cultural graces, among them
the habit of tea and coffee drinking, were spreading downward
to the financially limited but numerically vast members of
society and creating hitherto unsuspected markets which the
perspicuity of Isaac Babbitt enabled the company to exploit.
The wares which in 1827 attracted the curious to the little shop
window proved to be the mainstay of the company for over two
decades, and production, once established, survived many
changes in organization and ownership.

Such changes were not long in coming. The resources of
Babbitt & Crossman were strained by the 1826 expansion and the
construction of the Fayette Street works. In 1827 the need for
working capital became increasingly acute, and measures were
taken late in the year to relieve the long-felt want. It was not
surprising that under these circumstances the partners should
turn to William Allen West, their neighbor and close friend.

West was engaged in the retail dry goods business with a shop
on Merchants' Row adjacent to the Babbitt & Crossman jewelry
store. At the same time he followed with continuing interest
Babbitt's search for a Britannia mixture and seems often to have
strolled into the jewelry store to discuss with Porter, Crossman,
and Babbitt their latest efforts. From this point West's participation in the Babbitt & Crossman venture became gradually
more active, until his optimism over the future of the Britannia
business induced him to invest in the partnership. Some time in
December, 1827, in return for an unspecified amount of capital,

THE FAYETTE STREET SHOP
Built by Babbitt, Crossman & Company in 1826

West was admitted to the company as clerk and financial agent. Babbitt & Crossman was dissolved, and a new partnership was formed which took for its title Babbitt, Crossman & Company. There are also certain indications that about this time Babbitt & Crossman disposed of the Merchants' Row store.[9] In February, 1828, further funds were made available to the new partnership by mortgaging the company property to Joseph Dean, Jr., of Taunton, for $1,900.[10]

Throughout 1828 some of the promise of early years seems to have faded. Scattered hints lead to the conclusion that Babbitt, Crossman & Company had begun almost immediately to encounter difficulties. One account says that inexperience in mixing the metals made the sale of the company's products difficult.[11]

An examination of the Babbitt, Crossman & Company wares, however, fails to substantiate that excuse for such marketing difficulties as existed. The products which came from the Fayette Street works constitute some of the finest examples of Taunton Britannia in existence, surpassing in quality of craftsmanship and design much of the work of other manufacturers. Surviving specimens of this period reveal such an excellent grade of metal and such finished technique as to give rise to the suspicion that high manufacturing costs rather than poor quality may have been responsible for the decline in sales. This suspicion is partially borne out by the fact that the rotary-valve steam engine installed in the new mill proved to be much more expensive to operate than had been anticipated.

At the same time a number of general conditions existed outside the company which added to the difficulty of transacting profitable business with limited capital. Declining price levels, a shortage of specie, and depressions in the local textile industry were capable of contributing substantially to the Babbitt, Crossman & Company difficulty, while the tariff of 1828 provided no direct assistance.[12] The universal adoption of English style and

BRITANNIA TEAPOT, BABBITT, CROSSMAN & COMPANY, 1827
One of the first lot manufactured by the company

BRITANNIA TEA SET, BABBITT, CROSSMAN & COMPANY, ABOUT 1828
The fluted pattern is characteristic of work of this period

design by American manufacturers in this period, furthermore, indicates a prevalence of English ware in this country and hints at formidable foreign competition.[13]

Domestic competition also existed in 1828, but was at an early and ineffectual stage. American Britannia manufacturers were few and scattered over a wide area. Marketing facilities were still in an embryonic state of development, and the small resources of early Britannia companies tended in most cases to confine the sale of their ware to limited geographical boundaries. The purely local character of the industry is revealed by the fact that, as late as 1829, Taunton citizens were under the impression that Isaac Babbitt and William Crossman were engaged in the first and only Britannia manufacturing enterprise in the country.[14] It is probable that such competition as was encountered came more from pewter-making establishments, which were still firmly entrenched in many areas, than from Britannia shops. In any case, domestic competition would seem to have been a minor factor in the 1828 decline in Babbitt, Crossman & Company sales.

Until 1828 the only direct and first-hand record of the progress of the partnerships consists of the wares which have survived. The complete absence of company account books for the period is regrettable and restrictive, but in October, 1828, the long silence ends, and a withered, indistinct time book tells some of the small details of day-to-day operation.[15] In October, 1828, according to the time book, besides the three partners, fifteen hands were employed. The record of days worked, while rather inconclusive as a source of reliable summary labor statistics, does indicate a general increase in plant activity toward the end of the year, and a measure of recovery from the 1828 depression.[16] Like the company itself, most of the employees in this period were young. As far as can be ascertained, William Crossman, thirty-four years of age, was the oldest man on the payroll, the majority of workmen were in their twenties, and one apprentice was only sixteen. Of the other partners, William A. West was twenty-seven years old in 1828, and Isaac Babbitt, twenty-nine.[17] Perhaps the youth of the whole organization had much to do with the ambition of these early years, and may explain the vigorous expansion which was undertaken so soon after the start of the business in 1824. The time book also reveals the facts that while a holiday was granted the workmen on Thanksgiving day, the factory stayed open on December 25, and all hands worked through Christmas Day. This was usual practice at the time and deserves only passing comment. More significant as a clue to future labor policies is the appearance in the roster for December, 1828, of Miss Caroline Cobb, who was hired to wash the wares of the factory, and was the first woman employee of the company.

Growth and New Management, 1829–1830

On February 19, 1829, a simple annotation to the records appears in the time book: "New consearn Began 19 Thursday." The story behind this scrawled line is largely a mystery, but the sequence of events, if not a complete interpretation of their significance, may be related. On February 18, 1829, Isaac Babbitt sold his interest in the partnership for $1,030, and Babbitt, Crossman & Company was dissolved. Zephaniah A. Leonard, of Taunton, purchased for $5,000 a one-third interest in the Britannia works, and the partnership of Crossman, West & Leonard was formed. Babbitt remained with the new company in the capacity of plant superintendent.

No explanation can be given for Babbitt's financial withdrawal, nor for the discrepancy between the amount of money paid to him for his interest and the amount received from Leonard for an apparently equal interest. Zephaniah Leonard's admittance to the partnership, however, is partially explicable in terms of the history and resources of the family. The Leonards had played a remarkable part in the financial and industrial

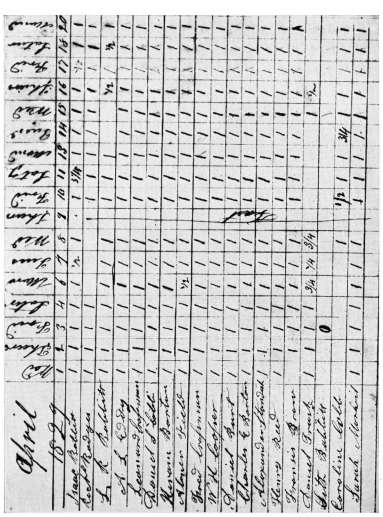

PAGE FOR APRIL, 1829, FROM THE CROSSMAN, WEST & LEONARD TIME BOOK

The earliest known company record

Amt. bro't up

	2	1900	Teas	6 h.p.	2.37½	4.75
	4	"	"	5 h.p.	2.12½	8.50
	2	2500	"	6 h.p.	2.25	4.50	27.50
97	3	2000	Coffees	10 h.p.	3.25	9.75
	2	"	Teas	6 h.p.	2.37½	4.75
	4	"	"	5 h.p.	2.12½	8.50
	4	2500	"	5 h.p.	2.00	8.00	31.00
9?	6	24	Lamps (handle)		6/9	0.75
						$105.25

May 4th 1831
Invoice Ware sold John Jones & Co.

99	12	20	Lamps		7/	14.00
	11	24	"		6/9	12.37½
	5½	15	"		7/6	6.17½	35.25
100	3	12	" (handles)		10/6	5.25
	1	24	"			1.12½
9?	6½	15	"		7/6	8.12½	15.50
						$48.75

May 4th 1831
Invoice Ware sold Churchill & Collamore & Co.

101	1	2000	Coffee	10 h.p.	3.25	3.25
	4	"	Teas	6 h.p.	2.37½	9.50
	1		Sett Sugar & Cream			2.75
	3½?	9	Lamps		9/	4.50
	4	20	"		11/	4.67
	4	20	"		6/9	4.50
	4	12	Lamps (handles)		10/6	7.00
	2		Branch Lamps		9/	3.00	37.17

May 5th 1831
Invoice Ware Con. John Bailey

102	4	70	Teas	8 h.p.		10/	6.67
	1	2500	"	5 & 6 h.p.	12½ & 2		4.25
	1	1800	"	5 & 6 h.p.	8¾ & 2¼		4.50
	1	2500	Sett Sugar & Cream				2.50
	1½	12	Lamps (handles)				1.75
	2	9	"			9/	3.00
	1	15	"			6/9	1.12½
	½	24	"			6/7	.56	24.35

PAGE FROM THE SALES BOOK, 1831, TAUNTON BRITANNIA
MANUFACTURING COMPANY

history of Taunton, commencing in 1652 when Henry and James Leonard established their iron foundry. From that time on, the family was prominent in the metal and textile trades and built up a reserve of capital which was vital in the financing of many early Taunton enterprises. Leonard capital flowed freely into faltering local industry, injecting new life into financially starved establishments and profiting greatly from the general need for working funds. Only the Panic of 1837 put an end to this dramatic personal story of high finance in a small community.

The admittance of Zephaniah Leonard into the Britannia firm gave a distinctly new tone to the management. Leonard's interests were financial and his knowledge of Britannia manufacturing seems to have been limited. Up to 1829 the partners managed the affairs of the company and actually worked as artisans in the shop. Even William West, with his retail cloth business, was an experienced metallurgist and brought to the office of financial agent a thorough knowledge of production methods. Zephaniah Leonard's name, on the other hand, never has appeared in any connection with production. He was the first stockholder, in the modern sense of the word, and the formation of Crossman, West & Leonard marked the end of an era. William Crossman still remained doggedly at his workbench, but a part of the proprietorship was assumed by interests outside the factory doors.

The transition was to a more flexible organization better adapted to expansion. The sale of a one-third interest in the Britannia works to Leonard was undoubtedly dictated by financial stringency, but the move was well timed. With manufacturing techniques fairly well worked out and valuable manufacturing experience built up, only capital and a larger organization had been wanting for the profitable exploitation of the products resulting from Isaac Babbitt's experimentation.

Crossman, West & Leonard was during its brief existence a

successful enterprise, and certain reliable accounts, which add greatly to the historical value of this period in the company's growth, give a picture of what was happening at the Fayette Street works in 1829. The following editorial, though incorrect in ascribing the founding and exclusive operation of the Britannia business to Crossman, West & Leonard, is revealing as a contemporary comment on operations.[18]

American *Britania* ware . . . is a still more recent experiment, and, we believe, there is but one Manufactory for that article, in the United States, and that is probably but little known. It is but a short time since, three enterprising young men, Messrs. Crossman, West & Leonard, attempted to introduce this valuable branch of manufacture amongst us. Their establishment, which for neatness and adaptation to its purposes, is admirable in all its parts, is situated in the thriving village of Taunton, Massachusetts. A short time ago we noticed the attempt in that village to establish the manufacture, but had doubts of its success, supposing, that at least for the present, it must be confined to the artizans of that country where it was originally discovered and from which it derives its name. An examination of the establishment of Messrs. Crossman, West & Leonard, is sufficient to dispel all doubts of its success, and the visitor who may be indebted to their politeness for a view of the process, will be surprised and gratified at the beauty of the specimens he will there find, which for neatness and elegance of model, and brilliancy of polish, we venture to say, would not suffer in comparison with the most highly finished articles of the same description from the shops of Great Britain.

The enterprising proprietors have thus far confined their labors to those articles usually made of the material known as Britania metal; such as Urns, Coffee and Tea pots, &c. Their success in that branch has induced them to extend their operations to the production of articles, hitherto formed from the harder metals; such as stirrups, the mountings of carriage harnesses, door plates, latches, &c. For such articles, from the specimens that have been produced, we should think it decidedly preferable to any kind of plated work. Its beauty is at least equal, and its durability incomparably greater, as a little labor will readily restore it, when tarnished, to the original polish. It is also recommended by its cheapness, as well as by those considerations connected with home policy, that should induce us to give a preference to our own, over foreign skill and labor, where the products of the former are equal in excellence and less in cost. On this, as well as the excellence of their workmanship, the Taunton Manufacturers may rely for entire success.

The following descriptions are those of Edmund W. Porter. They are given here in full because he quotes directly from record books long since lost, bringing us personal reminiscence of infinite value and interest when related first-hand.[19]

In February, 1829, an inventory of the plant was taken and stood as follows:

Land, buildings, machinery and fixtures	$11,103.96
Tools and mis. articles	942.58
Dies and moulds	1,050.15
Stock, finished and unfinished	1,855.55
Total	$14,952.24

There were fifteen hands at work at this time beside the superintendent and foreman, and not one of them is now living. It may be a matter of interest to some Taunton families to give a copy of the payroll for that month, giving the names of the employes and showing what wages skilled labor once commanded in those days.

	Per Day
Isaac Babbitt, superintendent	$2.00
W. W. Porter, foreman	1.00
Richard Rodgers, diemaker	1.50
Luther R. Babbitt, machinist	1.17
A. L. Eddy	1.00
W. H. Cooper	.92
Daniel S. Cobb	.83
Fred. Crossman	1.00
Leonard Crossman	.61
Abner Field	.75
Hiram Barton	.50
Sanford Smith	.46
Daniel Burt	.46
Henry G. Reed	.42
Alexander Standish	.38
Charles E. Barton	.31
Caroline Cobb	.22

In the company's accounts some items are noted, viz:

Man's   board, $2.00 to $2.25 per week
Woman's "   , $1.25 per week
Carpenter, $1.25 per day
Engine Coal, $10 per ton

Goods were ordered from Boston to come by "first wagon."

When the agent went into Boston to "drum the trade" he took a horse and chaise for two days, and the cost for the team was $5.33. We can imagine him starting out, not on the electrics for the Central Station with his neat gripsack or suit case, but rather with his new style, up-to-date "tea set" neatly packed in an antique round trunk safely lashed inside the thorough-braces of his "one horse shay."

These were picturesque years in the history of Reed & Barton, but they were productive years as well. Much remained to be learned about the manufacture of Britannia ware, and the workbench was the textbook. Foreman William Porter was never so happy as when he was experimenting, and a persistently curious mind questioned each process in the shop. In 1829 the technique of shaping hollow ware with a screw press began to try Porter's patience. At this time all hollow ware had to be "drawn down" into shape by a tedious process involving several dies in order to prevent the edges of the pieces from wrinkling. Porter decided that, if he could hold the edges down in some way, articles could more easily be drawn smooth. Experimentally, he flattened off the top of a deep iron ring, placed a metal disc on it, and placed a second ring on top of the metal disc. A set of wooden braces held all in place, and pressure from the screw press was exerted on the disc. Porter succeeded by this means in drawing the disc down into the form of a basin without a wrinkle. Isaac Babbitt was hastily summoned, and the results of the experiment were carefully examined by the two men. "Porter, you've done it, and I'll have a set of dies made at once!" exclaimed the superintendent. He did so, and thus began stamping with ring dies, a process which later became universal in sheet-metal work.[20] In the same year the old screw press was discarded, and a drop press installed in the shop. This latest innovation was proudly referred to as an "automatic" machine, since the operator's only function was to insert the metal blanks and hoist up the striking hammer by a hand crank. Gravity accomplished the rest.

Production techniques gradually were progressing from the archaic, but a degree of quaintness continued to characterize certain business methods employed at the Fayette Street shop.[21]

There was one business method practiced . . . which was a common custom in the early factories in various lines, that contrasts strangely with the present methods of a regular pay day and prompt payment of wages, and that was the giving of orders to the workmen upon the various stores in town for groceries, dry goods, clothing, meat, furniture, fuel and other supplies needed. Money, evidently, was scarce at times, and then the company gave its hands notes for their labor, and these notes were "shaved" by certain ones who had money to loan, and frequent credits and charges as "discounts" appear in the books, showing where and how the workman sometimes "kept the wolf from the door." It also shows that the business in early times was often up-hill work for the manufacturers.

The variety of wares which are listed as company products[22] indicates that a broad policy of experimentation with the uses to which the metal could be put was under way in 1829. Actual sales, however, seem to have been confined very largely to teaware. Of significance, furthermore, is the optimistic note which contemporary accounts strike in regard to current business and future prospects of Crossman, West & Leonard. That the company was experiencing a mild boom in business is further confirmed by the 1829 time book, which reveals a more fully employed working force in this than in the preceding year and an increase in number of employees from fifteen in October, 1828, to twenty-two in October, 1829.

Marketing the Wares, 1829–1830

The existence of an account of sales dating from March, 1829, throws additional light on the extent of the trade and on the nature of the products sold. From March through December, 1829, shipments were made to the customers and in the amounts shown in Table 1.

TABLE 1
Shipments to Customers, March–December, 1829
Crossman, West & Leonard

Charles Scudder	Boston	$ 73.85
Proctor & Palmer	Boston	97.56
Geo. H. Potter & Co.	Providence	105.90
Sampson & Tisdale	New York	652.35
Field Fobes & Co.	Philadelphia	606.83
Gad Taylor	New York	1,420.22
Daniel Boyd	Boston	525.95
Homes & Homer	Boston	130.10
I. S. Copeland	Zanesville, Ohio	68.70
Sm. B. Pierce	Boston	554.75
Read & Olcott	New York	28.75
Steamship President Co.		228.00
Charles Fletcher		9.50
James Fassett	Philadelphia	9.50
John F. Mackie	New York	2,642.00
Edward Watson	Boston	62.00
John Bailey	New Bedford	39.35
James Eames	Providence	2.75
		$7,258.06

Source: Reed & Barton Mss., Baker Library, Harvard University, Invoice Book, 1829–31.

These figures, though probably incomplete, are valuable for the picture they give of the geographical dispersion of sales. At this period in the company history a concentration of sales in the local area might be expected, yet wares to the amount of $5,359.65 were shipped to New York and Philadelphia customers, as against shipments of $1,592.21 to Providence, Boston, and New Bedford customers. Transportation facilities may have had much to do with this distribution. New York and Philadelphia markets were easily and cheaply accessible to Taunton by a sheltered water route. Schooners sailing daily out of Taunton — literally from the center of the town — brought the southern markets nearly as close as Boston, which could be reached only by expensive stage and wagon or by an often risky passage by boat around Cape Cod.

Crossman, West & Leonard appears not to have directed selling efforts through any one channel of distribution, and such limited conclusions as can be drawn about the 1829 customer list from trade directories of the period reveal no clear-cut company policy in this regard.[23] Among the buyers listed in the sales account are three hardware dealers, one hardware dealer and importer, three commission merchants, one importer of watches, one dealer in crockery, eight dealers in glass, one tin-plate and sheet-iron worker, one jeweler, and one watchglass manufacturer. No discounts are quoted, nor is any distinction made in prices between the various customers. The account book does reveal, however, that the company shipped a considerable amount of wares on consignment. This fact is of special significance and reveals one method by which Crossman, West & Leonard (and possibly the earlier companies) introduced its wares and achieved wide distribution. It was much easier, then as now, for a manufacturer to persuade merchants to accept goods which need not be paid for until resold than to sell merchants those goods outright. To the manufacturer who was willing to assume risks and who had sufficient working capital to be able to forego immediate payment for his wares, the method had much to offer.

The 1829 account book is valuable also because it enables us to make at least a partial analysis of the types of wares manufactured and prices quoted. (See Table 2 on page 44.)

The demands of fashion did not weigh heavily on Crossman,

West & Leonard's policy. Perhaps the most significant social movement of the 1820's and 1830's was a wholesale adoption of the democratic ideal, and the subsequent attempt to make less obvious the differences between rich and poor.[24] From the growing demand of the common people for more comfortable

TABLE 2

SHIPMENTS BY ITEMS, 1829

CROSSMAN, WEST & LEONARD

Item	Number Sold or Consigned	Approximate Average Price to Customers
Teapots	1,784	$2.00
Coffeepots	556	3.00
Cream and Sugar Sets	256	2.50
Lamps (pairs)	41	1.50
Coffee Urns	46	16.00
Lather Boxes (dozens)	48	4.50
Tumblers	158	2.50
Slop Bowls	2	1.25
Goblets	2	
Pitchers	1	
Bowls	1	

Source: Reed & Barton Mss., Invoice Book, 1829–1831. The majority of shipments in this account book are consignments, indicating that regular sales records were kept elsewhere. This may explain the fact that many of the products mentioned in the *Rhode Island American* article do not appear here.

living a great popular market was beginning to arise. This movement, however, was more concerned with expanding existing styles and fashions over a larger number of people than it was with actually changing those styles and fashions. The growing middle class was more anxious to get than to change, and it demanded cheap replicas of the once exclusive possessions of the wealthy rather than a style of its own. Consequently, the forms through which American taste found expression varied but little during the 1820's and 1830's. The wares of Crossman, West & Leonard, in so far as we know them, exhibit the same

BRITANNIA TEAPOT, CROSSMAN, WEST & LEONARD, 1828–1830
An early departure from the traditional fluted forms

BRITANNIA TEA SET, CROSSMAN, WEST & LEONARD, 1828–1830

well-proportioned restraint and classic refinement that characterize the products of Babbitt, Crossman & Company. Little
fundamental evolution of design took place between the earlier
company and the later, principally because no such change was
called for by the public. The Greek revival strongly influenced
styles of the day, and it was not until the late 'thirties that the
new mass market began to show signs of possessing an individ-
uality of its own.

A universal lack of originality in design characterizes this
period, and the lack is particularly noticeable in the American
Britannia trade. Throughout the years when America had little
manufacturing or art of its own, the cultured classes of society
patronized Europe and England. When this necessity existed
no longer, the habit remained and was adopted, along with other
superficial manifestations of culture, by the middle classes.
Thus perpetuated, the English tradition presented a formidable
obstacle to American manufacturers. The most obvious and
widely adopted remedy was to imitate as closely as possible the
English forms which the public demanded. The wares of both
Babbitt, Crossman & Company and Crossman, West & Leonard
were patterned after English contemporaries, and native
originality appears only in the technical processes by which
those wares were manufactured.

Relatively large sales by Crossman, West & Leonard outside
the local area indicate considerable promotional effort, but no
evidence has been uncovered of any newspaper advertising at
this time. The work of the salesman, however, was augmented
by the company policy, first noted in 1829, of placing its wares
in the exhibitions of various organizations and societies. This
means of achieving recognition was successful and continued to
be employed by the company long after the more usual advertising methods had been adopted. Even before 1829, wares were
exhibited in the Bristol County Agricultural Society fairs, and
at the annual exhibition of this society held October 7, 1829, the

merits of Crossman, West & Leonard's Britannia ware commanded a $5.00 award.[25]

A small beginning, surely, but soon followed by more impressive triumphs. At the American Institute fair of 1829, in New York, a "discretionary premium" was awarded the company for "superior Brittany ware." [26] This constituted important recognition, for prominent manufacturers exhibited at these fairs and the prizes carried weight in important markets. At the same fair the following year the Institute awarded: "A premium to Crossman & Leonard, Taunton, Massachusetts, for an assortment of very handsome Britannia ware." [27] Another account of the same exhibition says that the company's wares attracted particular attention and possessed "all the brilliancy and finish of Silver Ware." [28] No other premium for Britannia ware was awarded by the Institute, and Crossman, West & Leonard could justifiably lay claim to national recognition.

Judged by any standard, the progress of the three partnerships over the brief span of five years was remarkable. These years saw a product brought forth and manufacturing techniques developed from the depths of inexperience. The end of this period saw technical problems yield to financial ones and a bitter struggle for working capital strain the abilities of men who were mechanics first and financiers only incidentally. The close of the year 1829 found Crossman, West & Leonard financially well supported, its wares established over a wide geographical range, a sales agent employed, and a substantial volume of business built up. The close of the year also saw the company cramped for manufacturing facilities, its source of power costly and inadequate to meet the demands of the increased volume of business. With a high degree of optimism prevailing among the partners, plans for expansion began to be laid before the new partnership was a year old.

CHAPTER IV

YEARS OF CRISIS, 1830–1836

TAUNTON in 1829 presented a picture of uncertain prosperity. Spindles stopped in the textile mills and workers were let out to search for employment elsewhere. Sloops of the river fleet rode higher in the water than in other days, and less cloth and iron and fewer bricks left the Green for coastal markets. But at the Fayette Street shop of Crossman, West & Leonard the lathes spun with brisk activity, and orders accumulated as the reputation and popularity of Britannia ware increased. Collections, however, were slow, and cash was scarce. Stringent money markets and the further expansion of an already active business provided Leonard capital with still another opportunity for investment in the partnership. In July, 1829, only six months after Zephaniah Leonard's purchase of a third interest, Crossman, West & Leonard mortgaged the Fayette Street land, buildings, and equipment to Horatio Leonard [1] for $5,000. This additional Leonard capital seems to have been used to finance day-to-day operations, and the necessity for plant expansion remained unsatisfied.

The expansion issue was a controversial one. The Leonards, whose effective interest in the company by this time equaled that of Crossman and West, wished to reorganize the company and build new manufacturing facilities. Inertia, the evident instability of the times, and a heavy investment in the Fayette Street plant worked against the move. The conflict was a short one, however, and the speculative spirit of expansion, together with the optimism engendered by past profits carried the day.

The Leonards further proposed that steam be abandoned in favor of water power or, at least, that water power augment steam. Such a recommendation was undoubtedly wise, in view of the inefficiency of the James rotary-valve engine, but involved the acquisition of water rights and the construction of a dam and wheel. These objections were promptly countered by the Leonards, who proposed to lease to the company a site owned by Horatio Leonard at Hopewell, an outlying section of Taunton.

The Leonards carried all their points, and the partners consulted on methods of financing the move to Hopewell. The resources of Crossman, West & Leonard were still inadequate, and it is extremely doubtful whether the Leonards were willing to bear the cost of expansion alone. It may, in fact, have been impossible for them to do so because of their heavy investments in the Taunton iron industry. The familiar and almost constantly pressing need for more capital, which had brought in partners one after another to share in the benefits of Isaac Babbitt's experiments, operated again to enlarge the concern and widen still further the financial interests involved.

Formation of the Taunton Britannia Manufacturing Company

On August 18, 1830, the partnership of Crossman, West & Leonard was dissolved, and a joint-stock company, to be called the Taunton Britannia Manufacturing Company, was formed to carry on the business on an enlarged scale. The articles of agreement for the new company provide both explanation and description of the reorganization.[2]

The Subscribers, proprietors of an Establishment for the Manufacture of Britannia Ware in Taunton, having had several propositions made to them for admission into their Concern and feeling satisfied that the business is worthy of an enlarged Capital, have given the subject their serious consideration and are of opinion that with the facilities which would be afforded by an addition of Capital they would be enabled not only to increase their Manufacture in a ratio far exceeding the increase of Capital, but would be able by a proper extension of the business to Manufacture at a much less expense than at present.

They would therefore propose to form a new concern with a capital stock not exceeding Forty Thousand Dollars to be divided into Forty shares to be taken up by subscription. Of this amount they would subscribe Nineteen shares and would stipulate that the new concern shall purchase on terms which will not subject them to any sacrifice of property, common wear and tear excepted, all their real Estate, Fixtures, Machinery, and Tools upon the real Estate, altho the Buildings were put up in an economical manner there would probably be a sacrifice in case of the removal of the Establishment.

Dated August 18th, 1830

Wm. W. Crossman
Wm. Allen West
Z. A. Leonard

We the subscribers agree to take the number of shares affixed to our respective names in the concern above proposed subject to such assessments as may be made agreeable to the By Laws hereto annexed, and we pledge ourselves to the performance of the conditions and stipulations in the foregoing article offered by Crossman West & Leonard.

Dated August 18th, 1830

James W. Crossman	Eight Shares
Haile Wood	Six Shares
Horatio Leonard	Five Shares
Daniel S. Cobb	One Share
Haile N. Wood	One Share

The final details of reorganization, concerned with the terms of transfer of equipment and property, were not completed until well after the formation of the new company. The assets and liabilities which Crossman, West & Leonard turned over to the Taunton Britannia Manufacturing Company may be computed from the books of the latter company as follows:

Engine, etc.	$ 5,500
Stock, tools, etc.	12,000
Ware in hands of dealers	4,112
Old mill, land, and Buildings, Fayette Street	4,632
Total Assets	$26,244
Less	
Outstanding drafts, mortgages, and other liabilities	$ 4,039
Net worth	$22,205

In return Crossman, West & Leonard received:

Cash .... $ 8,744
12 Shares of nonassessable stock of the T. B. M. Company   12,000
                                                         ──────────
Total Cash Value $20,744
Plus:
7 Shares of assessable stock of the Taunton Britannia Manufacturing Company.

On the basis of valuations given, the exchange involved an immediate sacrifice by Crossman, West & Leonard of $1,461, plus whatever amounts might in the future be demanded on the seven assessable shares of stock. Against present loss in exchange, however, prevailed the expectation of future profits from nineteen shares of stock representing a 49 per cent interest in the new enterprise.[3]

With the 1830 reorganization, control passed from technicians to financiers, and the majority interest resided outside the factory for the first time. Of the eight shareholders of the new company only William Crossman, Haile N. Wood, Daniel Cobb, and William West were experienced in the Britannia business and had worked in factory or office. James Crossman, a successful merchant tailor who had turned to real-estate investment, was a director of the Cohannet Bank in Taunton. Haile Wood, Sr., seems to have been extensively involved in real estate, and the Leonard investments in textiles and iron have already been noted. Such diversity of interests among the stockholders imparted an element of strength to the organization, but raised managerial problems and called for new methods of regulating company affairs.

Between 1824 and 1829, company policies had emphasized production. This emphasis began to weaken only when Zephaniah Leonard was admitted to the partnership in 1829. Formation of the Taunton Britannia Manufacturing Company in 1830 and the creation of a stockholding group outside the factory reduced the technical emphasis still further, giving voice to demands for more intensive sales promotion and greater profits. James Crossman, the Leonards, and Haile Wood exhibited no particular interest in the workbench, but each had acquired wide trading experience and each was endowed to a certain extent with the useful ability to make money. With competition increasing and the complexities of trade multiplying, such stockholders might contribute much to the strategy of survival.

No proxy voting characterized the new organization. Unfamiliar though some of the new stockholders were with the details of Britannia manufacturing, they all evinced a strong desire to participate to the limit of their time and ability in the affairs of the company. Each of them served the company in some capacity, but because of other interests none could give his entire time to this enterprise, and a means had to be provided to bridge the widening gap between ownership and management. Article 3 of the bylaws of the new company contemplates such a purpose.[4]

Article 3d There shall be one or more general Agents appointed by the proprietors who shall superintend manage and carry on the active business of the Company subject to the control of the proprietors — They shall have power to purchase Stock, to manufacture and sell ware, to collect assessments, to receive and pay debts, to repair buildings and generally to conduct the pecuniary concerns of the Company to the best of their judgment —

They shall keep the Money and funds of the Company distinct from other funds.

They shall give and take Notes and secureties [sic] in the name of the Company which name shall be used only for and in behalf of the concerns of the Company They shall also keep books of account in a clear and perspicuous manner which shall be always open for the inspection of the proprietors and of which abstracts shall be made and exhibited to the proprietors upon request.

James W. Crossman was chosen as general agent for the ensuing year, and plans for the move to Hopewell proceeded rapidly. The site for the new factory was secured by a deed drawn on August 13, 1830.[5]

> Horatio Leonard, Charles Richmond and Ezekiel B. Leonard farm let to William W. Crossman, William A. West and Zephaniah Leonard: First right of water in the water privilege at Hopewell in the north part of said Taunton on mill river, alias canoe river . . . ; together with sufficient land on the south side of the public road for the erection of Factories and buildings for the improvements of said Water Privilege. . . . Also the land adjoining on the northwest side of said privilege the right of a wood yard . . . together with a right of way across the saw mill dam from said land to such Factories as may be erected. Also a piece of Land fronting the public road of two hundred feet in length, and 100 feet in breadth . . . in the vicinity of said privileges suitable for the erection of dwelling houses. . . . And the said William W. [Crossman], William A. [West], and Zephaniah A. Leonard . . . do hereby covenant promise and agree well and truly to pay or cause to be paid the sum of three hundred dollars rent yearly and every year during their possession. . . .

The Hopewell site on the Mill River offered excellent water power on a small scale, and history itself designated the location as a good one. Long before the Revolution low-slung, wooden mills sent grain and lumber and iron to Taunton Green. With the passing years a growing industry pushed farm lots and grazing fields away from the river banks and up to the surrounding hillsides. Marshy grassland along the valley gradually disappeared as dam after dam backed mill ponds upstream. By 1830 each available mill site had its own wooden water wheel, and the valley presented a scene of bustling activity unlike any other spot in the whole Taunton area. To the Taunton Britannia Manufacturing Company, however, the location presented inconveniences not found in the earlier shops on Spring Street and Fayette Street. Mill River was not navigable and wagons carried the products of the mills to Taunton Green for sale or reshipment, but mud in spring and snow in winter made narrow

dirt roads difficult and the distance at times formidable. Hopewell in 1830 offered no supply of labor, and a scattering of cottages and farms provided but inadequate housing for Taunton
laborers. Whatever the shortcomings of the location, however,
the company proceeded with its plans, and in the fall of 1830
construction of the new mill was under way. Records show
that the first proprietors' meeting of the Taunton Britannia
Manufacturing Company was devoted to the details of mill
construction.[6]

Voted
   That James W. Crossman shall be Treasurer of the Building committee
Voted
   That the Treasurer be authorized to hire money if necessary to defray
   the expenses of the Building and to sign the notes as Treasurer
Voted
   That Horatio Leonard be empowered to bargain for and purchase a
   Water Wheel of the dimensions and power granted us by Lease from
   C. Richmond and others
Voted
   That Horatio Leonard be authorized to purchase Timber for the Floom
   and Race Way such as he may judge suitable and proper

The water wheel installed in accordance with the terms of the
lease was a bucket wheel fourteen feet in diameter and seven
feet wide, to operate on a dam of ten-foot head and fall.[7]
   At this same meeting Haile Wood and James W. Crossman
were authorized to make contracts for the building, and it was
formally voted that the new structure be solidly constructed of
brick, one hundred feet long and forty feet wide, three stories
high.[8] This building stands today in active use — ample testimony to careful planning and sound construction.
   At a proprietors' meeting held on September 16, 1830, at the
old Britannia works on Fayette Street the question of housing
was considered, and a vote taken to build "one or more houses
as may be deemed necessary." At the same meeting additional

capacity for the new plant was also voted, to consist of "a building 50 feet long . . . 15 feet to be two Stories high for Jappaning Furnace &c the remainder to be 1 story high for Woodshed &c." [9]

The cost of the new works is not revealed by the records. In September, 1831, the main building, japanning furnace, fixtures, machinery, and stock were insured for $12,500 — the only indication of the value of the Hopewell investment.

While the new company planned to rely on water for the main source of its power, the Fayette Street steam engine was also installed in the Hopewell works, presumably to provide power when summer drought should lower the river. With this exception, however, the equipment of the new Britannia works was of the most modern design. Charcoal stoves were discarded for soldering purposes, and foreman William Porter introduced Professor Silliman's Diamond Fuser or Compound Blowpipe, which burned whale oil. As a final bow to modern efficiency, whale-oil lanterns of the latest design were installed to light the factory.[10]

Construction proceeded rapidly through the fall and winter of 1830, and early in 1831 the manufacture of Britannia was shifted from Fayette Street to suburban Hopewell. The move climaxed a remarkable six years of progress, during which brief span the company enlarged its capital three times, changed location three times, built a new factory and immediately outgrew it, and built a second and larger new factory. These facts alone provide the most fitting tribute to the enterprising spirit of the Taunton Britannia men.

The Taunton Britannia Manufacturing Company seems to have taken over the business of Crossman, West & Leonard intact and without any immediate change in methods. Existing precedents were adhered to in most cases, and the stockholders of the new concern wisely provided a continuity of experienced management to ease the transition to larger-scale operations.

H. Ballou

Factory Buildings, Taunton Britannia Manufacturing Company, 1830

From left to right: Two employees' cottages, the Lincoln homestead, japanning building, main factory building. Foreground: West Britannia Street

Immediately after the new concern had been formed, and at the same meeting which saw the acceptance of the articles of agreement and the bylaws, a formal contract was made with Isaac Babbitt to continue in his capacity of superintendent for a term of five years. Babbitt agreed to work diligently for the new company,[11]

... for and during and unto the full end and term of five years next ensuing ... and faithfully according to the best and utmost of my power skill and knowledge exercise and employ myself in the trade and business of the manufacturing of Britannia Ware ... that I will be just true and faithful in all things whatsoever relating to said business and will faithfully keep all the secrets relating to the said business so that the said William W. William A. Zephaniah A. James W. Horatio and Haile their heirs and assigns shall have the full profit and advantage thereof together with all the profit and advantages arising from my skill and labours during said term.

Babbitt posted a $1,500 surety for fulfillment of the new contract, and agreed to a salary of $1,000 a year, plus a $1,000 bonus at the end of the five years. William Crossman and William West, together with most of the employees of the old concern, also remained with the company, and helped make the first year of the Taunton Britannia Manufacturing Company simply an extension of the last year of Crossman, West & Leonard. The scope of operations, however, was enlarged as a result of the increased capital and the avowed purpose of the new organization to extend profits by an increased volume of business.

DESIGN AND PRODUCT DEVELOPMENT

The new company made several additions to the product line, and a shift in emphasis began to make itself apparent. Throughout 1831 the manufacture of coffin plates, castor frames, tankards, church cups, christening bowls, soup ladles, and candlesticks apparently was undertaken, and in 1832 toast racks, soda dispensers, and fruit dishes were added. Teaware sales, the backbone of 1830 operations, declined after 1831, and two major product developments became evident. An increasing supply of whale oil on the market was instrumental in promoting the improvement of lighting devices. Pewter and Britannia lamps enjoyed a great boom in popularity, in which the Taunton Britannia Manufacturing Company shared. At the same time, public fancy was captivated by a new table utensil, and the castor set came into its own. Soon almost every well-appointed table boasted a set of castor bottles containing salt, pepper, mustard, and relishes, all neatly contained and prominently displayed in a shiny metal frame. Luxurious living ascended to new heights when some manufacturers produced castor sets that revolved, and the Taunton Britannia Company was not far behind in catering to public taste.

A comparison of the 1830 shipments of Crossman, West & Leonard with the 1834 shipments of the Taunton Britannia Manufacturing Company, given in Table 3, on page 58, graphically illustrates the progress of product line evolution.

The wares shown in Table 3, which may be designated as the standard company line, accounted for a great majority of sales. Certain unfamiliar items, however, occasionally appear in the records and would seem to be special order or experimental products. Throughout 1833 and 1834 the company sold locks, latches, and door-knobs. An individual account on the books separated these items from the regular line, and they may possibly have been manufactured outside the factory. In 1833 the company filled an order for "1/2 Doz. Mouth Pieces for Claronets," and in 1834 the steamboat *Benjamin Franklin* was supplied with twelve Britannia egg boilers.

In matters of design the Taunton Britannia Company, in common with most other manufacturers in the trade, followed closely the example set by Dixon, of Sheffield, England, whose wares achieved a great reputation and popularity in America. The English tradition remained virtually as strong in the 1830's as it had been in the 1820's, nourished perhaps by large imports which followed the 1833 tariff reductions. English wares remained the pattern for American manufacturers, who copied each other's work by way of diversion. This subtle pressure

TABLE 3

COMPARATIVE ANALYSIS OF SHIPMENTS
CROSSMAN, WEST & LEONARD, 1830
TAUNTON BRITANNIA MANUFACTURING COMPANY, 1834

Wares	Number Shipped		Per Cent of Total Shipments		Per Cent of Change from
	1830	1834	1830	1834	1830 to 1834
Teapots	2,429	787	40.1	15.8	−67.6
Lamps (pairs)	1,395	2,861	23.0	57.6	+105.1
Sugar & Cream Sets	870	129	14.4	2.6	−85.2
Coffeepots	760	62	12.5	1.3	−91.8
Slop Bowls	345	123	5.7	2.5	−64.3
Looking-glass Frames	143	20	2.4	0.4	−86.0
Urns	64	43	1.1	0.9	−32.8
Glasses	42		0.7		
Tumblers	8		0.1		
Castor Frames		410		8.2	
Tea Sets		328		6.6	
Candlesticks		77		1.5	
Church Cups		12		0.2	
Church Plates		42		0.8	
Church Tankards		31		0.7	
Fruit Dishes		24		0.5	
Ladles (dozens)		21		0.4	
			100.0	100.0	

Source: Reed & Barton Mss., Invoice Books, 1829–31, 1833–47. This table includes consignments as well as sales and does not contain cash sales at factory. The figures presented, however, adequately show relative demand for the various wares and the changes occurring between 1830 and 1834.

to imitate seems to have arisen, in part at least, from the fact that most of the early Britannia men were technicians, primarily concerned with the development of mass-production methods and the factory system. Lack of time and talent made necessary the appropriation of already existing designs, and it was not

BRITANNIA TEA SET, TAUNTON BRITANNIA MANUFACTURING COMPANY, 1830–1836

Illustrating the "pigeon-breasted" style of design. Reproduced with permission from *Pewter in America*, by Ledlie Irwin Laughlin. The set is owned by Judge and Mrs. George V. Smith, West Willington, Conn.

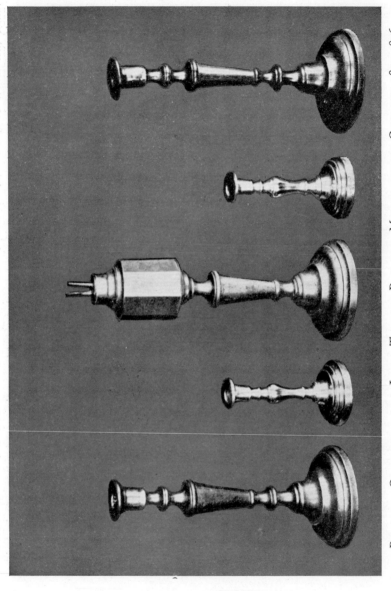

BRITANNIA CANDLESTICKS AND LAMP, TAUNTON BRITANNIA MANUFACTURING COMPANY, 1830–1836

Reproduced with permission from *American Pewter*, by J. B. Kerfoot

until production problems had been largely solved and creative artists employed that any marked degree of originality began to appear.

With the exception of oil lamps and castor frames the wares of the Taunton Britannia Manufacturing Company did not differ greatly from those of the earlier companies. Popular demand still called for English styles, and the company was forced to copy them. The classic spirit and a refined simplicity still continued to characterize the Britannia ware of Taunton. Evolution, however, was not totally absent. A certain modification of classic forms and an elaboration of simple detail appears in some patterns. A relatively new development, the "pigeon-breasted" teapot, is shown in the illustration opposite page 58. As in the past, however, the inspiration was not a local one and seems to have been patterned either after contemporary American work or, more probably, after some of the Dixon pieces.

Marketing Conditions and Methods

Public approbation greeted the first wares from Hopewell. In Philadelphia solemn judges of the Franklin Institute once more tipped their hats to the village craftsmen in the North, with the following comments on the goods entered in the Institute's seventh exhibition:

No. 22. An extra premium is due to the Taunton Britannia Manufacturing Company of Massachusetts, for its handsome display of Britannia ware (specimen No. 1). It is, in every respect, a superior article, and was frequently mistaken for a more costly metal.[12]

No. 1.P. The handsome specimens of Britannia ware from the Taunton works, are well worthy of particular attention; the quantity exhibited, and the workmanship of the article, together with its silvery appearance, display in bold relief, its near approach to the more costly metal.[13]

For several years after 1831 the Britannia Company did not exhibit at the annual fairs of the Franklin Institute or of the American Institute of New York. Wondering at the abandonment of this inexpensive and modestly successful promotional practice, we turn to the records for an explanation of sales methods adopted by the new company. The sales ledgers do not tell a complete story, however, nor do columns of figures adequately reveal those tremendous uncertainties which imparted to trade in the 1830's a flavor quite alien to present-day concepts of the term.

New England spring came late and chilly, and a bitter wind swept up Narragansett Bay in April of 1831. Captains of the Taunton coasting fleet paced their wharves impatiently[14] and scowled downstream over a monotonous vista of dirty river ice. Bales and cartons and barrels continued to accumulate, overflowing from storage sheds and mounting in growing piles on none-too-capacious docks. An atmosphere of impatience also pervaded the counting room of the new Britannia works in Hopewell as the isolation by mud and ice extended beyond its normal seasonal limits. Customers' stocks, shipped south before the December freeze-up, were exhausted, and a reviving trade in New York and Baltimore markets brought complaining letters to Taunton. This was commerce at its worst, but even in mild July, when mud of the Boston Post Road caked to a hard, fast surface and schooners quartered a crisp breeze down Long Island Sound, southern markets measured their distance from Taunton in more than miles. Slow and often uncertain communication separated the Britannia Company from customers by frequent gulfs of misinformation and ignorance. There resulted a leisurely tempo to trade and a certain casualness about sales relations which can well be excused in the light of contemporary conditions.

By mid-April of 1831, the last of the ice had slipped out of Taunton River, and heavy wagon loads of Britannia, the first shipments of the new company, churned the muddy lane from Hopewell to Taunton Green. For the most part, the names and addresses scrawled in black crayon on the wooden casks of ware were familiar ones to the old employees, but one day, late in the spring, a shipping clerk bent over a large barrel and laboriously spelled out a new address across the top: "Sandwich, Mass., Boston & Sandwich Glass Co." Thereafter, and throughout 1831, barrel after barrel of castor frames and bottle tops rolled from the shipping room to waiting wagons — many ad-dressed to Sandwich, only a few less to Cambridge for the New England Glass Company, and an occasional one to the Providence Flint Glass Company. These shipments represented the only new business obtained in the first year of operations, but the addition was an important one. In 1831 the Sandwich Glass Company purchased the unprecedented amount of $2,129 worth of frames and caps and became the second largest customer, while the New England Glass Company rolled up an impressive purchase total of $1,065 for the year. Taunton viewed the new contacts with great satisfaction, for the glass companies pur-chased outright, paid cash, and settled promptly — rare virtues in 1831.

With these exceptions, the managers of the Britannia Com-pany indulged in the complacent luxury of believing that sales promotion consisted of retaining old customers. Crossman, West & Leonard's strong New York connection through the firm of John F. Mackie was continued by the Taunton Britannia Manufacturing Company, and in 1831 shipments to the suc-cessor concern, Mackie & Murdock, were larger than to all other customers combined, amounting to over $14,000. As in the past, there were relatively few large customers. These custom-ers, however, took a substantial part of the Britannia Com-pany's output. In 1830 two companies (Mackie & Murdock, New York, and Fuller & Norton, Providence) received 96 per cent of the total recorded shipments! In 1831 four customers (Mackie & Murdock; Sm. B. Pierce, Boston; Boston & Sandwich Glass Company, Sandwich; and New England Glass Company, Cambridge) received 81 per cent of total shipments.

The total number of customers remained small, and surprisingly little effort appears to have been made to enlarge the sales territory. Dependence upon a very few customers was perhaps unavoidable at the time. Limited working capital restricted promotional efforts and made new contacts difficult to obtain. The Taunton Britannia Company saw positive advantages, moreover, in concentrating sales and purchases in such a manner as to make most effective the limited means of communication at its disposal. An easy informality, therefore, pervaded the marketing activities of the company, and no clearly defined sales organization or procedure seems to have existed. A salesman was employed, as formerly, to canvass the Boston, New York, Philadelphia, and Baltimore customers. His efforts were augmented by impromptu performances of some of the company stockholders who, apparently working in the interest of company dividends, turned in some rather surprising orders. Active selling effort ended here. With huge orders rolling in from Mackie & Murdock in New York through 1831 and the plant working at capacity, further promotional exertion or expenditures seemed unnecessary.

Terms of sale offered by the company were calculated to retain old customers, rather than to attract new ones. Here, too, a lack of formality characterized procedures. Customers received such terms as their purchasing power commanded, and the company earnestly prayed that small buyers would never learn what rates large buyers were obtaining. The majority of discounts granted in 1831 were at either 9 per cent or 10 per cent. Mackie & Murdock, however, commanded 13 per cent, and received, in addition, a percentage of their selling expense and a fee for collecting Taunton accounts in New York.

This latter function was no small task at the time, for cash transactions were comparatively few in number and were made difficult by a great scarcity of money.[15] Most trade was carried on by means of long credits, and few collections were made

immediately upon sale of wares. The Britannia Company habitually granted credit for from one to nine months, or longer, and
filled its books with paper transactions designed to offset the
shortage of specie. When the company desired immediate
funds, customers' notes or drafts were discounted by James W.
Crossman, acting in the capacity of private banker, or by the
Cohannet Bank of Taunton. The practice of discounting, or
"shaving," as it was somewhat bitterly referred to at the time,
was extensively employed by the Britannia Company. Paper
surrendered was "shaved" of about 10 per cent of its face value,
and the company subscribed to the idea that $90 of cash in hand
or bank credit was fully as tempting in those times as $100 of
notes. A multiplicity of such paper transactions forged a strong
bond of dependence between the company and the bank and
materially reduced the need for cash in the process of ordinary
business.

The necessity of economizing cash lay heavily upon the
company, and a glance at any page in the sales register reveals
the reason: "Invoice of Ware Consigned Mackie & Murdock"
began to appear with increasing frequency throughout 1831.
Consigned shipments to other customers as well mounted
higher and higher. Crossman, West & Leonard had experimented with consignment selling in 1829 and 1830, but the
Taunton Britannia Manufacturing Company literally pounced
on the system in 1831 as the answer to a poor concern's prayer.
Here was sales promotion without cost. Buyers eliminated their
inventory risks and were willing, therefore, to stock more wares
than otherwise they would have contemplated. Large shipments and big inventories in dealer hands made recourse to
faltering communication systems less frequent. The Britannia
Company, to be sure, had to wait for payment, but production
in the waiting period was financed by cash sales, by borrowing,
and by credit purchases. The whole trading world revolved
around credit — credit to dealers, credit from suppliers, credit

from employees. Payment to all waited upon disposal of consigned stocks on the shelves of customers. And business for the Hopewell enterprise boomed through the first year of operations.

Shipments, which had hovered around $8,000 in 1829 and increased to $13,000 in 1830, the last year of Crossman, West & Leonard, mounted abruptly in 1831 to a grand total of $23,000. New business from the glass companies contributed $3,000 of the increase, and greatly augmented consignments to Mackie & Murdock brought in most of the rest. Volume of shipments seems to have been an end in itself, on the assumption that consigned wares would rapidly become sold wares. This assumption led to further refinements in the technique of consignment selling, and in 1832 certain customers were designated as agents of the company in their respective cities and given virtual control of sales there. Mackie & Murdock continued to handle business in the New York area; in Boston the firm of Hosmer & Grew was appointed agent; in Providence, Pliny B. Fuller; in Philadelphia, F. V. Krug; and in Baltimore, William Tileston. This step marked the first designation by the company of a definite marketing channel and followed closely the general trend in contemporary American trade toward the employment of specialized middlemen.

Concentration of the company's sales efforts in four large markets and a simplification of accounts were achieved. The strong contacts thus built up bore early fruit, and shipments for 1832 soared above previous records to an all-time high of $34,000. Of these, however, actual sales amounted to only $10,000, while consigned wares accounted for the remainder. The stockholders could point with satisfaction to the fact that the company policy of consignment selling had resulted in a more than twofold increase in plant activity.

The Taunton Britannia Manufacturing Company seemed destined for growth, and started briskly to fulfill the hopes expressed and implied in the 1830 Articles of Agreement. The number of employees increased from fifteen in February, 1829, to an average of forty-two in 1831, and in May, 1832, an employment record of fifty-five workers was established. This, for Hopewell, verged on big business, and the form which this early organization for mass production assumed is an interesting one.

The Factory People and Their Work

The 1830's were part of an age in which, in the minds of a hardy race, morning was synonymous with daybreak, and the light of the sun was given to work by. The lathes and rolls turned early at Hopewell, and before the sun cast shadow on the mill pond, smoke from the Britannia works was drifting south to mingle with the smoke of other shops and lose itself in the morning mists of Taunton Great River. The men and women who entered the brick mill at dawn did so with some pride and faced their working day with reasonable equanimity. Long hours were accepted — these people were still close enough to the farm and the frontier to remember what work could be. Wages were not only adequate to live on, but represented a greater return for the labor expended than ever before. Industrial revolution was far more than a schoolbook phrase to men who could sit down and earn $1.50 a day without leaving their bench — this was progress, and a fine new age.

Labor at the Britannia works was quick to organize itself into a hierarchy of varying skills and trades. Different occupations received different compensation, but there seems to have been a tendency for individuals and even families to remain on one job, developing an intense pride in the skill with which it was performed. There was an air of dignity attached to work, and a personal pride in personal performance which made every occupation in the factory a skilled one in the minds of the employees.

For March, 1833, the company time book records a grouping

of occupations for the forty-one employees. Rates of pay at this
time, and for many years afterward, were usually given in
shillings and pence.[16] Wages varied somewhat in accordance
with seniority, but tended to maintain a pattern for each occupation.

TABLE 4

RATES OF PAY ACCORDING TO OCCUPATION
TAUNTON BRITANNIA MANUFACTURING COMPANY, MARCH, 1833

		Maximum Daily Rate	
10	Machine and casting hands	8/	($1.33)
11	Fitting and pressing hands	6/9	($1.12)
9	Soldering hands	6/9	($1.12)
5	Polishing hands	6/	($1.00)
6	Finishing hands	3/	($0.50)

Source: Reed & Barton Mss., Time Book, 1831–39.

The basic production processes hinted at in the occupational
classification differed little from those of the present day, although, in the details of operation, 1832 was a different world.
We can easily visualize Davenport's wagons rolling into Hopewell from Boston heavily laden with tin ingots and antimony,
which were soon to be unloaded and later carried to the casting-
room. Here the watchful eye of William Crossman guided the
melt, the mix, and the pour, while cousin Leonard Crossman,
perhaps, manipulated the heavy cast-iron furnaces as the com-
ponents fused and hardened in secret proportions into Britannia metal. Ingots flattened into sheets as the force of the river
spun wheel and rolls, and under the skillful touch of Noah
Williams and his companions flat discs of metal felt the force of
foot-manipulated drop presses, which transformed them into
fluted halves of teapots. Abner Field and a row of fitters — serviced by the same spittoon — assembled piles of parts and bound
them with wires into completed units, which a young man
named Barton carried to another bench. Here jets of flame from
the Silliman whale-oil burner flickered briefly, solder ran

through seams, and the wares moved into the custody of Mervin Chace, Horatio Williams, and the other polishers. Practiced feet pumped buffing and polishing wheels into activity. A whirling disc of buffalo or moose hide removed mars and scratches, and dusting from a softer wheel gave light and glow to the gray metal. Deft fingers of the Cobb sisters and Ann Mason swiftly wiped the ware for final finish. Wrapped in tissue, the pots and lamps and frames slipped easily into waiting barrels filled with meadow hay, and Davenport teams moved off toward the Green with new wares for distant markets.

The easy informality characteristic of sales methods of the Britannia Company also appears in the factory. Working hours apparently were not definitely fixed but, rather, tended to vary with the length of daylight and the time of year. Work commenced as soon as it was light enough to see and continued until dusk, with a half-hour respite for breakfast and an hour for lunch. The long hours may have passed not unpleasantly, however, amid a youthful good company of relatives and friends. The men and women who worked together at the benches of the Britannia shop were a closely knit group of brothers, cousins, sons, wives, and neighbors. A bond of common concern operated strongly, for community isolation restricted outside interests and concentrated attention upon the immediate environment. Even romance blossomed among the teapots, and on October 13, 1831, employees Hiram Barton and Caroline Cobb were united in marriage.[17]

No formal set of laws operated to protect the workers from unemployment, disability, and the results of old age. The only safety device standing between an employee and the crude machine he operated was his own heedfulness, and this was easily dulled by long, concentrated attention. At the Britannia works the obligation of management implied by these facts was fulfilled to a greater degree than practices of the times demanded. The right to discharge at will was freely exercised, and as yet no occasion had arisen involving care of aged em-

ployees, but on January 8, 1832, a meeting of the company
stockholders formally voted "to pay Andrew Barton Thirty
Dollars for Injury received in Mill." [18] There are, in addition,
many entries on the books recording payment for overtime and
night work. Usually such payment was at regular rates, but in
certain instances extra compensation was paid for what the
company appropriately called "over-work." Lucretia Strange,
who put in twenty hours of overtime in one period, washing
and wiping wares, was paid nearly double her daily rate for
the labor.

Wage settlement policies of the Britannia Company seem
strange to us today, but cash was scarce in the 1830's. As in the
previous decade, settlements had to be arranged in such manner
as to provide a minimum of strain upon the company's small
reserves. Wage payments during 1831 were almost exclusively
paper transactions. The payroll was reckoned monthly and
settled quarterly by a credit transferred from the company's
books to the books of James W. Crossman, or the Cohannet
Bank. Employees then were free to draw against the credit so
deposited.

The bookkeeper of the Britannia Company for this period
deserves everlasting fame and glory. He recorded, apparently
with success, a multiplicity of credit transactions involving not
only regular company affairs but also a considerable proportion
of the private negotiations of forty-odd employees. Workmen
did most of their purchasing in Taunton on credit, and bills were
settled by exchange of drafts and transfer of credits among merchants. Purchases of Britannia ware by the employees were
charged by the company against payroll, and many other miscellaneous transactions were effected without cash by similar
methods. In 1832 the company began to settle wage accounts in
cash, although there was little diminution in other types of
credit transfers.

The bookkeeper recorded, in addition, at least five different methods of wage calculation. Workers were paid day rates, hourly rates, job rates, and piece rates. In addition, contracts were entered into by the company with workmen outside the mill, and frequently employees were loaned to other concerns.

The most widely used basis of pay was the day rate, the workman agreeing when he was hired upon the amount he should receive per day. These rates, as did others, varied with skill and

PAY CHECK, TAUNTON BRITANNIA MANUFACTURING COMPANY

seniority. In the machine and casting department, for example, rates of 3/6, 4/6, 5/, 6/, 6/9, 7/, 7/6, and 8/ per day ($0.59 to $1.33) were in effect in 1833. The lowest of these rates seems to have been that of the department apprentices, and in certain other cases these boys were paid as little as $60 a year. The privilege of learning the trade was a considerable one, however, and the professions of solderer, machinist, fitter, and spinner were among the most honorable in industrial Taunton — attainable only by men of decided ability. Apprentice boys, moreover, received their board and the promise of rapid advancement. In the first quarter of 1831 the company paid Haile Wood $126 for boarding nine boys. We may surmise that life at the Wood house was seldom dull! The books record for us the progress of one of these apprentices. William Wood (probably a son of Haile Wood) started in the polishing department in March, 1831, at a rate of $6.00 a month. In April he was advanced to

$8.00, and a year later, in May, 1832, he was getting $10.00, which was advanced in July to $12.00.

More unusual than the regular hour and day rate methods of compensation was the company practice of contracting with its workmen for the performance of specific jobs. In such cases a formal agreement was entered into and recorded on the books. These transactions were almost like orders placed with another company, yet were confined entirely within the factory walls. In some cases one or two employees agreed to perform a certain task, the company charging their account with materials used, and crediting them for the ware completed. Time worked by other employees on such jobs was charged against the earnings of the contracting men. This time was kept in the company record book, paid for directly by the company, and deducted from the account of the contractors before final settlement. One such settlement reads as follows:[19]

A. Standish and C. E. Barton

June 30, 1831	Charges	Credits
for work partly finished when job commenced ...	$25.00	
for work of Thomas Babbitt	48.38	
for work of Seth Wood	15.24	
for work of B. W. Gardner	63.50	
for am't of work on job to date		$277.06
for unfinished ware. July 1		45.00
[Balance in favor of Standish and Barton]	169.94	
	$322.06	$322.06

Methods of contracting for job work varied considerably. Sometimes the contracts regulated only prices for each type of piece worked on and ran for a definite length of time, usually a quarter or six months. On October 1, 1835, Noah Williams agreed "to do Fitting at the last quarters prices discounted 10 pr cnt." [20] In many instances a stated number of pieces was undertaken: "John Allen & B.L.B. [Barnas L. Burbank] agree to make 6000 Castor Frames @ 6 ct. ea, beginning Sept. 7, 1835 Monday." [21]

As time went on, job contracts tended to evolve into straight piecework, undertaken without formal agreement as to time or number of pieces. In certain cases group rates were put into effect: for instance, in April, 1833, when four girls were credited with washing and wiping 847 castor frames, payment for which was divided equally among them. Other piece rates in effect at various times include the following: [22]

September, 1831, C. E. Barton,

                    soldering small lamps, 8¢ each

                    soldering large lamps, 15¢ each

        Wm. and B. Porter

                    making socket lamps, 6¢ each

                    making looking glasses, 42¢ each

December, 1831, Geo. Presbrey

                    raising pieces, $\frac{3}{4}$¢ each

February, 1833, W. W. Porter

                    setting looking glasses, 1¢ each

April, 1833, Harriet Cobb

                    wiping No. 5 tea pots, $\frac{7}{10}$¢ each

Outside the Hopewell shop, too, men nominally engaged in other occupations were earning piecework pay by whittling out the wooden handles which the company used on its tea- and coffeepots. Rates varied somewhat, but the average was about eight cents for tea handles and ten cents for coffees, and the men were charged for the beech boards from which the handles were cut. For years this work was done by Jarvis Smith, a farmer in Rehoboth, [23] although at times as many as four different handle contracts were in effect simultaneously.

The Hopewell shop, it seems, was more than adequate to house the Britannia business, for in 1832 a room on the first floor was hired by Crocker Brothers & Company, probably for rolling copper sheets. This arrangement provided the Britannia Company with a convenient method of profiting from the spare time of workmen and the idleness of certain pieces of equipment, as the following entry testifies:[24]

Crocker Brothers & Co. dr.
 for 11½ hours work by L. R. Babbitt $1.50
 for use of our Furnace 1½ Days Essaying Copper Ore ... .50
 for 6 Bush. Coal used at the Same Time 20 .... 1.20

Science of the day failed miserably in its attempt to heat and light the shop. A number of small, cylindrical wood stoves lifted the winter temperature only from frigid to cold, and in periods of extremely bitter weather the workmen were sent home. The new whale-oil lamps were a great improvement over the candle, but, says Porter, for the evening work they barely served to make the darkness visible! [25] Such handicaps apparently were not so bad to work under as they are to contemplate, for there seems to have been no complaint at the time, and considerable progress in manufacturing techniques was effected by the Taunton Britannia Company.

INVENTIONS OF FUNDAMENTAL IMPORTANCE

In 1832 Benjamin Pratt, the company sales agent, experienced difficulty in selling looking-glass frames in New York because a competitor was making or importing frames of a much lighter material and selling them at a considerably lower price. When this condition became known in the shop, foreman William Porter commenced experimenting to see whether, instead of casting a solid, heavy, and expensive article, he could make light and hollow frames by spinning. An account of his success has been handed down to us.[26]

He said to Pratt one day, "I think I can make them a better way than we are making them now." Pratt answered rather curtly: "We don't hire you to teach us how to do our work." Notwithstanding the cutting rebuff, Porter finished up three by spinning, and Pratt coming around soon after, saw them and carefully examined them and said, "How did you make these?" "By that new process I named to you," was the quiet answer. Pratt came down off his high horse at once and said, "Get us 300 dozen as quick as you can."

William Porter must have been a talented mechanic, for in 1833 he is credited with another invention. The bearings of the large rolls began to wear badly, and Porter made new ones of a very hard Britannia metal. These wore well, and Isaac Babbitt was much interested — so much so, in fact, that he later took out a patent on certain applications of the alloy, which has been known ever since as Babbitt metal.[27]

Even more important ideas were brewing in the Britannia shop, however, and in the following year William W. Crossman perfected, probably with Porter's assistance, a revolutionary process of spinning. We are fortunate in having a complete description of the new technique,[28] for it was destined to effect far-reaching changes in many metal industries.

Specification of a patent for an improved process for manufacturing Tea Pots, and other articles of Brittania Ware. Granted to WILLIAM W. CROSSMAN, *Taunton, Bristol County, Massachusetts, March 12, 1834.*

To all to whom these presents shall come, be it known, that I, William W. Crossman, of Taunton, in the county of Bristol, and state of Massachusetts, have invented a new and improved process in the manufacturing of tea pots, coffee pots, sugar dishes, cream jugs, and other articles, which are capable of being formed in the lathe, and are made of that kind of metal, alloy, or mixture of metals, of which those vessels are constructed, which are denominated Brittania ware, or any other similar metal, or mixture of metals, capable of being so wrought; and I do hereby declare that the following is a full and exact description of the said process.

The ordinary mode pursued in making such ware is to raise, or stamp up, from the sheet metal, such parts, say one-half, of these vessels, as will relieve from the mould or die after stamping, and then to solder such parts together. By the process which I have adopted, I rub, or burnish up, the required vessels, from a single flat plate, or sheet. Thus, suppose it is intended to form a tea pot, the middle part of which is intended to be bulging, or bellied; I fix in the common turning lathe a chuck, the outer end of which I turn into the form intended to be given to the lower half of the tea pot, leaving the inner end, which is fixed to the mandrel of the lathe, cylindrical. I then take the circular plate of metal and place it centrically against the outer end of the chuck, and against this, a flat piece of wood, against which the front centre of the lathe is to be brought up, so as to keep the metal in its place, and to allow it to revolve with the lathe. When put into rapid motion, I bear against the metallic plate with a soft piece of wood, or other suitable substance, so as to turn it over into the chuck, by which means the lower half is formed. In order to finish its upper part, I fix the lower end in a hollow, or female chuck, and by bearing against the upper end with a soft piece of wood, I give to it such form as I desire, which I can readily do by steadying the piece of wood on the rest. It is not necessary, in this case, that there should be any solid substance within the part of the pot to be so formed. But should this be in any case desired, such a piece may be very readily placed there, passing it in at the open end of the pot, like the end of the T of a rest, and sustaining it in a similar manner, where the metal may be brought up to it by the pressure of the piece of wood on the outside.

I have thus fully described the manipulation in such a way as will enable any competent workman to follow it without difficulty, and to produce any of the forms required in such ware, or vessels, to which the latter is adapted. When it is desired, beads, rims, or edges, may be afterward added to vessels so formed, so as to meet the requirements of taste, or fashion; but in doing this, there is nothing peculiar in the mode of procedure.

What I claim as my invention, and for which I ask a patent, is the forming of the bodies of tea pots, coffee pots and other articles, of Brittania or other metallic ware, or vessels from one piece of any metal capable of being so wrought, without the necessity for soldering seams, by taking flat plates of metal, and giving to them the required shape in the lathe, whether the same be done precisely in the manner herein described, or in any other dependent upon the same principle, and producing a similar effect.

WILLIAM W. CROSSMAN.

Spinning had been used for several years prior to Crossman's patent, but chiefly as an auxiliary to other processes. Halves, tops, and bottoms of hollow ware were often spun up. Crossman proposed, however, to spin a complete form in one operation, thus eliminating the stamping of halves and much of the fitting and soldering.[29] The perfection of his process represented a long stride in technical progress, both in the company and in the industry. Isaac Babbitt could still, in 1834, recall the day when he sat in a tiny alley workshop and laboriously hand-hammered his pewter ware into existence. Nor were the days of cast ware and pressed ware long past. The rapidity of progress from hammer to mold, to die, to lathe had been remarkable indeed.

Important though the new invention was, however, Crossman soon found it impractical for many purposes. Experience proved that the new technique had limited application in the Britannia business. Only objects with smoothly rounded walls could be spun complete, and as style moved out of simple forms into fluted, gadrooned, and angular shapes, spinning again became relegated to an auxiliary position. Crossman found, moreover, that all that his patent secured was a trip to Washington for himself and nation-wide publicity for his invention. The process was adopted enthusiastically and without acknowledgment or tribute by many other metal workers throughout the country.

LEAN YEARS AND A NEW COMPANY

Though great technical progress was being made in 1832 and 1833 at Hopewell, affairs were not proceeding quite so smoothly in the shop as the stockholders might have wished. On May 3, 1833, it was voted "That the Clerk address a letter to Mr. Isaac Babbitt for the purpose of learning his present disaffectedness toward this, the Taunton Britannia Manufacturing Company." [30] Shortly after this Babbitt left the company for good.[31] No explanations can be given of the motives involved. Were Babbitt's talents too diverse to be confined to the immediate necessities of the business? Were purely personal feelings behind the move? Was loss of ownership and control distasteful to him? Such questions, offering possible explanations, can never be fully answered. Only the fact remains that the founder of the company departed from Taunton, apparently in a flurry of ill will. His work was capably carried on by Crossman and Porter, but the loss inevitably was a serious one. The brilliance, foresight, and courage of this village mechanic, as well as his part in the founding of the enterprise, can hardly be overestimated.

The early 1830's witnessed still other important changes, and a vague sense of uneasiness pervaded the whole Hopewell organization. On April 4, 1832, for unknown reasons and without previous intimation, William Crossman, William West, and Zephaniah Leonard sold their interest in the Britannia company to Horatio Leonard for $15,000. Crossman stayed with the company, later taking Babbitt's place as superintendent. West and Zephaniah Leonard apparently severed company connections completely. We cannot say with certainty that it was premonition which caused these men to pull their financial stake, nor are we sure that the purchase was the consummation of a Leonard plan to acquire control of the company. Some evidence supports both suppositions. This fact is clear: here was the break with the past, and the last of the original partners was out. Horatio Leonard now held a majority of stock, and the Leonard infiltration, which began with Zephaniah's entrance in 1829, was complete.

The next step in organization was a departure from tradition. On December 24, 1832, the remaining company stockholders voted: "That Jas. W. Crossman shall see to getting a Petition drawn to send to General Court for our incorporation for the Taunton Britannia Manfg. Co." [32]

On February 16, 1833, the Act of Incorporation was passed by the Massachusetts House of Representatives and Senate, and signed by the governor. Horatio Leonard, James Crossman, Haile Wood, Daniel Cobb, and Haile N. Wood were designated a corporation — to be called, as before, the Taunton Britannia

Manufacturing Company. Liabilities under the Act were defined as follows:[33]

Section 2: Be it further enacted, that the said corporation may be lawfully seized and possessed of such Real Estate as may be necessary and convenient for the purposes aforesaid not exceeding the value of fifteen thousand dollars, and of personal estate not exceeding twenty five thousand dollars.

On April 22, the first meeting of the new corporation voted that Horatio Leonard be president, that Benjamin Pratt be clerk and treasurer, and that Horatio Leonard, Haile Wood, and James Crossman be the directors. The capital stock was first fixed at $36,000, but later altered to $40,000. Forty shares of $1,000 each were issued, each share entitling the owner to one vote, and division was as follows:

> Horatio Leonard .... 24 shares
> Haile Wood 6   "
> James W. Crossman 8   "
> Daniel S. Cobb 1   "
> Haile N. Wood 1   "

Incorporation was unquestionably a wise move at the time, and took advantage of a law passed in Massachusetts in 1830 which limited the liability of stockholders. Again, uneasy premonition appeared to underlie a major company change. Whatever the other motives behind incorporation, it was not inappropriate that in 1833 stockholders should seek to protect their personal property to the full extent allowable by law. Conditions in Hopewell had begun to point in one direction with increasing clarity — and with ominous portent.

While statistical data are incomplete, the course of events after 1832 is clearly marked. Shipments declined sharply from the 1832 high-water mark of $34,000. In the following year they dropped to $24,000, and, while 70 per cent of the 1832 total represented consignments, in 1833 the proportion went to 83 per cent. Actual sales in the latter year apparently were only a little above $4,500. The decline reflected both increasing competition and the general business uncertainty of the period. Competition increased rapidly in the early 1830's. Britannia-making establishments in the United States multiplied in number, grew in size, and widened their spheres of influence greatly. In 1833 a Meriden, Connecticut, Britannia manufacturer reported the employment of 250 hands and an annual output of $200,000,[34] while Burrage Yale, in South Reading, Massachusetts, employed 55 men in 1832.[35] No domestic competition on a scale such as this had been encountered before. Moreover, in spite of the progress of domestic producers, prejudice in favor of foreign articles remained strong. English manufacturers continued to ship ware in over the tariff and appeared to be supplying the bulk of the American market with its tea- and coffee-pots.[36] General business pessimism added to the depressing effects of increased competition, and money shortages came in rapid succession. Business men complained that government financial policies were ruining both enterprise and the nation.

The Britannia Company foresaw impending trouble, and, without sensing exactly where it would strike, employed the usual methods of curtailment. As early as May, 1832, the stockholders voted "To discharge such Hands as Wm. Crossman thinks proper." [37] In December all but six employees listed in the time book had 10 per cent deducted from their pay, and in March, 1833, a similar payroll deduction was made. In May, prices on many lines and patterns were reduced approximately 10 per cent.

The Britannia Company waited impatiently for the huge 1832 shipments to be sold as bills incurred in the manufacture of those wares began to fall due. But on January 1, 1833, $20,000 of consigned goods gathered dust on dealers' shelves. By April the company owed $19,400 — payment pending until wares were sold. More orders to fill, more borrowing—the great credit spiral accelerated. Cash sales declined as cash became scarcer. Customers must be retained by some means—consignments continued, and even expanded. Factory operations carried through on credit and a sprinkling of cash, and debts mounted to $24,500. The urgent necessity for large cash sales in the new year became increasingly evident. The year 1834 was ushered in by a flurry of orders, but all to be shipped on consignment. The trickle of cash into Taunton dwindled still further, and suddenly a crisis gripped the country. A contemporary editorial complained that "Every day adds failure to failure, misery to misery, and reduces the means of the most solvent persons. . . ." [38] Thousands of spindles came to a standstill in Providence, machine shops and foundries closed their doors,[39] banks faltered, 6,700 Boston citizens petitioned for restoration of government deposits, withdrawn in March from the United States Bank by Presidential order.[40] For the Britannia Company consignment orders declined precipitously. Total shipments for the year barely exceeded $18,000. Receipts, which on paper had exceeded expenses by $5,100 in the preceding difficult year, almost ceased in 1834, and in the last nine months of that year plunged $7,500 below expenses. On June 30, 1834, the stockholders examined a crucial balance sheet.

General monetary conditions throughout the country improved during the summer, but hope for the Britannia Company faded fast. Down went the payroll, and the number of workmen grew smaller and smaller. Thirty hands reported for work in March, then twenty—fourteen—twelve—four. In November, 1834, the doors were finally closed and the Taunton Britannia Manufacturing Company failed.[41]

Heavy debts and an almost total lack of cash with which to finance the daily needs of the business were the direct causes of failure. Behind these lay an organization ill adapted to conditions of the times. The stockholders of the Taunton Britannia Company correctly surmised that technical progress had gone far enough by 1831 to show results in profits. Unfortunately for the future of this new emphasis in company policy, however, the owners insisted on the end but neglected the means. The men retained to manage the business after 1830 were mechanics, not salesmen. Both Babbitt and Crossman stayed at their work-

TABLE 5

BALANCE SHEET, JUNE 30, 1834

TAUNTON BRITANNIA MANUFACTURING COMPANY

Current Assets		Current Liabilities	
Cash .... $	3.47	Bills Payable $22,860.46	
Finished Ware on hand, unfinished stock, materials, etc.	14,908.32	Miscellaneous Payables	9,957.56
Ware Consigned	27,284.45		
Receivables	2,980.95	Total Current	
Total Current Assets	$45,177.19	Liabilities $32,818.02	
Fixed Assets		Net Worth	
Company Horse	95.00	Profit & Loss	
Tools	14,474.79	Account	693.73
Real Estate	13,764.77	Stock	40,000.00
	$73,511.75		$73,511.75

benches, showing neither inclination nor ability to direct sales activities. Benjamin Pratt was entrusted with sales promotion in 1832, but his efforts suffered markedly from lack of adequate supervision and control. Sales promotion was for the most part left in the hands of a few large customers, without adequate incentives to insure that promotion. The concentration of consignments placed the fate of the Britannia Company squarely in the laps of not more than four dealers who had little or nothing to lose, whatever happened in Hopewell. Consignments created a tremendous boom in plant activity and high paper profits, but the bubble burst in 1834 when credit could no longer be obtained. In one sense we cannot indict the Hopewell men to any greater degree than we can indict businessmen throughout the country, for what happened in Hopewell happened elsewhere as well. Credit was at best a highly uncertain base for expansion, but the times offered no other.

The stockholders abandoned the enterprise, and throughout the winter of 1834–35 no Britannia ware left the works. Credit gone, money lacking, contacts lost, machinery rusting — the venture indeed looked hopeless. One asset alone remained undepreciated, the virtually indomitable spirit of the workmen.

This generation had brought from farm to factory a highly developed sense of individualism and a supreme confidence in its own ability to smash adversity by the sheer force of manual labor. Defeat came hard to the little group in Hopewell, for their occupation was their life. Two young men who had worked near each other in the shop conceded no defeat. Nor did company agent Benjamin Pratt.

Early in 1835 a remarkable plan evolved, and the records tell us the story of a great gamble — of how Pratt approached Henry Reed and Charles Barton with the proposition that they take over the Britannia business and rent the shop from Horatio Leonard; of how Pratt offered his services as salesman, and how in April of 1835, the doors of the shop were opened and the water wheel began to turn again. But the records tell us little of young Reed, the spinner, and his friend Barton, the solderer, who optimistically believed that they could succeed where older, wiser, and wealthier men had failed.

In contrast to most of the men in the Britannia shop, Charles E. Barton was a "foreigner," who had migrated to Taunton from Warren, Rhode Island, probably at the instigation of his brother-in-law, William Crossman. Barton started work in 1827 at the age of nineteen, as an apprentice in the Fayette Street shop, and proved an apt pupil at the soldering trade. Wages were not much those first years, but 55 cents a day and board at Wood's kept him hard at work. Barton made rapid progress through the years of his apprenticeship, and emerged in 1831 a skilled craftsman commanding a wage of $1.12 a day. Just as little is known of this early career as of the part C. E. Barton played in the later history of the firm. Fortunately, H. G. Reed is a less mysterious and legendary character.

It might be expected that Henry Gooding Reed would enter the Britannia works, for his name could have commanded an entry into most of the thriving industries of Taunton. The son of a family prominent in government, law, and church for five generations in Taunton was almost certain to receive the consideration of prospective employers. We may be sure, however, that family influence was not so used, and that the eighteen-year-old youth who walked into the Fayette Street shop with William Crossman one morning in May, 1828, was there on his own initiative.

"Here, Porter," said Crossman to the foreman, "is a boy that wants to learn a trade; you set him to work and see what he will amount to." [42] Not so impressive a threshold crossing as that one seventy-three years later when Henry Reed closed the factory door behind him for the last time!

As a matter of fact, Henry Reed was by no means an impressive boy. Quiet and of a somewhat retiring nature, he seems to have found greater capacities for amusement in personal hobbies than in the social life of the town. A flair for making things became apparent early in Henry's boyhood, but the simple wood-carving tools and toys he constructed certainly bore no traces of genius. The trait on which neighbors commented most was an earnest liking for manual labor. Henry's father, John, was not one to let such a commendable inclination become flabby, and, for the time being, the boy was enlisted as a clerk in his father's store at a tender age. Nor did the money which the family possessed in very modest amounts ever find its way into Henry's pockets, for what he had he earned himself. Spending money in trifling amounts came from evening labors, when, after school

HENRY GOODING REED, 1810–1901

CHARLES E. BARTON, 1812–1867

and store, the boy hiked two miles to Grandfather John's black-smith shop to hammer out shoe nails which could be sold in the village.[43] The value of hard work and keen appreciation of qual-ity in manual performance were the lessons Henry Reed's boy-hood had taught him. The family, however, countenanced no neglect of book-learning, even in the manually inclined, and at Bristol Academy Henry received the best schooling the town afforded. This was the background and equipment of the new apprentice.

William Crossman had no occasion to regret his choice, for Reed rapidly mastered the techniques of spinning and was soon entrusted with the position of timekeeper as well. By 1831 Reed's earnings, like Barton's, had risen to $1.12 a day, and an increasing amount of reliance came to be placed by Crossman on the young man's steadiness and ability.

The great opportunity which the events of 1834 presented to these men found Reed and Barton without capital, and com-pletely inexperienced in the difficulties of managing an enter-prise. An intimate knowledge of Britannia manufacturing was their chief asset — to which Benjamin Pratt contributed a com-prehensive acquaintance with the wider field of customers and sales. Thus equipped, the three men made hopeful plans for the 1835 season. Admittedly the venture was a desperate one, but Reed, Barton, and Pratt had nothing to lose — much to gain. Horatio Leonard, visualizing a rental return from other-wise idle equipment, and perhaps some small reduction in the Britannia Company's huge debt, gave the enterprise his blessing.

On the morning of April 1, 1835, ten men and one woman filed into the Hopewell shop and took their places at the benches. This marked the official start of the Taunton Britannia Manufacturing Company, New Concern, and it was not an auspicious one. Even with the working force at a bare mini-mum there was little assurance that wages could be paid, and only a stock of old material on hand made production possible at all. Loyalty rather than the hope for gain brought old hands back to the shop. Barton and Reed returned to their places at the bench, and conferences on company policy took place to the tune of the lathes.

The New Concern does not seem to have been an independent legal entity, but rather the old company under new management. Barton and Reed hired such tools and equipment of the old company as the small scale of operations demanded, while Pratt sold the wares on hand and endeavored to collect bills owed the Taunton Britannia Manufacturing Company. The inheritance of the New Concern from the old was largely one of suffocating debt, and operations in 1835 barely survived the crushing load. Reed and Barton were constantly at their benches, working day and night on tasks for which they could afford to hire no help. William Crossman also returned to the shop and offered the service of experience.

But neither experience nor determination nor toil was capable of imparting a more optimistic tone to the workbench conferences. Heads wagged in Hopewell as reports on increased English imports came in, or when Pratt returned from his trips with a few scattered cash orders and reported the progress of the Connecticut factories. Money remained scarce, and credit came hard to the stricken Hopewell enterprise. From New York came disturbing reports.[44]

. . . there is no risk in anything but collecting debts. In New York you cannot collect a debt without a man chooses to pay . . . we must be in debt on an average of from 30 to 50 thousand dollars, this they do not consider much in York State . . . but would make me feel very uneasy.

The situation was an ironical one. People still wanted teapots, castor frames, and lamps, and wanted them badly. Trade could be extremely brisk on credit terms, but there was no credit for the Britannia Company, nor could much be granted by it.

Not all the news in these discouraging days was bad, however, and a rumor drifted through Taunton which caused men to gather in stores and shops throughout the town in hopeful discussion. Uncertainty at length yielded to fact, and Taunton hailed the coming of the railroad. In July, 1836, the Taunton Branch Railroad was opened to the public, and local comment was both proud and optimistic.[45]

The Opening of the Taunton Branch Rail Road, on Wednesday last, forms a new era in the history of our town. It brings Boston within one and a half hour's ride from this town, and will enable its citizens to visit the city, transact their business, and return the same day.

. . . . The cars left at a quarter before five o'clock in the afternoon, and arrived at the juncture with the Boston and Providence Rail Road in Mansfield, in less than half an hour. The branch rail road is about seven miles in length, and is one of the best constructed in the country.

Lowering of the barriers of distance was a great service to the Taunton area, but its effect was cumulative rather than immediate. To the Britannia Company the branch railroad offered winter communications and a hope for further development of overland routes to the south. Trade still proceeded slowly, however, and, contrary to expectations, no great increase in cash sales resulted.

Progress, though it was slow, was by no means imperceptible. Pratt worked hard and well, and consigned wares on dealers' shelves gradually began to move. Barton and Reed labored as effectively in the factory. Operating costs were held to poverty levels, and seldom throughout 1835 and 1836 did the working force exceed 14 hands. In 1835, $9,500 worth of bills were incurred and $14,400 worth of settlements made. In 1836, operations dwindled, but the favorable balance of payments was maintained. Both Reed and Barton advanced money out of their own pockets to tide the company over embarrassing shortages. The January 1, 1836, balance of accounts was one of which Henry Reed and Charles Barton could be justifiably proud, even though it made only too plain the laborious road ahead.

Orders were sporadic through 1835 and 1836; activity in the Britannia shop often came almost to a halt. But day after day, evening after evening, two determined men worked intently. Experiment followed experiment as Henry Reed and Charles Barton sought better techniques, new alloys, finer quality. Slack

TABLE 6

BALANCE OF ACCOUNTS, JANUARY 1, 1836
TAUNTON BRITANNIA MANUFACTURING COMPANY

Stock, supplies, metal etc. on hand	$5,996.31
Ware in the hands of Hosmer & Grew	106.69
Ware in the hands of Gilbert Clark & Co.	153.19
Ware rec'd from R. & Danforth	5.00
Company horse and waggon and harness	150.00
Tools now on hand, say	3,000.00
Am't of debts due us considered good	10,305.77
	$19,716.96

The above is all the assets of the concern Jany 1st 1836 except the Real Estate

Debts which the concern owes $20,386.16

Source: Reed & Barton Mss., Waste Book, 1833–36.

periods in company activity were never unproductive for the two men, for it was then that they acquired their technical mastery of the business. Improvement in quality came to be a passion through these hard years, and the narrow circle of company customers began to show appreciation. By 1837 Henry Reed's metallurgical experiments bore fruit, and customers of the New Concern remarked approvingly, "Their metal has the right ring!"

All progress was technical progress, however, and the company for the most part continued to follow the inspiration of others in matters of taste and design. No artist sat in the shop as yet, and the responsibility for product conception remained entirely with the partners. Henry Reed and Charles Barton imitated others as freely as did their contemporaries. Reed insisted only that the copies made should be at least equal and preferably superior in quality to the originals.

[Handwritten copartnership agreement, transcribed as follows:]

An Agreement this fifteenth day of Feby Eighteen hundred and Thirty seven — made and concluded between Gustavus Leonard on the first part and Henry G Reed and Chs E. Barton on the second part — Witnesseth — That Gustavus Leonard of the first part agrees on his part to take all the Tools belonging to the Taunton Britannia Mfgrs New Concern at their cost. and further agrees to deliver to the parties of the second part as follows — viz — one Third part to H G Reed and the same to Chs E Barton. in the same proportion as to price and terms as will have any exact bearing to the first cost of the same —— And the parties of the second part agree to take from the party of the first part. the said Tools according to the terms above written on the 1st day of May Next and then enter into Copartnership on such terms as has been agreed upon by this instrument — viz — the party of the first part to hold one third. and the parties of the second part to hold one third each —

Signed Sealed. & Delivered
in presence of —
B. W. Pratt

Gustavus Leonard
Henry G. Reed
Charles E. Barton

COPARTNERSHIP AGREEMENT, LEONARD, REED & BARTON,
FEBRUARY 15, 1837

Horatio Leonard looked with increasing favor on the New Concern and watched the tenacious struggle against debt and hard times slowly swing in favor of young Barton and Reed. In the back of his mind, too, were plans for the career of his son, Gustavus. When Pratt, Reed, and Barton proved that the business could survive, at least on a limited scale, Horatio transferred to his son all right, title, and interest in the stock and tools of the Taunton Britannia Manufacturing Company. To the New Concern the full significance of this change was not at once apparent. Charles Barton and Henry Reed must anxiously have pondered their fate and the future of their hard-won gains as it became increasingly apparent during the closing months of 1836 that a reorganization of some sort was imminent.

Gustavus Leonard soon dispelled any doubt that may have existed, and it became apparent that his interests lay in other directions than the iron works of his father or the dry goods store of Atwood, Smith & Leonard, in which he had hitherto been an active partner. The prospective position of landlord held too passive an interest for young Leonard, and his father speedily summoned Henry Reed and Charles Barton to an historic conference. Would they, in consideration of skillful service rendered and money loaned, consent to a partnership on equal terms with Gustavus? They would — and the articles of agreement were speedily drawn up.

The agreement left ownership of the real estate in the Leonard family, but granted to Reed and Barton one-third ownership each in the tools of the Taunton Britannia Manufacturing Company, as well as a one-third interest in profits of the reorganized company. The Taunton Britannia Manufacturing Company remained in legal existence, but only in a landlord capacity, owning and receiving rent for the Hopewell real estate. The operating company was henceforth to be the partnership of Leonard, Reed & Barton.

For Henry Reed and Charles Barton the years of crisis appeared to be over. If patient labor alone could bring them this far, the future prospects of patient labor and active financial support seemed bright indeed, for the long evening hours when lights burned in the Britannia shop had built a strong and lasting foundation for success.

PART II

GROWTH AND INDUSTRIAL LEADERSHIP
OF THE FIRM UNDER HENRY G. REED
1837–1860

CHAPTER V

PROFITS AND PROGRESS, 1837–1860

FEBRUARY, 1837, launched a fresh effort in the trial and error process of American industrial evolution. The partnership of Leonard, Reed & Barton was new in name, but its counterpart existed in hundreds of companies, small and large, throughout the manufacturing country. This beginning merits study, therefore, not only because it marked the start of the modern Reed & Barton organization, but also because it furnishes a concrete, graphic example of the remarkable powers of regeneration inherent in the American business enterprise of the day.

Many organizations and experiments failed in the difficult 1830's, but rarely did failure stifle initiative. A new generation of energetic business men profited from mistakes of the past to build new companies and conduct new experiments. Each failure taught fresh lessons, and an accumulating body of proven principles of business administration guided the efforts of would-be industrialists. To Leonard, Reed & Barton the history of the Taunton Britannia Manufacturing Company held much of value, and the new partnership was quick to appreciate the opportunity for comparison. The pitfalls which ended the career of the old company, therefore, were negotiated successfully by the new.

The period of years extending from 1837 to 1860 constitutes a definite unit in the history of Reed & Barton. These years mark the struggle by the new partnership to achieve a size and success equal to that of the Taunton Britannia Manufacturing Company of 1833, the surpassing of that high point, and a final consummation of the long-sought transition from workshop to factory. These years witness, moreover, the maturing of Henry

Reed's genius and designate, in a general way, the period of his greatest effectiveness. From 1837 to 1859 Reed & Barton was Reed's company, and the history of the period reflects the power and influence of one man's control. After 1859 this situation, in so far as Henry Reed was concerned, existed no longer.

The two decades which followed the 1837 founding of Leonard, Reed & Barton constitute one of the most successful and progressive eras in the history of the company. These were years of truly great accomplishment, when managerial talent, disguised in shirt sleeves and a bench apron, guided the company from obscurity to absolute leadership in the Britannia industry. Good fortune played a part in the story of success, but hard work and the immovable resolve to produce only the best urged on the 1837–1859 evolution.

RAGS TO RICHES

Some information about the founding of the Leonard, Reed & Barton partnership is lacking, but many of the details have survived. According to the terms of the agreement, Gustavus Leonard paid in to the treasury of the new company $3,719 in return for his one-third interest.[1] Henry Reed and Charles Barton appear to have put up no cash for their respective third-interests, but contributed their skill and knowledge of the Britannia business, together with such stock, tools, and materials as they owned at the time. Reed and Barton also seem to have held certain small claims against the Leonards for expenses incurred in operating the Taunton Britannia Manufacturing Company — New Concern. These were also surrendered.

Leonard, Reed & Barton came into existence as a legal entity distinct and separate from the Taunton Britannia Manufacturing Company. This fact augured well for the 1837 partnership, which, unlike the "New Concern" of Henry Reed and Charles Barton in 1836, was thereby free to commence operations unburdened with the debts of previous failure. By February, 1837, all the essential preliminaries had been completed, obligations of the partners defined, articles of agreement drawn, signed, and witnessed, and a few necessary repairs in the mill completed.

On Monday morning, February 20th, Leonard, Reed & Barton opened its doors and commenced manufacturing operations.

The company as of that day consisted of the three partners and one employee. The production line was Henry Reed, spinner; Noah Williams, fitter; and Charles Barton, solderer. On Tuesday the number of employees doubled as polisher Mervin Chace reported for work. By the end of the week eight men, including Reed and Barton, were laboring at their benches in the second-floor front room of the brick building. Gustavus Leonard presumably was on the road interviewing customers, or in the office writing letters or balancing accounts. A less modest start than this would have been impossible, for a smaller force could not have carried through the necessary sequence of manufacturing operations. So small was the scale of production those first few weeks that the loss of any one man in the shop would have forced a suspension of output! In this elementary stage of development the duties of the partners were clearly defined and immediately essential. The time book reveals what the partnership agreement fails to state. To Gustavus Leonard fell the duties of selling and bookkeeping. He was the "financial agent and outside business man." [2] Henry Reed was metallurgist, general superintendent, and boss spinner. Charles Barton assisted Reed in supervisory functions and presided as chief of the soldering department. Both Reed and Barton received regular day wages, their accounts being kept in the time book with the other workmen. Leonard received a yearly salary. Profits, if any, were to be divided equally among the partners.

These were weeks of empty titles. Henry Reed was "boss" spinner, but he was also the only spinner. Barton was "foreman," but his "department" consisted of one workman, Charles

E. Barton! Gradual growth, however, had by the end of March eliminated some of the one-man departments, and Henry Reed soon found he had a real shop to supervise. There was much optimism at the Britannia works as output began to increase, and the working force grew from eight hands to thirteen in little more than a month. Early April saw the company successfully established and on the verge of expansion to a profitable level of operations.

But April, 1837, brought profits neither to Leonard, Reed & Barton nor to other American manufacturers. Bitter, paralyzing panic swept out of the South, and spring ushered in "a commercial revulsion, such as the country had seldom witnessed." [3] Excited speculation and reckless extension of credit terminated in a monetary crisis which gripped New Orleans in March and grew in breadth and intensity, striking New York in May and reaching into every phase of the commercial and industrial life of the country. A general slackening of trade deepened to depression — a depression replete with more failures, greater unemployment, and more complete prostration of commerce than the country had ever witnessed. More than six hundred banks closed their doors, specie payments were suspended,[4] and money to satisfy even the minimum requirements of life became difficult to obtain. Signs of improvement were hopefully sought through the summer, but the progress of post-panic events made only too clear the fact that here was national disaster on a tremendous scale. By fall nine-tenths of the factories of the eastern States were said to be closed.[5] Taunton, like other towns similarly devoted to trade and manufacture, was hit hard by the events of 1837. *Niles' Weekly Register* reported that on April 13th the extensive house of Crocker & Richmond, of Taunton, failed for $600,000.[6] On that same day a committee of ten was appointed in Taunton to consider the financial state of the community. The report submitted by this committee to a public gathering later in the day stated:[7]

The extraordinary scarcity of money which has caused so many and such disastrous embarrassments in every section of the country for some-time past, has at length reached our flourishing village, and caused several of our enterprising and spirited citizens to suspend payment. But the failure of men in a time of such extraordinary embarrassment, pervading the whole country, is no evidence of their insolvency. Property, however valuable, will not now command money.

The committee urged the necessity for public calm so that the credit of the solvent should not be destroyed by undue pressure on the part of the timid. But, in spite of all, assignees' notices and advertisements requesting payment of delinquent accounts multiplied. Several merchants stated that they would do business on a cash basis only, which to all practical intent and purpose meant that they would do very little business. The Cohannet Bank, fortunately no longer the depository of the funds of the Britannia company, quietly expired, though its affairs were not terminated for several years. Horatio Leonard declared himself insolvent, in consequence of the failure of Crocker & Richmond, and assigned his property to a trust for the benefit of his creditors. The firm of Horatio Leonard & Company failed, tying up a substantial part of Gustavus Leonard's capital which was invested there. The losses of the Leonards were severe, but Gustavus escaped the fate of his father and remained solvent. For that fact the struggling partnership of Leonard, Reed & Barton had cause to be thankful.

The passing months brought scant comfort and no relief to manufacturers. The depression deepened, wages declined, and unemployment spread. A profound social unrest shook the country. Contemporary with a general antipathy toward big business arose the feeling that the rapid growth of luxurious habits among all classes was detrimental to the industry, the resources, and the morals of the people. Clearly, this was not an auspicious time for the sale of teaware! But Leonard, Reed & Barton did not fail, and sufficient capital was obtained, either from the company treasury or more probably from Gustavus Leonard, to eke out a meager existence. Output was necessarily curtailed, and the number of workmen declined. In July, 1837, the working force consisted of Henry Reed, Charles Barton, Mervin Chace, Noah Williams, and Lucretia Strange. In August seasonal dullness combined with the depths of depression to close the shop, but September found the doors open once more and five men at their benches. In defiance of the trend of business, October found the Britannia works of Leonard, Reed & Barton still open and employing eleven persons. By December business had become almost brisk, and twenty workmen labored at the task of producing teaware for a market which loudly was renouncing luxury in any form.

Available evidence shows that Taunton recovered from the crisis of 1837 more rapidly than the severity of that crisis would seem to have permitted. Small companies in general possessed the flexibility to absorb severe shocks and apparently suffered less than large enterprises. In many cases small manufactories like Leonard, Reed & Barton simply closed their doors until panic had subsided and reasonable equilibrium had been restored. Most of the April insolvents in Taunton eventually settled their debts and resumed operations. Business, restored by necessity to a cash or short-term credit basis, was more soundly conducted than before 1837. Thus, though times continued to be bad, the immediate environment in which the Britannia works existed was by no means dismal; indeed, hopeful sentiments were frequently expressed.

Operations during the first year of the Leonard, Reed & Barton partnership were largely experimental, designed to establish the name and line of the company. This purpose was achieved, for sales expanded sharply in 1838, in spite of continued depression. In the spring of the year came restriction — not of manufacturing, but of selling![8]

Taunton May 22ᵈ — 1838

B. W. Pratt Esqr.

Sir

Yours 19ᵗʰ is at hand am sorry to say I cannot hold out inducements to you to take orders for Wares — I am at present fearful we cannot fill our orders for delivery between this time and Sept — It will require about one Thousand Dollars worth pr. month in Boston alone. . . .

Respy Yr Servt

Gustavus Leonard

Other such letters followed in rapid succession.[9]

June 4, 1838, " . . . will be impossible to give you Teaware in time for Autumn Sales We consider our existing Contracts to fill orders for Autumn as *binding*. . . ."

October 11, 1838, "It will not be expedient to take orders for any more Ware until further advice as with our present contracts on direct sales we shall not be able to furnish the article this autumn"

February 16, 1839, " . . . must decline offering you a supply of our Ware in consequence of our present agreements to supply being quite as large as we can fulfill."

Demand for company wares continued strong, and their growing popularity through the years of deepest depression formed a legitimate basis for the expansion of manufacturing facilities. This great opportunity for expansion was permitted to go begging. To create the immediate means of satisfying the market, Leonard, Reed & Barton would have had to borrow. Such a loan could undoubtedly have been negotiated in the improved money market of 1842–43. The reputation of the company was good, and its prospects excellent. But no loan was negotiated. Instead, a slow, cautious growth was financed out of earnings only, and Gustavus Leonard continued to send company regrets to disappointed customers. Behind this policy lay the completely conservative personality of Henry G. Reed, who practised in private life the virtue expressed in his favorite motto, "Work and Save," and who applied that same motto with equal enthusiasm to the affairs of the firm. Still vivid in the minds of the partners, moreover, was the disaster which expansionist practices had wreaked on the Taunton Britannia Manufacturing Company in 1834. Capacity production in the early 1840's appeared to create no great amount of optimism in the Britannia works, nor did it awaken visions of quick riches among the partners.

Slowly the company gained back the eight to ten thousand dollars which, according to Gustavus Leonard,[10] had been lost in five years of experimental operation. Scrupulously avoiding the use of borrowed money, the partners turned back income into the treasury to finance cash purchases of more materials and the employment of more help. The year 1843 created still greater opportunities for rapid expansion as trade in general began to recover and signs of prosperity gave rise to increasing demands from company customers. A heavy tariff placed on imported Britannia products lent further optimism to the domestic trade, but Henry Reed continued throughout 1844 and 1845 to enlarge production facilities only to the extent permitted by company earnings.

Growth, though restrained, was far from insignificant, however. The number of employees increased from twenty in December, 1837, to thirty-three in December of the following year.[11] From this time to 1845 the average number of workmen employed remained between twenty and thirty, and despite urgent calls for more goods, only occasionally exceeded the latter figure. The partners' equity in the business grew from $9,646.51 in September, 1840, to $14,114.54 in July, 1845, while inventories increased in the same period from $6,724.48 to $10,732.56.[12]

Sound growth was accompanied by sound policies in finance and sales. From the moment when Leonard, Reed & Barton began business the partners avowed their intention to make only cash sales. The Panic of 1837 and the five subsequent lean years made such a policy impossible. Lack of specie and extremely slow collections throughout the commercial world forced the company to grant credit. The balance sheet for April 16, 1841, shows a total of $9,042.92 owed to the company, as compared with an estimated annual sales volume of between $20,000 and $30,000.[13] Slow collections in turn forced the company to purchase on credit and even pay wages in notes rather than cash. With returning prosperity these conditions, which must thoroughly have aroused Henry Reed's Yankee instincts, were promptly eliminated. By 1846 business had largely been restored to a cash basis, and the balance sheet for July was prosperous and sound.

TABLE 7

BALANCE SHEET, JULY 10, 1846
LEONARD, REED & BARTON

Current Assets		Current Liabilities	
Cash in Bristol County Bank	$2,350.20	Payables	$192.70
Material and Finished Ware on Hand	8,860.58		
Receivables	940.00		
Total Current Assets	$12,150.78		
		Net Worth	
Fixed Assets		Owners' Equity in	
Tools	4,000.00	the Business	15,958.08
	$16,150.78		$16,150.78

Source: Reed & Barton Mss., Account of Stock, 1840–57.

The balance sheet appeared to satisfy even Henry Reed, and in August, 1846, almost ten years after the start of the business, the first dividend, of $1,500, was divided among the partners.[14] Scant reward for the labors of management through some of the most difficult years in the history of American business! Further rewards were in store, however, and on July 7, 1847, another $1,500 dividend was declared. The profit for this year, after deducting the dividend, was stated to be $3,229.95.[15] This latter sum, in accordance with past practice, was immediately reinvested in the business.

After 1847, profit and dividend information is unfortunately scarce. The prosperity of the company, however, continued to increase, despite a temporary business recession in 1847, and the partners apparently continued to withdraw only a small part of their profits in dividends. These were good days, not only for Reed & Barton, but for Taunton as well. Profitable business and general optimism were the keynotes sounded both by the retailers on Main Street and by the manufacturers along Mill River. New shops and freshly painted signs bore silent testimony to prosperity, while shiny hacks and well-groomed horses clattered a noisy welcome to rising gains. Taunton's population increased from 7,645 in 1840 to 10,441 in 1850,[16] and the receipts of the local railroads reflected greater traffic, both passenger and freight. From 1843 to 1849 the receipts of the Taunton Branch Railroad increased 32 per cent, while for the same period the New Bedford Railroad, opened in 1840 and giving Taunton its first direct rail connection with a seaport, increased its revenues 63 per cent.[17] The prosperity of 1849, however, was merely a stepping stone to the boom years to follow. Taunton citizens caught their breath sharply as the cholera epidemic of 1849 struck into New England, then, as the threat subsided, lapsed into the undisturbed enjoyment of good times.

For Reed & Barton the 1849–54 period was one of unparalleled expansion, as Britannia ware achieved the peak of its popularity and the company found itself the largest and best known in the industry. California gold flowed freely, prices rose, and profits soared, but conservative management enabled the Britannia concern in Taunton to survive the sudden success and emerge well fortified for whatever events might follow.

In July, 1854, the partners looked at their account books to

MAIN STREET, TAUNTON, IN THE 1840's

The jewelry store of Isaac Babbitt and William Crossman was in the building at the far right

find that their investment had almost quadrupled in five years.
Sales during this unprecedented period abruptly increased out
of the $20,000–$30,000 level, at which they had consistently
held during the 1840's, to a volume exceeding $90,000.[18] In-
vestment in tools doubled from 1849 to 1854, and inventories
tripled.[19] The year 1854, however, brought a sharp financial
panic and a short depression to the country. Reed & Barton
confessed to a depressed state of trade and uncertainty as to what
the future might bring,[20] but a prompt revival in the following year dispelled all doubts. Sales for 1855 reached
$93,835.00,[21] and on May 18th a dividend of $4,500 was declared.
The revival extended through 1856: " . . . a very active and
busy year. The Factory business has been good, requiring constant attention. . . . "[22] Sales volume exceeded $100,000, in
spite of growing competition and the increasing popularity of
electroplated silverware. A contemporary critic remarked,
"Their wares are regarded by the trade as among the choicest
and most saleable in market. . . . "[23]

Cautious management, however, was not always proof against
the extremities of cyclical fluctuation. A sharp panic in August,
1857, resulted in many failures. The ensuing depression, though
short, caused acute suffering in Taunton and forced Reed &
Barton to curtail operations. E. W. Porter records the following
account of the hard winter of 1857–58 in Taunton.[24]

A financial panic swept over the country this fall. Many manufacturing
concerns went to the wall. J. K. Mills & Co. of Boston suspended, carrying Mr. W. Lovering of Whittenton with them. The Wm. Mason Works
and many others were crippled.

Reed & Barton sent nearly all their hands home by November 15, and
they were not called in again until the middle of February. Hundreds of
men worked digging stumps on the pine lands around Mayflower Hill,
just for the fuel. . . . Some dug several cords. Fortunately I had work
with N. B. Leonard and a few others all winter on 3/4 time.

Appointed on a committee of 3 by the Mechanics' Literary Association
to investigate the condition of the "poor & unemployed."

The workmen of Reed & Barton, however, sustained themselves with a wholesome independence that asked no charity and were well rewarded for their winter hardship. In the fall of 1858, just one year after the panic and shutdown, Porter recorded the following entry in his diary.[25]

Geo. Brabrook has been having a splendid success as salesman and our Factory has been rushed all the fall. During Nov & Dec we have had to run *two shifts* of hands, working day & night. In Dec. Peleg Francis made 22 days of *overtime*. He is a roller in Fathers department, & had to roll metal for both day & night hands.

In 1859 the company was again refusing orders. One customer, frantic for wares of any type, offered to clean the garrets of the obsolete products of other years. Sales for the year amounted to $129,000,[26] and the partners' investment in the business grew to $107,597.31.[27]

The close of the year found the firm in eminently sound condition, with a remarkable record of conservatively financed growth. Any appraisal of this highly successful period in the company's history must, of necessity, acknowledge the general upward trend of business as one important explanation for such progress. Yet of more importance, perhaps, was the influence of Henry Reed, for it was he who dictated the policies which brought success. The story of managerial and ownership evolution which gave Reed control of the company is therefore an integral part of the history of profits and progress from 1837 to 1859.

THE COURSE OF OWNERSHIP

The 1837 partnership of Leonard, Reed & Barton was short-lived, and in the summer of 1838 Henry Reed left the company. Much mystery clothes this event and also the motives involved, but apparently Reed felt that the business was not large enough to support all three partners. A year later, however, when prospects looked somewhat more hopeful for an enlarged trade, he returned and sought to rejoin the partnership. Charles Barton was agreeable and anxious to have him do so, but Gustavus Leonard objected strenuously. Leonard claimed that since Reed had left the company in a period of temporary adversity, he should not be taken back when times were good, even though the act of leaving had been prompted by the belief that all would benefit therefrom. Barton mediated successfully between the conflicting factions, and in 1839 Henry Reed became a partner once more. An undercurrent of conflict persisted, however — a conflict which apparently had its origin in the early days of the Taunton Britannia Manufacturing Company. Since 1830 an intangible atmosphere of friction between manufacturing and financial interests had hung over the company. If the control of the Leonards was never openly opposed, at least it was secretly resented in the factory. Perhaps the little group of Britannia men was too closely bound by ties of common interest to admit of domination from outside the workshop. Whatever the causes, the fact remains that early in 1840 Leonard, Reed & Barton was split open by a cleavage of interests which saw Henry Reed and Charles Barton bargaining with Gustavus Leonard for control of the company. One proposal was drawn up, according to the terms of which Reed and Barton were to sell to Gustavus Leonard their interest in the partnership and to work for $2.00 a day for one year, "Reed to show how to mix metal & japan and any other information that may be required. Reed & Barton not to engage directly or indirectly in making Britannia ware for one Year." These terms apparently were not acceptable, and the agreement was never signed. Finally, some months later, Leonard proposed to withdraw from the firm, and an equitable settlement was arranged whereby Henry Reed and Charles Barton purchased his interest in the tools and stock on hand. For this interest Leonard was paid $8,178 [28] — not an inconsequential increase over his 1837 investment of $3,719! The agreement does not seem to have affected the ownership of the mill buildings and real estate, which remained in the possession of the Leonards. Gustavus Leonard continued to work for the company as salesman-treasurer, and the Leonard, Reed & Barton mark continued to be used on some company wares. But it was, nevertheless, a new firm which came into existence on August 26, 1840.[29] With

---

NOTICE,

THE Copartnership heretofore existing under the firm of Leonard, Reed & Barton, was dissolved by mutual consent, on the 26th inst.

GUSTAVUS LEONARD,
H. G. REED,
C. E. BARTON.

THE undersigned, having taken the establishment formerly occupied by Leonard, Reed & Barton, are prepared to execute at short notice, orders for all kinds of Britannia Ware. No expense having been spared to prepare their Factory for this purpose, and being determined their Ware shall be composed of the best materials, and executed in good style, trust by diligent attention to their business, to merit a share of public patronage.

HENRY G. REED,
CHARLES E. BARTON.

Taunton Sept 2, 1840.

NOTICE OF THE DISSOLUTION OF THE LEONARD, REED & BARTON
PARTNERSHIP
From the Taunton *Whig*

the passing years the memory of Babbitt & Crossman, the Taunton Britannia Manufacturing Company, Leonard, Reed & Barton — important names all — sank into oblivion. The coming century brought fame to a new name, and the white-smiths of Taunton from this time on were to be known as Reed & Barton.

The 1840 agreement brought past resentments to the surface,

and relations between Henry Reed and Gustavus Leonard remained strained. Edmund Porter admits that for a time a "ring" existed in the factory consisting of Alfred Brabrook, J. Allen, F. A. Harvey, and William Barker, who joined Leonard in opposing, more or less openly, the newly formed partnership. "All good worthy men," said Porter, "but in this case evidently *a little off.*" [30] The friction appears to have disappeared harmlessly, and Leonard's friends became among the most competent and faithful employees of the company. Leonard himself served the company well, and his premature death in the spring of 1845 left a vacancy difficult to fill.

The year 1847 brought further changes in ownership, connected in some way not ascertainable with the settlement of Gustavus Leonard's estate. At this time Henry H. Fish, dry goods merchant and banker of Fall River and brother-in-law of Gustavus Leonard, purchased a third-share in the Reed & Barton partnership. Fish showed no immediate interest in the company except as an investment, but sent his son George to Taunton to learn the trade. Simultaneously with this transaction the Leonard, Reed & Barton mark on company ware was completely eliminated in favor of the Reed & Barton stamp. [31] No evidence has survived to explain the admittance of Henry Fish to the firm. It is not unreasonable to suppose, however, that the added financial backing thus assured was sufficient justification for the move.

After Gustavus Leonard's death the task of keeping the company sales and financial accounts fell to Alfred Brabrook, who had been hired by Henry Reed in 1837. Through Alfred's influence a new apprentice reported for work in 1850. The young man was George Brabrook, Alfred's brother. With a background of rugged life on the family farm in Acton, and a year of civil engineering training behind him, George came into the factory completely naïve concerning the complexities of trade and manufacture — nine years later he was a partner in the business. Brabrook's career led from the packing-room, where he served his apprenticeship, and followed the course of the great sales boom of the 1850's. So successful did he become as a salesman that Henry Reed and Charles Barton had no alternative but to admit him to the firm. On March 20, 1859, George Brabrook became the fourth partner.[32]

Rumour says that he took one quarter for $5000 paying in $500, and giving his note for $4500.

His excellent record as a Salesman made him sought after by certain Connecticut parties and Reed & Barton did this to keep him.

Brabrook's entrance into the firm was by no means the last ownership change in the company history, but it did mark the establishment of the last of four interests, the interplay of which was to constitute the story of control for the next forty-five years.

THE ACQUISITION OF THE PLANT

Great company growth was accompanied not only by the succession of partnership changes described above, but by an expansion of manufacturing facilities as well. The evolution of the Reed & Barton plant during the 1837–1859 period constitutes an important chapter in the history of profits and progress of these years, and is closely allied in many particulars to the withdrawal of Leonard interests from the partnership. The history of the Britannia works property remained closely connected with the fate of the Taunton Britannia Manufacturing Company, whose last days it is therefore desirable to outline briefly.

In 1837 the Taunton Britannia Manufacturing Company performed no active function other than the collection of rent from the various parties, including Leonard, Reed & Barton, who were operating on the premises of the Britannia works. Gustavus Leonard served as treasurer, clerk, and agent for the landlord company, and his father, Horatio, proceeded to purchase all the shares which were not at that time in the possession of the Leonard family, with the exception of eight shares retained by James Crossman. In 1840 Horatio appears to have sold or transferred his majority interest in the company to Gustavus. In 1844 the Taunton Britannia Manufacturing Company consisted of stockholders Gustavus Leonard and James Crossman, the Britannia works property, and a large unsettled debt — grim reminder of the 1834 failure. On August 31, 1844, a stockholders' meeting was called in the store of James Crossman. The company property was sold to Cyrus Lothrop, of Taunton, and the Board of Directors (Crossman and Leonard) voted "that the proceeds of the sale be appropriated to cancel out the demands against the company." [33] On December 24, 1844, the Taunton Britannia Manufacturing Company was formally dissolved and passed out of existence.

Reed & Barton paid annual rent of $580 to the Lothrops for the use of a part of the Britannia works property. In 1854 most of the Lothrop interest in the real estate was acquired by C. E. Albro, and, in so far as property ownership was concerned, Reed & Barton remained a homeless waif. With an increasing volume of orders to fill, this situation could not be tolerated for long. The increase bred congestion, and the space available to the Britannia company was both limited and scattered. In 1845 Reed & Barton used half of the first floor of the brick building for casting ovens, rolls, and presses, and the second floor for the spinning, fitting, soldering, and polishing workers and equipment. Also competing for space in the none-too-large structure was the tack and shoe-nail shop of Stephen Rhodes, employing twenty hands, and the textile machinery works of William Mason, with thirty workmen. Henry Reed appropriated for his japanning oven the kitchen of the old Lincoln homestead on Tucker's Island; and the long wooden building below the raceway housed the japanning furnace, the company office, Alfred Brabrook's packing-room, a blacksmith shop, and a tenement.

In 1852 the pressure of expansion combined with the accumulation of adequate capital reserves to institute a building and buying program. Two brick double tenements were erected on Britannia Street beside the three wooden 1830 houses, while in the mill yard itself new ground was broken. A brick addition was appended to the main factory building to take care of the growing requirements of the healthy young plating department. Across the river another brick structure was erected to furnish much needed space for burnishing. In the five succeeding years various small purchases of land and buildings increased the real estate account of the company from nothing in July, 1852, to $4,820 in July, 1857.[34] In September of that year a new dam was built, and William W. Porter carefully cut the date inscription for posterity to admire. It was October 24th, however, which saw the climax of expansion, for on that day Charles Albro, in consideration of $13,500, transferred all right, title, and interest in the Britannia works to Reed & Barton, and the company at last had a home of its own.

The purchase of the plant and the great sales boom in 1858 and 1859 fittingly culminated an amazingly progressive and profitable score of years. At the beginning of 1859 Reed & Barton was more strongly entrenched marketwise than it had ever been before and was enjoying a financial position which few later periods were to surpass. The popularity of Reed & Barton wares is easily understood, but the financial strength of 1859 might be termed surprising. For, since the death of Gustavus Leonard in 1845, Reed & Barton had drifted along its course virtually deprived of the benefit of financial management. Fortunately the current of the times required not financial, but technical, skill. For Reed & Barton the happy coincidence of the right man at the right time spelled success. Henry Reed was a technician and a manufacturer. He was, moreover, cautious in fields where he recognized his limitations. Most important of all perhaps, he was left free to apply his skill and to exercise his caution virtually unrestricted by dissenting voices of ownership and management. Reed & Barton, 1859, was Henry Reed's masterpiece, and we may say of his management that he turned genius in production, indifference in selling, and thriftiness in finance into great profits.

CHAPTER VI

NEW METHODS AND IMPROVED WARES

CIRCUMSTANCES bequeathed Henry G. Reed the domination of company management, but he rejected that part of his inheritance which centered in the company office. The bench, rather than the desk, was the focus of his operations between 1837 and 1859, and our attention therefore naturally focuses on events in the factory — on the development of product, of design, of manufacturing technique, and on the men who made that development possible.

TRANSITIONS

The 1837–1859 period was perhaps the most difficult in Reed & Barton's history, and demanded of the company three great transitions. The first and most important requisite for survival was the transition from workshop to factory. This called for more than mere growth in size and involved the widespread adoption of power machinery, specialization of men and equipment, and the delegation of authority downward from top management to a foreman class. The physical obstacles to be surmounted in achieving high-speed, low-cost output were formidable, but even more so was the change in viewpoint demanded of management. The annals of American business are filled with this struggle of artisans and small shop-owners to survive initial success, to discard their concepts of business on a small scale, and to master the attitudes demanded by business of factory size.

Success in the 1840's and 1850's required, secondly, a transition through a series of important product changes. The score of years which followed 1837 witnessed one of those great division points at which a whole class of products reaches the height of its popularity and is displaced, sometimes abruptly, by something new and better. The introduction of electroplated tableware foretold the end of Britannia ware as such and tore a complacent, well-established industry out by its roots. So superior did the new article prove to be that the eventual displacement of Britannia ware was inevitable, and the remaining life of the older product was plainly to be bounded by the length of time it took manufacturers to learn to make the new.

The third great transition required of Reed & Barton and the industry was through an upheaval in American taste which was destined to carry design the length of a downward path from Colonial refinement to the threshold of the Victorian débâcle. This was the most spectacular transition of all, from which, for the individual producer seeking profit, there was no opportunity for escape.

The fact that Reed & Barton had successfully negotiated the workshop-to-factory transition causes little surprise. Henry Reed's talents were such as to make this evolution not only possible but easy. There existed, moreover, a wealth of precedent and contemporary experience upon which to draw. Almost all trades were deep in the process of becoming industries, and contemporary examples in the manufacturing world clearly illustrated the problems of growth. In Taunton, moreover, a supply of mechanical talent, released by the decline of the iron industry and the frequent failures of the textile companies, was awaiting reëmployment and a chance to apply its knowledge of large-scale operation.

The product and design transitions, however, were not easily negotiated, for the Taunton Britannia men in general and Henry Reed in particular were mechanics by natural inclination, and connoisseurs of public taste only by laboriously acquired experience. No professional interpreter of market demand was employed, and no artists were consulted. Specialization in the company did not begin to approach that highly refined point until 1860 or later. The men at the factory bench felt competent to turn out wares which would sell, and experience proved their confidence to be justified.

New Designs

The choice of a line with which to begin business in 1837 was a crucial matter, for on it depended the immediate fate and future prospects of Leonard, Reed & Barton. No minute books record the anxious discussions which preceded the February opening, but consideration of product was a major concern of the partners. The experimental work of Henry Reed and Charles Barton in 1835 and 1836 formed an invaluable background of knowledge for the new partnership, and the Britannia metal formula developed and proven in those hard years provided a highly satisfactory foundation for the line.

The first samples released by Leonard, Reed & Barton to the trade in early 1837 consisted, to a considerable extent, of the old Taunton Britannia Manufacturing Company line — a matter of necessary economy in the use of existing dies and molds. Three teaware patterns new to the company, however, carried the burden of responsibility for Leonard, Reed & Barton's initial success. Soon destined for fame were the patterns numbered 2700, 2800, and 2900.

As spring arrived and commerce yielded to panic and depression, the wisdom of the partners' choices became evident. Only an extremely popular line of wares could wring sales from a market such as this, and the buying temper of the times left no room for mediocrity. Orders trickled in to Taunton, " . . . business gradually increased, more hands were employed, and a better command of the market was held, the roots of the enterprise striking deeper and deeper, and its branches producing healthy and satisfying fruit." [1] Even the 1837 market greedily absorbed the new teapots, and chiefly to the No. 2700 octagon

BRITANNIA TEAPOT, NO. 2900

BRITANNIA TEAPOT, NO. 2700

These two patterns contributed substantially to the success of the Leonard, Reed & Barton partnership. They were made under this stamp between 1837 and 1847

BRITANNIA TEAPOT, No. 2700, LEONARD,
REED & BARTON

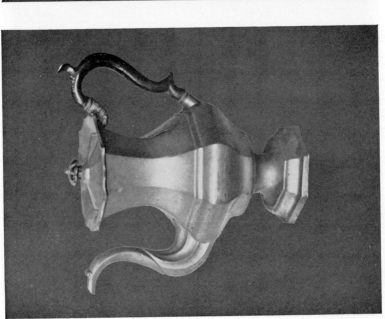

BRITANNIA TEAPOT, JAMES DIXON & SONS,
SHEFFIELD, ENGLAND

Ten half-pint size

pattern did Leonard, Reed & Barton owe its continued existence.

The success of the great gamble of 1837 clearly proved the ability of the Taunton Britannia men to produce a line which would sell, but success came, not from any great feeling for design, but from a complete willingness to adopt that which had been proved successful. Leonard, Reed & Barton placed before the market a line of faithful copies of popular Dixon patterns. The famous trinity, Nos. 2700, 2800, and 2900, were admittedly English in origin and obviously adopted because they had shown their worth. The year 1837 was no time to experiment with untried wares or to dabble in the dangerous field of original product design! As in the previous decade, imitation of proven products continued to be the key to success for American manufacturers, and servile copying ran unrestrained through nearly the whole fabric of art and industry during the 1840's. In the Britannia industry, particularly, the origin of product design continued to be predominantly English and the firm of James Dixon & Sons, of Sheffield, led the field. Plagiarism in those times was not so serious an indictment as in our own, for attention was then still focused on machinery, while the wealth and leisure necessary to fertilize original thinking along cultural lines was largely lacking.

America in the '40's was still a lusty young country — too energetic to be artistic and forced by that circumstance, as well as by tradition, to borrow from older and more sophisticated civilizations. Originality was largely confined to the development of mechanics, and was absorbed in that vast and profitable field. Far more incentive existed for young talent to become a good machinist than a master craftsman, and until after 1860 industrial artists in America were few in number, and, for the most part, meagerly patronized. Men like Henry Reed who were busy with manufacturing problems thus had no reservoir of trained designers, such as existed in England and France at the time, to draw upon. The only possible course, therefore,

was to imitate. "The subtle poison of the nineteenth century —
the pressure to copy someone else," [2] — was a universal characteristic, and Henry Reed was no worse than his contemporaries.
He was, in fact, better than most, for, while all too many
American copies of English wares were cheap mockeries of the
originals, the Britannia of Taunton was universally acknowl-
edged to surpass its English progenitors in quality. Henry
Reed bent every effort to perpetuate this situation.

In this commendable ambition Reed was remarkably successful, and it took Leonard, Reed & Barton little more than a
year to achieve national recognition. Patterns 2700, 2800, and
2900 were shown in the 1838 exhibition of the American Institute in New York, and the reception accorded them was
enthusiastic.[3]

BRITANNIA WARE

The following letter and the appended statement, from an active
member of the Institute, speaks great things for our progress in the useful arts. It exhibits another step taken towards our real and lasting independence. These wares are wanted in every family in the Union, and
it is a great triumph to be able to produce them among ourselves cheaper
than they can be afforded by importers. The public are invited to call
and examine the specimens at the Repository, 187 Broadway.

T. B. Wakeman, Esq. Corresponding Secretary, &c.

Sir, — I send herewith several specimens of the manufacture of Britannia Ware, from Taunton, Mass., which I am satisfied will bear comparison with any in Europe, for neatness and elegance of finish.

In calling the attention of the Institute to them, I beg leave to express
my firm conviction, that if such specimens of American manufactures
are properly encouraged, it will lead in a few years to an entire independence of foreign nations for articles of necessity and use, which I
trust may be the case, as the time has arrived when the experiment
should be made.

With my best wishes for the prosperity and welfare of the Institute,

I am, very respectfully,

Your obedient servant,

CHARLES H. DELAVAN.

P.S. The cost of this Britannia is,

For the coffee-pot, ...$2.65
For the sugar and cream pots, ... 2.40
For the tea pot, ... 1.78
                                                  ————
                                                  $6.83

The cost of English Britannia, no better in quality, and the same pattern —

For the coffee-pot, ...$4.06
For the sugar and cream pots, ... 2.57
For the tea-pot, ... 2.53
                                                  ————
                                                  $9.16
Deduct price of American from English 6.83
                                                  ————
Leaving a balance of $2.33

You will perceive, Mr. Secretary, that there is a saving of two dollars and thirty-three cents on the set — which every American ought to be proud of.

                                          C.H.D.

Manufacturers: Leonard, Reed & Barton.
St. John & Wetherell, Agents, New-York.

Even without benefit of a 25 per cent tariff protection, the Taunton wares could have undersold the imported by a considerable margin. English Britannia was forced to compete on the basis of reputation and quality. Reed apparently was quick to appreciate this fact, and continued unabated his experiments to surpass in quality both foreign and domestic wares. Success appears not to have diminished in the slightest degree the constant effort to produce a better product, and the whale oil lamps at the Britannia works still burned late at night as the partners worked out new ideas.

In the summer of 1838 the rolls which Elias Strange had made for Babbitt & Crossman in 1824 were relegated to tasks of minor importance, and a new set was procured from Boston which gave a vastly improved surface and made a finer finish possible. The company was prompt to inform customers of the fact.

Taunton, June 28th 1838 [4]

Mssrs. Krug & Colladay,

    Gent

    Annexed you have bill and Invoice Tea ware about the balance of your order of April which we think you will find more satisfactory finished than that alluded to in your last letter.

    We are now takeing all pains to give you your 200 setts better than *any ever* has been sent into market as yet, and we hope and trust better than Dixsons. First by a new pair hardened Steel Rolls to give the metal a smooth surface. Secondly by selecting all our polishing earth, and lastly to spare no pains to affect a perfect polish. . . .

                Yours Resptly
                Leonard Reed & Barton

The new surfacing process was noted by the Massachusetts Charitable Mechanic Association, which awarded the company a silver medal in the second Association exhibition in Boston and drew a favorable comparison between Leonard, Reed & Barton teaware and the imported article.[5]

The favorable recognition accorded the company's three new English patterns through the years of depression reënforced Reed's determination to follow the English manufacturers in matters of design. In every case the acknowledgment was open and unashamed. On June 5, 1839, the company said in a letter to a Philadelphia customer, "We are about getting up Dixon's latest pattern for the fall trade." [6] And a week later, to a Boston dealer, "You ask if we have seen the new Importers pattern Tea Ware. *We have them all* at our Mill and shall make the best and put them into the market much less than the English. . . ." [7] New patterns were brought out, not on a predetermined schedule or according to any fixed policy, but rather, depending on whether Dixon had done anything in the trade. A new Dixon pattern in the American market was cause

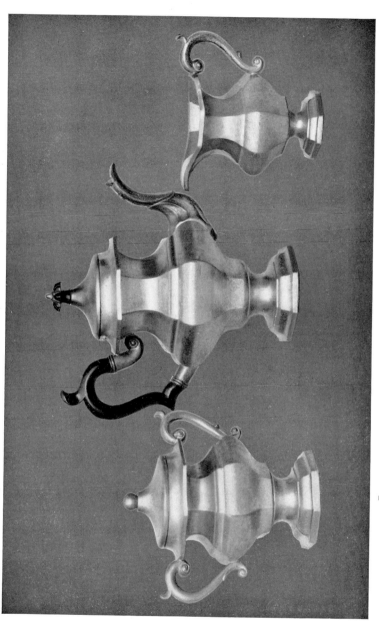

BRITANNIA TEA SET, No. 3000, LEONARD, REED & BARTON, 1837–1847
Illustrating a further departure from the early fluted patterns

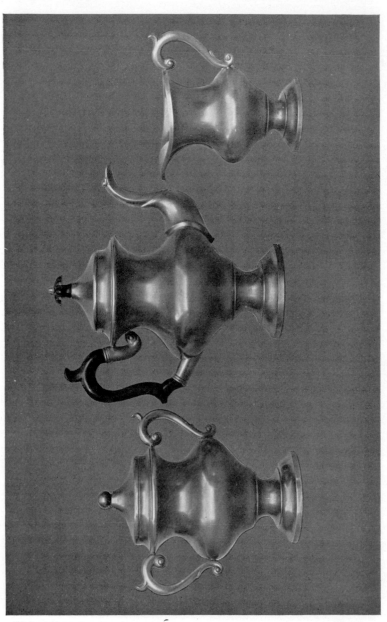

BRITANNIA TEA SET, No. 3400, LEONARD, REED & BARTON, 1837–1847
An example of rugged simplicity characteristic of the period

for brisk activity in Taunton, and Reed trod hard on the heels of the English agents.

Taunton Oct. 23^d 1840 [8]

Mrss Young Smith & Co
    Gent

. . . .

. . . . In regard to making a new sett from Dixon pat. We may think it expedient providing one is in Market superior in taste to ours.

Should like it if You will procure for us and send immediately two setts of his latest or best patterns — We will soon decide and advise You if we think it expedient to make them.

Respy Yours
Reed & Barton

Constant alertness to market innovations made up for the dearth of creative talent. Such alertness became increasingly vital to success as markets began to emerge from the stagnation of the 1820's and 1830's. Change was in the air, and the patterns on which the Taunton Britannia Manufacturing Company had founded its venture in 1830 began to be looked upon with some disdain by the hoop-skirted hostesses of 1840. Such items as were new in the Leonard, Reed & Barton line exhibited certain innovations in design, although the chasteness and severity of past years persisted. A new spirit was present, but it was not a radical spirit. That some of the old forms survived was due in part to the strength of tradition, and in an even greater degree to the fact that machine techniques were still incapable of complex maneuvers on an economical scale. The main development in the field of design to 1840 was the decline of the fluted and the substitution of less delicate, more virile, and sturdier patterns. Broad planes, sweeping curves — a bolder and somewhat less refined touch — became increasingly popular as memories of the gracious Georgian era faded. But the new work was not unpleasing, and much of it was well proportioned.

New Products

Alertness to change in design, however, was but a footnote to the more vital and far-reaching problem of change in product. Reed proved himself to be astute, not only in shaping his teapots to meet popular fancy, but also in placing the proper emphasis on the proper product at the right time. The company had already witnessed first-hand the immense power of social custom and the profits accruing to those who successfully rode the crest of fashion. In the early stages of Leonard, Reed & Barton's existence no great exercise of ingenuity was required to discern what the market was calling for. Teapots and castor sets were taproots of the 1837 partnership, and the "healthy and satisfying fruit" which the company first produced had a definitely familiar flavor.

The growing web of communications, however, gave wings to new ideas. Here and there appeared the insignificant beginnings of important product developments, and more than ordinary discernment was required to keep abreast of growth in the Britannia industry after 1840. In no case was Henry Reed caught off guard, and without exception the company either pioneered in new fields or immediately followed the pioneers.

The early 1830's saw a new alloy, German or nickel silver, introduced into America from England. The properties of this metal, great durability and freedom from corrosion, were early recognized, but tardily applied to practical fields. Reed was among the first in America to see the potentialities of the alloy, and by 1838, almost ten years ahead of the trade, Leonard, Reed & Barton were regularly manufacturing nickel-silver castor frames, and building up a fund of experience which was later to prove of great value.

The spreading popularity of gas-lighting devices also appears to have attracted the attention of the partners, not so much it would seem because of the possibilities involved as because of

BRITANNIA COMMUNION SET, LEONARD, REED & BARTON
Manufactured between 1837 and 1847. Reproduced with permission from *American Pewter*, by J. B. Kerfoot

BRITANNIA TEAPOT, No. 3550, LEONARD, REED & BARTON
First made in 1844

an implied threat to the established oil-lamp business. In 1838 steps were taken again, well in advance of the market, to modify Leonard, Reed & Barton lamps to permit their use with gas as well as with oil. When gas lighting finally swept the smoky,

TABLE 8

SHIPMENTS OF WARE, JANUARY–DECEMBER, 1838
LEONARD, REED & BARTON

	Units Shipped	Average Price	Value of Shipments	Percentage of Total Shipments
Castor frames (without bottles)	7,416	$ 1.75	$12,978.00	41.6%
Tea Sets	706	10.50	7,413.00	23.8
Teapots	2,749	2.00	5,498.00	17.6
Urns	143	11.00	1,573.00	5.0
Sugars and Creams	710	1.50	1,065.00	3.4
Coffeepots	359	2.90	1,041.10	3.3
Coffin plates (doz.)	298	2.50	745.00	2.4
Lamps	736	.75	552.00	1.8
Slop Bowls	74	1.00	74.00	
Plates	82	.75	61.50	
Cups	60	.75	45.00	
Tankards	18	2.50	45.00	1.1
Bowls	12	1.25	15.00	
Shaving boxes (gr.)	2	18.00	36.00	
Pepper caps (gr.)	12	5.00	60.00	
Total	13,377		$31,201.60	100.00%

Source: Letters and invoices, 1837–39, and Day Book, 1837–39.

picturesque whale oil lamps from the market the company was in a position to profit greatly.

The great depression of 1837–43, one of the severest in our history, seems to have sharpened the acumen of the Britannia men of Taunton, for during those uncertain years diverse markets were tapped. The campaign year of 1840 brought a short but vigorous trade in Harrison mugs, which served the two-fold purpose of increasing company profits and of expressing the

Whig party sentiments of Henry Reed. At the same time an incursion was made into the industrial market with the sale of Britannia metal sheets and miscellaneous supplies to small workshops in the vicinity of Taunton. Leonard, Reed & Barton also experimented with flatware, a field of vast possibilities which the company had hitherto ignored. An 1840 letter mentions the fact that at that time facilities existed for manufacturing up to 100 dozen spoons per week.[9]

While the market for new products was expanding, manufacturers of staple items of Britannia tableware were constantly pushing prices downward in an attempt to reach purses which had been closed to the best grade of metal. Many factories, among them Reed & Barton, added a group of "common metal" articles to their established line in an effort to tap the low-price market. It was this practice which attached a stigma to the term "Britannia ware" and elicited the scorn of later generations, which often failed to realize that good Britannia was the rule and cheap Britannia the exception. By 1843 Reed & Barton was making both "good" and "common" metal teaware and castor frames, the inexpensive line designed to sell at slightly more than half the price of the regular line.

This downward growth and spread of the market for metal tableware was also manifested by an increasing demand for a class of wares sold largely by tin peddlers to the country trade. To acquire for themselves a share of this market, Britannia manufacturers adopted a line of cheap but substantial "block tin" ware, which in composition and appearance strongly resembled the pewter of earlier days. The alloy had to be cast rather than rolled and stamped and hence did not lend itself well to mass-production methods, but in its inexpensive sturdiness block tin met the requirements of the trade for which it was designed.

Reed & Barton laid plans to commence the manufacture of block tin, and early in 1847 bought out the shop of Nathan

Lawrence, who was practising that branch of metal work in Baltimore. According to the terms of the agreement Lawrence was to move to Taunton, bringing with him his two employees, James Williams, a journeyman, and John MacDonald, an eighteen-year-old apprentice. On August 31 the Baltimore contingent arrived, and the Taunton workmen stared aghast as MacDonald walked into the shop clad in a black broadcloth dress frock coat, with very tight fitting pants closely strapped down — on his head a tall silk hat! The ensuing demoralization was apparently short-lived, and Lawrence soon had his department installed on the third floor of the main building, in the rooms formerly occupied by Mason's machine shop. Teaware, castor frames, lamps, pitchers, and candlesticks formed the bulk of the block-tin line, in which Reed & Barton had a good run of the trade for several years.

At no time did Henry Reed relax his watch on the English Britannia industry. Samples of metal taken from Dixon teaware were sent to New York for analysis,[10] and other close checks maintained on developments across the ocean. In 1847 it was discovered that ware of a very superior finish was coming into the country, possessing a lustre and color nearly equal to that of silver. Subsequent investigation revealed that the finish was imparted by a laborious process of hand-rubbing. As in the case of block tin, Henry Reed lost no time in experimenting. Immediate arrangements were made whereby a Mrs. Morris and her three sisters named Barber, who understood the process, agreed to leave their homes in England and come to Taunton. In due course the Englishwomen arrived, and were installed in a polishing-room in the japanning building.

The importation of Mrs. Morris and the Barber sisters set a precedent in the company. It caused far less of a sensation than had John MacDonald and his dress frock coat, for English workmen and women were numerous in Taunton, and the practice of bringing in skilled foreign labor went back at least as far as 1823, when the calico print works of Crocker & Richmond imported nearly a thousand workers. In 1848 Reed & Barton again had recourse to the English labor market, and induced John Fletcher and the two Furniss brothers to come to Taunton from Sheffield to teach the Reed & Barton workmen English methods of soldering. Edmund Porter reveals, however, that results did not always measure up to expectation, in so far as the Englishmen were concerned. They were, he confesses, skillful in hand work, but were unable to show the Yankees anything in the line of labor-saving appliances or up-to-date methods. "For soldering they all used the jewelers mouth blow pipe that had long since been discarded in the metal trade in this country." [11]

If England failed in some respects, she did, at least, continue to inspire the American market with new product ideas. The Birmingham metal trades, which supplied so many of the living wants of the British people, did not desert them in death, and an extensive business in coffin furniture — name plates and handles — flourished there from 1760 on.[12] Americans, however, do not seem to have become "splendid in ashes, and pompous in the grave"[13] until pine box necessity began to yield to the luxury of walnut, elm, and mahogany. To the Taunton Britannia Manufacturing Company, in 1831, fell the honor of presenting the coffin plate to the mass American market. Leonard, Reed & Barton found that by 1838 the idea had taken vigorous root. By 1845 ill-bred, indeed, was the citizen who went to his last resting place without benefit of a Reed & Barton plate. The business was profitable and the market was limited only by the extent and health of the population.

New Skills

Product change and development, which played so important a rôle in the early days of the Reed & Barton partnership, was coincidental with and partially a result of the development of

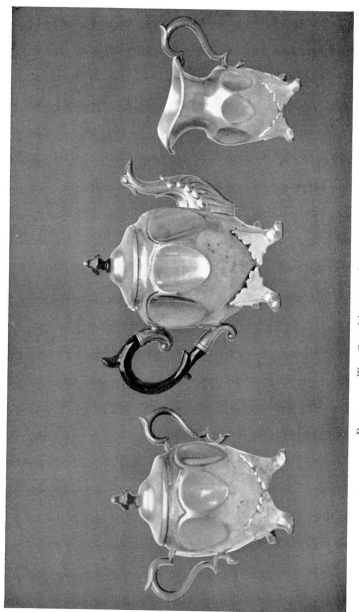

BRITANNIA TEA SET, NO. 1505, REED & BARTON

A further variation from traditional forms. Probably first made in 1846

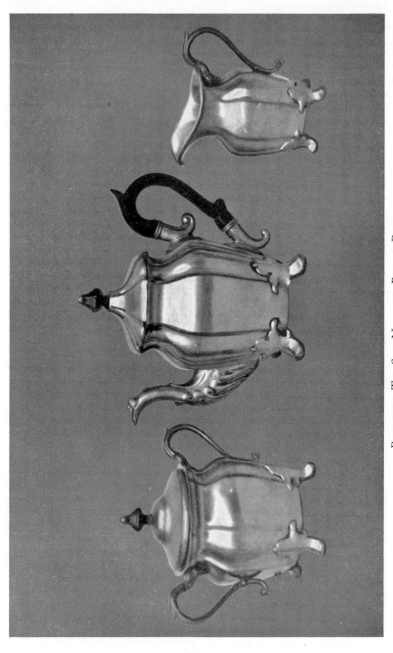

BRITANNIA TEA SET, No. 1507, REED & BARTON

This pattern and its contemporary, No. 1505, were probably among the first wares to bear the Reed & Barton stamp

new factory skills. Most basic processes in the manufacture of Britannia ware remained unchanged, but the refinements were numerous. Attention first turned to the wooden handles of tea-ware, which in 1845 were still being laboriously carved by hand. Competition at length forced the company to abandon the fine birch handles and adopt the more usual cast metal forms, with pearl shell insulators. Reed, having brought the manufacture of handles into the factory, insisted likewise that the company should not trust outsiders to make even so small a part as the insulators. One morning in April, 1849, Henry Reed appeared in the shop carrying a huge pearl-oyster shell, which he and Edmund Porter experimented upon until a satisfactory method of cutting out insulators had been discovered. From that time onward, all pearl cutting was done by the company, under Reed's vigilant supervision.

Certain improvements in manufacturing technique made shop tasks easier and the manipulation of the metal more adroit. The old whale-oil soldering lamps with mouth blow-pipes had passed out of existence unlamented. On September 14, 1837, machinist J. W. Strange was paid $50, an extremely liberal bounty at the time, for an improvement in soldering lamps. This improvement appears to have been the substitution of bellows for the mouth blowpipe. In 1845 Porter describes the lamp then in use as follows:[14]

The soldering lamp at this time was a banjo shaped article, filled with whale oil, there were two wicks and the *wind was raised* by a pair of blacksmiths bellows, the air being blown into a barrel emersed in a cask of water and heavily weighted to get a pressure. Tho' rude, it worked very well and good work was done. The blaze of the lamp was blown thro' an iron nozzle & the rays concentrated, making an intense heat.

Early in 1847 a further refinement in soldering was effected by the introduction of the "fluid lamp," which replaced smoky whale oil with a mixture of turpentine and alcohol. In 1854 gas was installed in the factory, which, by making possible both a hotter flame and less bulky apparatus, greatly facilitated the work of the solderers.

The implications of these and other improvements in technique were far-reaching. Greater skill in metal working led

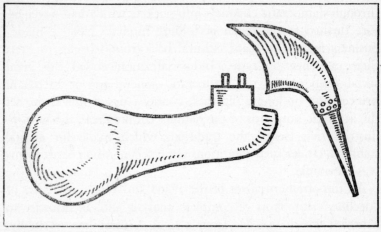

SOLDERING LAMP IN USE IN 1845

naturally to the greater use of that skill. Unfortunately, the growing ability to manipulate metal was not matched by a growing appreciation of appropriate decoration. With new-found tools and talent the Britannia manufacturers attacked the underpinnings of American taste with the same innocent enthusiasm that a child with a new toy saw devotes to the legs of the family heirloom. The middle 1840's and thereafter saw more and more elaboration upon old forms, more and more experimentation with new. Ornateness of design increased in direct proportion to the increase in metal-working ability, and by 1859 decoration had largely supplanted form as the medium through which beauty was sought.

Aesthetic Standards

The blame for an ever increasing superficiality of design, however, should not be placed entirely on the shoulders of the manufacturer. The consumer himself was accomplice before the fact. The wealth of the nation was growing; it was also flowing through democratic channels into pockets which had never before thrilled to the touch of folding money. Newly "made" business men with scant cultural background began to exert their influence on taste. Industrialization ended the great social influence of the aristocratic generations of merchant princes, and no longer did these connoisseurs of fine living set the aesthetic standards of the nation. Unlike these, the new industrial rich lacked the traditions which made for artistic stability. Under such conditions some degeneration of art forms was inevitable.

All too often criticisms of the 1840's and 1850's, the years of "decline," stop short of complete analysis and do injustice to a period which was far from a total cultural loss. Actually, much was accomplished in the field of design. What the young era of manufacturers lacked in taste, it attempted to make up in vigor. First and most important, a break was made with Europe, as growing wealth made for a growing national consciousness. To be sure, English fashions still predominated, and an Italian movement gained a considerable foothold; but here and there American manufacturers dared to ignore tradition and were loyally supported by the American market. Original thinking made its long delayed entrance in the 1850's, and consumers began to develop a personality which, if it was uncouth in its early stages, was at least partially independent. The middle years of the century witnessed a quest for betterment, which, though blind and groping, was energetic and sincere. Restlessness characterized the age, and the living standards of fathers were spurned by sons. Greater comfort and greater luxury were constantly sought, and the American home, while becoming uglier on the outside, became steadily warmer and better lighted within. The Britannia tableware which had served one generation so well was rejected by a new generation, and the cry was for something new and finer. English knowledge and American ingenuity stepped forward and met the demand. Electroplated silverware ended the thirty-year reign of Britannia ware in America, placed the Metal of Kings on the workman's table, and opened up a virtually unlimited new field of enterprise.

PLATED SILVERWARE

Experiments in electroplating were being conducted long before the founding of Babbitt & Crossman in 1824, and the process owes its existence to a series of discoveries made at the beginning of the nineteenth century. Independent experiments in England from 1801 to 1803 established the fact that a current of electricity passing through a conducting liquid decomposed the ingredients of that liquid, and caused their elements to be set free at the two immersed electric poles. By applying this principle, it was found possible to deposit a layer of one kind of metal upon another; and the art of electroplating was born. The deposition of metals by electricity was regarded at first as a curiosity, and no commercial application of these discoveries appears to have been made until the 1830's. In 1838 the firm of G. R. & H. Elkington, of Birmingham, England, was engaged in electroplating buttons, and to this firm is due much of the credit for developing the process and applying it to a wide range of products. Soon several English firms were profitably engaged in the trade and exporting considerable amounts of electroplate to America.

J. O. Mead, Britannia ware manufacturer of Philadelphia, was the first to commence electroplating in America. In 1837 he traveled abroad and brought home with him a Smee battery, one of several existing devices to generate electrical current. In the span of five years Mead developed a workable plating technique, and in 1845 formed a partnership in Hartford with William and Asa Rogers under the name of Rogers & Mead. This company, the first to manufacture electroplated silverware in the country, was soon dissolved. Mead returned to Philadelphia, where he reëstablished his business, while William and Asa Rogers in 1847 founded the firm of Rogers Bros. and took the lead in placing electroplate before the American market.

Less than a year after the formation of Rogers Bros., Henry Reed was laying plans for a plating department. As in the case of block tin, no time was spent in experimenting. In January, 1848, Deforest H. Peck was brought from Connecticut to set up his jars and vats in Taunton. Little is known of Peck's background and training. It is most probable that he was an employee of Rogers Bros. and learned his trade from them. He appears to have been a competent plater, for results were soon forthcoming.

Peck was installed in a small room on the third floor of the brick mill, scarcely larger than a good-sized bedroom. In these cramped quarters, and amid the ill-concealed skepticism of the old hands, he set up a Smee battery and a small jar of plating solution. "Mr. Peck soon had a cup with a pearl white coating of silver upon it that elicited the wonder and admiration of the britannia boys." [15] Further treatment of the plated wares was necessary, however, in order to convert the frosted, opaque color to clear sheen. "Taunton had neglected to educate any for this work, so the Nutmeg State was again placed under tribute, and Manning W. Fox, an experienced burnisher, was sent for to teach the Cohannet Yankees how to burnish silverware." [16] William Abbott and Frank Farrows, both from Connecticut, were added to the burnishing force, and were joined in short order by Elizabeth Hodgdon, the first girl burnisher in Reed & Barton's employ. Also in 1848 Reed sent to England for a family named Rogers, with several daughters who were skilled burnishers. Eventually, as in other factories, female help became the rule in the burnishing department of Reed & Barton.

Deforest Peck stayed with the company for only a year, at the end of which time Reed, with a consuming desire to learn all that was known of electroplating, brought from England an expert plater named Brown. So skilled did Reed himself become under Brown's tutelage that when the Englishman left the company, Reed did all the plating himself, and in 1850 educated George Smith of Taunton to be the next plating boss.

Much mystery surrounds the methods employed by the early electroplaters. The trade in its infancy bordered on dark alchemy, and the men who manipulated the unfathomable forces of electricity were regarded with awe and respect. The platers themselves did little to dispel this atmosphere, guarding jealously the knowledge which they had acquired through hours of patient experimenting. No two methods were exactly alike, and each man was possessed of secret formulae which made his process, in his own opinion, better than any others. An air of furtiveness emanated from behind the closed doors of the plating-room as mysterious powders were slipped into steaming brews to form the solutions and baths. Few of these trade secrets have survived, and all too often the details of early processes used by the various companies are no longer known. A battered notebook of 1850 vintage, therefore, preserves a rare segment of the Reed & Barton history, for in it is recorded in Henry Reed's handwriting a minute description of the company's first plating experiments.

To obtain the necessary electricity for plating, Reed employed the Smee battery, which was based on the principle that copper and zinc plates suspended in a jar of sulphuric acid generated a current, the intensity of which could be increased by employing additional jars in the battery. His instructions called for the use of six jars. The plating solution, contained in a separate vat connected by wires with the battery jars, was a laboriously concocted mixture of silver and potassium cyanide, twelve ounces of silver to twelve pounds of cyanide dissolved in twenty-four quarts of water.

After the object to be plated had been carefully cleaned, it was immersed in the plating vat and connected to the zinc of the

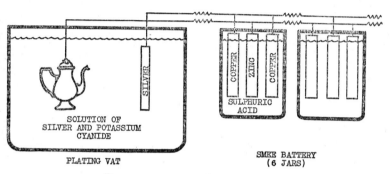

PLATING WITH THE SMEE BATTERY

Smee battery to form the negative pole in the plating solution. A sheet of silver attached to the copper of the battery formed the positive pole in the plating vat. Electrolytic action deposited the silver dissolved in the solution on the negative pole, and the silver sheet which formed the positive pole replenished the solution. Pages of instruction on how to avoid "roughness," "slightly brownish appearance," "dirty, furry appearance," and a host of other ailments to which the plated ware was subject reveal the great uncertainties of these early efforts. Chemicals were crude and impure, current was uncertain, and no body of proven information was available for reference. But even under handicaps such as these, electroplating throve and the wares became popular.

Reed & Barton applied its plating process to the regular line of Britannia ware. Coffin plates were particularly suitable for plating, and in this new finish sold extremely well. Much plating

TABLE 9

SALES BY PRODUCT, SEPTEMBER 1–OCTOBER 20, 1857
REED & BARTON

| | Plated Wares | | Unplated Wares | |
	Units Sold	Value	Units Sold	Value
Tea sets	2	$53.26	88	$1,354.98
Teapots	14	71.00	231	374.64
Urns	2	26.00	24	216.32
Coffeepots	3	20.75	24	89.71
Sugars	1	3.46	39	72.58
Creams	4	9.13	28	31.75
Slop bowls	1	2.50	30	37.29
Castor frames	28	206.63	710	876.17
Cake baskets	11	82.18	100	257.25
Coffin plates (Dozens)	116	213.25	145	237.49
Pitchers	3	19.62	48	178.91
Kettles	4	55.83	13	115.25
Meat dishes	5	257.00	3	70.77
Entrée dishes	4	84.00	8	132.00
Vegetable dishes	2	35.54	5	54.75
Dish covers	4	40.00	10	76.91
Tureens	1	33.50	5	83.75
Cups	127	141.49	32	20.32
Butter plates	3	15.00	2	5.50
Plates	6	11.28	12	11.50
Flagons	2	10.26	4	17.00
Goblets	60	99.50	..	..
Music plates (Dozens)	..	..	87	601.00
Pepper tops (Dozens)	2½	2.50	147	61.74
Mustard tops (Dozens)	..	..	83½	83.50
Salts (Pairs)	..	..	90	154.91
Waiters	..	..	20	36.00
Milk pitchers	..	..	20	32.50
Bowls	..	..	2	3.17
Syrup tops (Dozens)	..	..	1½	3.43
Water dish	..	..	1	4.00
		$1,493.68		$5,295.52

Source: Reed & Barton Mss., Day Book, 1855–57.

continued to be done on a Britannia metal base, but nickel silver was found to be even more durable and satisfactory for the purpose, and its use spread. Not only was this alloy a good plating base, but unplated it served admirably for a low-price line and quickly displaced block-tin ware in this capacity. Nickel silver presented new manufacturing problems because of its toughness, but in 1857 after several unsuccessful attempts Edmund Porter learned how to spin the metal, and the way was clear for development of the line.

Britannia ware clearly was doomed. The better grades of Britannia encountered increasingly severe competition from electroplated silverware, while "common metal" Britannia yielded to unplated nickel silver. For a dying institution, however, Britannia ware gave a good account of itself throughout the 1850's, and an analysis of the Reed & Barton line in 1857 reveals the fact that electroplate was still in its infancy. The sales analysis reveals also a prolific growth in the variety of articles manufactured.

Designing

The late '50's brought not only a multiplication of products, but also a flowering of design — literally. Increasing skill in two techniques gave impetus to decoration. In 1852 Reed & Barton hired Eli Smith, the first chaser to appear on the payroll. Floral patterns, carefully incised by the chaser's art, appeared in ever increasing profusion after this time. Plain surfaces began to disappear with even greater rapidity as machines were devised to cut fine geometric patterns into the metal and engine-turning came into its own. Reed & Barton sent its wares to Boston to be completed when such ornamentation was desired, but by 1860 the demand for high design required that the company install a lathe of its own to perform the task.

Now, at last, the necessity for copying existed no longer. With the new tools available, and a market demanding such wares, manufacturers proceeded to outdo each other in the variety and quantity of adornment. In the middle 1850's patents on tableware design began to be recorded in appreciable numbers — an evidence of the new originality, though not, unfortunately, a guarantee of good taste. Henry Reed soon showed that he could make scrolls and curlycues along with the rest and best, and the first Reed & Barton patent, a tea service design, was recorded on January 12, 1858.[17]

The patent marks an important shift in emphasis behind the scenes at Reed & Barton, a shift which began to occur early in the 1850's. Slowly the attention of the management turned from techniques and methods to results. Growing recognition was accorded the idea that design of the product had become at least as important as the design of the machinery to make it. Henry Reed, the metallurgist and mechanic, became Henry Reed, the designer.

Profits and progress explained the transition. With the successful establishment of the plating department no adequate outlet existed for Reed's creative energy. Sales were increasing daily, and profits were high. All except the most minor production difficulties had been brought under control, and no company in the field surpassed Reed & Barton in modern equipment and processes. Competent men in the factory handled routine problems with great skill, and a loyal, highly efficient workforce made management simple. Thus did circumstances in this great peak of prosperity leave Henry Reed without a function. He turned quite naturally, therefore, to the virgin field of design, and sought, with versatile mind and manual dexterity, to compensate for inadequate training.

By 1854 a designing room had been set up and placed under the direction of William Parkin, who was brought from England to make dies for the teaware department. In addition to die-sinking, Parkin also seems to have done considerable designing, and his room became Henry Reed's favorite haunt.

PLATED FRUIT BASKET, No. 1963, REED & BARTON

PLATED VEGETABLE DISH, No. 1941, REED & BARTON
Early examples of Reed & Barton's electroplated ware, probably first
made in the 1850's

PLATED SUGAR BOWL, No. 1760, REED & BARTON   PLATED TEAPOT, No. 1950, REED & BARTON

The sugar bowl appears to have been first made in 1849, the teapot in the early 1860's

Neither Reed nor Parkin was a drawing-board designer, and few of the patterns created at this time originated on paper. Like the shipbuilders of an earlier day, Reed carved his ideas in wood and did his sketching with a jackknife. In this medium his prowess became a byword, and Taunton knew him as the "champion whittler."

The change in emphasis from processes to products — from the means to the end — was characteristic of the industry, and by the late 'fifties it was evident that the initiative in originating designs for the American market had been completely assumed by American manufacturers. The taste of independence was intoxicating. Henry Reed in 1859 was whittling out his ideas with the same enthusiasm and sense of destiny with which Isaac Babbitt in 1823 had mixed his metals.

In one respect it was unfortunate that Reed's interests and energies turned to designing, for Reed, like other manufacturers who were doing the same thing, was little qualified for the task. Judged by present-day standards, much of the work of mechanics in the field of art was of dubious quality, the full effects of which were to become apparent in a later period. Reed's devotion in the late 1850's to matters artistic should be associated only with that later period, and in no way be allowed to obscure the great achievements of the preceding two decades.

The transition through the technical and product changes required by the age was successfully accomplished by the application of skill in known fields and caution in unknown. Henry Reed performed an even greater task, however, when, with great keenness and understanding, he adapted the organization of the company to meet the requirements of enlarged trade and solved the problems of personnel arising out of growth.

CHAPTER VII

A FACTORY AND ITS PEOPLE, 1837–1859

THE 1837 partnership of Leonard, Reed & Barton marked the beginning of a new effort on the part of the Britannia men of Taunton to achieve a genuine factory organization. Caution in finance and great skill in production might alone have made this effort a success, but it was Henry Reed's ability to organize and effectively manage his men which made the effort a truly great success. The start which Leonard, Reed & Barton made in 1837 was not a hopeful one, however. It resembled far more the Spring Street shop of Babbitt & Crossman than it did the highly specialized and flourishing works of the Taunton Britannia Manufacturing Company.

INTERNAL ORGANIZATION IN 1837

Once again, in 1837, small size went hand in hand with an almost completely unspecialized management. Rarely was one man assigned a single function. Henry Reed kept the time book, spun metal, supervised the shop, designed company wares, or repaired to the kitchen of the Lincoln house to brew odoriferous batches of japanning lacquer. Alfred Brabrook kept most of the company accounts but hardly could be called "bookkeeper" because his other duties included traveling as a salesman, painting japan on teaware handles, and packing orders for shipment. This situation remained substantially unchanged throughout the 1840's. Small size continued to demand diverse functions of workmen and partners, and the latter supervised the activities of the former through direct contact. Administration meant merely the exchange of words between friends.

WORK AND WORKMEN

Management remained on a personal basis not only because the group was small, but also because the men and women first added to the 1837 work force were almost exclusively local. The Taunton Britannia Manufacturing Company trained a large

CHART I

ORGANIZATION CHART, 1837, LEONARD, REED & BARTON

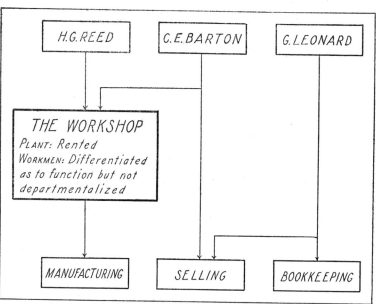

number of Taunton and Hopewell inhabitants in the trade, and these were the first to be reëmployed as Leonard, Reed & Barton began to expand. Family groups, well known to Henry Reed and Charles Barton, remained remarkably faithful to the Britannia trade. Tradition and training, handed down through such groups, materially simplified the problems of supervision and permitted the competent treatment of personal peculiarities.

After 1840, however, expansion and the need for special skills required the company at times to seek workmen outside the Taunton area. The practice was a healthy one, and brought new blood and vigorous talent to the community. There was apparently a more or less regular exchange of help between Reed & Barton, Roswell Gleason's in Dorchester, and the Connecticut Britannia establishments. Most of the exchanges proved to be of a permanent character, and there is no evidence that a class of migratory workmen existed. The men who came to Taunton established homes and became accepted parts of the local life.

One example of this uprooting and replanting process has survived in some detail. In 1848 B. F. Knox made his decision to leave the employ of Roswell Gleason and come to Taunton. Reed & Barton's offer of employment at $8.00 a week reached Knox at an opportune time, for the Gleason apprentices, of which he was one, were in great disfavor. Allegedly in protest over the quality of Mrs. Gleason's cooking, the apprentice boys, with a rare sense of the spectacular, rolled a large chopping block down the Gleason front stairs and out through the closed front door.[1] It is not known whether this incident actually hastened the departure of Knox from Dorchester, but if it did, he seems to have liked Taunton cooking better, and the family name, first inscribed on the Reed & Barton payroll in April, 1848, remained there until the death of his son, Frank, in 1942.

The practice of bringing in "outsiders" created definite problems of adjustment in certain cases, for the old hands at the Britannia works tended to resent new arrivals. The Englishmen were particularly hard for the community to assimilate. Serious though never entirely successful efforts were made to convert the "foreigners" to American habits. One noteworthy incident in the conversion process has been recorded:[2]

1850

June 28 The Furniss Brothers, Tom & Ed., Englishmen, have a knock down in the yard back of the Saw-mill. We go out from the shop as soon as we hear what is going on, & put a stop to it without ceremony. They claimed that was the way Englishmen settled their disputes. We told them, "we would *not allow* any such work on *Yankee soil,* and *dont you forget it."*

The workmen of Reed & Barton considered they had been *highly insulted* by the transaction, and *told them so.* They never tried it again.

Henry Reed's quiet manner of speaking and innate humor, however, eased many a delicate situation in the plant, and in most cases the new employees had only temporary difficulty in becoming adjusted to their surroundings.

There was, indeed, very little to disturb the equanimity of the Britannia works. Leonard Crossman, Noah Williams, Lucretia Strange, and the other old employees must have looked with satisfaction upon the régime of Leonard, Reed & Barton, remembering, as they so easily could, other years and other conditions of work. Porter's diary reveals some of the changes which twenty-five years produced: [3]

In 1829 when my father commenced housekeeping, he was getting 1.00 per day of 13 or 14 hours as a skilled Mechanic & foreman of the shop. no. 37 School Street. Now the same talent commands 1.50 to 2.00 per day of 10 to 11 hours. But let us make a list of a few items.

	1829		1854
Skilled Mechanic	.75 to 1.00		1.50 to 2.00
Hours of labor	13 to 14 hrs		10 to 11
Feather Bed	$12.00	Mattrass	$5.00
Brass Clock	1-day $20.00		8-day $5.00
Stove	$30.00		$15.00

Wages have raised about 100 per ct. while articles of furniture are very much lower & $100 will go much farther in house furnishing. While hours of labor greatly reduced. This change is owing largely to labor saving machinery & yet all have plenty to do. The rise in wages, creates new wants, and former luxuries have become necessities.

The upward trend of wages at the Britannia works was part of a general increase in the earnings of labor throughout the country and the world. At the same time other manufacturing costs were increasing. Both the price of metals and the prices received by Reed & Barton for their wares should be considered as a partial explanation of the prevailing wage level at the Britannia works.

The cost of tin, chief raw material used by the company, increased more or less steadily from 14½ cents per pound in August, 1843, to well over 30 cents per pound in June, 1859.[4] Growing efficiency in production appears to have offset these rising costs of materials to a certain extent.[5] The company was, nevertheless, forced to seek frequent upward revisions of its price lists, and upon the ability of Reed & Barton to obtain higher prices for its wares depended both wage levels and profits. This ability to command higher prices in the market, as well as the growing speed and efficiency of production in the shop, enabled Reed & Barton to pay what were considered generous wages for the time. Porter's statement of rising earnings in the Britannia company are borne out by the records, although his 100 per cent increase figure seems to refer to particular cases rather than to the company average. In 1829 the average daily wage paid was 80 cents. Thirty years later that average had increased more than 50 per cent to $1.22. Rates for individual jobs are difficult to compare because they are quoted for specific patterns of ware, few of which remained in the line long enough to provide a basis for comparison. The highest pay received by a solderer in 1823 was $1.12½ per day. By 1838 this rate had increased to $1.42, while at the same time solderers on piecework were earning $1.75, a far higher wage than in any previous period.

The custom of paying extra for overtime work, in which the company as early as 1832 had set an example for industry to follow, appears to have been continued by Leonard, Reed & Barton and Reed & Barton. Apprentices benefited particularly

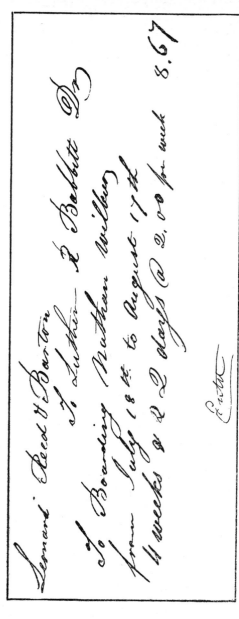

Accounting Entry Showing Settlement of an Apprentice's Board Bill, About 1837

in this respect, receiving as much as 178 per cent of their regular pay for such work.[6] Aside from this dispensation the apprentices received much the same as they had in the past. Standard rates of pay were $30 for the first year, $40 for the second, and $60 for the third, with board furnished to the amount of $2.00 or $2.25 a week.[7]

Women employees fared exceedingly well after 1837, and their position became more firmly established in the company as an enlarged scale of operations created new jobs and raised earning power. In the early days of the company the only employment open to women was in finishing, washing, and packing wares. Caroline Cobb was receiving 22 cents a day in 1829, and the highest pay earned by women in the plant was 32 cents a day. In the 1840's women took over jobs in the soldering and polishing departments, with pay increasing in direct proportion to the higher degree of skill required. With the advent of plating, women were employed at hitherto unheard-of rates, earning as much as $1.50 a day by 1859.

Records of the polishing and burnishing departments fortunately have survived, and reveal much about the place of women in the Britannia works. In September, 1858, polishing boss Fred A. Harvey supervised a force of ten men and six women polishers. The record shows a long list of rates paid for polishing various articles and patterns, wages being figured for the most part on a piece-rate basis.

Rates paid for polishing:

No. 1756	coffeepots—	25½ cents per piece
" "	sugars —	6 " " "
" "	creams —	6 " " "
" "	teas —	5–10 " " "
" "	baskets —	16–19 " " "

Earnings throughout the department varied widely according to the different degrees of ability shown by the employees. Rates for women were the same as those for men, and the type of work was virtually the same. In September, 1858, the women polishers averaged 68 cents a day, while the men earned $1.02. Certain of the more expert, however, received considerably more. Eliza Morris was earning 80 cents, while Harriet Johnson and Mary Greene received an average of 83 cents a day.[8]

The important rôle played by women in the factory is reflected in the total employment figures. In October, 1857, there were eighty-two men and thirty women on the regular payroll. Of these thirty, possibly five were polishers. Several others must have been solderers, for as early as 1845 Edmund Porter tells of learning this job from Aunt Becky Robinson and indicates that other women as well were similarly engaged. It was the burnishing department, however, which furnished the greatest opportunities for female employment.

By April, 1857, the burnishing department, still under the direction of Manning Fox, boasted a force of nineteen women. The trade was both difficult to learn and delicate to practice. Great skill and no small degree of physical strength were required to manipulate the polished steel and agate tools so as to gloss over the metal evenly, without wave or mar. The unexcelled work of these women and their successors became one of the great Reed & Barton legends, and no finer work in this line has ever been done.

Burnishing was at best a lengthy, tedious task and accounted for much of the difference in price which existed between plated and unplated wares. The prices for a five-half-pint No. 1799 teapot, for example, were $5.25 plated, and $3.10 plain. The cost of burnishing accounted for $1.00 of the $2.15 difference. Some idea of the work involved may be gained from the fact that fruit baskets, tea- or coffeepots, castor frames, and articles of a similar size each required slightly more than a day to burnish, even in the most skilled hands. Creams and sugars each took about a day to complete, and the average burnisher could turn out perhaps three or four cups or two butter dishes in this time.

The burnishing process, therefore, constituted a serious bottle-
neck in the production of plated ware and required a large department in order to keep pace with more rapid operations in
the plant.

Earnings of the burnishers, who like the polishers worked on
a piece-rate basis, were the highest of any received by Reed &
Barton women employees. In September, 1858, the four most
skilled women working under Manning Fox received the following average daily wage: [9]

E. O. Fisher	$0.95
Emeline Burbank	0.90
Mary Jane Paull	0.91
M. Westcott	0.85

The earnings of the fitters, casters, spinners, and other male
employees averaged considerably higher than those of the
women burnishers and polishers, and the wages received by the
foremen and others with special talents seem to have been especially liberal.[10]

	Daily Earnings
George Brabrook, Salesman	$4.66
Alfred Brabrook, Bookkeeper-Treasurer	3.93
W. W. Porter, Boss Roller	2.57
J. J. Burbank, Press Boss	2.47
E. W. Porter, Foreman, Teaware Dept.	2.27
Fred Harvey, Boss Polisher	3.64
George Smith, Boss Plater	1.95
William Parkin, Diesinker	2.94
I. W. Thayer, Boss Caster	2.35
Nathan Lawrence, Boss of Block-tin Dept.	2.76

In addition to dividends, Henry Reed and Charles Barton received a regular daily wage of $3.00, compensation for the not
inconsiderable amount of work they performed at the bench.

There is no reason to suppose that Reed & Barton employees
were paid any better or any worse than the general average of

the industry. The frequent interchange of workers between Taunton, Dorchester, and Connecticut suggests a fairly uniform wage level throughout, although definite proof of this surmise is lacking. But in comparison with other industries the men and women in the Britannia works fared well. The daily wages of Massachusetts cotton-mill operatives between 1851 and 1860 averaged $1.03,[11] a level greatly exceeded by full-time Reed & Barton employees and even surpassed by the 1859 Reed & Barton average wage of $1.22, a figure far from representative because of the part-time earnings included. The average daily wage of Massachusetts metal workers in general, 1851 to 1860, was $1.35,[12] while all but a few of the Reed & Barton male employees appear to have received more than this amount in the sample year of 1859. Even the earnings of some of the women employees of Reed & Barton equaled or exceeded the average paid to male metal workers in Massachusetts. In so far as comparisons are possible, it would appear that Reed & Barton wages tended, in the late 1850's, to approximate the highest averages received in skilled occupations.

Hours and Payment of Wages

As in the case of wages, a comparison of hours worked by Reed & Barton employees with hours worked in other firms and industries is very difficult. The ten-hour-day movement received much publicity in the 1840's but there is little to indicate the extent of its adoption. At this time the working day at the Britannia works appears to have averaged about twelve hours in length, although, as in earlier years, working hours varied both according to the time of year and to the activity of the company. Usual practice was to divide the year into two schedules. From March 20 to September 20, employees went to work at 5:00 a. m. and remained until 7:00 p. m., with a half-hour off for breakfast and an hour off for lunch. On September 20 the schedule changed and the factory began "lighting up." Work then commenced after breakfast, at sunrise, and continued until 7:30 p. m., with an hour off at noon. March 20, which saw the end of "evening work," was always an occasion for a celebration. In 1849, for example, all the Reed & Barton employees repaired after work to John Leonard's hill, where a "grand blow-out" was held, to the tune of fireworks and a tar-barrel bonfire.[13] In the 1850's a reduction in the length of the working day seems to have been made. According to payroll records of 1858 the eleven-hour day had become the standard, with overtime rates apparently being paid for work in excess of that time.

Each employee was responsible for reporting his own time. Accounts were settled at the end of each quarter, and the workmen were paid by check, which they cashed at Taunton Green. Local grocers and market men adapted their methods to this system and let their bills run three months. Not until the 1850's did local storekeepers begin to make regular and substantial cash sales. The growing prevalence of cash transactions finally led Reed & Barton to abandon the quarterly payoff, and in July, 1858, workmen began to be paid monthly.[14]

Loyalty and Group Consciousness

The outstanding feature of the maturing years of the Reed & Barton partnership, however, was neither wages nor hours, but rather the high degree of unity, efficiency, and intense loyalty of the working force. The presence of these virtues in the 1840's is easily explained, for, as previously shown, the small size of the business created a natural cohesiveness and made direct personal management not only possible but necessary. But ten years later, despite the tremendously accelerated pace of business and a working force enlarged five times, we find the same feeling of solidarity and permanency among the workmen and a continuation of personal administration.

Tangible evidence of devotion to the company is not difficult to discover, and the service records of the employees are revealing. Of the twenty-eight men and women at the workbench in 1845, nineteen were still employees in 1859; of these, seven had worked for the company since 1831, and at least four had served Babbitt, Crossman & Company in 1828. Nearly all the 1849 working force were still at work ten years later.[15] Even more significant was the prevalence of two-generation records, which began to appear surprisingly early in the company history. The eagerness of fathers to bring their sons into the business reflected in the most genuine manner the desirability of employment at the Britannia works. Of the eight apprentices who appeared on the 1858 payroll ledger, five were sons of regular employees.[16] Blood relationships were comparatively as numerous in the 1859 factory as they had been in the 1839 shop. The Babbitts, Burbanks, Stranges, Chaces, and Cobbs were essentially Britannia families and remained so through many branches of their family trees.

The length of time required to master a trade in the Britannia works, moreover, also contributed much to the permanent character of the working force. A three-year apprenticeship with promises of highly remunerative and eminently respectable employment at the end was not an investment to be lightly thrown away.

These factors, explanatory of the most happy state of personal affairs in the Britannia works, have a familiar ring, and recall the continuous existence of a comparable state of affairs in the company almost since 1824. By 1850, however, a situation new to company history had been created by great growth — a situation in which mere size alone threatened to cleave a gap between management and labor.

No gap ever appeared. Reed & Barton management continued to be almost synonymous with labor. Great growth and success failed to lure either Henry Reed or Charles Barton into the front office. Most of the white-collar tasks usually required of busy and prosperous business owners were thrown in bewildered haste upon the shoulders of others. Charles E. Barton remained a solderer to the end. Henry G. Reed's interests grew broader, but were bounded on one side by the plating vats and on the other by the teaware department and Parkin's designing room. Visitors to the factory frequently expressed surprise at seeing members of the firm engaged in manual labor. One day some ladies from the Green were looking through the plant and chanced to come upon Charles Barton busily engaged at his soldering bench. One of them was heard to exclaim, "Why, Mr. Barton, I didn't know you *worked!*" [17]

Both Reed and Barton lived among their employees, and the two families occupied for many years an old double tenement house on Bay Street. Their living habits varied but little from the standards of the workmen, and each pursued a conservative, almost frugal existence in the best New England tradition.

The acid test of familiarity enhanced rather than impaired Henry Reed's position as leader, and the measure of discipline necessary to high morale and efficiency was at all times maintained. If Reed's sympathy commanded affection, his ability commanded respect. At no time, after the death of Gustavus Leonard, was there any question of authority. Reed administered as he thought right, and he invariably was right because he knew his men and he knew his business. But his word, while law in the factory, was usually soft spoken.

Reed practised characteristic Yankee thrift and expected others to do likewise. "Work and Save" were still the words heard by advice-seeking young men, and Reed, remembering the beneficial effects of his own thrifty boyhood, never entirely approved of giving apprentices cash wages over and above their board. That philosophy never interfered with paying a liberal day's wage for a fair day's work, however, and assistance in times of distress flowed naturally and without stint from firm to employees.

A foundation of confidence underlay the mutually satisfactory relationship between company and employees. Reed trusted the integrity and ability of his men and women in the factory, and they had faith in the firm. In both instances this confidence was justified. No legal obligation required the firm to pay accident compensation or even pay extra for overtime work. Yet these customs, not altogether familiar or accepted ones in an age of rugged, developing industrial society, continued to be observed in the Britannia works. And neither Henry Reed nor any other member of the firm ever discharged an employee because of old age or physical infirmity. In the complete absence of bargaining and concession, workmen gave their best efforts to the company and took a tremendous pride in the skill with which they performed their jobs. Behind all this lay one simple formula: the ties and obligations of personal friendship were not discarded at the factory door.

Yet the workmen were far from pampered. Periodic layoffs were considered a normal and necessary misfortune, and somehow a spirit of sturdy self-reliance was built up. The factory people asked no favors of the firm and turned in times of depression to odd jobs and to the farm for support. Where each workman was able to dictate his own destiny, individual enterprise flourished and initiative found many outlets. Not security, but opportunity, was sought. The men of Reed & Barton were constantly branching out into business for themselves — a sign of healthy freedom and a gauge of the caliber of the men employed.

Elijah Braman, in 1834, set up his own shop in Warren, Rhode Island, to sell Britannia ware and apparently also manufactured castor frames. In 1837 Alexander Standish was apparently running a business of his own, making tops for castor bottles, and renting equipment from Leonard, Reed & Barton. Eli Eldridge, with his son, left Taunton some time after 1841 to become superintendent at Roswell Gleason's; in 1848 he returned to Taunton and established his own business. In 1852 Jirah Strange and

Peleg Francis fitted up a shop on Washington Street, Taunton, to make coffin trimmings.

The presence of individualism, however, in no way impaired the strong community feeling, which persisted long after the company had grown large. Reed & Barton was a social as well as an industrial entity, and the working force exhibited the voluntary unity of a church parish or lodge. A wistful glance a hundred years into the past reveals a self-sufficient little settlement in Hopewell, or, as a part of it came to be called, Britanniaville. The company constituted the center of community life — a state of affairs already extinct in city factories of the day, but which was destined to persist in small and relatively secluded communities until the advent of the automobile. This phase of the company history is an important one, for it concerns the happiness and well-being of the workmen.

By 1848 the first of a long series of illustrious Reed & Barton organizations had been formed — the Ciceronian Debating Society. With great formality and proper decorum the spinners, solderers, fitters, and other company employees gathered to discuss the affairs of state. In 1848 Edmund Porter was chosen president, and membership included Nathan Lawrence, John MacDonald, Edwin Reed, J. W. Thayer, Luther Babbitt, and other well-known names from the Britannia works. About this time the Saturday Evening Club was organized by Edmund Porter, Jahaziah Burbank, and others for the less formal but perhaps more vital function of repairing to Taunton Green after work, consuming huge quantities of pastries, and escorting fair company home.

Conflicts of a social nature inevitably flared up in this small community. Most of these arose out of differences between the habits of the newly arrived English workmen and those of the old residents. Temperance was the ground upon which battle was joined, and Edmund Porter led the forces of abstinence. The Saturday Evening Club had an English equivalent in the more spectacularly informal Ale Club, and Porter waged unceasing warfare on the deep-rooted love of the Englishmen for their evening pot of brew. This conflict grew out of practical as well as moral considerations, and Porter bitterly complained that Johnny ———, an excellent solderer, was frequently so full of beer that he could scarcely do a decent job before afternoon! In these sentiments Porter was joined by Henry Reed, who served as treasurer of the Total Abstinence Society. Reed, however, with his usual mildness, left to Porter the more active work of pledging the wayward.

By 1856 the Circeronian Debating Society apparently had talked itself out. A new debating society called the Mechanics Association was formed in the factory as a joint-stock company with a capital of $500. The old District 15 schoolhouse was purchased, became Mechanics Hall to three generations of employees, and was at last converted into the present Reed & Barton carpenter shop.

Other gatherings of a less pleasant nature also brought the workmen together outside the factory: [18]

1849

Sep 6 James C. (Chandler) White, *a shopmate died today*, only 20 yrs & 7 mos. old. leaves a wife and one child (married very young) Funeral on the morrow — 32 hands from the mill in procession with crape on their arms, to the grave. The general custom of the shop at a hands funeral.

The group consciousness of Reed & Barton employees created a great loyalty toward the company and helped to ease the transition from workshop to factory. This loyalty was carefully, though unconsciously, nourished by the skill and tact with which Henry Reed molded his organization after 1850 to meet the requirements of increasing size. The days when one man could supervise all men and all activities clearly were over. Tacit recognition of this fact was made by the partners, and a definite foreman group grew into existence. The increased volume of business tended to crystallize the company organization into definite departmental units, and growth became synonymous with specialization.

RISE OF FACTORY ORGANIZATION

The Leonard, Reed & Barton workshop of 1837 and the Reed & Barton factory of 1859 are two extremes which stand out in sharp contrast when directly compared. The transition from one to the other, however, was so gradual that it is impossible to say precisely when "workshop" was no longer the appropriate name for the enterprise at Britanniaville.

By 1850 specialization had appeared along two distinct lines. Certain segments of the company had become organized on a product basis. Nathan Lawrence's department, for example, turned out block-tin ware almost independent of the rest of the shop. At the same time specialization was taking place according to jobs performed rather than products made. Fitters, solderers, spinners, polishers, and other functional groups rapidly attained the status of full-fledged departments, each with its own foreman and assistant foreman. Specialization went even further, and certain men within these departments began to devote their attention to one kind of metal or one type of ware. When this point had been reached, Reed & Barton possessed both the size and organization of a true factory.

A description of the plant in 1856 lends support to this conclusion: [19]

The works of Messrs. Reed & Barton are extensive, and divided into different departments or rooms for the different processes, as the machine room, rolling room — in which the blocks of metal are rolled between cylinders into sheets of any required thickness, — the burnishing room, plating room, press room two general work rooms, two buffing rooms, polish room, and others. In their press room they have a number of presses of immense power — one screw press weighing about seven tons — for stamping designs and figures upon the different articles of their manufacture; and their stock of dies is most complete. Their show room contains samples of their manufactures, embracing urns, vases, cups, tureens, plates, salvers, &c., which in brilliancy, beauty, exquisite taste and skill in design and workmanship, would attract attention amid the most magnificent displays in the windows of the large jewelry stores in our cities.

Henry Reed was forced to abandon exclusive attention to the spinning lathe and to occupy a substantial part of his time with

CHART II

ORGANIZATION CHART, 1859, REED & BARTON

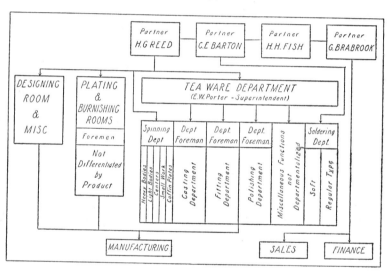

the supervision of the teaware department. By 1854, however, the growth of other branches of the business forced Reed to delegate the management of teaware to Charles Barton, while he turned his attention to one new department after another. Ill health soon restricted Barton's activities to the soldering department, and the position of teaware superintendent fell to Edmund Porter. Both Henry Reed and Charles Barton occupied a most unconventional place in their own administration. Barton, though an owner of the business, functioned as a working foreman. Reed formulated company policy at the highest level of management in the factory, but at the same time directed the spinning department in a foreman capacity and worked at the bench as a regular laborer. The resulting organization was complex, and lines of authority frequently overlapped, but in practice, management was direct, personal, and highly effective.

The year 1859 found Reed & Barton organized in the usual and necessary factory hierarchy of workmen, assistant foremen, foremen, and superintendents, but the change from no organization at all to a mass-production basis was accompanied by few of the usual growing pains. Henry Reed exhibited great organizing ability in making the transition successfully. His intimate knowledge of the workmen enabled him to pick competent foremen, and his preference for factory over office enabled him to follow carefully the work of the men he chose. Most important of all, it was devotion inspired in employees by close personal contact with a sympathetic leader which carried the company through one of the great crisis periods in its history.

CHAPTER VIII

GROWTH OF A SALES POLICY, 1837-1859

THE DEVELOPMENT of the Reed & Barton marketing organization paralleled in certain respects the building up of a factory organization. In both fields the company followed a pattern which was characteristic of business growth throughout the nation — the general trend toward specialization. In marketing, the passage of time and the accumulation of experience established an ever clearer definition of distribution channels. Special agents arose to perform special functions, and a great increase in trade made possible concentration of individual efforts upon one line of goods or one function. The great class of merchant middlemen gradually became divided, and the wholesaler, the retailer, the commission agent, the importer, and a host of other specialists emerged.[1]

WHOLESALERS AND COMMISSION AGENTS

Middleman specialization had progressed far enough by 1837 to provide Leonard, Reed & Barton with a group of dealers who confined their efforts mainly to the field of household hardware. Certain of these, to be sure, still carried on the multiple functions of importing, wholesaling, and retailing, but the trend toward selectivity was clearly established and promised the Britannia company that the efforts of their sales representatives were not to be dissipated over too wide a range of products. Leonard, Reed & Barton hoped with justifiable optimism that before long the large hardware houses might abandon importing, retailing, and other functions irrelevant to the wholesale distribution of Britannia ware. Even the achievement of the ideal goal — an agent devoted exclusively to the interests of the company — was not beyond the realm of possibility.

Leonard, Reed & Barton's wares were placed in the hands of two types of middlemen — the wholesaler and the commission agent. The arrangements effected soon showed that what the company lacked in marketing experience it made up by observing the mistakes of its predecessor, the Taunton Britannia Manufacturing Company. Wholesale houses were considered safe, for they purchased outright; but still vivid in Henry Reed's mind were the credit crisis of 1834 and the long rows of dust-covered teapots on the shelves of southern commission agents. The 1837 partnership would have preferred to have nothing to do with the commission-agent type of dealer, but necessity demanded otherwise. The depression which followed 1837 was a difficult time to persuade dealers to purchase large inventories. Wholesale houses were not numerous. Most of the few market contacts which Leonard, Reed & Barton possessed, moreover, were the customers of the Taunton Britannia Manufacturing Company, and for the most part these were commission agents. A compromise between the desirable and the necessary was at length negotiated, which eliminated the proven dangers of a large unsold inventory on dealer shelves. Sales were made on a commission basis, but an ironclad restriction guarded against a recurrence of the events of 1834: "It is a rule of our concern not to consign." Agents received a sample line only, from which orders were taken and forwarded to Taunton to be made up at the factory as received.

Leonard, Reed & Barton policy called for distribution of wares through one large wholesale house or commission agent in each of the principal market cities. Formal agreements were drawn up in each case, and the exclusive distribution privilege was extended for a minimum of twelve months. In return for granting this privilege the company insisted that agents should not ". . . buy or sell wholesale or retail in England or the United States the Tea Ware of any manufacturer or Company but ourselves." [2] In Boston, Deming Jarves, founder and agent of the

Boston and Sandwich Glass Company, was granted the exclusive right to purchase and sell castor frames, bowl covers, and jug tops. No such agency for the distribution of teaware was granted in that city, however, and several wholesale houses carried the line. Southern markets were served by commission agents, also with exclusive rights in their own cities. In 1837 St. John & Wetherell was company agent in New York, Krug & Colladay in Philadelphia, and Stickney & Noyes in Baltimore. All were listed as commission agents, and all carried a more or less diversified line of hardware, glass, and Britannia ware.

These were the principal outlets for company products, and Leonard, Reed & Barton was firm in its attitude toward other dealers in these cities.

Taunton Aug 1 1839 [3]

Mess H. B. Hall & Co.
  Gent.

   We have before us yours of 29 ult — and can only say our ware at present is engaged to B. & Shipman of your city and must therefore decline arrangements for the sale of it elsewhere in Phila as multiplying Houses for the sale of it would be inpolitic

Respy. Yr. Obt. Servts.
Leonard Reed & Barton

The exclusive agency arrangement was stated by the company to apply not only to sales in Boston, New York, Philadelphia, and Baltimore, but to sales everywhere. In January, 1839, Elijah Braman, of Warren, Rhode Island, was informed that "in consequence of an arrangement with some wholesale Dealers in Brittannia we cannot sell any Tea Ware excepting in large Cities say New York Boston &c and cannot therefore fill any orders from you." [4]

Company policy in this respect was flexible, however, and actually substantial sales were made outside the metropolitan areas. Usually such sales were made only to wholesale customers who ordered well in advance and in substantial amounts, a wholesaler's rating being assigned any dealer who purchased more than $1,000 of goods a year. Occasionally these restrictions were relaxed to favor old and well-known customers.

Taunton Jany 13th 1844[5]

Mr S. H. Williams

. . . .

You inquire if we require a certain amount of goods ordered to make the greatest Dist., we reply that we have not so much refference to the amount ordered at a time, as to the class of dealers to whom we sell.

We should make the same dist. on an order of 100$ as we should on a larger one if it was from one of our regular customers, and did not often occur, but should require the orders generally to exceed that amount to make the above dist.

. . . .

Resply Yours
Reed & Barton
By A. Brabrook

These restrictions on sales had very obvious advantages at the time they were imposed. Slow and uncertain communications continued to make market contacts difficult to maintain. Gustavus Leonard was the only "salesman," yet his time necessarily was divided between shop and road, and he was unable to make calls on large numbers of customers. The company felt, quite rightly, that the promotional efforts of dealers could best be supervised if the number of those dealers was small. Finally, the demand for company wares was more than adequate to crowd production facilities to the utmost, and there was little apparent need for seeking new outlets. Yet in the end the confining of sales was destined to prove both unnecessary and undesirable.

TERMS OF SALE

The terms on which the company did business with its agents are quite clearly defined by the correspondence which has survived. One fact stands out with great clarity. A definite plan was in use, which, though frequently inadequate and often changed, did constitute the first attempt by the Britannia company to pursue a consistent and reasoned market policy.

In an effort to substitute order for the haphazard bargaining of earlier years an attempt was made to set up a standardized scale of discounts which would apply with consistency to all dealers. In 1837 Leonard, Reed & Barton was quoting the following terms to wholesalers:

Teaware 25%	discount from list price
Nickel-silver castor frames 17%	" " " "
Plain frames (Britannia) 10%	" " " "
Lamps 20%	" " " "

Commissions given to agents are not clearly defined, and terms appeared to vary considerably. The commission agent assumed no inventory risks and therefore received a smaller discount than regular wholesalers. In regard to a contract with Berkley & Shipman, of Philadelphia, the company stated, "We were to allow them 10 pr. ct. as profit, take Banca Tin at Cash price and allow 2½ pr. ct. for buying." [6] Since the usual fee for commission agents dealing in domestic products was from 2½ per cent to 5 per cent,[7] the Leonard, Reed & Barton representatives seem to have been waxing fat on their agreement; but too little information has survived to make any final appraisal of the rates paid.

Usual practice was for the company to pay shipping expenses to the wharf in New York, Baltimore, or Philadelphia, the customer assuming risk of shipment or paying insurance charges thereon. The matter of shipping terms was a legitimate field for bargaining, however, and all degrees of compromise were arrived at. Great was the relief and clearer the air in Taunton when a penny-wise negotiation over some large shipment was at last concluded!

One of Henry Reed's most cherished desires was for a cash

business. In an endeavor to achieve this end the company offered a liberal discount of 5 per cent for cash payment in 10 days. In 1838 working capital needs became acute in Taunton. "We must sacrifice on something to get *Money,* as we can get no Disct. at Bank," states a letter to Krug & Colladay,[8] and an 8 per cent discount for cash is quoted. "Necessity compels us to make this offer." A revealing letter of three years later confesses a motive behind the cash policy which has a very familiar ring.[9]

Taunton Nov. 18th 1841

Mr. Nathaniel Witherell Jr.
    Dr Sr.
. . . .

    It may look a little singular to you that we should have adopted the course of selling all our wares for cash. It was mainly because Dixons custom was a similar one and we think thus far the terms have been the best that could have been adopted for our interests — and also better for the interests of the purchaser — as we have made and still shall continue to make a liberal Discount in consequence

Resply Yours
Gustavus Leonard
for Reed & Barton

However firmly the company stated its policy of cash business only, the times made this impossible, and credit was frequently extended to tried-and-true customers. Six-month terms were quoted, usually with the stern admonition that future business must be for cash, and customers' notes were taken to the Taunton Bank to be discounted. As in past years, the matter of collecting accounts required delicate negotiations and no small amount of patience. Scarcity of specie and the periodic contraction of banking facilities between 1837 and 1843 added greatly to the difficulties of trade, and the exchange of funds was often expensive. When exchange rates between cities became excessive, prices of wares were raised to cover the difference between the value of money in Taunton and in the southern markets. Gustavus Leonard frequently complained that, "As it is with difficulty we make Tea Ware nett the Cost of manufacture [we] cannot save ourselves in selling the article and losing the exchange." [10]

Customers themselves performed valuable services for the company in collecting accounts and furnishing credit information. The usefulness of the New York, Philadelphia, and Baltimore agents, however, went far beyond this. Leonard, Reed & Barton made frequent inquiries of its dealers on the state of local trade and sought advice from those close to the market on matters of styling and pricing. Usual practice in deciding whether to undertake a new line or pattern was first to ask dealers what the market would be willing to pay, then to see if the article could be manufactured to yield a profit at that price.

PRICE POLICY

In general, the pricing practice followed by the company consisted of a rule-of-thumb policy, having reference on the one hand to direct costs of manufacture, and on the other to the bargaining position of the buyer. In certain cases, customers were successful in holding prices down; in other cases, the company succeeded in getting either higher prices or lower discounts. In all cases, pricing was a continuous process of bargaining, with both parties pleading poverty. The popularity of Taunton Britannia ware gave the company an edge in the dickering and usually made higher prices obtainable in the periodic emergencies created by sharp rises in the cost of metals. In so far as the No. 2700 octagon pattern was concerned, for example, the company was able to name its own price. The quotation on this particular item went from $22 per dozen in 1837 to $25 in 1838, and to $29 in 1841. In 1841 rising costs required that the company ask, and the popularity of the pattern enabled it to receive, a general increase of 25 cents per tea set. Again, in 1853 and 1857, small upward price revisions were conceded by the market as the cost of metals soared.

The southern agents performed a further vital function in

procuring for the company a substantial part of its raw materials. Tin, antimony, copper, wrapping paper, polishing earth, hides, and other articles were purchased by customers and shipped to Taunton, the cost of the purchases being credited to the customer's account. In fact, a very substantial barter trade was taking place during the 1837–43 depression and did much to alleviate the difficulties imposed by lack of cash.

Taunton March 2d 1838 [11]

Mr. George Manning

Your letter of the 19th Feb. is at hand offering to sell Lamps for us on commission. . . . We will exchange for *Banca* or Streights Tin or for cut nails at 9 mos. market prices and furnish with what Lamps you may want at the 6 mos. proposed prices. This last offer is such an one as would need little or no capital to comply with and on our part is offering the Lamps at a very low rate. We will take nails of H. Leonard & Co Brand, Lazelle Perkins & Co. Fall River Iron works or Boston Iron Co at their market prices

Respy Yr. Servt

Leonard Reed & Barton

The company also expressed a willingness to accept scrap metal in payment of outstanding accounts, and as late as 1859 old coffin plates, teaware, and pewter at predetermined rates per pound were being used by customers to settle bills or pay for new orders.

Occasionally dealers wrote and expressed a desire to exchange their stock for newer models. Reed & Barton disclaimed all responsibility for style obsolescence, but at the same time recognized the problem which dealers faced. Gustavus Leonard informed Davis, Palmer & Company, of Boston, in 1840 that the company did not consider that justice demanded exchange of new stock for old, since ". . . the main advantage of selling over consigning we deem to be the sale being final at time of delivery." Leonard conceded this much to an old customer, however: "We are prepared to fill small orders at same dist. we have formerly allowed on larger ones — so that the loss by change of style or by Interest for goods on hand shall after this come on us." [12] Several years later, company policy relaxed somewhat to allow one customer to return some remnants of unsalable patterns, the sacrifice being made with the expectation that he might thereby revive his flagging promotional efforts.

The one company practice which admitted of no bargaining, and which seems to have operated absolutely without exception, was that which pertained to Reed & Barton's right to regulate prices at which dealers disposed of company wares. Any company representative who underbid "ticket" quotations in selling to retailers stood in imminent danger of losing his agency.[13]

We have determined to make no article excepting we can regulate the price at which it shall be offered from the wholesaler to the Retailer and that must be a uniform price whether it be offered to the retailer in N. York, Phila. or Boston.

The company stated that wholesale dealers might make a discount of 5 per cent to retailers or purchasers of small lots, and 10 per cent to other wholesalers, ". . . but maintain the ticket prices when you retail or sell not to sell again. . . ." [14] Later, the retailers' margin was increased to between 7 and 10 per cent.

Firmness in some respects was matched by leniency in others, and many favors were extended to customers over and above the contractual requirements involved. Misunderstandings between Reed & Barton and its dealers invariably were settled promptly, and usually in favor of the latter. Customarily the company acquiesced with the dealer's viewpoint on any first complaint, but at the same time made clear the terms under which the same situation would be settled should it arise again.

At all times was Henry Reed willing, and even anxious, to make up special orders to meet special wants. The boast of Leonard, Reed & Barton and later of Reed & Barton was that the company could and would make anything in the line of

Britannia ware that its customers desired. Such special orders were made up, however, with the understanding that after a certain period of time had elapsed the articles should be made available to all the trade. Certain dealers resented having designs which they sent to Taunton thus released to competitors, but the company agreed in turn to bear the cost of making up the dies and molds and often gave a special discount to the house which originated the pattern. In this way a compromise equitable to both parties was usually effected.

It is most unfortunate that so little information has survived about prices, terms, and trade practices in the Britannia industry prior to 1850. There is little basis for a comparison between Reed & Barton and competing firms, but there seem to be no complaints from customers that the Taunton company was undersold. In 1841 Leonard boasted to a New York dealer, "As to prices and terms we shall make the terms better to you than you can do with Dixon — or better than we find others do in the English trade. . . ."[15]

Changing Channels of Distribution

The relations between Reed & Barton and its agents, though cordial under normal circumstances, were not completely satisfactory. Less than a year after Leonard, Reed & Barton had commenced operations, the commission agency system and exclusive representation began to show signs of inherent weaknesses. Some agents and some exclusive houses proved more satisfactory than others, but the eventual fate of these methods of distribution was to be the same.

Wherever the company had made a happy choice of agents, the granting of exclusive privileges worked out very well. Deming Jarves, for example, accounted for many thousands of dollars' worth of frames and bottle tops, and his promotional enthusiasm left little to be desired. A poor choice of agent, however, meant a great loss in that agent's territory, for there

Prices of Ware
Manufactured by
LEONARD, REED & BARTON.

FANCY TEA WARE.

PATTERN	Tea Pots Half Pints 5	Coffee Pots 6	Ten Half Pots	Sugars	Creams	SLOP BOWLS No. 1	No. 2	
700	22,50	25,50	34,50	18,00	12,00	15 00	12 00	p doz
800	22,50	25,50	34,50	18,00	12,00	15,00	12,00	"
200	22,50	25,50	34,50	18,00	12,00	15,00	12,00	"
400	22,50	25,50	34,00	18,00	12,00	15,00	12,00	"
500	22 00	25,50	33,00	16,50	11,00	15,00	12,00	"
700	23,50	26 50	35,00	19,00	13,00	15,00		"

FANCY URNS.

	ROUND STAND. Half Pints 10	16	SQUARE STAND Half Pints 10	16	ROUND STAND Half Pints 24	32	SQUARE STAND Half Pints 24	32
	5,50	8,00	6,75	9,00	11,50	13,50	13,00	15 00
	5,50		6,75					
	5,50	8,00	6,75	9,00	11,50	13,50	13,00	15,00
	5,50		6,75					
	5,50	8,00	6,75	9,00	11,50	13,50	13,00	15,00

LAMPS.

HIGH STAND, plain. Pattern No.	per dozen.	DISH STAND, handled. Pattern No.	per dozen.	HIGH STAND, handled. Pattern No.	per dozen.	DISH STAND, plain. Pattern No.	per dozen.
7	10,50	12	11,50	9	11,50	14	9,50
9	10,00	14	10,00			12	10,50
15	6,75	24	6,75			20	7,00
19	7,50	26	5,00			18	8,00
13	7,50	18	8,50			24	6,25
		20	7,50				

CASTOR FRAMES.

SILVER and TUTANIA—Revolving. Figured.	Plain.	Square.	Round.
7 Rings per dozen	31,00	20,00	12,00	12,00
6 " " "	29,00	19,00	12,00	12,00
5 " " "	29,00	19,00	11,00	11,00
4 " " "				

	No. 1.	No. 2.	No. 3.	No. 4.
CANDLESTICKS,	11,50	8,50	6,75	
TUMBLERS,	2,50	2,00		
SOUP LADLES,	4,50	4,00		
COFFIN PLATES,	2,50	1,75	1,50	
FRUIT DISHES,	24,00	24,00	21,00	21,00
BEER MUGS,	7,50	5,50	3,75	
SOCKET LAMPS.	5,00	4,50		

COMMUNION WARE.

TANKARDS,	per dozen,		60,00
PLATES,	" "		9,00
BOWLS,	" "		30,00
CUPS, (plain.)	" "		11,00
" (handled)	" "		12,00

EARLIEST KNOWN COMPANY PRICE LIST, 1837

were no other dealers there to augment his efforts. Actually the practice of appointing one representative in a district began to break down in the southern markets as early as 1839.

The commission agent, when chosen as the sole means of distribution, proved exceptionally unsatisfactory and failed in most cases to provide promotional effort adequate to satisfy the company. Selling from samples, moreover, involved many delays and brought complaints from purchasers who did not wish to wait for their orders to be forwarded to Taunton and made up there. As time went on, Reed & Barton inclined more and more toward the wholesaler, and experience proved that the dealer who purchased a stock of wares outright exhibited far greater vigor in pushing the line than did the commission agents, whose sense of responsibility rested upon ethical rather than monetary grounds.

The practice of granting exclusive agencies resulted in almost constant bickering among agents and invoked the ill will of dealers who were not favored with an agency. In New York the firm of St. John & Wetherell complained bitterly when, at the expiration of its contract in 1838, Young, Smith & Company was given the agency. Krug & Colladay in Philadelphia reported that its exclusive rights in that city failed to protect it from New York competition, and then was completely alienated when Reed & Barton granted Berkley & Shipman the Philadelphia area.

The appointment of Young, Smith & Company as New York agent soon proved to have been a bad mistake: [16]

Taunton, June 11 — 1840

Messrs. Young, Smith & Co.

    Gent.

        We wish to know from you decidedly, and we wish to know immediately what course you are calculating to pursue in giving us orders for this Summer and the coming Autumn. That we cannot content ourselves with New York Sales as they have been under our existing contract with you (Being lately only about one Quarter of those of Boston) You will readily perceive. *Something must be done* and that very soon too — You may tell us if you choose of the general stagnation of Business. You may detail if you wish the dull sales in the City of New York — We have various sources of information which substantiate the fact that a good deal of Brittannia Ware has been retailed and wholesaled in New York the two past Seasons. That it has been but a very small part ours you must admit. We have wated patiently for you to give us orders, but we have wated in vain.

We want a decided and immediate answer as to the inducements you offer for a trade in New York the coming Summer & Autumn. If you are willing to give up the contract we are allowing you the privelige of ordering ware to close up what you have on hand. . . .

> Resply yours
> Leonard Reed & Barton

Nevertheless, the contract was renewed for 1841, but the results were even less satisfactory. The company complained that in New York ". . . sales were limited much more so than was anticipated at the time the contract was made, leaving us a chance to dispose of less quantity of goods . . . than we should do if no such restriction existed." [17] At the same time it became evident that Young, Smith & Company was selling wares below ticket, and when this fact had been confirmed by cautious investigation, the agency was terminated.

One more attempt was made to sustain a commission agent on an exclusive-distribution basis in New York, and Nathaniel Witherell was nominated in place of Young, Smith & Company. In 1843, however, Reed & Barton announced its determination not to have a commission house in Philadelphia, and the same policy appears to have been put into effect in New York. Henceforth company wares were sold outright, mainly to wholesalers. The number of dealers in the large cities multiplied rapidly, indicating the abandonment, once and for all, of exclusive privileges.

The reviving prosperity of trade after 1843 undoubtedly

played an important part in hastening the change from commission agents to wholesalers, and from limited to general distribution of Reed & Barton wares. Better times created means to finance outright purchases, and wholesale dealers regained confidence, at last daring to place stock on their shelves. When general business emerged from its six-year depression, the demand for Reed & Barton wares quickly outstripped the limited provisions for distribution which had been made in less prosperous times. Pressure from within the trade at length became so strong that it smashed through all artificially imposed restrictions on the market.

The story of distribution in Boston during the 1837–43 period is a far brighter one than that in the southern markets. The commission agency gained no foothold in Boston, and the explanation for this fact can be made in terms of miles. With the Britannia works only two hours distant by Boston & Providence and Taunton Branch Railroads, dealers there were able to keep small stocks on hand, reorder frequently, and receive their orders with practically no transportation delays. With inventory risks virtually eliminated, little incentive existed to sell from samples on the less profitable commission basis.

The choice of representatives in Boston was far more fortunate than it had been in New York or Philadelphia, possibly because the Boston dealers were better known to the Taunton men.

Davis, Palmer & Company, Sumner & Hopkins, and Jones, Lows & Ball piled up substantial teaware sales. Deming Jarves soon became the company's largest dealer, and trade with this firm held at a high level until well into the 1850's. Jarves was a sharp trader, however, and Reed & Barton paid dearly for his patronage. Dealing with him was from start to finish one continual dicker, and Jarves coaxed, pleaded, and threatened in order to obtain an extra 2 per cent, or a shilling off ticket. Sheer persistence of his demands, plus an unexcelled sales record, eventually obtained for him better terms than any other dealer was getting, and it was Deming Jarves who first broke through the sacred limit of 27½ per cent discount, cash.

The performance of the Boston dealers between 1837 and 1843 brought the center of company sales back to New England for a brief time, but with the multiplication of New York, Philadelphia, and Baltimore houses after 1843 the southern markets once more began to assume great importance. The results of abandoning the commission-agency type of business caused considerable satisfaction in Taunton.[18]

> The class of customers to whom we sell . . . are wholesale dealers, and were formerly large importers of Dixons ware — they have now abandoned the sale of English ware, and buy their Tea Ware, Urns, and Communion Ware of us. We have sold more Tea Ware to that class of customers in Maiden Lane for the last 8 months than we have sold to all our other customers united — We of course feel under some obligation to them — no other dealers probably in the United States would have done so much to establish the reputation of our ware. They are a class of dealers who buy their goods direct from the manufacturers — and if they buy frames at all they would not buy them through any Agent.

Transportation and Sales

Success in the 1840's inspired many changes in the Reed & Barton organization, but trade methods and customs savored strongly of the beaver hat era. Communications southward were still slow and uncertain, and the company continued to ship its wares by coasting schooners. The wharves of the Taunton River fleet still echoed to the rumble of wagons from the Britannia works, and winter continued to place a chilly interdict on trade.

Both railroad and steamship lines facilitated travel, but rates were too high to allow the shipment of sizable orders for long distances. Direct communication was always an object, and the company preferred to ship by Taunton vessels sailing a through route to New York or Philadelphia. Steamship freighting required unloading at Providence, for these vessels could not

Shipped in good order and condition, by *Russ & Barton*
on board the good *Brig* called the
Acorn whereof *Harwood Barton*
is Master, for the present voyage, now lying in the PORT of *Boston*
and bound for *Philadelphia* **To say:**

Eighteen Boxes & one Bbl
Britannia ware

Being marked and numbered as in the margin, and are to be delivered in the like good
order and condition, at the aforesaid Port of *Phil a*
(the danger of the seas only excepted) unto *Messrs. Jno. & Jacob Snider*
or assigns, he or they paying Freight for the said Goods, *ten cents.*
per box

with — Primage and average.

In Witness Whereof, the Master of said vessel hath affirmed to three
Bills of Lading, all of this tenor and date; one of which Bills being accomplished, the
others to stand void.

Dated at *Boston*
Sept 25th 1840

Harwood Barton
For Mr. Master

BILL OF LADING, 1840
Reed & Barton

J. Marsh, Stationer.

Jno. Snider &
Phil a

negotiate the Taunton River, and the company complained of ". . . the detention almost always attending the latter way of sending." [19] In winter when the river was closed or when no through vessel was scheduled to leave Taunton, wares were sent by the recently constructed New Bedford Railroad to that port for reshipment, and in time New Bedford captured permanently much of the river fleet business.

The ways of trade were still informal, exhibiting only a minor acceleration in tempo from the previous decade. Beyond extending permission to a few houses to represent them, Reed & Barton exerted no great effort to cover the market or systematically canvass for orders. The general sales philosophy, apparently, was to let the mountain come to Mahomet. The regular commercial drummer was an institution of the future, and merchants frequently visited the factory to place their orders for the season. It was no uncommon sight at this time to see some stylishly clad merchant prince from Broadway perched on an empty box by the side of one of the members of the firm in the mill, as he made his contract for the holiday goods, the talk mingling with the rattle of busy artisan tools.[20]

Few new experiments were attempted by Leonard, Reed & Barton or by Reed & Barton in the line of advertising. In 1842 the New York agent placed small advertisements in certain newspapers, but in general this medium of promotion seems to have been ignored. The practice of showing company wares at exhibitions of the Massachusetts Charitable Mechanic Association, the American Institute, and the Franklin Institute was continued and resulted in much beneficial publicity and a formidable accumulation of first-award medals.

The 1840's, however, terminated the Rough and Ready period of distribution, and after 1850 the picturesque yielded rapidly to the practical. In time the railroads displaced the river sloops, and the telegraph sliced through the isolation of distances. Change-provoking growth altered the marketing structure of Reed & Barton, and the appointment of George Brabrook as the first full-time company salesman since 1834 heralded great expansion.

Brabrook's career set a splendid precedent for future generations of Reed & Barton salesmen to follow. Up from the ranks

☞ **Taunton Britannia Ware.** —— The subscriber having made an arrangement with a Boston house to supply him with this celebrated Ware, is prepared to furnish dealers and the trade generally with every variety, manufactured by them, at their lowest prices, for cash. Samples can be seen at 93 John st. between Cliff and Pearl.

j10   **NATH. WITHERELL**, jr. Agent.

ADVERTISEMENT BY THE COMPANY'S NEW YORK AGENT
New York *Tribune*, January 10, 1842

through a hand-soiling apprenticeship, Brabrook soon proved his worth on the road, and orders piled up at the factory in ever increasing volume. New terms were instituted to meet both greater competition and the enlarged scope of Reed & Barton trade. Discounts on teaware were extended from 25 per cent to 27½ per cent, and occasionally to 30 per cent. The cash-in-ten-days policy of 1845 became cash in thirty days, and large customer balances began to be carried on the books. The increasing demand of dealers for credit forced the company into short-term borrowing, and by the late 'fifties the Taunton Bank began to provide Reed & Barton with working capital.

POSITION IN THE INDUSTRY

Most important of all market circumstances after 1850 was the development of domestic competition. A backward glance reveals the fact that almost since its beginning in 1824 the Taunton company had either led the domestic Britannia industry or had been among the leaders. Certain shops achieved greater recognition in their own district, but available evidence strongly indicates that Crossman, West & Leonard, the Taunton Britannia Manufacturing Company, Leonard, Reed & Barton, and Reed & Barton led domestic manufacturers in the national market. At times this leadership was undisputed; occasionally it was seriously challenged. In its best days the Taunton Britannia Manufacturing Company was unrivaled by any American Britannia firm, but 1834 brought decline and oblivion. In 1837 Leonard, Reed & Barton was one of several twenty-employee shops, but the following years brought success at the expense of competitors, and 1850 brought to Reed & Barton absolute and unquestioned leadership (even over the English) in the Britannia field.

Proof of this fact lies in both the size and the reputation of the Taunton company. So far as can be ascertained Reed & Barton in 1850 was much the largest organization in the industry. The average Britannia manufactory at this time employed fourteen hands, with capital invested of $6,507.14,[21] while the Reed & Barton working force numbered over one hundred, and capital invested in the business exceeded $30,000. Competition came principally from Roswell Gleason in Dorchester and Hall, Boardman & Company in Philadelphia, neither of which appears to have been as large as Reed & Barton, although Hall, Boardman & Company was reputed to possess a modern and efficient factory.[22] This firm, moreover, turned its attention to the far-southern and western markets rather than to the New York area. Significant perhaps is the fact that in all the surviving Reed & Barton correspondence of this period, only Roswell Gleason's firm is mentioned. Rufus Dunham in Maine, Israel Trask, of Beverly, Massachusetts, Smith & Company, of Boston, and a host of smaller Britannia shops in Connecticut seem to have provided some competition, but for the most part on a local scale.

Certain it is that no other company in the industry received

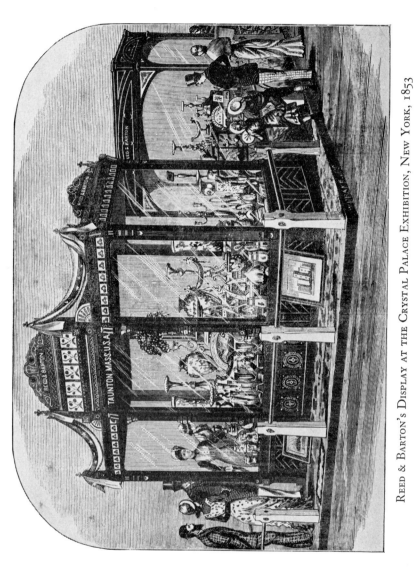

Reed & Barton's Display at the Crystal Palace Exhibition, New York, 1853

greater national recognition from impartial judges than did
Reed & Barton. The most lavish praise and highest awards of
the American and Franklin Institutes consistently went to the
Taunton company, and very few other manufacturers received
any notice whatsoever in these important exhibitions. Gleason
was commended for his coffee urns by the Massachusetts Charitable Mechanic Association in 1841,[23] and the Franklin Institute
recommended the work of Hall, Boardman & Company in
1844, 1845, and 1846, though stipulating that ". . . the forms or
patterns might, perhaps, be improved." [24]

By 1850, too, the importation of foreign Britannia ware had
decreased to an insignificant level.[25] The preoccupation of the
English houses with electroplate made Reed & Barton not only
the most important American Britannia manufacturer but the
most important Britannia manufacturer selling to the American
market. This honor promised to be a doubtful one, however,
and it speedily became evident that success after 1850 was to de-
pend not on Britannia but on electroplate.

CHALLENGE OF A RIVAL

The 1850's saw a revolution in the Britannia and plate industry, and 1852 was the crisis year. Then occurred one of those
events which abruptly jar the gradual process of evolution far
from its normal course, and inspire great changes almost overnight. The formation of the Meriden Britannia Company in
Meriden, Connecticut, produced truly electrifying effects upon
the trade.

From any point of view the founding of this company was an
inspired achievement. The Meriden Britannia Company was
a merger of several small Connecticut firms, most of which
appear to have been employing only eight or ten workmen
and doing business upon a more or less local scale. In 1853, the
first full year of operation, the new company sold $300,000 of
wares and shortly declared a 50 per cent dividend.[26]

The Meriden Britannia Company was essentially a selling organization, and the four small factories which it owned could not have produced a quarter of the wares sold.[27] The amazing results achieved are explicable only in terms of market conditions in the industry at the time. Prosperity prevailed, and a tremendous latent demand for Britannia and plated ware existed which the obsolete selling practices of manufacturers had failed to exploit. The Meriden Company immediately embarked on an aggressive marketing program. The vigor of this fresh effort swept competition off its feet and seized the sales initiative which Reed & Barton had only just inherited from the English. The effect on Reed & Barton was abrupt and, in the long run, exceedingly beneficial. Almost immediately the Taunton company's leadership in size of output was lost and its marketing methods outmoded. Scattered and ineffective competition suddenly coagulated into an intensely energetic and progressive rival unit.

It was inevitable that Reed & Barton should respond sharply to the challenge. The formation of the Meriden Britannia Company came at one of the highest peaks of power in Reed & Barton's entire history. The foundation for successful resistance had been carefully laid by Henry Reed: the wares of Taunton enjoyed the highest reputation for quality of any in the market, an adequate financial reserve had been built up, and a highly efficient manufacturing organization developed. Reed's foresight had given the company valuable experience in the field of plated ware, and Reed himself was at the peak of his efficiency.

But while the basis for successful competition with Meriden existed, the fate of Reed & Barton was in the last analysis to be decided in a field alien to Reed's disposition and training. In the future it was to be sales effort, rather than product quality, which would determine industry leadership. In this crisis of marketing the last, and perhaps the greatest, of Henry Reed's talents stood clearly revealed. Kind Providence may have provided the company with a salesman in its hour of need, but it was Reed's insight into human character that recognized the potentialities of George Brabrook. With a rare ability at diagnosing his own limitations, Reed turned over to his young salesman the job of meeting the Meriden Britannia Company on its own ground. Brabrook succeeded, and in the face of intense competition Reed & Barton throve and grew stronger than ever.

The years which followed the Meriden merger gave rise to a confused competitive situation. With a market organization creating demands far beyond its own producing capacity the Meriden Britannia Company began to purchase large quantities of wares from other manufacturers. The fashion once set was followed by others, and many companies sought to round out their lines in this manner. Reed & Barton itself purchased certain articles, notably flatware, but for the most part the company's function seems to have been that of a supplier. Large sales were made to Rogers Bros.; the Meriden Britannia Company; Lucius Hart, of New York; J. O. Mead & Company, of Philadelphia; and others. During 1854 and 1855 purchases by Rogers Bros. appear to have been larger than those of any other customer. As a result of this practice, manufacturers found in short order that they were competing with their own goods. Reed & Barton Britannia ware went to Hartford, received a coat of Rogers Bros. silver plate and a Rogers Bros. stamp, and appeared in regular market channels to compete, usually at a lower price, with the regular Reed & Barton plated line.

The formation of the Meriden Company foretold other changes in the industry, and the increasing influence of large firms virtually ended the workshop era of Britannia ware and electroplate production. The industry picture first resolved itself into a three-sided competition between Reed & Barton and the Meriden Britannia Company in the Britannia field, and between Reed & Barton and Rogers Bros. in electroplate. At the end of the decade the assimilation of the Rogers concerns by the

Meriden Company narrowed the field of competition, and left Reed & Barton and the Meriden Britannia Company the outstanding contenders, with several smaller manufacturers picking the bones of the market feast.

Through these years of keen competition, Reed & Barton pursued a cautious program, and Henry Reed's conservative nature shadowed the progress of the marketing organization. Cautiously the Meriden precedents were examined. Reed did not agree that they all were good and insisted that his company avoid entangling alliances of any kind. A proposal by Smith & Company, of Boston, was disposed of with this guarded comment: [28]

> We are aware that Manufacturers have in some instances agreed upon certain prices for their goods and doubtless expected the result would be higher prices and greater profits. We think however good the plan in theory it has been found impracticable, and usually resulted in the injury rather than advantage of the parties —
>
> You will not understand us to say there is no occasion for an advance in prices, we only express our decided conviction that we had each better fix our prices from our own judgement and independent of each other

Nor did Taunton match the pace of the Connecticut firms in pricing, quoting discounts, or advertising. Reed & Barton's prices seem to have been a trifle higher and discounts slightly lower than either Rogers Bros.' or the Meriden Britannia Company's, and the amount of advertising done by Reed & Barton was negligible in comparison with that of the Connecticut firm.

The Meriden Britannia Company usurped that leadership which the firm of Dixon had held for so long; and, as in former years, Reed & Barton followed the precedent set by another. This rejection of leadership was a policy too consistently followed and too deliberately courted to have been a result of mere accident or lack of initiative. At no point in the company's development between 1837 and 1859 was an untried experiment resorted to. Henry Reed rejected the spectacular successes and escaped the disastrous failures which fell to the lot of the pioneer in this and other industries. The prospect of inordinate gain did not particularly attract Reed and never became during his administration an objective of the company. Conservative policies yielded adequate dividends and assured a long-continued existence. Because of the application of already tested methods and processes Reed made virtually no mistakes — certainly no serious ones. Yet so closely was the market followed, and so alert was Reed, and later, Brabrook, to developing trends, that often the company shared the profits of invention with the inventors.

In one field only was Henry Reed intolerant of competition. The wares of Reed & Barton continued to lead the market in quality of craftsmanship. The Britannia and electroplate which came out of the Taunton factory were equaled by few other manufacturers and surpassed by none. Reed & Barton products in 1859 constituted the highest standard of workmanship in the industry.

*   *   *

The complete story of this fruitful period becomes clear in retrospect. Standing solidly on the policy of manufacturing the best in the market, Henry Reed's deliberate caution in other spheres of action built a sturdy organization which never experienced the demoralization of costly mistakes. Reed considered himself a production man, yet he achieved fully as great success in the field of general administration by preserving through years of great growth a warm personal relationship between workmen and management. Expansion was the most severe test of Henry Reed's ability. It was not to be expected that a man so used to doing things himself could ever successfully tolerate the efforts of others, yet Reed did consistently recognize talent and give it room in his organization to thrive, thereby inspiring the loyalty of his men and assuring the continuing success of the firm.

PART III

GEORGE BRABROOK AND THE SHIFT TO A MARKETING EMPHASIS
1860–1900

CHAPTER IX

WORKING HARDER TO SELL, 1860–1880

THE OPENING SHOTS of civil strife constituted an appropriate and prophetic overture to the last four turbulent decades of the century. For the Britannia, electroplate, and silverware industry, and for most industries these were years of great competition. It was a period which for many companies meant more activity than profit, and which for all companies meant great efforts and prolonged trials. These trials and efforts are nowhere better illustrated than in the luxury-product industries, supersensitive as they were and are to the slightest environmental changes. The Reed & Barton organization reacted quickly, though not always predictably, to the often painful stimuli of the times. That company's history presents, therefore, not only a story of individual labor under adversity, but a unit of measurement for the changing aspects of general industrial life. The forty years of George Brabrook's administration, extending from before the Civil War to the turn of the century, constitute as distinct a unit in the company history as the Reed administration which they succeeded. From a marketing viewpoint, however, the 1860–1900 period divides itself into two great selling efforts, with 1880 the division point or breathing space between.

That widespread changes in the business world were destined to appear became quickly evident with the close of the Civil War. Even contemporary business men sensed the change. The prewar decades had seen a great preoccupation with experimental and inventive manufacturing. Some important development occurred in the field of marketing even at that time, but the manufacturer, for the most part, was busy with his machines.

Technological development in certain fields continued unabated, or even at an accelerated pace, but after the prosperity of Civil War years manufacturers were forced to devote increasing attention to marketing the products they had learned to produce in such great abundance.

The postwar decades brought a tremendous growth of population which the railroad converted into a growth in markets. But if markets increased, so, too, did the number and size and efficiency of competing industrial units, and probably at a faster rate.[1] The general level of prices, driven hard by increasing competition, a slowing increase in gold production, and other factors, declined more or less continuously from 1865 to 1897. The fall in the price of metals and metal products in the period was particularly severe.[2] For the Britannia and electroplate industry, with technical development already brought to a point of high operating efficiency, there commenced an era of unprecedented competition for markets scarcely large enough to support the optimum output of all the companies involved. Frequently this competition took place against the dark background of depression. Faithful to the trend of the industry, the administrative emphasis of Reed & Barton became focused on marketing, and in this field the company's fight for existence and recognition took place.

The viewpoint and interest of Henry Reed, the man at the bench, did not change with the times. The shift of emphasis in the company and in the industry found him still absorbed in technical matters about the factory and in the design aspects of product policy. His greatest work finished by 1860, Reed appeared willing that new men should grapple with the new problems. To no small extent, however, the very presence of the stocky, bearded figure of Henry Reed in the factory was influential in company management. Never far from the workbench he understood so well, Reed appeared through these years as the kindly but determined guardian of fine craftsman-

ship. But the immediate fate of the company Reed placed in
the hands of George Brabrook, first assigning to him full
responsibility for marketing the company's wares and later
entrusting him with the financial management of the company
as well.

CIVIL WAR MARKET

Reed & Barton in 1860 faced the future with three great assets:
a tested product and an unsurpassed market reputation; sound,
adequate financial resources; and George Brabrook, a man who
could sell. The stress of a war market almost immediately made
demands upon these assets and provided a test for the new sales
management. The first effects of war were reflected in delays,
apprehension, and uncertainty. Many companies suffered
severely from the loss of southern markets and the forfeiture of
southern debts. Reed & Barton felt the ill effects, not from any
loss of customers or bad debts, but from the generally poor state
of business and a universal feeling of pessimism. "The opening
of the war puts a damper on all business & Manufactories go
very slow & but little is done, for it is a time of great uncertainty.
All trade is at a standstill except for the bare necessities," wrote
Edmund Porter in 1861.[3] Reed & Barton countermanded large
orders of English glassware because of "present very extraordinary circumstances."[4] During this period Reed & Barton
seems to have employed no salesmen, nor engaged in much
promotional activity. Brabrook himself did whatever selling the
market called for.

The depressed phase of war-time business rapidly yielded to
government purchases and currency inflation, however, and an
excited and speculative prosperity descended upon the North.
Reed & Barton sales mounted from approximately $148,000 in
1862[5] to $256,472 in 1863, and in 1864 to $341,456.[6] Edmund
Porter, whose long experience in the trade qualified him as a
competent observer, stated that during these years the drummer

or traveling salesman was not needed by the factories.[7] Merchants ordered their goods by letter or visited the factories to select their supplies. Dealers from the large cities would visit Taunton and actually beg for goods, so great were the demands upon them. Porter records one incident illustrative of the urgency of war trade which occurred in the Porter Britannia & Plate Company, of Taunton.[8]

The writer recalls one New York merchant who called one day and complained that we were not sending his goods fast enough, as "he was losing trade every day." Said he, "Have you any old or unsaleable goods on hand? Let me see what you have, perhaps I can use them, for anything will sell in these times." So we took him up in the attic and showed him a lot of odds and ends that we had expected to melt up, and he took the lot at regular prices and was glad to get them. This was a frequent occurrence in those days.

George Brabrook himself related of this period that on his infrequent visits to the large cities he found it unnecessary to leave his hotel. Customers, informed of his presence by card, would flock to his room to try to place orders.[9]

Porter also noted certain fundamental changes which occurred in the market structure of the electroplate industry.[10] Many manufacturers, swamped with orders from jobbers, withdrew their salesmen, abandoned retail contacts in the trade, and devoted their attention to meeting the demands of the wholesale houses in the large metropolitan markets. Many jobbers installed complete silver-plating departments in or near their stores, where a plater and a number of burnishers were kept busily at work. These houses purchased goods "in the metal" (unplated) from manufacturers, stamped them with their own mark, and plated the wares as ordered by customers. The jobbers, moreover, placed their own drummers in the field and pushed the trade in their own name, taking over the territories and customers abandoned by the manufacturers. Apparently the Taunton electroplate factories were thus selling a large percentage of their output unstamped and unplated to meet the jobber demand.

Reed & Barton sales records confirm Porter's statements. From April, 1865, to June, 1866, three pieces of unplated ware were sold for each piece of plated ware. In value, unplated wares comprised 62 per cent of the factory output.[11] Most of the largest Reed & Barton customers for that year were the jobbers and retailers who operated their own plating establishments and purchased goods "in the metal." Purchasing heavily from Reed & Barton and identified by Porter as houses of this type [12] were the following: Palmer & Bachelder, Boston; Newell Harding & Company, Boston; Ball, Black & Company, New York; E. V. Houghwout & Company, New York; Hiram Young & Company, New York; Bancroft, Redfield & Rice, New York; Lucius Hart & Company, New York; Garrett & Sons, Philadelphia; and others.[13]

In this period also the terms of trade altered considerably, and much more business than formerly was being transacted on a cash or short-term credit basis. During November, 1865, shipments by the Porter Britannia & Plate Company were $30,000. By February 1, 1866, all these goods were paid for in full.[14] At the same time 88 per cent of the notes received by Reed & Barton from customers were for no more than six months, 56 per cent were for two months or less, and 35 per cent were for fifteen days or less.[15] Such terms were in marked contrast to prewar years when, in spite of Henry Reed's efforts, credit of six months and longer was frequently extended. Reed & Barton continued, however, to be lenient with old customers, one of whom was informed, ". . . our terms are cash — we cannot sell you six ms. . . ." but, "If you should order we are disposed to make the payments as easy in regard to time as we can consistently, and we may let the bills stand in a/c longer than 30 days. . . ."[16] In the winter of 1863, advances in the price of plated goods were made which ranged from 5 to 10 per cent, and at the same time discounts were lowered 5 per cent. The company refused to predict what prices would be in the spring.[17] In January, 1864, Rogers & Brother was informed by Reed & Barton that ". . . we make 10 pr ct dist. in place of 27½. . . .;" that prices on cake baskets were to be advanced 5 per cent; and that "Some of our goods that are sold at net prices are a little higher."[18] The number of customers on the company lists declined considerably as the market for wares was more and more taken over by jobbers. Orders, smaller in size than before the war, greatly increased in number and reflected both more rapid communications and the inability or unwillingness of the company to fill orders for large amounts of ware.

Prosperous times yielded to boom times, and 1865, "the most profitable year known in the history of New England states,"[19] accentuated the prevailing tempo of trade. The jobbing trade became even more vociferous in its demands for unmarked, unplated goods. At the same time manufacturers began to purchase of each other in considerable quantities. The value of a complete and well-rounded line appeared particularly great at a time when customers, pressed by an impatient market, sought to fill their needs from one source of supply. It became plain, too, that a customer whose total needs could be filled by one manufacturer was forestalled from patronizing others. And yet, so diverse had the products in trade become that in 1865 practically none of the Britannia and electroplate makers could boast of a complete line. Reed & Barton and the Meriden Britannia Company offered the greatest assortment of wares, yet Reed & Barton purchased the bulk of its flatware from Rogers & Brother and the Hartford Manufacturing Company. At the same time the Meriden Britannia Company was purchasing both flatware and hollow ware.[20] Indeed, the flatware lines of almost all manufacturers bore a resemblance that was far from coincidental. The Oval, French, and Olive patterns turned up in many different catalogues and bore many different stamps.

George Brabrook, 1828–1908

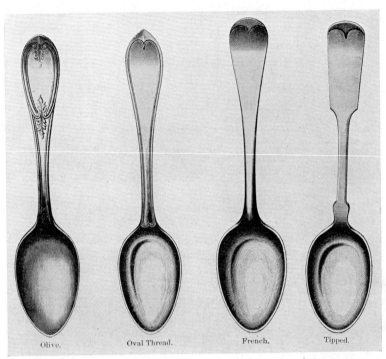

Olive.   Oval Thread.   French.   Tipped.

ELECTROPLATED FLATWARE PATTERNS POPULAR IN THE 1860's AND 1870's
Manufactured chiefly by the Connecticut factories; plated and sold by all
manufacturers in the trade. From a Reed & Barton catalogue

Unmarked and unplated blanks of these patterns were turned out by the thousand by Rogers & Brother and sold to any and all in the industry who wished to buy. This inter-trading in the industry was reciprocal, however, and the Connecticut flatware houses made extensive purchases of Reed & Barton hollow ware. In 1865 Rogers & Brother was one of the largest company customers, ordering 416 baskets, 32 pitchers, 37 fruit dishes, 25 vases, 38 syrups, 184 castor frames, 103 butter dishes, 28 urns, 307 goblets, 24 card stands, 131 napkin rings, 104 cups, 70 tea sets, and a large number of other items.[21] It was not unusual for two identical sets of teaware to be seen side by side on a store shelf, one marked Reed & Barton and the other Rogers & Brother.

DISLOCATIONS AND ADJUSTMENTS

The end of the war brought as great changes to the trade as the war years themselves had brought, for in many ways the end of the war was the end of an era — a great and prosperous era when the manufacturer's chief concern was manufacturing, and sales tended to take care of themselves. The end was not unheralded. The formation of the Meriden Britannia Company sounded the first warning in 1852, but the lush 'fifties and the war prosperity unfortunately concealed the full implications of the merger. Not until postwar conditions momentarily lifted the veil did the industry get its first clear glimpse of an inherently ugly competitive condition.

A depression in 1866 and 1867, the natural aftermath of the fever of war years, caused sales of electroplated wares to drop sharply and at last brought the latent forces of competition to the fore. Great confusion appears to have characterized this market. Curtailed customer lists, neglected retail contacts, and rusty sales organizations rose to haunt the plated-ware manufacturers, who looked in dismay at the dominant market position of the large jobbing houses. The manufacturers paid a heavy price for the great war sales of unmarked goods. In many markets the name of the manufacturer who made the wares now carried less weight than that of the middleman who marked, plated, and sold it.

The pinch of hard times in 1866 caused factories once again to send their salesmen on the road, and there began in that year a slow and painful struggle to regain lost markets — to establish once again the prestige of the maker's name stamped on his own products. Porter states that there ensued a bitter conflict with the jobbers, who were naturally loath in time of depression to withdraw from the lucrative fields and practices of war days and to abandon the trading value which had come to be attached to their names.[22] The conflict was decided in favor of the manufacturers, who regained most or all of their old markets and prestige. Many jobbers failed; a larger number abandoned plating and confined themselves exclusively to wholesaling activities. A few continued, with fair success, to maintain their own plating departments and to stamp with their own marks the wares which they purchased. Never from this time on was the dominance of the manufacturer in the field of sales challenged, nor did the jobber ever again rise to the position of power he enjoyed in 1865. The conflict of 1866 dealt a severe blow to the middleman in the trade, and the functions he performed henceforth were considered by many manufacturers to be useful but by no means indispensable.

The trade between manufacturers, selling and buying goods to be sold, continued on a fairly extensive scale after the war. A well-rounded line appeared to be as necessary to manufacturers in bad times as in good, and few factories had seen any opportunity for expanding their facilities to produce every article demanded of them. The chronic complaint arose once more that manufacturers were encountering their own goods in competition. The need for a full line was greater than the evils attendant upon the methods of acquiring one, however, and the manufacturers continued to purchase and sell the wares of other factories on a substantial scale until the late 1890's.

The Growth of Markets

For Reed & Barton, as for the industry, the depression which followed the war meant the immediate need for decisive market action. Sales declined from $475,800 in 1865, the highest peak ever attained up to that time by the company, to $441,891 in 1866 and to $350,890 in 1867.[23] George Brabrook was faced with the necessity of working harder to sell, and his efforts took many forms new to the company.

Brabrook's first efforts were directed at building an organization for selling (Chapter XI). With the workable nucleus of such an organization formed soon after the war, new markets were sought, and Reed & Barton reached out through stretches of country hitherto barren of sales. Slowly at first, but at an accelerating rate, orders began to flow in from Kentucky, Missouri, Minnesota, and Iowa. The California trade, rejected in 1861 on the inconsequential pretext that its merchants refused to transact cash business, began to show signs of promise, and Taunton ware began to cross the Rockies in quantity. By 1869 Reed & Barton had caught up with the growth and movement of population, and the distribution of sales assumed a nationwide aspect. The company name penetrated into what then were remote, almost frontier, communities, and sales were made wherever families with the means to afford an electroplated tea set existed.

The growth of markets was qualitative as well as quantitative. While new geographic markets were being found, new types of customers were also being introduced to the merits of electroplate. One of the most promising new sources of sales was the hotel trade, a trade destined to assume vast importance in the industry. Reed & Barton first seems to have experimented with the hotel market in 1860, when large numbers of heavy nickel-silver spoons and forks were ordered from the Hartford Manufacturing Company, plated and stamped by Reed & Barton, and sold to a "Merchant's Hotel" — location unknown. The great expansion of this market, however, occurred some years after the Civil War, and grew directly out of the spurt in railroad construction in the late 'sixties and early 'seventies. Railroads meant travel, and travel meant accommodations. Many an imposing hostelry was opened to profit from the increasing mobility of the nation's people. The Tremont House in Boston, the Astor House and the Park Avenue Hotel in New York, Willard's in Washington, the Palmer House and the Sherman House in Chicago were great establishments, and their business meant much in fame and fortune to the electroplate industry.

The hotel trade called for a durable line of flat and hollow ware, but elegance as well as sturdiness was required. Many of the large new hotels boasted exceedingly luxurious appointments, and for them a line of heavy silver plate or solid nickel-silver ware was required. The more modest establishments purchased thinner plate or unplated white metal. In almost all cases the hotels enjoyed a favored place in the market because of the size of their orders, and price concessions were usually asked and obtained. Middlemen saw little of this trade, for most of the orders were placed directly with the manufacturer. The electroplate factories went after the expanding hotel trade with great aggressiveness and enthusiasm: Reed & Barton, the Meriden Britannia Company, Gorham, and a host of smaller houses competed with vigor for a share of the business.

A large new hostelry nearing completion was an irresistible magnet which with silent force attracted silverware men from near and far. A salesman's letters tell of one such experience. In the spring of 1875, as the finishing touches were being put on the Palace Hotel in San Francisco, salesmen mysteriously began to arrive in town. Long before bidding was opened by the owners, salesmen from Tiffany's, the Meriden Britannia Company, Gorham, and Reed & Barton had installed themselves and their samples. Tension mounted as the time for submitting bids

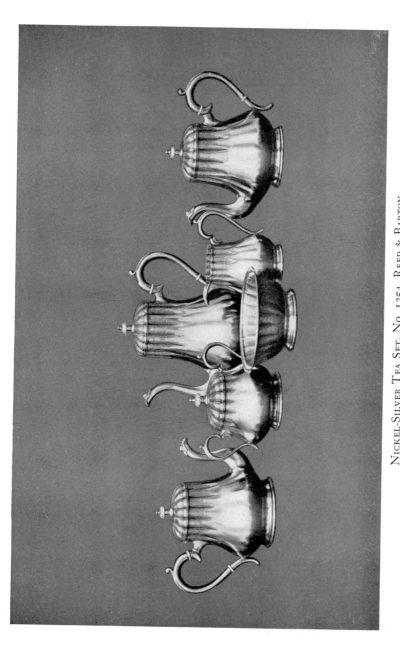

NICKEL-SILVER TEA SET, NO. 1254, REED & BARTON

First made in 1857, this pattern is reputed to be the first nickel-silver service produced by the company. From a company catalogue

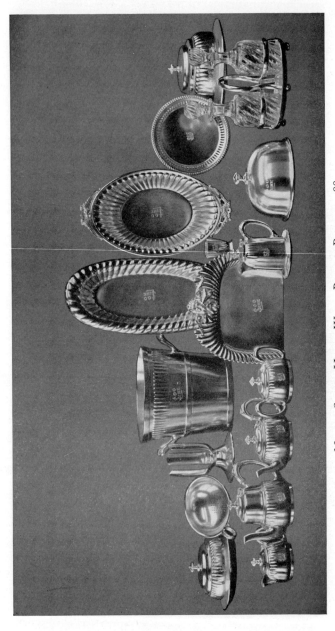

NICKEL-SILVER HOTEL WARE, REED & BARTON, 1889

Made for the Minneapolis, St. Paul and Saulte Ste. Marie Railroad Company. From a company catalogue

approached, and devious pressures were exerted to obtain "inside" information and assistance. Each salesman watched with guarded suspicion the movements of his competitors. J. H. Rines, representing Reed & Barton, wrote, "The dealers here all enquire every day if its decided yet, and I would prefer that you should not lose the order as your sales would probably be affected by it." [24] Rines did his work well, however, and the order went to Taunton, as did many another in the following years. In spite of the difficulty which the company experienced in matching certain competitors' prices, Reed & Barton was extremely successful in the hotel market, possibly more so in these early years than any other manufacturer.

The hotel trade not only provided in itself a flourishing source of sales but also encouraged the development of certain lines for household use. Manufacturers rapidly began to appreciate the fact that flatware, originally sold in quantity only to hotel customers, had vast possibilities in wider markets. One of the most far-reaching product developments of the times was the increasingly prominent place that flatware came to occupy in the American home. Reed & Barton flatware sales rose from an insignificant level before 1860 to $119,179 in 1872,[25] and the company, whose flatware manufacturing facilities were limited to spoons, began to consider ways and means of making itself independent of the Connecticut supply houses.

A Beginning in Advertising

Brabrook's expansion of the company's markets resulted from effort on a scale hitherto untried, but it was not enough. The Meriden Britannia Company pushed sales just as vigorously, and advertised extensively in newspapers and periodicals of the day. The rapidly growing Gorham Manufacturing Company, of Providence, also began to realize that craftsmanship was not enough, and in the late 'sixties launched a vigorous advertising campaign which featured its electroplated wares and acquainted the buying public with the merits of "Gorham Plate." In 1866 Brabrook made the inevitable concession to competitors' practice, and what appears to be the

---

REED & BARTON,

TAUNTON, MASS.
ESTABLISHED 1824.

Manufacturers of the new Patent

SEAMLESS-LINED ICE-PITCHER.

Pronounced by Dr. Hayes, State Assayer of Massa-chusetts, to preserve water perfectly pure; while the water in others made in the usual manner of two different metals soldered or welded together (thus forming a galvanic arrangement), after standing for one hour, was found to contain traces of lead and copper, and in four hours sufficient metal had been dissolved to render the water deleterious to health.

Are also Manufacturers of the finest quality of

ELECTRO-PLATED NICKEL SILVER,
AND

WHITE METAL TABLE-WARE

of every description, including a large variety of new and elegant designs, which are sold by the principal dealers in the United States, with our guarantee that the goods are made of the best quality of metal, and plated full weight of silver.

The Highest Prize for Silver-Plated Ware was awarded to Reed & Barton by the American Institute, New York, in 1867.

Office and show-rooms at the factory, Taunton, Mass., and 194 Broadway, New York.

REED & BARTON ADVERTISEMENT
Harper's Weekly, 1868

first Reed & Barton advertising copy was prepared and inserted in the *Dunkley & Woodman Business Directory*. In 1868 a more ambitious program was launched in *Harper's Weekly*. Two years later the sum of $3,921.90 was spent on newspaper and periodical advertising.[26] The results of this experiment apparently failed to convince Brabrook that these media had any possibilities for Reed & Barton, and little additional copy was placed for several years.

While Reed & Barton was advertising in *Harper's Weekly* the practice of exhibiting company wares was continued whenever the opportunity presented itself. Other manufacturers in the industry also patronized the exhibitions and fairs, and rivalry for the gold medals and first awards was often keen. These awards are of more than passing interest, for they present the only surviving impartial judgment on the relative merits of the various manufacturers who competed for them and furnish a valuable clue to the contemporary market reputation of wares beyond the memory of any man now living. Limiting the significance of these awards, however, is the fact that some of the fairs exhibited at the same time examples of no more than three or four electroplate manufacturers. Subject to this limitation, the exhibitions of the American Institute, of New York, through the 'sixties and 'seventies reveal the esteem in which Reed & Barton products were held.

In the Annual Fairs of 1863 and 1865 E. D. Bassford received a bronze medal and honorable mention, respectively, for silver-plated wares which he exhibited. These wares apparently were of Reed & Barton manufacture, for in later exhibitions Bassford was listed as the company representative. The following comments are characteristic and self-explanatory:

Annual Fair of 1867: From the report of the judges.[27]

> Between the goods of Messrs. Kitchen & Co. [made by Rogers, Smith & Co.] and those of E. D. Bassford, made by Messrs. Read & Barton, your judges had great difficulty in deciding, both being eminently worthy of premiums. More of the goods of Read & Barton were plated on white metal, a material on which workmanship cannot be shown with the same facility as on German silver. Both exhibitors show goods of exquisite finish and design, but your judges are compelled to award the first premium a first class medal to the goods manufactured by Read & Barton, entry No. 600.

Annual Fair of 1869: Awards for silver plated ware.[28]

> Reed & Barton, Taunton, Mass.; E. D. Bassford, Cooper Building, exhibitor, for silver plated ware. First medal and diploma.

Holmes, Booth & Hayden, 27 Reade street, New York, for silver plated ware.
First medal and diploma.
Simpson, Hall, Miller & Co., 19 John street, New York, for plated ware.
Second medal and diploma.
Manning, Bowman & Co., 60 John street, New York, for silver plated ware.
Third medal and certificate.

Reed & Barton also received, in 1869, a First Award at the Mechanics Fair in Boston, with an enthusiastic citation.[29]

The judges are warranted in pronouncing this display of Ware to be of superior merit, unsurpassed in quality and style. The Dᴜʀᴀʙɪʟɪᴛʏ ᴏꜰ Reed & Barton's ware has been so long known to the Judges that they feel it their duty to accord them the position of *first* among the manufacturers of ᴘʟᴀᴛᴇᴅ ɢᴏᴏᴅs.

In 1870 the company received another American Institute medal for the best silver-plated ware exhibited. In 1878 the judges of the Mechanics Fair in Boston stated that Reed & Barton plated white-metal goods were unsurpassed in "design, style and finish by any other manufacturers." At the American Institute Fair of 1878 Reed & Barton received the Medal of Progress, highest award made by the Institute for electroplated wares. The judges reported: [30]

We have carefully examined the wares exhibited by REED & BARTON, and find the quality of plating unsurpassed by that of any other manufacturer in the country. This firm has shown marked progress in the art by originality of design, solidity in the metallic deposit, and in the perfection of finish.

Pʀɪᴄᴇ Cᴏᴍᴘᴇᴛɪᴛɪᴏɴ

Aggressive salesmanship, a constant seeking for new markets, and advertising were resorted to in varying degrees by all the electroplate manufacturers after 1865, but competition took one final form which was easier, more universally adopted, and of all competitive practices the most disastrous to the industry. The 1866 depression brought ruthless price cutting, a practice which, once established, defied virtually all remedial measures. Discounts were forced steadily upward, and Reed & Barton found that for plated hollow ware on which a wholesaler's discount of from 20 to 25 per cent was granted in 1864, it was necessary in 1867 to allow 25 per cent plus 5 per cent, and in 1869, 25 per cent plus 10 per cent.[31] Cash sales appear to have declined after 1865, and paper running from two to six months was common, with an occasional nine months' note being accepted. In 1868 only 13 per cent of the notes received from company customers were for less than a month, and 15 per cent for two months or less.[32]

Postwar competition was bitter, but it developed all possibilities, and considering the times, Reed & Barton and the industry fared well. The hotel trade did much to relieve what otherwise might have seemed a drab half-decade of indecisive markets and general uncertainty. After the 1866–67 depression had subsided, high prices, expansionism, and heavy consumer buying, plus an almost blind faith in the resources of the country, tended to conceal the fundamentally speculative basis of business.[33] Unemployment continued high, and living costs outran the increase in wage levels, but 1868 and 1869 brought a semblance of recovery and prosperity. Reed & Barton sales mounted steadily through these two years, although the cost of doing business in 1869 was stated to be inordinately high, collections were slow, and many failures occurred among customers.[34] A brisk and increasing trade through the next three years led the industry to hope that the flare of ruthless competition of 1866 and 1867 had been but a temporary condition and that there might, after all, be plenty of profits for all. In 1872, on the threshold of a fresh national disaster, Reed & Barton sales achieved a new peak of $686,771.[35]

The panic of September, 1873, and the general collapse of an

over-expanded system of credit in the business world put an end
to the implied promise of the 1869–72 prosperity and ushered in
five hard years of depression, which in the electroplate industry
as in many industries brought out all the worst elements of the
1866–67 period. Prices were cut, and then slashed. Discounts
increased. A buyers' market forced manufacturers to grant
longer credit than ever before, and Reed & Barton carried its
best customers through lean months when payment was next
to impossible. Complaints arose in the trade that old systems
were crumpling into dishonorable practices — that many jobbers, desperate for business, were betraying their retail customers and selling goods indiscriminately at wholesale prices
to anyone who might ask for them.[36] Large electroplate manufacturers, their selling organizations built up by the trials of
postwar years, systematically set to work to drive small competitors and, if possible, each other out of business. The evils of
excessive "free competition" became painfully apparent to all
concerned, and a remedy characteristic of many other industries
in the same predicament was at length adopted.

Early in 1876 the Silver Plated Ware Manufacturers Association was formed, apparently a combination of the Connecticut
flatware factories. A circular sent to customers in January, 1876,
graphically summed up conditions in the trade in these words:

To Dealers in Silver Plated Ware

Gentlemen:

As you are doubtless aware, Silver Plated Forks, Spoons, and other
Flat-Ware have, for a long time past, been sold by the manufacturers at
ruinously low prices; brought about, not by an increased production, or a
lessened demand, nor by a proportionate reduction in the cost of goods,
but simply and solely by a suicidal competition.

In view of the unfortunate results of the past two years' business, the
manufacturers, at a meeting held in New York, January 18th, 1876,
unanimously adopted the following discounts and terms:

FIRST QUALITY SPOONS, FORKS, and other FLAT-WARE.

40 per cent discount,

four months' note for approved credit, or 5 per cent cash discount if payment is received within 30 days; or 6 per cent if within 10 days of average date of invoice

FIRST QUALITY GERMAN SILVER SPOONS,

30 per cent discount,

four months' note, or cash discounts as above.

This advance yields to the manufacturers but a fair margin, and affords to the dealer a *liberal* profit on staple goods.

Trusting you will appreciate the necessity of the action which enables us "to live and let live," we remain,

Yours respectfully,

In addition to these established terms, the association members agreed to pay rebates of as much as 10 per cent to customers who stated that over a specified period they had not sold wares below the established rates and discounts of the association.

Two years later the Silver-Plated Hollow-Ware Association was formed for a similar purpose, its membership consisting of the Derby Silver Company, Hall, Elton & Company, Meriden Britannia Company, Meriden Silver Plate Company, Middletown Plate Company, Reed & Barton, Rogers & Brother, Rogers, Smith & Company, Simpson, Hall, Miller & Company, and the Wilcox Silver Plate Company.

Associations, mergers, and coöperative action of various kinds were the usual panacea for industries harassed by the competition of the 1870's and later years, but in relatively few instances did the expected results follow. Vigorous attempts were made in the fields of finance, manufacture, and transportation to eliminate "the evils of competition." When this aim was achieved, it was often found that competition itself was eliminated, and anathema in the form of the Sherman Anti-Trust Act at length descended on the heads of the participating groups. Other and less drastic attempts were made, usually by smaller companies, to remedy the more unscrupulous prevailing trade practices and at the same time to preserve the independence of all units concerned.[37] Loosely knit associations of this type depended for the most part on the voluntary coöperation of the members. Methods of enforcing agreements were limited or nonexistent, and the inherently individualistic tendencies of the member companies often obstructed effective coöperation. The silver-plated ware associations were of this nature, and while they constituted the first hint of group consciousness in the industry, their tangible and lasting results appear to have been small. Price competition continued to exist and, in the unplated and hotel-ware lines particularly, caused Reed & Barton much difficulty and annoyance. A company letter directed to the New York office in 1878 commented: [38]

We are in receipt of the enclosed letter from Messrs. *Rogers and Bro* but as you see they do not state whether the goods are wanted plated or in metal & am instructed to request you to see them & quote them such prices as will be high enough so they will not want them as we don't *like* to sell them on account of always meeting the goods in competition afterward & to R[eed] & B[arton]'s disadvantage in price

INTENSIFIED PROMOTION

Rivalry between the electroplate manufacturers increased rather than slackened, and the late 'seventies brought more salesmen, increased advertising, better market coverage, and a constant quest for new markets. Although the number of establishments engaged in the trade declined precipitously in this decade, the technical progress of the remainder was so great that the total output of the industry increased.[39] Coupled as it was with stagnating markets from 1873 to 1878, the enlarged capacity of electroplating establishments made competitive pressure more acute, in spite of all collective efforts to remedy the situation. The growing size of the competing units, moreover, furnished the means for promotion on a more ambitious scale than ever before. In this further expansion of effort the Meriden Britannia Company led the market, forcing competitors to

H. Ballou

THE REED & BARTON FACTORY, 1875

The Reed & Barton Factory

The large building at the left is the original 1820 structure. From the New York *Daily Graphic,*

follow suit or become hopelessly outsold. Reed & Barton pursued a conservative course, but when the need for action became acute, the company moved swiftly and with the great effectiveness which a careful study of other concerns' mistakes made possible.

A new advertising campaign was launched in 1875 by a $600 contract with the *Daily Graphic* (New York), in which Reed & Barton specified that, in addition to the regular space engaged, the *Graphic* agent should write a "description of our works and business of such character as he may think interesting to your readers and advantageous to us." [40] This description was to be accompanied by several large sketches of the factory, executed by the *Graphic's* artist.

In the same year Reed & Barton also approached various publishers with the proposal that certain of the company wares be used as premiums for advertisers. From this time on, some advertising was done each year, and 1878 and 1879 brought a particularly vigorous campaign in which a variety of religious periodicals were used to supplement the newspapers and general magazines. In these two years, quarter-, half-, and full-page copy was placed in at least seventy-five different newspapers and periodicals ranging from the *Baptist Weekly* to the *American Statistical Review*.[41]

The ambitious extent of the 1878–79 campaign, coming so closely on the heels of a period characterized by casual advertising, indicates an abrupt reversal in the promotional viewpoint of Reed & Barton management. It may well be that the Philadelphia Centennial Exhibition of 1876 effected this change. The great five-months-long demonstration in Fairmont Park of the arts and manufactures of the world stirred the enthusiasm of the American people as no similar event had ever done before, and on a scale quite unprecedented. Men, women, and children from every section of the country thronged the exhibition halls. The American manufacturer was brought suddenly and dramatically face to face with his market, and the experience was not one to be easily forgotten. A keener awareness of the consumer appears to have pervaded Reed & Barton sales methods from this time forward.

Manufacturers of electroplate were quick to realize that the Centennial Exhibition presented an unparalleled opportunity for publicity, and preparations were made on a costly and elaborate scale. Reed & Barton set up an ornate glass cabinet nineteen feet long and eleven feet high, in which were placed 1,040 gilded and silver-plated pieces valued at $24,500.[42] The exhibits of other manufacturers were on a comparable scale, and in addition each prepared at great cost some magnificently wrought centerpiece for his display. W. C. Beattie designed for Reed & Barton the "Progress Vase," a massive piece of symbolism four feet long and three feet high, depicting the progress of centuries from savagery to idyllic peace and culture.

In a less formal vein another piece of well-executed statuary depicted a trotting horse and sulky. Both received favorable comment from the judges of the exhibition and the Progress Vase was given a first award. Gorham presented an even larger chef d'œuvre in the form of a monument five feet long and four feet high entitled the "Century Vase," its motif similar to that of the Reed & Barton piece. The Meriden Britannia Company offered the "Buffalo Hunt" on an equally massive scale.

Reed & Barton's exhibition expenses amounted to $15,250, but immediate returns were forthcoming. Much favorable comment was made on the Progress Vase, and the remainder of the display stimulated admiration and sales. One tea set of heavy electroplate, profusely decorated with repoussé chasing and gilt was seen and admired by members of the Japanese Commission, who purchased it for presentation to the Emperor of Japan. When all the repercussions of the Centennial had at last subsided and a calm appraisal of results was possible, George Brabrook came to realize that publicity of the right sort echoed

FLATWARE ADVERTISEMENT WHICH APPEARED IN VARIOUS
PERIODICALS ABOUT 1879
Typical of the promotional campaigns of George Brabrook

sharply in the Sales Ledger and he determined to keep the name of Reed & Barton before the market.

This ambition was furthered by developments in a sales-promotional field which history has far too often consigned to insignificance, but which, in reality, profoundly influenced the course of much business evolution. The growth of the illustrated catalogue occupies an important place in the marketing history of Reed & Barton.

The difficulties and limitations of trade without benefit of illustrative processes is difficult to comprehend in this day of sleekly groomed catalogues. Trade with distant customers waited upon the means whereby manufacturers could show those customers their wares. Photography antedated the Civil War but its commercial application was limited by the quality of the negatives, the cost, and the lack of means by which prints could be transferred effectively to newspapers and periodicals. Various engraving processes were available, but here too the cost was high. Manufacturers depended upon direct visual means to demonstrate their wares, and trade in all but highly standardized products was largely restricted to markets where sample lines could be displayed to customers. The growth of far-flung national and international sales areas made a great need still greater, and science, as usual, provided a remedy. The perfection of electrotypography made possible the large-scale commercial application of relatively inexpensive wood engravings, and in the late 1850's the illustrated catalogue was born. That a tremendous expansion of markets occurred at approximately the same time that electrotyping came into universal use is more than mere coincidence. For the electroplating and silverware industry the development of means of illustration was almost as vital a factor in growth as had been the railroad.

Between 1858 and 1860 the Rogers Bros. Manufacturing Company and Rogers, Smith & Company each brought out small, cloth-covered catalogues containing price lists and a few woodcuts of flatware patterns. From this time on, the growth of the catalogue in both size and quality was rapid. In 1861 Reed & Barton was respectfully regretting to customers that it had no regular line of illustrated catalogues, but would be glad to furnish photographs of ware. By 1868 Reed & Barton catalogues had been made up, but seem to have been given only to company salesmen and not distributed to the trade. These first catalogues contained surprisingly well-executed photographs, individually mounted by hand on stiff sheets of paper ten inches long and five inches wide, bound in heavy, gold-embossed leather. Customers, however, continued to demand books for their own use, and one salesman wrote back to the factory, "These people *all* ask for *books,* and photographs *are not the thing.* They need a book to which a ready reference can be had to anything you make." [43] About 1870 a small paper-bound catalogue was printed containing a few woodcuts and price lists of flatware. But in the following year the Meriden Britannia Company, which had been distributing catalogues freely to the trade, prepared a collection of woodcuts of a size hitherto unheard of and handsomely bound in heavy cardboard and cloth. The challenge was accepted in the trade, and catalogues grew steadily larger and more sumptuous as each company sought to outdo the other. Reed & Barton's first catalogue in the grand manner appeared in 1877 — a magnificent volume of two hundred and twenty-four pages, thirteen inches wide, eighteen inches high, and one inch thick, containing finely executed woodcuts, one-third actual size, of the entire line. The Meriden Britannia Company matched this publication with a similar one in 1878 and an even larger edition in 1883, whereupon Reed & Barton brought forth two years later one of the most ambitious examples of book-making that American publishers had yet seen.

The 1885 catalogue, assembled by the Springfield Printing Company, contained four hundred pages, fourteen inches by

THE PROGRESS VASE
Awarded first prize at the Centennial Exposition, Philadelphia, 1876

CLOSE-UP VIEW OF ONE OF THE GROUPS OF THE PROGRESS VASE

Showing detail of sculpture

seventeen, and nearly four thousand wood engravings, as well as a steel-engraved frontispiece of the Reed & Barton factory and four lithographic plate pages in color of some of the company's more ornate products. All engravings were half actual size, printed on extra heavy plate paper, and each book weighed sixteen pounds! The binding consisted of heavy paperboard covered with the best English muslin, elaborately ornamented with gold and silver leaf. All the wood engravings were made by craftsmen in the factory, a task which consumed the entire time of twenty-seven engravers for three years. The total cost of the seven thousand volumes which were printed and distributed to customers was rumored to have exceeded $100,000.

The Reed & Barton catalogues were the most spectacular of the various measures which Brabrook designed to meet the efforts of competing firms. Reed & Barton promotion in general was of a far more conservative nature. The absence of elaborate advertising methods characteristic of some companies in the industry, however, was far from disastrous for Reed & Barton, and once again a cautiously pursued policy led to moderate success, particularly during the difficult years of the 1873–78 depression. The success of the depression period, however, was of a negative variety, consisting of moderate shrinkage in sales volume at a time when many firms and industries were experiencing severe shrinkages. Suffering no more than nominal hardship during the lean years, Reed & Barton stood ready to profit greatly when recovery set in. The years 1879 and 1880, therefore, were good years for the company, and returning prosperity coupled with a bolder-than-usual advertising program pushed sales up from $521,577 in 1875 to $592,100 in 1879 and to a triumphant total of $771,117 in 1880.

That the company survived the difficult span of years with such success in the field of sales is a great tribute to George Brabrook. Neither an inspired promoter nor a brilliant personality, Brabrook turned a disposition for hard work and a thorough knowledge of design and salesmanship to good account. The men under Brabrook worked hard, for he had scant patience with idleness in any form. Like Charles Barton and Henry Reed, he was a shirt-sleeve manager, familiar to every section of the factory and constantly in evidence. One of the most characteristic sights in the Reed & Barton establishment of the 1870's was George Brabrook dashing at top speed across the yard from office building to factory and back, a stub of pencil in one hand and an order book in the other. Even in his

CHART III
REED & BARTON DOMESTIC SALES, 1861–1880

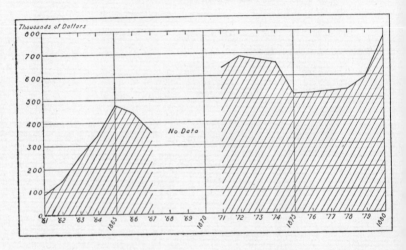

later years impatient vigor characterized his activities. Brabrook never commanded the almost legendary devotion accorded by the men in the factory to Barton and to Reed, but his ability was profoundly respected by all who worked with him. On occasion he could be the heartiest and most gracious of companions. In later life his appearance and bearing suggested, with a not unbecoming dignity, the importance of his position in company and community. With the exception of a single trip to Ger-

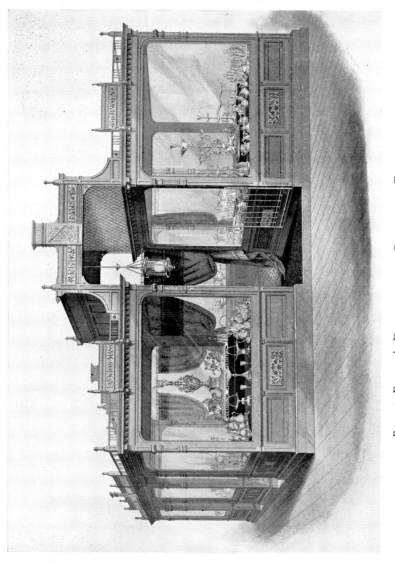

Reed & Barton's Display at the Centennial Exhibition
Philadelphia, 1876

A Page from Reed & Barton's 1885 Catalogue

many, George Brabrook scarcely ever left Taunton after the Reed & Barton salesforce had been organized. Yet few persons were more cognizant of current trends in the American business and artistic fields. Brabrook eagerly scanned scores of newspapers and periodicals, always receptive to new ideas and capable of interpreting them wisely. In his high-pitched, nasal voice, so inappropriate to the frame of the man and the text of his utterances, Brabrook drawled his instructions out of a profoundly cultured background. It was this intimate understanding of contemporary developments which enabled Brabrook to direct the company successfully through the crisis years of the 1860's and 1870's.

The year 1880 was a prosperous one in sales returns, but it by no means terminated the necessity for working harder to sell. This year constituted a brief and refreshing pause — a pause which, if it induced a complacent attitude, invited disaster in the years to come. This year marked the end of one difficult half of Brabrook's administration. Brabrook's keen vigor tolerated no slackening of effort, however, and it is scarcely conceivable that he was not aware of great problems to be solved in the future.

CHAPTER X

THE CHANGING MARKET, 1880–1900

Silverware manufacturers were prosperous and optimistic in 1880. Their prosperity was a part of the generally active state of trade throughout the country; their optimism grew out of the realization that a great depression had come to an end. Few business men would have predicted at that time that the years to come would be as difficult as those just past. Yet the silverware industry was on the brink of a great reorganization, and individual producers like Reed & Barton were immediately to be faced with extensive changes in the methods and direction of distribution. Far-reaching decisions on product policies were soon to be made, and serious business recessions would complicate all trade problems. In 1880, however, there was good reason to hope that the improved facilities for transacting business, coupled with even moderate prosperity, might usher in a period of growth such as the American business man had never before seen.

Taunton in 1880 was no longer an isolated community depending on its uncertain river life line for existence. The New Bedford Railroad and the Taunton Branch connection to Boston had been augmented by Old Colony branch lines to Fall River and to Boston via Middleboro. The river fleet was but an emaciated ghost of its former self, and coasting schooners now carried few barrels of Reed & Barton ware. The Fall River Line operated two luxurious steamboats, the "Bristol" and the "Providence," on the New York run,[1] and the "detention almost always attending the latter way of sending" in 1838 had yielded to modern speed and efficient freight handling. The telegraph and the cable imparted a snap and briskness to trade and brought world markets to Britanniaville. Taunton's population had increased to 25,448 in 1880, and its prosperity was measured in new houses, stores, and factories. Paved streets laid the dust of Main Street, and horsecar lines transported citizens in stylish dignity, if not with speed. A growing line of mansions on Dean Street bore testimony to past profits and future expectations.

The sales department and the shipping-room of Reed & Barton rejoiced in the new conveniences and yet took pride in certain customs and traditions of a much earlier day which were destined to continue to a much later one. Davenport & Mason wagons still rolled into the yard in the evening for their daily load of crates and barrels, although five or six wagons now were to be seen where one had appeared before. The packing-room force had yet to make the acquaintance of such niceties as corrugated cardboard and excelsior; the "meadow hay clerks" prepared company wares for shipment in much the same manner as their fathers had done before them. Even in the rapidly growing stockroom, progress touched but lightly, and for many years after systems had been installed in other departments the company proudly called attention to the phenomenal George Harvey, stockroom boss, who boasted that he knew by memory the location and inventory count of every variety and size of company product — and made good his boast. Months after he had retired and a "system" had been installed for checking inventory, Harvey continued to be called back into the factory to locate odd lots of ware which had temporarily disappeared during the transition from the old methods to the new.

A prosperous growth of business in the Reed & Barton factory and in Taunton in 1880 reflected the general state of commercial affairs throughout the country. A more or less steady expansion of population and trade had been taking place before, but good times in 1880, 1881, and 1882 gave added strength to growth.

Railroad construction increased rapidly; immigration spurted; the Middle West, West, and South invited commercialization on an increasingly larger scale. Reed & Barton found a booming trade in the coal, steel, oil, and mining cities which had sprung into lusty existence. Two great movements crystallized which affected sales organization in the electroplate and silverware industry. The first was a steady drift of population toward the city, and the development of great metropolitan markets. The second was the spread of city culture and the comforts of life outward, first to suburban and then to country communities. Neither of these diametrically opposite movements was new, but both accelerated in the last two decades of the century.

The growth of great city markets far from the factories which supplied them necessitated a certain amount of decentralization in sales administration, and most of the electroplate manufacturers established branch offices. On the other hand, the increasing demand from small and scattered country communities called for a vastly enlarged salesforce and a more intensive use of illustrated catalogues. George Brabrook met these diverse requirements successfully, and his organization progressed with the trade in size, activity, and territory covered.

The trend of Reed & Barton distribution through the 1880's and 1890's was toward direct contacts with retailers and away from the jobbing trade. A considerable number of wholesale customers, however, were retained, their function being to sell in the narrowing areas which Reed & Barton salesmen did not cover.[2] At the same time large sales were being made to independent contractors in the hotel, railroad, and steamship trades. A few sales may have been made to other manufacturers, but this once common practice was being terminated rapidly. Selling through an ever increasing variety of outlets was potentially a source of much customer ill will, and yet with a few exceptions the company successfully avoided trouble. The key to the prevention of market confusion was a carefully preserved range of discounts. Jobbers received jobbers' rates, and retailers received retailers' rates. In all cases it remained highly desirable to keep individual terms secret, and in most cases this was possible. In few trades were discounts so jealously guarded. Occasionally a retailer succeeded in obtaining a wholesaler's rating by subterfuge, but such cases were few indeed. Brabrook insisted that a careful check be made on each applicant for a catalogue, in order that his business status should be established beyond all doubt.

One of the most delicate problems in customer relations arose with the growth of the large department stores. This movement was observed with alarm by independent retail jewelers — hitherto the principal outlet for electroplate and silverware. In 1883 the *Jewelers' Circular* complained that huge bazaars were swallowing up the old specialists.[3] Manufacturers were faced with a dilemma. Should they forfeit the good-will of the retailers, or ignore the big orders of Macy, Ridley, and A. T. Stewart? Sixty years later the trade was still to be seeking a completely satisfactory answer to this situation.

The large manufacturers inclined to side with the jewelers from the first and strove to keep their reputation immaculate by refusing to sell to department stores and by endeavoring to prevent such stores from obtaining their wares. A surreptitious flow of merchandise occurred, however, and the department stores occasionally managed to obtain through wholesale channels the wares of manufacturers committed not to sell to them. Unhappy was the predicament of the producer when such lots of ware appeared on the department-store counters, often at substantial discounts! Irate jewelers served notice that such offenses against trade convention would not be tolerated often.

Gradually, as certain of the department stores discarded their bargain-counter atmosphere, built a reputation for quality merchandise in a refined setting, and guaranteed to maintain prices, some electroplate manufacturers lost their prejudice against this type of outlet. Jewelers, however, did not, for in the department stores' lower prices they saw a serious menace to their existence. At this time Reed & Barton appears to have avoided the department stores conscientiously, preferring the older and more conservative distribution channels. This policy was strongly reinforced by an experience in Philadelphia at the turn of the century, when misguided zeal on the part of a Mr. Flood, the Reed & Barton representative, resulted in the sale of a large order to a department store in that city. A new Reed & Barton agent in Philadelphia, investigating the affair, reported, ". . . several of the local dealers have today brought the matter to my attention saying that if we intend to let department stores have our goods they will close their accounts. I informed them that such was not the case and that Reed and Barton would not sell or allow department stores to handle their goods. . . ." [4]

Problems in customer relations were vexing at times, but throughout the 1880–1900 period other and more fundamental difficulties were destined to tax the abilities of company management. If 1880 appeared to Reed & Barton as a prelude to continued prosperity in which new markets were to yield a continuing increase in sales volume, the years which followed were a distinct disappointment. Company sales declined steadily through 1881 and 1882, in spite of the generally prosperous state of the industry. One possible explanation of the decline was the keen competition which existed, together with a sharp curtailment by Reed & Barton of the vigorous advertising campaign of 1879 and 1880. A further and more fundamental explanation lay in the changing nature of company markets. It became apparent that even the tremendous popularity of electroplated ware was not immune to the shifting whimsy of taste. The "new and better" product which had displaced Britannia now began to lose a part of its markets to solid silver.

Sterling Silver for the Mass Market

Of all the transitions from old and familiar to new and better which took place in American metal-craft history, the change from electroplate to sterling is perhaps the most interesting — certainly the most complex in all its ramifications. Up to the Civil War period solid silver was practically inaccessible to the middle-class market. To be sure, domestic silverware had been produced since early Colonial days, and most American families of moderate means could boast of a coin-silver spoon or two, but the market for silver services was not a mass market and the producers were craftsmen rather than manufacturers. The price of the metal effectively discouraged large demand and the application of machine methods to its fabrication into tableware.

Several factors combined to alter all this and to make sterling ware accessible and popular. The mining of silver, after a period of modest growth, assumed formidable dimensions in the middle 'seventies. The famous Comstock Lode, discovered in 1859, swung into peak production, and new mines yielded an increasing supply of the precious metal. Improved metallurgical processes lowered costs of production and permitted the utilization of lower-grade ores. Silver prices, which had maintained a steady level at between $1.32 and $1.36 an ounce from 1850 to 1872, began a more or less steady decline as supplies increased and demand from Europe for monetary silver fell off.[5] With each new slump in the price of the metal, solid silver tableware edged farther into the upper limits of the electroplate market.

Coincidental with, and partially as a result of, the growing availability of silver, appeared the old desire of moderately prosperous people to own the hitherto exclusive possessions of the wealthy. By those same mysterious processes through which first pewter, then Britannia, then electroplate had become "fashionable," sterling silver assumed a halo of social approbation. Contemporary events did much to publicize the metal. The endless dialectics of the Free Silver movement assured the metal public attention, while the glamor of the prospecting West and the fabulous silver services of the mining barons lent an atmosphere of romance. With the stage thus set for a flourishing trade, only one further development was called for to make latent demand active. Just as the small shops of the pewterers had been inadequate to meet the manufacturing requirements of a mass market in Britannia ware, so too were the establishments of the silversmiths of the 1860's ill adapted in size and organization to supply sterling wares on a large scale. The lowering price of silver meant little without factories to convert the relatively inexpensive silver into equally inexpensive silverware.

Among the first to augment hand craftsmanship by factory methods of production in the silverware field was the Gorham Manufacturing Company, which even before the Civil War had done much to spread the market for solid silver wares. Once a successful precedent had been established, other firms were quick to follow. In the postwar years an increasing number of silversmiths became silverware manufacturers. The fall in silver prices after 1875 hastened the movement, and while neither the artisan nor his skilled craft disappeared (as did the pewterer and his trade), yet to an increasing extent the power press of the factory displaced the hand hammer of the workshop.

The extension of the market for solid silver differed in one important respect from the growth in popularity of electroplate some thirty years earlier. Electroplated wares almost completely eliminated the use of the unplated Britannia metal tableware with which they at first competed. Solid silverware, on the contrary, has never displaced electroplate. Competition between the two centered at first only in the field of highest-quality electroplate, and here the triumph of solid silver was absolute. Electroplated wares slipped down a notch on the social scale, and those manufacturers who sought only the quality trade found, after 1880, increasing difficulty in obtaining it without a sterling silver line. Ornate sterling services graced wealthy New York tables and set a mark for envious society all over the country to aspire to. Special orders on a magnificent scale received great publicity and paced the world of fashion. The dies alone for the Bradley Martin service cost $11,000; those for W. K. Vanderbilt, over $10,000; J. W. MacKay's, over $9,000. One New York matron boasted a silver service which, "if melted down again, would pretty well furnish a Mexican Mine." [6] Sterling, however, did not continue for long to confine itself to the high-price markets, but exerted a constant pressure on the retreating upper limits of the electroplate market and penetrated into more and more "middle-class" homes.

Solid silver rapidly became the conventional gift for weddings, and in the last fifteen years of the century the wedding market grew so vigorously that it altered the whole seasonal pattern of manufacturers' sales. The traditional November and December periods of factory activity began to be copied on a smaller scale by an early spring peak as June nuptials made increasing demands on the spring-season gift market. Even brides of moderate means were expected to possess a minimum of three dozen sterling pieces.[7]

George Brabrook Stands His Ground

In the early 1880's Reed & Barton had already begun to feel the effects of the demand for something better. One fact became increasingly apparent. Reed & Barton products were having greater difficulty in exclusive markets they once had dominated and were being forced by the solid silverware of other manufacturers into lower income levels of demand. That Reed & Barton was being forced into fields where price competition was keen could hardly be disputed. Nor could it be disputed that these fields were alien to the abilities and experience of the management. The salesmen were the first to report difficulties, and they complained to George Brabrook that lower prices and higher discounts must be quoted if the company was to continue in the electroplate market. Brabrook heard the complaints with scant sympathy and allowed the necessary price concessions with grudging reluctance. On one occasion his salesmen banded together in joint protest over the price of a new water pitcher and forced him to change it from $4.00 to $3.50. "Damn it all," Brabrook exclaimed, "Now we'll have to sell four thousand more of these things to get our money back!" [8]

Surrounded by a business environment which fertilized concepts of mass production on a grand scale, Brabrook, the craftsman, stolidly resisted the trend. Brabrook, the salesman, held firmly to the belief that fewer goods sold at a higher price meant less selling effort and expense for the same total sales returns. Few companies in the industry had depended for so long a time and so exclusively upon quality as the basic selling appeal. Before the Civil War this appeal had been valid in all markets, but in postwar years the hotel trade, the mass market for inexpensive electroplate, the depression of 1873–79, and the vastly increased output of the industry brought many changes. Reed & Barton continued to seek its customers with the quality appeal. Neither Henry Reed nor George Brabrook, imbued as they were with half a century of tradition, would concede that quality could under any circumstances be secondary to price.

Stubborn adherence of the company to an ideal had established an unsurpassed reputation for craftsmanship. Many of Reed & Barton's outlets, however, were beginning to become less conscious of craftsmanship and more conscious of price. The Philadelphia office manager wrote home: [9]

Wallace's prices are away below those quoted by us, however I have gone at the Company with the quality argument and seem to have impressed them, however the prices quoted by Wallace seemed to interest them as well.

REED & BARTON'S DISPLAY WAGON
Taunton's 250th Anniversary Celebration, 1889

A Reed & Barton Trade Card, 1884
A popular early method of direct advertising

The position of Reed & Barton after 1880, therefore, was not altogether a promising one. With sterling manufacturers infringing upon the upper price levels and most electroplate manufacturers underselling the company in the lower, the necessity became acute for a definite decision on future product policies.

Brabrook's remedy for meeting increasing competition from electroplate manufacturers after 1880, however, involved no change in policy at all. Defying circumstances and trends, he merely intensified his selling efforts in every direction. This was the remedy characteristic of a salesman, and with superb salesmanship Brabrook carried it through. In one gigantic and prolonged effort he threw the whole accumulated weight of Reed & Barton's great reputation at a startled market which had echoed since the Civil War to the cry for lower prices, higher discounts.[10]

We trust that when you consider our estimates, you will take into consideration the quality of the goods which we propose to furnish and to secure an article of the first class in every respect we believe is impossible at a less price than those quoted by us, and our prices are low as is possible without sacrificing quality, finish and workmanship.

"Without sacrificing quality, finish and workmanship" — these words of one of Brabrook's office clerks, uttered in the last decade of the century, could as well have been those of Isaac Babbitt or William Crossman long before. They sounded a consistent keynote of policy down through seventy-five years of rapidly changing company history. They were echoed in spirit by the aging Henry Reed when he snatched an imperfect piece of ware from the hands of a workman, crumpled it on the floor with his heel, and exclaimed, "We don't make seconds in this factory!" [11]

Brabrook's defiance of low prices and cheapness succeeded when the tendency of the times indicated that it should have failed. A spectacularly vigorous salesforce stormed the hotel trade, capturing much of the top-grade business and convincing many a wavering customer that low cost at the expense of quality was poor economy indeed. The company soon rose to the position of leader in the hotel market, and that leadership was founded almost entirely on the Reed & Barton name for quality. Such being the case, a course of events which ran contemporaneously with Brabrook's selling campaign caused much bitterness in the company.

Trade-mark protection laws in the 1880's left many opportunities for unethical practices to flourish. In 1886 a company commenced an electroplating business in Taunton under the name of Reed, Barton & Company. Behind this organization lay the resources of Charles Barton's heirs, who appear to have been dissatisfied with the terms of settlement effected when, after Barton's death, his interest was purchased by the remaining Reed & Barton partners. Managing the new enterprise and lending their names to its title were Edward Barton, the son of Charles Barton, and Waldo Reed, a lawyer in Taunton who appears not to have been related to Henry Reed but who was the son-in-law of Charles Barton. Following an inconspicuous start, the venture gained momentum and distributed increasing quantities of inferior wares to the trade. The possibilities of confusion were endless — some dealers mistook the new company for the old; others, who were not on the accepted list of Reed & Barton accounts, purchased the ware of the new company to take advantage of the name. Reed & Barton brought suit against the new company, but after extensive legal proceedings Waldo Reed and Ed Barton established the right to use their own names in business, and in 1890 Reed, Barton & Company was incorporated. If these two men had, as was popularly believed at the time, set up their company with the idea of selling out quickly and profitably, they were disappointed. Reed & Barton exercised a judicious restraint and made no immediate offer. Reed, Barton & Company languished, and in 1892, on the verge of bankruptcy, it finally received and accepted a relatively modest offer from the older company. Ed Barton and Waldo Reed were given employment by Reed & Barton as salesmen, and the affairs of their company were terminated.[12]

The cumulative effects of this incident appear to have been small, although feeling ran high at the time and mutual recriminations were the order of the day. Only the parties involved failed to see the humorous side of the affair, and with the termination of Reed, Barton & Company, even those customers who had been temporarily misled soon forgot the matter.

In terms of sales this period was a moderately good one for Reed & Barton. The 1881–82 decline extended through three more years as a new and severe depression curtailed demand, but Brabrook's efforts prevented the decline from becoming as precipitous as the state of general trade indicated it might be. With returning prosperity in 1886, company performance improved noticeably, and by 1892 sales volume reached $1,012,-343.[13] In terms of market experience the period was a most significant one. While Brabrook's efforts to reach the hotel trade with quality merchandise were successful, those efforts forcibly revealed to him the fact that there was a market level below which the company could not go and that competition in the electroplate field was limited by the extent to which the company was desirous of maintaining its reputation for quality.

With the low-price markets thus blocked by self-imposed standards, the quest for customers inevitably led Reed & Barton into the sterling market. Carrying out the tradition which led Babbitt to abandon pewter for Britannia, and Reed to abandon Britannia for electroplate, George Brabrook forged ahead on his own initiative and, brushing aside the doubts of many in the factory, commenced the manufacture and sale of sterling silver products in 1889. This line, providing as it did a fitting medium for the expression of the company ideals of fine craftsmanship, was immediately successful. Sterling sales expanded from

$66,055 in 1890 to $217,950 in 1891 and to $312,005 in 1892.[14]
The performance of the new line testified to Brabrook's keen
understanding of the requirements of the quality market and
indicated that at least one phase of a difficult situation had
been successfully solved.

The Industry Organizes for Growth

While George Brabrook was endeavoring to decide in which
sales area the future of the company lay, new problems were
developing. To those whose vision was keen it was becoming
apparent that a rapid increase of American population was
dividing markets. Just as earlier growth had taxed distribution
channels and forced middlemen to specialize, now even greater
market expansion was taxing the capacity of manufacturers to
reach all the customers whom they had served in the past. One
of two remedies was commonly adopted. Some producers relinquished all but a part of their hitherto general markets and
concentrated their efforts on a narrower range of goods or a
smaller group of consumers. In other cases great consolidations
and trusts were organized to continue to reach the whole expanded market.

Manufacturing specialization had long existed in the electroplate and silverware industry — frequently to the detriment of
concerns which continued, like Reed & Barton, to turn out a
wide range of products. The most familiar examples in the
industry of the advantages of concentrated effort were the
Connecticut flatware houses, notably efficient in their narrow
field and capable of underselling most of the general-line producers. In another section of the market certain sterling
specialists occupied a similar position, and with similar results.
As yet, however, there had been no great merger designed to
reach the whole market, both mass and exclusive, on a grand
scale.

Reed & Barton, the Gorham Manufacturing Company, and

REED & BARTON STERLING WARE, ABOUT 1889

Among the first manufactured by the company. From a company catalogue

the Meriden Britannia Company were all, to a certain extent, in a similar position. All three sought the general market and reached out with a range of products which extended from inexpensive plated white metal to superb hand-wrought sterling silverware. Of the three, Reed & Barton was in the least favorable position to compete with specialists. The Meriden Britannia Company was much larger and, with greater resources, was better able to promote sales vigorously in many markets. In addition, the Meriden company controlled certain of the flatware specialists and thus stood to profit rather than suffer from their competitive abilities. Moreover, an expansionist policy extended this control and placed more and more resources at the company's disposal. Gorham, on the other hand, exhibited an increasing tendency toward specialization in the field of sterling and expensive electroplate.

While the Meriden Britannia Company and Gorham were evolving their own solutions to problems of a widening market, Reed & Barton continued on its middle course, refraining from drastic moves in the direction of either specialization or expansion. The rapid growth in volume of total sales from 1885 to 1892 seems to have discouraged a critical appraisal of the company's competitive position. The large foreign sales to 1889 and the even larger sterling sales after 1890 tended to minimize the fact that sales of electroplated flat and hollow ware had been declining more or less steadily since 1880, despite the successful trade in hotel ware. The spring of 1893 brought a violent money panic, collapsing price structures, and widespread business failures which introduced four years of deep depression. Reed & Barton sales declined sharply, and the depression revealed competitive trends which the prosperity of 1892 had obscured.

Conditions in the electroplate and silverware industry after 1893 bore a striking similarity to those which after 1873 led to the formation of the two trade associations. Competition took on a harsh aspect, and the struggle for sales ignored established price levels and trade practices.

The impotence of the Silver Plated Ware Association in the earlier depression, however, militated against the adoption of such a remedial technique in the later. By 1897 rumors had begun to circulate that a great trust was being contemplated. The movement to organize some kind of consolidation apparently originated among certain of the smaller Connecticut electroplate manufacturers, who saw in such a scheme an opportunity to improve their weak financial condition.[15] One firm after another joined in the movement, most of them being prompted to enlist because of the difficulties of competing with the large companies in the industry. When the Meriden Britannia Company at last showed interest, the proposed combine assumed formidable dimensions. Its purpose changed from defensive to offensive, and the organizers talked of controlling the whole output of electroplate and silverware in the country. It is said that at one point in the negotiations Reed & Barton was approached. George Brabrook emphatically refused to coöperate. "Not when they have ten votes to our one!" he remarked.

Late in 1898, after prolonged bargaining among the companies interested, the consolidation became a fact, and the International Silver Company came into existence. In its final form the organization was composed of sixteen companies including the Meriden Britannia Company, Rogers & Brother, Holmes & Edwards, and most of the Meriden electroplate manufacturers. It was believed that the combination would be able to control over 75 per cent of the electroplate manufactured in the country.

This event was analogous in many respects to the formation in 1852 of the Meriden Britannia Company. Those outside the merger found that a group of hitherto comparatively weak companies had, by combining with each other and with stronger units, organized themselves into an intensely vigorous competitive force. The 1898 combine was especially potent because it was backed by the resources and organization of the Meriden Britannia Company. The results of the combine exerted a far-reaching effect upon Reed & Barton and upon the industry. While the effectiveness of the Meriden company was impaired somewhat by association with weaker firms, those firms achieved greater strength and renewed energy. The over-all result was a net increase in the competing strength of the Connecticut factories.

The International merger was so extensive in scope that it embraced all branches of the industry from "flash" plate for the cheapest bidders to sterling silverware. It was the very antithesis of specialization and the ultimate in the expansionist theory of dealing with enlarged markets of the times. Reed & Barton now found itself competing, not only with intensive specialists both on a price and a quality basis, but with a huge organization equipped to sell on an extensive scale in many fields. Possessing neither the resources necessary to push all markets effectively nor the unity of product to concentrate upon one, Reed & Barton perched precariously on a compromise between the powerful diversification of International and the equally powerful specialization of Gorham. Great salesmanship and one of the finest salesforces ever to take the road preserved the market balance. The sheer vigor of Brabrook's marketing organization, plus the unsurpassed reputation of Reed & Barton wares, enabled the company to maintain its position in the trade.

The industry in general found, as did Reed & Barton, that the emphasis of the International combine was upon sales. Intensive promotional activity by the new company placed the whole industry under obligation to overhaul its selling techniques, particularly its advertising methods. Like the Meriden merger of 1852, the 1898 combination caught most of the industry off guard and forced many companies to take prompt defensive measures. Between 1888 and 1893 Reed & Barton did practically no advertising. From 1894 to 1900, however, the yearly expenditure ranged from $4,444 to $12,408,[16] ample testimony to the increased tempo of trade effort brought about by depression and the exertions of competitors.

The problem of providing effective promotion was not the only one which a diversified line of wares created for Reed & Barton in the 1890's. Questions of brand policy assumed increasing importance as the advertising campaigns of manufacturers went over the heads of the retailers and acquainted final consumers with factory trade names and marks. The efforts of Reed & Barton to sell in many markets called for a more careful consideration of company reputation than had been the case in days when lines were smaller and the spread was narrower between the highest and lowest quality produced. Implied in the action of many companies was the belief that manufacturers who produced both a quality and a cheap line of wares might find that the former was suffering from the promotion of the latter. The Gorham Manufacturing Company appeared to have recognized the danger to its sterling products inherent in the existence of an inexpensive plated line and placed much promotional emphasis on higher-priced wares. International also sought to prevent in consumers' minds the association of the good with the cheap by preserving the range of brand names of its component companies.

George Brabrook's policy again was one of compromise. Reed & Barton sacrificed much of the low-price market to protect its name in quality markets, and yet Brabrook was too much the salesman to withdraw completely from the lower field. Whether compromise was a wise course is difficult to judge. It was plain, however, that a company whose reputation through the years had been one for craftsmanship would do well to proceed with caution in lending its name to relatively inexpensive wares designed for mass markets.

Brabrook's wariness through forty years of sales administration undoubtedly cost Reed & Barton something in opportunities missed. By compromising between many markets the company renounced the chance to assume unchallenged leadership in any one field, and stood by to watch the spectacular growth of

CHART IV

REED & BARTON SALES BY MAJOR PRODUCT LINES, 1862–1900

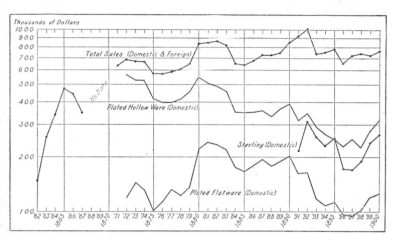

more than one competitor. These facts in no way constitute a condemnation of Brabrook or an adverse criticism of this era in the company management. Faced with the choice between speculative risk for great returns and conservative practice for the sake of safety, Reed & Barton chose the latter. When a company is faced with the necessity for making such a decision, the basis for criticism lies not in the choice made but in the success with which the decided course is adhered to. The steady upward trend of Reed & Barton sales in a period of frequent depressions, declining prices, and keen competition speaks more eloquently than words of the company's reputation and Brabrook's salesmanship. In spite of the self-imposed handicap of great caution, many genuine achievements were effected. A talented salesforce was built up, new markets were tapped, much commendable promotional work was done, and product lines were established which were to form the basis of company sales in years to come.

CHAPTER XI

THE SALESFORCE AT HOME AND ABROAD
1860–1900

INCREASING COMPETITION and expanding markets in the late 1860's were immediately responsible for creating the Reed & Barton salesforce. Underlying causes, however, went farther back. The selling organization, which appeared to be the spontaneous product of a trying age, was in reality the culmination of a gradual process of growth originating in more peaceful and prosperous times. The evolution of management in the field of sales was somewhat parallel to the evolution of management in the factory. In both cases growth was accompanied by increasing specialization of individual functions and the necessity for more and more detailed supervision. When the matter of timing is considered, the similarity between progress in production and in sales abruptly terminates. In comparison with general company growth the development of a salesforce was amazingly late and slow.

Reed & Barton had grown from a one-room shop to a factory employing two hundred workmen without benefit of a sales manager and with only part-time attention of the partners to problems of distribution. The overwhelming emphasis until this time had been on the development of manufacturing techniques, and this preoccupation left few resources of energy or capital available for marketing. So successful, indeed, was devotion to the workbench in establishing the reputation of company wares that an organization for selling was hardly necessary. A seller's market from 1843 to 1865 for Britannia ware and electroplate also delayed the necessity for market action. An exceptionally keen, long-range point of view might have foreseen the eventual intensification of competition to which accelerated factory output was leading, but in reality few manufacturers in the electroplate industry thus prepared in time of rain for the drought to come. Most selling organizations have dated only from the time when the need for them became acute.

A Sales Organization

After the Meriden Britannia Company merger in 1852, Henry Reed and George Brabrook recognized the necessity for marketing effort. By the time Brabrook became a partner (in 1859) Reed & Barton was on the verge of achieving the rudiments of a selling organization — a sales manager directing the efforts of one or more men under him. In the factory this same degree of specialization, in the form of foreman-over-workmen, had taken place more than thirty years earlier. The Civil War, however, arrested promising developments in sales management, and the 1860–65 period was one of suspended animation in this field. After 1865, evolution resumed its interrupted course. By the end of 1866 it had become apparent that the market could no longer support all companies in the industry in the manner to which they had been accustomed.

George Brabrook at first elected to assume the burden of increased promotional effort himself, and for several years following the end of the war he did all the traveling for the company. This burden proved to be too great. Since Henry Reed showed a disposition to entrust to Brabrook the management of finance as well as of sales, Brabrook's presence at the factory became increasingly necessary; and, accordingly, he began to choose the men who should replace him on the road. By 1867 the dense distribution of customers throughout certain sections of New England, the State of New York, the Middle West, and the South strongly suggests that as many as four salesmen were "drumming the trade." Brabrook's organization for the job at hand, however, went beyond this point.

The increasing importance of metropolitan sales areas was recognized as early as 1854 by the Meriden Britannia Company, which in that year established a branch office in New York. In 1861 and 1863 Reed & Barton turned down proposals by New York dealers to establish a similar office, but at last the necessity for closer contact with this important market became clear. Competition in New York was keen, and the Meriden Britannia Company, with an office and showroom on the spot, had Reed & Barton at a disadvantage. By 1867 the number of retail and wholesale customers served by Reed & Barton in New York City alone reached ninety-two and constituted adequate justification for an office. In that year a lease was signed for an office and showroom at 194 Broadway, and Calvin P. Harris was placed in charge of company affairs there.

The primary function of the branch office was to display the company line and to take orders from resident dealers and from those who periodically visited the city from outlying districts. Sales were made to both wholesale and retail dealers, with a careful distinction in discounts between types of customers. The sales office assumed functions which customers themselves formerly had performed for the company: Calvin Harris collected accounts, gathered credit information, supplied the company with news of trade developments, purchased supplies for Taunton, and supervised shipping and delivery of goods sold through his office. When Reed & Barton's foreign trade developed, the New York office handled all matters relating to shipments abroad and maintained close contacts with exporters and shipping agents. Calvin Harris' branch office offered one further service, of an intangible but immeasurably valuable nature: quite exclusive of the actual work performed there, the New York branch added much to company prestige. The advertising value of a sales office in a business world where New York offices were becoming fashionable should not be underestimated. When the Reed & Barton sign was hung out on

Broadway, the company became cosmopolitan in reputation as well as in fact.

In 1869 the office address was given as 2 Maiden Lane, in the heart of the jewelry and silverware district. By 1877 it was deemed advisable to follow the movement of fashionable stores uptown, and a showroom was opened at 686 Broadway, the Maiden Lane office being continued. Calvin Harris was placed in charge of the uptown store, the purpose of which was to sell at retail. In 1885 this store removed to 37 Union Square. Several other changes were made in the location of offices in succeeding years, and a branch was opened to deal exclusively in hotel wares. Two main offices continued to be maintained — one in Maiden Lane, possibly devoted to transacting business with dealers; the other farther uptown, where a retail store and showroom were located.

Selling in the New York area had by 1880 assumed a distinctly modern aspect, both in the extent of the trade and in the organization of facilities to expedite it. This was far from being the case in most sections of the country reached by Reed & Barton. Sales offices were a luxurious convenience as yet, and Brabrook relied on his slowly increasing force of drummers to make the sales and maintain the contacts. By 1875 Frank Cady was making the first of his many warm friendships among New England customers, and Oscar Lane was successfully justifying the expense of sending a representative to Chicago. At a slightly later date H. W. Graves was carrying the line through the Carolinas and Virginia. By the early 'seventies the possibilities of the Far West had been established, and this market, though not immediately large, promised much. In 1875 J. H. Rines was in San Francisco bidding on hotel orders for Reed & Barton. Four years later sales there had grown to a point where it seemed advisable to employ R. K. Haskell, formerly a salesman for Adams, Shaw & Company and for Gorham, as resident agent for Reed & Barton. In addition to the Reed & Barton line, Haskell also handled fine gold jewelry of Enos Richardson & Company, diamonds and pearls of Taylor & Bros., and sterling silver of Wood & Hughes.

SALESMEN AND THEIR RECORDS

In 1885, the first year for which reasonably complete sales records exist, the Reed & Barton selling organization appears to

TABLE 10

SALES BY DOMESTIC SALESFORCE, 1885
REED & BARTON

Salesman	Main Territory	Sales for 1885
Frank Cady	Boston	$76,714.27
Charles E. Hodges	Upper New York, New Hampshire, Vermont	36,398.61
J. W. Watson	Large cities in New York, Ohio, Kentucky	47,503.45
A. Brabrook	Baltimore	23,039.97
H. W. Graves	Georgia, Alabama, Louisiana	7,367.21
Luther Hyde	Wisconsin, Iowa, Colorado, Illinois, Kansas, Nebraska, Missouri, Minnesota, Michigan	35,194.19
William Bowdoin	Detroit, Chicago	9,984.32
George Kendrick	Canada, Nova Scotia	13,534.40
W. G. Tucker	Maine, Massachusetts, Connecticut	18,723.70
P. J. Godfrey	New Jersey, Pennsylvania, Kentucky, Illinois, Indiana, Ohio, Maryland, West Virginia	12,895.75
H. S. Follansbee	Pennsylvania, Ohio, Indiana, Illinois	13,240.90
H. M. Lane	Chicago	19,177.95
G. D. Lawrence	Ohio, Pennsylvania, Indiana, Illinois	4,342.61
T. B. Penton	Virginia, Georgia, Alabama, Louisiana	11,602.93
W. H. Kinnicutt	Ohio, Pennsylvania, Indiana, Illinois	976.77
E. A. Reed	Iowa, Nebraska, Minnesota	4,766.88
E. H. Adams	San Francisco	12,738.17
	Total sales by salesmen, 1885	$348,202.08

Source: Reed & Barton Mss., Agents' Sales, 1885.

have been well developed and flourishing. Table 10 indicates the extent and performance of the 1885 salesforce.

Behind these names and places and figures lies a dramatic story.[1] The Reed & Barton drummers were among the vanguard of commercial men who rolled back sales frontiers and penetrated, often under most trying conditions, to every section of the growing country. In many regions this was still the era of the stagecoach and linen duster, of travel by canal boat and river steamer and horseback, of hard-seated, unheated railroad coaches. The frontier spirit persisted not only in the physical appearance of many of the mining towns but in methods of selling. High stakes were the order of the day, with salesmen playing a win-all or lose-all game. Competition often was on a tooth-and-nail basis, and the niceties of trade in the eastern cities were but faintly echoed in the inland markets. Trade in the Middle West and West provided many opportunities for unscrupulous profit, and at the same time richly rewarded honesty and genuine ability. Commercial men emerged from this proving ground with their careers made or broken for life. In all cases "frontier" business was of a highly speculative nature, and companies were faced with the difficult necessity of appraising the future of new areas and new cities. Would the struggling young jeweler in Denver close his doors or blossom into an account worth many thousands of dollars annually? What was the future of the Chicago stockyards, the Twin City millers, the Pennsylvania oil wells, the Kansas farmers, the Northern Pacific Railroad lines? These questions could hardly be answered at the time, yet upon such questions rested the prospects of many an enterprise. The constant and rapid growth and decline of market areas made problems of distributional emphasis acute. Reed & Barton gambled heavily on the Middle West and, to a lesser degree, on the Far West. In both cases results were eminently successful.

The control which Brabrook exerted over his men was necessarily loose. Selling conditions varied so greatly throughout the country that a fixed procedure was virtually impossible. Wisely, Brabrook granted the Reed & Barton drummers great freedom in choosing customers, granting terms, and quoting prices. Contacts with Taunton were made by letter or, when the need was urgent, by telegraph. At the end of their trips the drummers made a verbal report to Brabrook upon the conditions

encountered and results obtained. In addition, each man was required to keep a record of hours worked, which was turned in
at the end of the trip.

SALARIES OF SALESMEN

Most of the salesmen appear to have been paid a fixed salary
with a bonus for keeping expenses below a certain percentage of
sales. Employment contracts usually were renewed each year,
the terms of the new contract depending upon the previous
year's performance.

In January, 1877, George Brabrook told salesman B. F. Merrill
that if, for the coming year, his sales exceeded the $19,000 total
of 1876 and that if his 1877 expenses were only 10 per cent of
sales (instead of the 15 per cent figure of 1876), his salary would
be raised. At this time Merrill was receiving $3.75 a day.[2] In
1880 a three-year contract was signed with Walter G. Tucker
providing for compensation at the rate of $4.50 a day in 1880,
$5.50 in 1881, and $6.50 in 1882. If the cost of selling should
exceed 7 per cent of the net amount of sales, then the pay for the
second year would be only $5.00 a day and for the third year,
$6.00.[3]

The Reed & Barton salesmen were by far the most highly paid
group in the company, their salaries substantially exceeding
those of foremen and department heads. In 1885 at least four
salesmen were receiving as much as, or more than, the $250
monthly salary of the plant superintendent. Among the 1885
salesforce the following monthly salaries were in effect: [4]

J. W. Watson	$250.00
A. Brabrook	260.00
W. Bowdoin	260.00
F. L. Cady	250.00
C. E. Hodges	166.67
H. M. Lane	166.67
L. Hyde	208.00
W. G. Tucker	100.00

The high pay received by the salesmen was an integral part of Brabrook's intensive selling campaigns and served, in part, to offset the limited amount of money expended upon advertising.

Caliber of the Salesforce

The Reed & Barton salesforce under Brabrook unquestionably was one of the finest in the field, and yet the high salaries paid were not the only, or even the most important, reason for the high caliber of the men employed. Almost without exception Reed & Barton salesmen came up through the factory. Many started as "meadow hay clerks" in the packing-room, while others served an apprenticeship in the manufacturing departments. In all cases a thorough knowledge of the factory and its products was gained through such a background, and the training proved its worth when the salesmen were called upon to explain the merits of their product. Moreover, by recruiting from the ranks, Brabrook was able to form in advance a fairly accurate judgment of the qualifications possessed by young candidates for selling positions.

By 1885 the pattern of the Reed & Barton selling organization had been established. From this time to 1900 expansion took place, but along already proved lines. In 1891 a Philadelphia branch office was opened with Mr. J. F. Dean in charge. The next year trade prospects in Chicago looked so bright that H. M. Lane was instructed to establish a branch office there. New faces appeared in the salesforce to take the place of Cady, Watson, and Bowdoin. Alfred Brabrook, known to factory and customers alike as "Old Mortality," retired after more than fifty years of service. The traditions of the '85 men were ably carried on, and at the turn of the century Reed & Barton could boast of salesmen who recognized no superiors in the trade.

Mr. E. H. Adams had already laid the foundations for a highly successful business in San Francisco with a spectacular, diamond-cut-diamond selling technique. In Detroit Mr. J. F.

Dean had purchased a membership in the Detroit Athletic Club with his bonus money and had cornered the Club's silverware business. At the same time his acquaintance with a restaurant proprietor named Statler was bearing fruit as plans for a chain of hotels across the country began to materialize and Reed & Barton received the contracts to supply them. In E. A. "Easy" Reed (no relation to Henry G. Reed) the company had one of the best and most cordially liked salesmen the industry has ever known. Kindly, sincere, and quiet, he counted among his friends some of the finest and wealthiest jewelers in the country. While he was frequently a guest in their homes, he never took advantage of friendship to force a sale. If a number in the line did not meet with the expected success, "Easy" Reed was just as quick to caution an inexperienced buyer not to stock it as he was to advocate the selection of a style which he knew would bring results. In Chicago Chauncey Smith carried on where H. M. Lane left off. Smith, keen-minded, slight in stature, and nervous, talked silverware every waking hour of his life. Back in Taunton he could and frequently did become vociferous over the slightest error with any of his accounts, but no one on the road could venture the least criticism of the company, its products, or its personnel without bringing down upon his head the whole force of Chauncey's invective. During his career he sold millions of dollars' worth of merchandise. Never would he discuss with a customer the qualifications of competing lines, and nothing but the outstanding merits of Reed & Barton wares interested him.[5]

Selling Abroad

The salesmen who carried the Reed & Barton line abroad are equally deserving of notice. Commercial traveling in the regions they visited bordered on high adventure and involved no small element of personal risk. The development of Reed & Barton's foreign trade, moreover, was as significant as it was spectacular, for it constituted the final phase of George Brabrook's sales administration and one of his greatest efforts to spread the market for company wares. In respect to timing, the Reed & Barton export trade was closely connected with a widespread movement by other American manufacturers to reach new markets beyond the national boundary. In the silverware and electroplate industry this trend was strongly reinforced by the Philadelphia Centennial Exhibit of 1876 as well as by exhibitions in Europe which had shown American wares to the world and had stimulated the demand for such goods abroad.

Until the 1870's very formidable handicaps existed to hamper an export trade, and these handicaps persisted stubbornly for many years. Tariff and language barriers, slow and uncertain communications, and exchange difficulties — all retarded trade. The high reputation of certain European houses discouraged many American producers who sought to sell there. In 1877 the *Jewelers' Circular and Horological Review* complained that domestic manufacturers were being deprived of promising South American markets by stringent trade regulations.[6] In spite of such difficulties, however, electroplated ware began to be shipped out of the United States in increasing amounts. In 1870 the total exports of plated ware amounted to only $29,679, but by 1880 great expansion in foreign trade had raised this figure to $292,563. In 1889 ware to the amount of $587,163 was shipped out of the country.[7] Reed & Barton's foreign trade paralleled this course through the 1870's and 1880's.

The first company customers outside the United States were those in Nova Scotia, New Brunswick, and other parts of Canada; but this business prior to 1870 was inconsequential. By 1873 a few scattered orders were being received from South America through New York commission houses, and Bailey, Gomez & Company in Rio de Janeiro was ordering on an experimental basis. In 1874 the first concerted effort was made by Reed & Barton to reach the South American market. A contract was made with Liedierd & Company, of New York, by the terms of which their agent, J. Harcourt Bagôt, was to take orders for Reed & Barton wares in the West Indies and South America. Liedierd & Company was to receive a 10 per cent commission on net sales. Bagôt's instructions were specifically stated in the contract: discounts granted to South American dealers on ware were not to exceed 40/5 per cent; freight and tin-lined packages were to be charged to buyers; payment was to be in cash in New York or Boston on delivery of invoices and bills of lading. The contract was to be for one trip only, and Bagôt was to be furnished a sample line free of charge.

This first attempt to tap the foreign market was little short of a fiasco: Bagôt proved to be a willing but incompetent agent; unbelievable misfortune and difficulty were encountered at every step; and Taunton policies proved inapplicable to the market. Letters which Bagôt wrote to the company survived this otherwise unfortunate adventure and present a graphic account of conditions encountered.

Bagôt's principal efforts were confined to Buenos Aires and Rio de Janeiro, his first stop being in the former city. The first letter Reed & Barton received from him was wildly optimistic; in fact, Bagôt stated his belief that he could sell at least $100,000 of wares in eight months. This was, however, the last optimistic note sounded in the correspondence. Bagôt's efforts to find reliable houses to handle Reed & Barton goods soon revealed the fact that European manufacturers were firmly entrenched in the market and spared no pains to prejudice the South American trade against United States houses. The English firms of Dixon and Elkington were apparently unknown, but "common trash" from Birmingham and fine silver of French manufacture found ready sales. Cristoffle & Cie, the most famous French firm in the field, had exclusive contracts with almost all reputable dealers. Commenting on the success of other American manufacturers, Bagôt stated, "Mr. Rorke of the Boston & Sandwich Glass Co.

was out here some time ago, he as well as Gorham's man went away disgusted."

Upon the many difficulties of transacting business Bagôt waxed eloquent. Delay in shipping caused much trouble, and the state of transportation from New York to South America was such that better time could be made by sending wares by way of Liverpool, England! Tariffs were high, particularly on Reed & Barton products, which were heavier than the European, and much damage was done to shipments when they were unpacked at the custom house. Delay attended the entry of goods, and Bagôt despairingly complained that his samples were detained three weeks by officials in Buenos Aires.

With justification and considerable astuteness Bagôt criticized the inability of Yankee manufacturers to adapt their concepts to the requirements of the trade. A cash trade, so uncompromisingly insisted on, was virtually impossible to obtain, for English and European firms granted twelve months' credit and did most of their selling on a consignment basis as well. In almost all cases American goods were far undersold by European, and Bagôt stated that unless Reed & Barton would abandon its policy of refusing to lower quality standards, nothing much could be done in this market. Unquestionably, the most serious criticism of North American houses lay in the fact that they failed to comprehend the South American temperament. Trade, remarked Bagôt, proceeded at a leisurely pace, with many holidays and innumerable minor delays. "Weeks to these people are only as hours. . . ." Selling was a ceremony which called forth all the social graces, and the Yankee trader's methods were looked upon with some distaste. French and Portuguese salesmen were far more fitted by temperament to meet the requirements of the region and were much more popular in the trade than drummers from the United States. Many of the European houses, moreover, employed resident agents, who became established in the South American cities and challenged the efforts of traveling men to obtain an important share of the market.

These difficulties might have been overcome in time, but there were others which defied remedy. "Yellowjack is in town!" exclaimed Bagôt on several occasions, as epidemics swept up and down the coast with deadly regularity, sending people hurrying into the hills and paralyzing trade. Revolution and financial panic as well greeted Bagôt upon his arrival in Brazil, and more than once during his trip merchants closed their doors as government or revolutionary armies marched by. "I guess its the weather which is warming these fellows up. They . . . multiply revolutions in place of words!" wrote the Reed & Barton agent in disgust.

Bagôt's experience led him to make certain recommendations to the company. Stating first of all that Reed & Barton wares enjoyed a great reputation and might be made to sell, he suggested extensive newspaper advertising in South America. This suggestion was complied with by the company only to an inconsequential extent. Reed & Barton did, however, exhibit wares in the Chilean Exposition of 1875, where they received a first award and favorable publicity. Bagôt also urged larger discounts to the trade. South American merchants were so unfortunately naïve as to reveal to each other the discounts they were receiving. Therefore, it was necessary to grant maximum discounts to all — an unpleasant contrast to trade practices in the United States. Bagôt's final recommendation was that Reed & Barton either establish a resident selling agency or sell through a European house which employed a resident agent in South America.

Before Bagôt had been in action for many months it became evident that he was no salesman. Good customers were alienated and poor ones solicited. Very few sales were made and his sample line itself was disposed of at auction at a considerable sacrifice. Finally a contract highly unsatisfactory to the company was negotiated by Bagôt, and he was recalled. It was unfortunate that Bagôt's trip came to such an ignominious end, and that he was thus discredited in the eyes of the company, for many of Bagôt's observations could have been of great value and his appraisal of the market proved in later years to have been keen and accurate.

Later experiences in the South American market were less unfortunate. Carlos Basseri covered the trade there in 1876 with some success. J. H. Rines established many contacts in Europe in 1875 and even placed orders in St. Petersburg, Russia. New York export houses also continued to order considerable quantities of ware. By 1879 Rines' efforts were supplemented by those of M. T. Thatcher, and it is possible that other salesmen as well were sent abroad. Foreign sales increased from $13,764.48 in 1874 to $103,128.70 in 1881. The list of active company customers in the latter year reveals the geographical extent of the trade.

The company was optimistic about the increase in foreign sales and saw in these markets a chance to bolster declining domestic sales of hollow ware. The foreign business, moreover, exhibited a different seasonal pattern from the domestic and enabled the factory to maintain a steadier volume of production throughout the year. Much of the summer slack in plant activity was relieved by heavy export orders through July, August, and September. Further enthusiasm was forthcoming when it was discovered that many of the company patterns which had become obsolete in the United States could readily be disposed of in South America. Large quantities of such wares were dusted off and shipped out — an entirely unexpected pleasure.

The encouraging trend of exports led Brabrook to still greater efforts. The 1885 catalogue contained pages of code words by which foreign customers could cable orders. Discounts appear to have been increased to a level beyond those quoted to domestic customers, and certain South American houses were

allowed 50 per cent or even 50/5 per cent. Orders from abroad
mounted to a peak of $174,916.54 in 1887; and Brabrook ex-
panded his foreign salesforce. C. A. Pope and Thomas Raddin

TABLE 11

GEOGRAPHICAL DISTRIBUTION OF FOREIGN CUSTOMERS, 1881
REED & BARTON

		No. of Customers			No. of Customers
Argentina:	Buenos Aires	5	Ireland:	Belfast	2
Chile:	Santiago	1		Dublin	1
	Valparaiso	10	Scotland:	Glasgow	1
Brazil:	Pernambuco	5	Germany:	Bremen	3
	Rio de Janeiro	7		Berlin	1
	Bahia	2		Hamburg	6
	São Paulo	1		Mayence	1
	Pará	1	Prussia:	Frankfort	1
Colombia:	Bogotá	6		Cologne	1
Venezuela:	Caracas	5	Austria:	Trieste	2
Uruguay:	Montevideo	4	Belgium:	Brussels	2
Bermuda:	Hamilton	2	Holland:	Rotterdam	2
Trinidad:	Port of Spain	3		Amsterdam	1
Cuba:	Havana	5	Denmark:	Copenhagen	1
Barbados:	Bridgetown	1	Sweden:	Stockholm	1
West Indies:	St. Thomas	1	Portugal:	Lisbon	1
	Martinique	1	Spain:	Malaga	1
Panama:	Panama	1		Seville	1
Hawaii:	Honolulu	2		Madrid	1
Australia:	Melbourne	1		Bilbao	1
	Sydney	3		Barcelona	2
	Adelaide	1		Cadiz	2
China:	Hong Kong	1	Hungary:	Pesth	1
Japan:	Yokohama	1	Bohemia:	Prague	2
England:	London	3	Russia:	St. Petersburg	1
			India:	Madras	1

Source: Reed & Barton Mss., Letter Books, 1879–81.

traveled for the company through India, China, the East
Indies, Australia, and Africa. Ed Barton, of Reed, Barton &
Company fame, covered Mexico, Central America, the west

coast of South America, and the Far East. H. N. Graves was sent to Australia for at least one trip, and in South America a resident agent, A. R. Werner, was finally established. Werner served the company well and made many friends in Taunton when he visited there. It was his intimate knowledge of Brazil which preserved such of the South American market as Reed & Barton retained. In 1898 the company offered him a permanent position on a straight salary basis instead of paying him a 10 per cent commission as formerly, and the next year Werner visited England and the Continent in the company's interests. Certain other salesmen as well were employed by the company in the late 1890's. Their contracts were for one trip, with 10 per cent commissions, and none appear to have stayed with the company long or to have achieved any spectacular successes.

In obscure corners of the earth Thomas Raddin did a selling job that was little short of miraculous, and the name of Reed & Barton was long remembered by many an Indian, Sumatran, and Batavian merchant. Defying plague, poor communications, inadequate banking facilities, and language difficulties, Raddin sold silverware from Palembang to Mangalore. His last order was placed in Surabaya, Java, and there he was stricken with the plague. The company received a notice of his death in April, 1897, and immediately dispatched Ed Barton to the scene. Barton, after much expensive conniving with native officials, succeeded in smuggling Raddin's body out of Java concealed in a shipment of logs, and Raddin was buried in the Mayflower Hill Cemetery in Taunton.

Raddin's place was taken by William J. Poetz, who represented both Reed & Barton and the Waterman Pen Company. Of interest are the instructions written to Poetz, in Sydney, Australia, by George Brabrook in the summer of 1901.[8]

Our idea would be for you to take a steamer from Sydney to Singapore, canvass Java and returning to Singapore, take in Rangoon (should reports on business be sufficiently favorable to justify it) then to India via

Colombo, Ceylon, and visit Bombay and Calcutta, and such other places in India as would seem to warrant a visit. . . .

You will please understand that we do not insist on your making this trip unless it is agreeable to you and you think that it will pay fairly well from such information as you are able to obtain. . . . Should you decide to make the trip you could, of course, return via the Suez Canal and England after finishing India.

In spite of all Brabrook's efforts, Reed & Barton's foreign trade did not prosper. After 1887, sales declined more or less steadily. It is extremely doubtful, moreover, if Reed & Barton, even in the peak years of the late 1880's, ever realized substantial profits from the trade. The expense of sending company representatives abroad was inordinately high, and the company had little success in locating reliable resident agents. Figures for William Poetz's trips reveal the cost involved and the returns realized.[9]

1898–1899 ACCOUNT OF W. J. POETZ

Sales in Africa:	Oct.–Dec., 1898; Jan., Feb., Aug.–Oct., 1899:	13 customers	$10,819.53
Sales in Australia:	Feb., June, Nov., 1899	14	2,694.06
Sales in New Zealand:	Jan., June-Sept., Dec., 1899	6	1,269.46
Sales in Tasmania:	Jan., July, 1899	1	449.46
Gross Sales	. . . .		$15,232.51
Less:			
Selling expense	$4,467.10		
Two years' salary	3,600.00		8,067.10
Net Sales			$7,165.41

In addition to undergoing prohibitive selling expenses the company found it necessary to grant increasingly high discounts in order to retain any foreign customers. By 1900 terms of 50/- 10/5 per cent were allowed some buyers. In an effort to dispense with costly sales trips by company men, Brabrook turned to the New York export houses, and by offering discounts as high as 50/20 per cent was able to induce some of them to carry the line.

After 1900, however, little effort was made to push the foreign trade, and the volume of business never again approached the 1887 level. Sales declined to $50,972 in 1900 and still further in succeeding years. Orders from abroad, however, continued to come in to Taunton in modest amounts, and the name of Reed & Barton was long remembered favorably in certain sections of the world.

CHART V

REED & BARTON FOREIGN SALES, 1874–1900

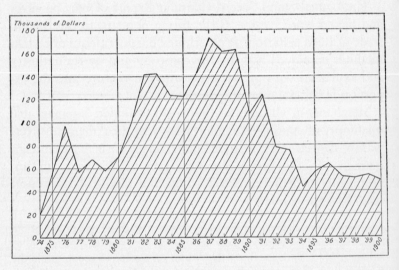

Brabrook's venture into the foreign market added more to the volume of company sales than it did to profits, but it was not a total loss. As advertising, this trade was of great value, and the company name was carried to the ends of the earth. In men like Werner, Raddin, and Pope the tradition of great salesmanship was ably sustained. Most important of all, the foreign trade brought Reed & Barton wares into competition with the best in the world. For the Taunton company the result of this competition was cause for much pride. By 1900 Reed & Barton's reputation for quality was established, not only in North America, but wherever silverware was sold.

The company failed to build up a foreign sales volume sufficient to justify the great expense of selling abroad. So, too, did many other American electroplate and sterling manufacturers who entered the trade. Yet at the same time that Reed & Barton foreign sales were sharply declining, total American exports in general were steadily increasing, and many industries were realizing fat profits from abroad.

The United States Special Consular Report of 1902 on silver and plated ware [10] came as the fitting obituary to the foreign trade of Reed & Barton. It constituted harsh criticism of certain methods employed both by the company and by the industry and explained with great clarity why the venture into the export trade was not more successful.

Merchants in all parts of the world exhibited a remarkable unanimity of opinion as to the reasons why the American silverware and electroplate manufacturers did not do better in foreign markets. In the first place, American houses were uncompromising in their terms, according to a report of the consul from Iquique, Chile: [11]

American merchants give the least commercial advantages of any of the large exporting countries, usually demanding cash in exchange for bill of lading at New York, or thirty days' draft on receipt of goods, while the English and German merchants give from three months to a year's credit. . . .

The practice of granting different discounts to different customers was also severely criticized. Both these weaknesses had been pointed out by Bagôt fifteen years before.

The fact was also made clear by the report that in almost all instances American wares were of too high a quality for the markets sought. England was the only nation of all those reporting in which this fact did not obtain. Reed & Barton was a notable offender in this respect. A letter to the consul in Santos, Brazil, from São Paulo says: [12]

> In speaking with Mr. A. Birlé here he informed me that the traveling agent of Reed & Barton, the well-known plated-ware firm of New York, was a good friend of his and had tried to sell him their goods, but that on account of their costing so much more than the German ware (50 per cent more, he said) they had never done anything with that company.

Both in Europe and in South America the cheap lines of ware put out by the French and German proved eminently more suited to the trade. The consul in Breslau, Prussia, said of American wares ". . . the old conservative idea appears to exist that such articles are things of superlative luxury. . . ." [13] From Bahia, Brazil, came the comment, "What is desired here is a cheap article rather than a good one. . . ." [14]

The most severe and universal criticism offered was that while American products were unexcelled in quality, their style was not suited to the markets to which they were sent. Certain excerpts from the Consular Reports are particularly revealing: [15]

Iquique, Chile: "German manufacturers will make any style of goods wanted. . . . Merchants here carry the idea that American manufacturers will not change their style of goods to secure the trade in these countries."

Nottingham, England: "The English market and English tastes are not studied."

Prague, Bohemia: "American patterns and styles do not generally suit local tastes and requirements."

Coburg, Bavaria: "So far American manufacturers have not taken sufficient care to adapt their products to the wants of the German market."

In Mexico and in certain parts of South America the patterns offered were acceptable to the taste of the times, but these areas were the exception. To this criticism the reply could be made that the cost of bringing out lines of wares acceptable in taste to many different countries was prohibitive. This does not explain, however, the failure of most American electroplate manufacturers to concentrate upon a single region and adopt a line of ware suitable to it. The blunt fact was that, by and large, local tastes were completely ignored.

In certain countries local regulations severely hampered American firms, and no reasonable remedial measures were possible. In France a maze of complicated regulations seriously impeded the importation of silverware. In England all ware was required to be hall-marked, and the stamp of quality thus applied was so deeply incised that ware usually had to be re-finished after marketing. This imposed a considerable hardship upon American houses and in some cases required the maintenance of a refinishing shop in England.

The combination of avoidable and unavoidable difficulties which terminated Reed & Barton trade abroad affected the whole industry, and George Brabrook was probably as skillful in his administration of foreign sales as most other managers. Any criticism of this epoch in his career should recognize that his methods were those of his contemporaries, and in many places where he failed, they failed.

In the field of domestic sales the balance of criticism is over-whelmingly favorable to Brabrook. Here his accomplishments were many and valuable. If his stand on matters of product policy was at times indecisive, his ability to direct an intensive selling campaign more than made up for the weakness. His greatest contribution, however, stands clear above all else and beyond all criticism or reproach: to George Brabrook alone must go the credit for creating the Reed & Barton marketing organization.

CHAPTER XII

PRODUCING FOR A GILDED AGE, 1860–1900

THE LAST THIRD of the nineteenth century has inspired more descriptive phrases than possibly any other period in American history. This, the so-called Victorian era, was unquestionably an amazing period in every respect — a period so prolific in bizarre characteristics that until recently it has been maligned, ridiculed, or politely ignored as a part of the American heritage. Like every period that has just closed, it is a much misunderstood age and therefore a fertile field for study.

Silverware was but a small part of the total artistic environment of these years, but it proved to be a completely typical part. The electroplated and sterling services of American manufacturers matched with perfect harmony their background of black walnut and horsehair furniture. The tea set of 1880 appeared remarkably well placed and at home among the plush-covered albums, the hand-painted china, and the corner whatnots of the day. In the Reed & Barton line we see reflected the whole cycle of fashion, which, from an unassuming beginning in the 1860's, whirled through a period of unprecedented ornateness in the 'seventies and 'eighties and culminated in a healthy reaction to its own excesses as the century drew to a close.

ARTISTIC TASTES AND INFLUENCES

The sweep of fashion was compelling in the silverware industry, and no company even contemplated resisting the trend of the times. This fact constituted something of a contrast to events in the world of art, architecture, and letters, where a few individualists like Winslow Homer, Henry Hobson Richardson, and Bret Harte scorned the malaproprieties of the age and

ELECTROPLATED TEA SET, REED & BARTON

Exhibiting the style of design characteristic of the 1870's and 1880's

ELECTROPLATED TEAPOT, REED & BARTON
High Design in the 1870's

founded new schools of thought and action.[1] Silverware manufacturers, bound by the stern requirements of commercial necessity, could scarcely afford to exert any artistic independence.
Staying in business meant catering to the questionable tastes of
the mass market rather than to the better taste of a scattered few
individuals. The position of the silverware designers was de-
fensible on more positive grounds than these, however. The
work of this period was sincerely applauded by those for whom
it was intended, and contemporary opinion held, with only a
few dissenting voices, that art forms had achieved a new pin-
nacle of culture. Many of the dissenting voices were English. In
1873 George Frank Jackson, of Birmingham, commented with
remarkable restraint, ". . . the manufacturers of other countries
[than England] seem to concentrate their attention upon
ornamental construction and decoration, which is often carried
to excess."[2] Typical of contemporary self-satisfaction, on the
other hand, are the remarks of the economist and historian
Albert S. Bolles, who in 1879 stated, "Within the last ten years
the United States have made a great advance in the beauty and
originality of styles of silver-ware."[3] There is no evidence to
show that the American manufacturers regarded their own
work with anything but great esteem. Once again, we should
exercise caution in using present-day standards as the basis for
criticizing the work of another and very different age.

The trend toward an ornate style had its immediate origin in
the 1850's, when manufacturers strove to prove their new skills
by superimposing a network of surface ornament upon old
forms. This movement continued in the following decade with
increasing intensity. War riches were translated into a demand
for lavish fashions. Postwar uneasiness and a "moral collapse in
government and business"[4] discouraged whatever wholesome
influences had survived in the artistic world. In silverware the
1870's brought no improvement. Styles, indeed, became much
more profuse than ever before; the buying public appeared to be

attracted more by brilliance than by fine craftsmanship. Ornamental detail which to us appears to be inappropriate to the point of vulgarity was then hailed as "original" by a nation which still continued to confuse bigness with greatness.[5] The call for high design took many of the hardheaded American factory men aback, however, and they turned to foreign sources of inspiration in order to meet the demands upon them. Egyptian, Chinese, and Japanese styles were largely drawn upon, their exotic nature finding ready acceptance. Conservative England was ignored, for English silverware resisted the excesses of the period, and its "durability, evenness of surface, and solid workmanship"[6] as well as a lack of complicated embellishment obviously rendered it unsuited to the American market.

Reed & Barton wares of the early 1870's reveal all aspects of contemporary trends. Floral patterns strongly tempered by Japanese motives predominated. At the same time many new shapes were introduced. The old-style, gracefully curved teaware handles yielded place to angular forms, while the bodies and covers of the ware displayed a confusing array of decorative detail. Classic allegory spread from literature to the decorative arts; mysterious scrolls were engraved upon teapots and detached heads peered out from the ware in unexpected places. A fashion for sentiment played its part; Victorian goodness found expression in the form of sculptured cupids, which capered over much of the electroplated tableware of the day. Paradoxically enough, the trend toward elaboration was allied with a nature movement. The simple, functional forms of nature, however, were ignored, and the superficial shrubbery adopted. Later, nautical subjects were widely employed, shell ornament and a dull water-finish with bright-cut decoration possessing great market appeal.[7]

Both Henry Reed and William Parkin designed the company ware, but after 1870 Reed appears to have done much less of this work than diesinker Parkin.[8] Reed's conservative nature

could scarcely allow him to continue his work in this field with
any great degree of enthusiasm. By 1874 it had become very
apparent that designing was no longer a secondary function in
the factory, and a specialist was at last employed. W. C. Beattie
was brought from England, and on September 4 of that year
became the first full-time Reed & Barton designer.[9] Beattie,
however, could no more resist the current of popular fashion
than could Reed, Parkin, or any of the silverware manufacturers
and designers.

A growing awareness of the precepts of mass production in-
vaded the field of design. Interchangeable parts were found to
be an economy not only in machinery but in ornament. Standardized handles, covers, feet, and finials were applied to many
different types of ware. Sometimes the results happened to be
attractive; oftener the practice gave rise to highly inappropriate
alliances. The confusion reached its peak in the 1880's, when
Japanese art, interchangeable parts, mysticism, allegory, sentiment, and nature motives clashed in one great discord. This
discord echoed in the Reed & Barton factory, and much of the
line exhibited the extravagant styles of contemporary manufacturers. Yet, even in these years, commendable work was
done. The wares of Reed & Barton were as restrained as those
of any other factory in the electroplate industry and undoubtedly
more so than many.

The climax of ornamentation in the middle 1880's was necessarily short-lived. The prevailing fashions in silverware were
too intense to be long popular, and cries of revolt were heard
even as the decorative cycle reached its peak. "People are tired
of the hackneyed Roman, Etruscan, Japanese and Egyptian
styles, and want novelties, something that combines originality
of design with richness of metal and artistic workmanship,"
complained the *Jewelers' Circular*.[10] The decade ended in a
transitional state of affairs, with most critics agreeing that some
new influence was required but with few constructive ideas as

to what it should be. Appraising the work of the lily-gilding years of the 1870's and 1880's is no easy task. Much that was praiseworthy, both in methods and in results, came out of this period. At its worst, designs of the era went to ludicrous extremes; at its best, the period exhibited a good feeling for ornament of a rich nature.

These years were far from wasted ones for Reed & Barton. One great achievement was the creation of a designing department; another was the enhancement of the company's reputation in the field of design.[11] Credit for both these accomplishments must be divided between Henry Reed and George Brabrook. Each contributed much, though in a different way. Reed, though lacking a polished artistic background, insisted that whatever was undertaken in the factory should be done with meticulous care. More important yet, he was there to see that it was so done, and knew in minute detail how to do it himself. One of Henry Reed's most cherished ideas was that there should be at least one masterpiece of metal craftsmanship in process in the factory at all times, to serve as an inspiration and stimulant to his men. Reed's influence in the factory produced electroplated wares of a quality which even modern technical skill cannot profitably surpass. Whatever the merits of the designs of the period, the workmanship displayed, particularly in burnishing and in casting, was superb.

George Brabrook contributed a wealth of artistic feeling and probably did as much as any one man could to restrain the improprieties of current design. Under his guidance the designing-room took on an added importance and grew rapidly in size. He accumulated a library of reference books on design which proved of greatest value in years to come. Brabrook himself had an uncanny ability in sensing what the market wanted and in making those almost imperceptible changes in ware which meant the difference between the fine and the mediocre. "Well now," he would say, taking a piece of ware from the hands of

Electroplated Wine Stands, Reed & Barton, about 1882

Superb glassware, purchased in England and France, appeared in these combination pieces

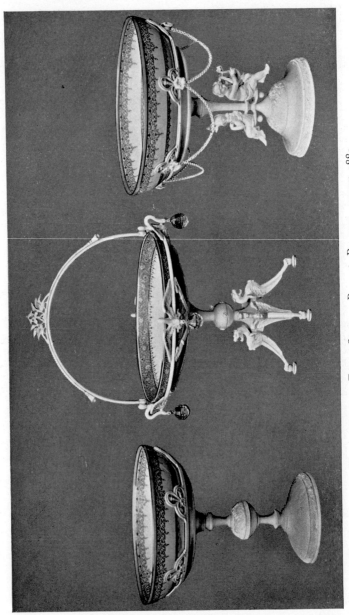

ELECTROPLATED FRUIT STANDS, REED & BARTON, ABOUT 1882

a designer, and squinting at it carefully for a moment, "I think maybe if you flared this edge out a mite, say an eighth of an inch, all 'round, these things would look a lot better." [12] Invariably his judgment in such cases proved to be correct, and the designing department came to rely heavily upon him for guidance.

The emphasis placed by both Reed and Brabrook on matters of design was reflected by the increasing number of designers and modelers employed. By 1889 twenty-four men were working in this department.[13] Every convenience was placed at their disposal, even to the extent of individual rooms to which each of the principal artists could retire and work, guarded by lock and key from any interruption. Only Henry Reed and George Brabrook had free access to these sanctums, and in this carefully cultured atmosphere the foundation for great artistic accomplishments was laid.

Those accomplishments began to be apparent by 1890, both in the Reed & Barton factory and in the industry. The attempt of silverware manufacturers to develop an original "American style" was abandoned. Concurrently, the public grew tired of ideas imported from civilizations far removed in taste and custom from their own. Chastened by their experience of the past thirty years, the designers of silverware turned back to the great master periods of European art. The French Renaissance was placed under heavy tribute, but the styles of other periods as well, notably the English Georgian, were widely adopted. Luxurious floral motives were also employed, though with far greater skill in adapting decoration to form than had been exercised in previous years. Ornateness characterized 1890–1900 silverware, but it was a new ornateness, most of it in eminently good taste.

Contributing much to this revival were the European draftsmen and artists who were brought into America by the large factories. These men, in turn, brought with them European concepts of artisanship far superior to the unrefined native product of their adopted country. The influence of the French and English artisans was a cumulative one, though at first it scarcely made itself felt amid the powerful eccentricities of American taste. As the number of foreign designers increased, so too did their power. By 1890 the conservative aesthetic traditions of these men dominated much of the American scene. In no field, commercial or artistic, however, was their influence felt with more force than in silverware. In the Reed & Barton factory the number of foreign-taught designers and modelers increased steadily. A. F. Jackson was brought from England and by 1889 had succeeded his fellow-countryman, W. C. Beattie, as head designer. At the same time Ernest Meyers, a Frenchman, was experimentally applying his classical Paris training to American conditions. At least ten others in the design department were foreign-born and trained. This condition was characteristic of the industry. In 1889 one-third of Tiffany's artists were Continental or English. The head designer at Tiffany's, Paulding Farnham, had studied abroad. Wilkinson, head designer of the Gorham Manufacturing Company, was an Englishman, trained in England. A large number of Gorham artists, moreover, were said to be foreign by birth or extraction. A similar situation prevailed in the Meriden Britannia Company at the time.[14]

Also a factor in the improved taste of the early 'nineties was the growth in size and influence of American art schools. The Art School of the Cooper Union in New York (founded in 1857), the National Academy of Design (1826), the University of Cincinnati School of Design (1869), the Rhode Island School of Design (1877), and several other similar institutions had begun to turn out competent artists. More important than the initial results achieved by these schools, however, was their implied promise that in the future the majority of American products might be designed by American artisans.

STERLING BOWL, REED & BARTON
Typical of fine craftsmanship in the 1890's

PLATED FLATWARE, REED & BARTON, MADE AFTER 1868
Roman Medallion, Gem, Pearl, Unique, Orient, Brilliant
These patterns were the first original flatware designs of the company,
and enjoyed great popularity through the 1870's

Product Development

The evolution of design throughout the 1860–1900 period was accompanied by widespread product changes. Reed & Barton experienced three great developments — the creation and growth of the sterling, hotel-ware, and flatware lines. The quantitative growth of these lines has already been noted; beyond this, however, a considerable evolution occurred in the character of the products themselves and in the organization of facilities to produce them. In each case progress was from an experimental lot of ware to products of consistently high quality; from the drawing board to a highly specialized manufacturing department.

The growth of the flatware line was closely allied to that of hotel ware. Throughout the early 1860's, in fact, the two were practically synonymous, for little flatware was produced except for the hotel trade. Departmental organization progressed more rapidly in flatware than in hotel hollow ware, and in 1868 some fifty employees were producing spoons, forks, and knives under the direction of Elijah Tolman. As this department grew and Reed & Barton began to patent designs of its own, the necessity of purchasing flatware from other factories declined. Until 1868 the Reed & Barton line consisted of six or eight patterns common to all the trade — Plain, Tipped, Threaded, Oval, Olive, Beaded, French, and Shell. In December, 1868, the first original Reed & Barton flatware pattern, called the Roman Medallion, was patented. Appropriately enough, its designer was Henry G. Reed. This was followed in the next ten years by the Gem, Pearl, Unique, Orient, and Brilliant patterns, designed by Parkin and Beattie. The ornate character of these patterns suggests that they were designed primarily for household rather than for commercial use. All Reed & Barton flatware was plated upon the best quality of nickel silver obtainable, the plate being deposited in four different grades of thickness. Prices per dozen teaspoons in the Roman Medallion pattern ranged from $4.25 for Extra Plate to $5.25 for Double Plate, to $6.25 for Triple Plate, and to $7.25 for Quadruple Plate. Extra heavy spoons in plain patterns for hotel and steamboat use were priced at from $5.75 per dozen for Extra Plate to $9.50 for Quadruple Plate.[15] Manufacturers tried to outdo one another in the variety of pieces produced, with the eventual result that almost every type of food had a piece of flatware designed especially for it! In 1880, for example, Reed & Barton manufactured twenty different varieties of spoons, twelve different forks, ten different knives. The complete flatware line consisted of fifty-seven distinct items. Inventory problems were enormous, for most of the pieces were made in four grades and more than a dozen patterns. When pieces, grades, and patterns were all taken into consideration the number of items in the flatware line alone totaled 3,560!

The evolution of the hotel-ware line was relatively detached from the general movements of fashion. Throughout the whole 1860–1900 period the hotel ware of Reed & Barton and most other factories exhibited a degree of simplicity absent in other lines. Necessity rather than choice dictated styles, and considerations of price, use, and care kept ornamentation at a minimum. The hotel ware of electroplate manufacturers preserved Colonial traditions of plain surface and simple line through the depths of the Victorian cycle and exerted an unquestionably beneficial influence upon other branches of manufacture. The first Reed & Barton hotel flatware orders were executed outside the factory, and the hollow ware was turned out in the regular teaware department. By 1883, however, a separate department employing twenty-six men had been organized by Henry Nickolds to fabricate nickel-silver hollow ware for hotels.[16] So rapidly did this business expand that six years later the department employed one hundred and nine men and was divided into two sections, one headed by Nickolds and the other by John Rogers.

CHARACTERISTIC PLATED FLATWARE PIECES ILLUSTRATED IN THE
1885 CATALOGUE

STERLING FLATWARE OF THE 1890's, REED & BARTON
Luxembourg, Trajan, La Reine, Majestic, La Marquise, and La Touraine
Ornateness applied with skill and good taste

The Reed & Barton line of sterling silverware exhibited a vigorous awakening to the dictates of good taste. A. F. Jackson, the designer from England, immediately set to work in the design department to establish the company name in the new field. The rapid increase in sterling sales after 1890 indicates that he was remarkably successful in achieving this objective, and in 1895 the *Jewelers' Circular* remarked that Reed & Barton sterling flatware upheld the maker's reputation as originator of design.[17] After 1890 the sterling output was prolific, with a strong emphasis upon flatware. In 1890 three patterns were brought out, followed by two more in 1891, two in 1892, and one each year thereafter, all of which were extensively advertised. In addition to these, Jackson designed, in 1891, several patterns of coffee spoons which found a ready market. In the late 1890's the line of sterling flatware was augmented to meet a great demand for souvenir spoons of all descriptions, and Mr. David Howe invented a process of etching upon metal which enabled both souvenir spoons and a new patented type of baby spoon to be inscribed with appropriate scenes and verses.[18] Sterling hollow ware was also produced in substantial quantities, with much of the effort in this line devoted to imposing trophy cups and statuary. Jackson's work in the designing-room was executed in the factory by Stephen Beckwith, the first sterling foreman. Beckwith was soon replaced by Alec Weir, a Scotsman of great ability, under whose direction the department rapidly increased in size and efficiency. By 1900 an entire factory building was being utilized for this branch of manufacture.

In addition to the growth of the sterling, hotel, and flatware lines, several other notable product developments occurred in the last forty years of the century. Reed & Barton did an extensive business in double-lined water pitchers, first patented in 1858 and extensively copied by other manufacturers. A great controversy arose in the trade regarding the harmful effects of metals upon liquids. Many customers complained that metal containers tainted the contents, while others maintained that metal poisoning was to be expected in the normal course of events. George Brabrook patented a papier-mâché lining, but this soon yielded to modern progress. In 1868 a china-lined pitcher was patented and placed on the market. This imposing article of tableware was highly praised in all quarters, and an extensive advertising campaign established it as one of the best known of Reed & Barton products. Massachusetts State Assayer, S. Dana Hayes, reported that "water remains cold, and ice keeps, nearly one third (or exactly 26 7/10 per cent) longer in your pitchers than they will in double walled pitchers made in the old way . . . ," and that in the Reed & Barton pitcher all danger to health was removed because liquids could in no way come in contact with metal.[19]

Another new idea which achieved great success in the 1870's and encouraged many imitators was the patent cutting-tined fork, the patent for which was acquired by Reed & Barton in 1869. This fork was designed with a sturdy cutting edge and was advertised as a combination knife and fork. While this article was building up a substantial sales volume, attractive associations of glass and silver began to find a market. Much beautiful glassware was imported from France and England to be fitted into electroplated metal frames in Taunton. Reed & Barton also acquired a considerable reputation for enameled and gilt hollow ware.

Changing social customs continued to be closely echoed in the Reed & Barton line, and in the 1880's the venerable castor set began to disappear from the fashionable tables of New York society.[20] When individual salts and peppers began to sell, the eventual end of another American household tradition was presaged. The table of 1880 was not to be devoid of an impressive centerpiece, however, for the spot vacated by the castor was promptly occupied by the epergne. In the manufacture of this article of elegance Reed & Barton spared neither expense nor

ELECTROPLATED, PORCELAIN-LINED WATER PITCHER, REED & BARTON
One of the best-selling items in the company line through the 1870's

EPERGNE, REED & BARTON, FROM THE 1885 CATALOGUE
Symbol of luxurious living and a peak in contemporary design

effort. For those who could afford one, the Reed & Barton grand epergne was the climactic symbol of sumptuous living.

TECHNICAL PROGRESS

As might be expected, the great diversity of products and the changes in style and fashion owed their origin in many cases to new manufacturing techniques. Henry Reed remained keenly interested in new results and in new ways of achieving old results; consequently many changes occurred in the factory. One of the most important of these transpired over a period of years in the burnishing department. This operation as it was originally practised in the factory was a throwback to the days of hand craftsmanship. As late as 1877 a force of sixty or more men and women were wielding their steel and agate tools by hand, with the consummate skill imparted by long practice. One old-timer eloquently described the work of this period with the proud remark, "When a Reed & Barton burnisher finished off a tray, a fly would break its legs trying to walk across it!" [21] The high cost of hand-burnishing was inappropriate, however, to a mass-production age. However superior in final results the process might be, the pressure of competitive practice gradually forced its abandonment. Burnishing on a lathe was rapid and economical, and Reed & Barton finished many of its wares in this fashion. Usual practice was to lathe-burnish all plain surfaces of an article, and then turn it over to a hand-burnisher, who "picked out" the spots which could not be reached on the lathe. Flatware was burnished mechanically by an ingenious machine which guided burnishing tools over the ware and finished several pieces simultaneously. Lathe-burnishing was limited, however, to ware with a relatively large expanse of plain surface, and a more universally applicable substitute was sought. Although much hand- and lathe-burnishing continued to be done, buffing gradually became the accepted finishing technique in the industry. The change resulted from one of those not too common occasions when modern progress failed, while lowering costs, to improve quality. The end of hand-burnishing on a large scale was a genuine, though unavoidable, loss to the silverware industry.[22]

American metal-working machinery in general was radically improved in design and performance throughout the 1870's and to the end of the century.[23] The development of high-speed steel

A SECTIONAL CHUCK.

An Invention of Lasting Importance

in Philadelphia paved the way for a great machine-tool industry. Agricultural implements, typewriters, and hardware were becoming increasingly efficient. "Standardization of machine parts, enabling speedy replacements and repairs, also became more general, and metal was worked to a much finer gage than before."[24] The skill of American watch factories in mass-production methods startled Europeans and deprived Swiss exporters of many of their markets.[25] This great progress was a feature of the silverware industry as well, and in no other period in Reed & Barton's history were so many new techniques put into practice in the factory. Many of these were discarded; others survived to form the basis for present-day operations.

Early in the 1870's N. B. Leonard, whose association with the company went back to the days of Babbitt, Crossman & Company, is said to have invented the sectional chuck. This seemingly simple type of collapsible wooden mold revolutionized spinning operations, was immediately adopted by the whole industry, and is in use today as an indispensable part of the spinner's equipment. Metal articles could be spun over and around the chuck, which was then collapsed by removal of a center pin and extracted piece by piece from the interior of the completed vessel.

Many new devices were evolved for ornamenting the surfaces of silverware, one of the most important of which was patented by Henry Reed in 1871. Explaining the old and new processes of ornamenting ware, the patent stated: [26]

It is well known to those skilled in the art that gold, silver, and plated-ware has always heretofore been partially finished, then engraved or chased by hand at great cost of time and labor, as well as risk of injuring the articles, and burnished and finished afterward.

. . . . The process which I am about to describe is one which is now in practical operation in Reed & Barton's manufactory in Taunton, Massachusetts, and by which it has been demonstrated that not only can a superior article of manufacture be produced, but it can be produced in so incredibly short a time as actually to diminish the expense of such ornamentation to less than one-twentieth (1/20) part of what it has been up to the present time, and, of course, to enable the manufactured article to be sold at a correspondingly reduced price.

The main feature of Reed's invention was the transference of designs to already burnished and polished ware from steel dies. The article to be ornamented was placed firmly on a polished steel bed or rest, and in that position the die, having the design upon its face, was applied by means of a drop-press. Reed &

Barton also acquired, about this time, a patent from James H. Reilly, of Brooklyn, New York, for a "satin-finish" process which was very popular in the trade. This patent covered the use of a revolving wheel of jointed wire needles, which produced the dull finish desired by inflicting a multitude of tiny scratches upon the surface of ware with which it came in contact.[27]

In the plating department many great improvements were effected, foremost of which was the substitution, about 1874, of an electromagnetic battery for the old Smee galvanic battery with its cumbersome paraphernalia of jars, plates, acids, and smells. By 1878 three dynamos had been installed in the Reed for certain types of ware. His patent was based upon the dis-& Barton factory for generating electricity, and the plating-room was considered as modern as any the industry boasted.[28] Howell W. Wright directed plating operations during the 1860's and contributed a process of "bright plating" which was widely used covery that if white metal was polished before plating, the silver would be deposited in a very fine state of division, so that when the ware was removed from the plating bath it retained its original brilliant surface and required little polishing or burnishing.[29] Nickel silver, however, brought unfamiliar problems to the Reed & Barton plating-room. Old, haphazard methods of mixing solutions proved inadequate, and the company experienced many difficulties. When, in 1872, teaware started coming out of the plating vats colored black, Reed & Barton decided that it was time to hire a chemist. On a trip from England, Charles Minchew stopped to visit in Taunton, and one evening brought his supper in to the factory to eat with a friend employed there. The visit was a long one, for Minchew was hired on the spot as chemist and served the company well until his retirement many years later. Minchew's first move was to inspect the plating vats. He found them to be rubber-lined, and deduced the fact that electrolysis was drawing the sulphur from the rubber, and that the sulphur was discoloring the wares in the bath. Cement vats were immediately installed and the difficulty disappeared. Minchew even saved the solutions themselves by devising means of removing the sulphurous infiltration.[30]

Technical improvements in methods of producing flatware were probably more prolific than those in any other branch of silverware manufacture. Developments in this line can be traced best, perhaps, by studying the evolution of spoon-making. Spoons originally were made almost entirely by hand. Whatever ornamentation was desired was produced by engraving or by striking the handles on flat dies with a hammer held in the hand. William Gale, who commenced business in 1821, invented a process of cutting ornaments on rollers and running the spoons through them to receive the pattern impression. This method was succeeded by the drop hammer, and flatware began to be made from flat dies, both the upper and lower dies containing the ornament.[31] Early Reed & Barton flatware was produced by this method. Through the 1860's, however, flatware-fabricating techniques remained relatively slow and crude. As late as 1862 the Gorham Manufacturing Company, for example, was shaping spoon bowls by laying the blank on a lead matrix of the proper form, resting the edge of a rounded steel punch upon it, and giving the punch a powerful blow with a sledge hammer.[32] In the 1890's the shaped die came into universal use, which gave shape to the flatware at the same time that it rendered the pattern. In this decade many process improvements were patented in the Reed & Barton factory. In 1895 Elijah Tolman invented a device for heating the end of the flatware, which was to be struck with a pattern die while at the same time keeping the remainder of the article water-cooled. In this manner the temper of the spoon or fork shaft was maintained.[33] Elijah Tolman, moreover, appears to have first begun hot stamping in the factory, probably in the early 1890's. In the manufacture of hollow handles for knives, a number of ingenious devices were patented by Reed & Barton men for securing the halves of the handles together and to the blade. George Brabrook himself devoted some time to the manufacture of flatware, and in 1898 patented a silver inlay invention for plated forks and spoons. This invention consisted of hollowing

PLATED SYRUP PITCHER, No. 2200, REED & BARTON

out the base metal of the article to be plated at the points of greatest wear and inserting a block of solid silver.[34]

For a product of an artistic nature, production in the Reed & Barton factory had become surprisingly well standardized. Operations were subdivided, and a high degree of specialization prevailed. Henry Reed kept careful account of each step in the manufacturing process. His personal record books tell in detail how each piece of ware in the factory was assembled and also give the direct labor costs of each operation. Table 12 illustrates the typical sequence of operations and the labor cost of each.

TABLE 12

SEQUENCE OF OPERATIONS, WITH LABOR COST OF EACH OPERATION, FOR
SPECIFIC ITEM, APRIL 1, 1875 [a]

REED & BARTON

	Direct Labor Cost in Cents	
Casting:		
Plate metal	0.75¢	
Handle	0.17	
Spout	0.20	
Joint	0.50	
Tip (2 parts)	0.35	
4 Lion feet	0.67	2.64¢
Rolling:		
Plate	1.25¢	1.25¢
Press Room:		
Stamping body	0.40¢	
Stamping cover	0.30	
4 circular parts	0.34	1.04¢
Lathe Work:		
Body spinning, first chuck	1.00¢	
Body spinning, sectional chuck	1.00	
Body turning	1.75	
Cover seat, making, fitting, etc.	0.75	
Cover seat, trimming off edge	0.25	
Cover ring, spinning	0.30	
Ball for tip, turning	0.25	
Plate, spinning & turning on chuck	3.00	8.30¢
Bench Work:		
Handle, scraping	0.40¢	
Handle, fitting on	0.80	
4 feet scraping	0.80	
4 feet scraping to solder	0.80	
2 plain mounts, cutting up	0.20	
Swallow tail, scraping & fitting to solder	0.20	
Spout, scraping	0.20	
Spout, fitting to body & cutting spout hole	1.60	
Spout cover, rough cutting	0.35	

```
Spout cover, dressing off .........................  0.50
Joint, fitting  ...................................  0.56
Top legs, scraping, etc ...........................  0.40          6.81¢
```

Soldering:
```
2 wire mounts  ...............................  0.20¢
Cover seat in body ...........................  0.75
Cover ring on  ...............................  0.30
4 feet on  ...................................  3.00
Handle on  ...................................  1.00
Spout on  ....................................  1.00
Joint to cover & ball  .......................  1.00
Spout cover on  ..............................  0.30
Tip & ball on  ...............................  0.50
Plate on  ....................................  0.75
Hole in handle up  ...........................  0.20          9.00¢
```

Buffing:
```
4 feet .......................................  1.00¢
Handle  ......................................  1.25
Spout  .......................................  0.75
Joint ........................................  0.25
For plating ..................................  4.00          7.25¢
```

```
Washing:  .....................................  1.50¢          1.50¢
```

```
Papering:  ....................................  1.50¢          1.50¢
```

```
Examining for Plating: ........................  1.00¢          1.00¢
```

```
        Total direct labor cost per unit ............          40.29¢
```

Direct material costs in cents:
```
Paper ........................................  2.00¢
Metal, 1 lb., 2 oz. ..........................  37.33          39.33¢
```

```
        Total direct labor and material cost per unit,
        exclusive of plating .....................          79.62¢
```

```
Retail selling price ..............................            $5.50
```

a Syrup pitcher No. 2200.
Source: Reed & Barton Mss., Piece rates 1862 and 1876. Not an exact quotation.

THE MODELING ROOM.

The Factory in Operation, 1878

FILLING ·THE MOULD.

THE MOULD AND PLATE.

THE FACTORY IN OPERATION, 1878

Factory Organization

The organization of the factory, which prior to 1860 had been partially on a product and partially on a process basis, evolved almost entirely to a product basis. Nickel silver, sterling, plated white metal, and other product divisions were largely separate from one another, each with its own spinners, solderers, casters, and foremen. A superintendent exercised general direction of the whole factory and reported to Henry Reed, though Reed himself was constantly in the factory and assumed many of the detailed functions of management.

Accounting Procedure

The minute breakdown of operations in the factory suggests accurate and detailed costing. This was actually the case in so far as direct labor costs were concerned, as shown by Henry Reed's operation analyses. Each department boss kept his own records of piece rates and hours worked, from which payrolls were computed. The only material which was charged into production on the basis of actual amounts used was metal. This was charged in, however, at a standard price which had little relation to current market values, and no reserve accounts were utilized to carry the difference between actual and standard costs. To the intense annoyance of his salesmen and some of the foremen, George Brabrook, who supervised the costing, habitually placed a value on the metal used far above either the current market price or the price the company had paid for it. The inflated cost resulting from such a practice, Brabrook felt, was an excellent cushion against the inevitable cuts in the price of the finished article forced on him by company salesmen and competitive action. All costs of manufacturing, other than the direct labor and metal costs, and all administrative and selling costs were considered as overhead. No further attempt was made to assign them to different products or departments, nor was

CHART VI
Process Chart of the Reed & Barton Factory, 1880

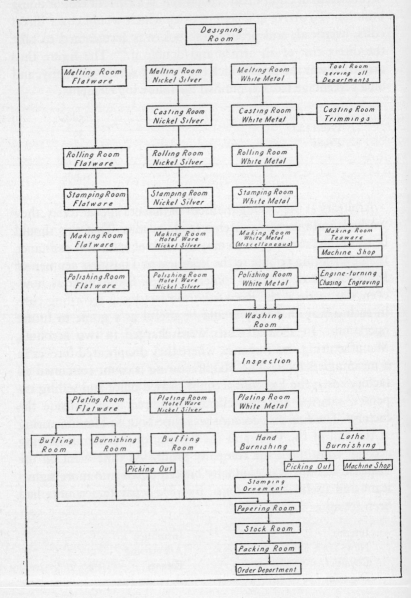

depreciation of equipment recognized as a current cost of doing business. To arrive at a selling price which would cover direct costs, overhead, and profit, Brabrook was accustomed to take the direct cost of an article and double it.[35] The figure thus arrived at was the price which the dealer paid the company, and on a percentage basis, contained the following elements:

Direct costs 50%
Overhead 30
Profit 20
                                            ———
                                            100%

Arbitrary as the costing methods of that era appear today, they worked, and business concerns made profits. That this should be so in the face of such a complete lack of statistical assistance is an everlasting tribute to the keenness and business acumen of Brabrook, Reed, and their contemporaries. Some progress, however, was made at the Reed & Barton factory in recording costs in such a way that they would be useful as a guide to future operations. In 1860 all costs were charged to two accounts, Manufacturing and Expense, where they disappeared forever in a meaningless total. The Manufacturing account contained all factory costs; the Expense account carried office and selling expenses, salaries, and miscellaneous indirect costs outside the factory. The Expense account was closed out to Manufacturing at the end of the year, and the balance of the Manufacturing account constituted the company profit. As time went on the Expense account was gradually broken down into more significant and useful subdivisions. By 1870 separate accounts had been set up as follows: [36]

Interest	Insurance
New York Office	Advertising
Royalties	Patents
Discount	Revenue Tax

By 1900 the following had been added: [37]

Attorneys	Philadelphia Office
Building	Chicago Office
Payroll	New York Office–Union Square
Charity	New York Office–Maiden Lane
Liability Insurance	Supplies
Fire Insurance	Selling Expense
Commissions	Packing and Shipping

Little progress was made, however, in analyzing manufacturing costs, and throughout the whole period cost-consciousness was noticeably lacking in the factory. This factor was closely allied with the high-quality standards in force. A detail which might double the cost of an item was not rejected when it made possible a better product.[38] Thousands of dollars were spent in the production of superbly wrought dies, many of which are still in use today. Many innovations were so costly that the company could never hope to profit by them, and yet such methods returned much to the company in the form of an enhanced market reputation. It might almost be said that the most effective advertising expenditures made by Reed & Barton at that time were made within the confines of the factory walls.

Every phase of the product history of the 1860–1900 period reflected the drive to produce wares of universally high quality. The equipment to accomplish this end was immeasurably improved, and that improvement constitutes tangible proof of the brilliant careers of many men. The growth of Reed & Barton through these forty years, as through the years preceding 1860, was essentially a democratic process, the result of joint efforts from every section of the factory and at every level of management from front office to workbench. The essence of manufacturing progress was loyalty to company ideals on the part of the workmen of Reed & Barton, and a careful cultivation of the talents of those men by an alert management.

CHAPTER XIII

LABOR, MANAGEMENT, AND A FINANCIAL CRISIS
1860–1901

THE MANAGEMENT OF MEN

MAURICE MCCARTHY, the elder, was a kind of odd-jobs man about the Reed & Barton factory. A devoted son of the "Auld Sod," his presence added color to the maintenance department for many years. Maurice, however, was an inveterate pipe smoker. After being repeatedly admonished not to smoke during working hours, Maurice was discharged. The next day he was back on the job — with his pipe. The matter was referred to the highest authority. Henry Reed walked out into the factory yard and told Maurice that he did not want to fire him, but that smoking was prohibited and he would have to comply with the rules. Squinting one eye, Maurice replied, "Mr. Reed, shure it's not what you put in your mouth that causes trouble in this world — it's what comes out." Reed looked thoughtful for a moment and then remarked that there was some real philosophy in that contention. Maurice stayed on the job and continued to smoke his pipe with impunity.[1]

There were very few factory rules that were not subject to revision under the pressure of extenuating circumstances. Of such circumstances Henry Reed was final arbiter, and appeal to him was neither difficult nor infrequent. The administration of labor was Reed's province and he performed his delicate functions in this field with fairness, tact, kindness, and conspicuous success.

Reed's task of personnel administration grew with the size of the working force. In the space of forty years employment doubled, tripled, and doubled again. The number of employees grew from 125 in 1860 to 336 in 1865, 425 in 1871, 500 in 1878, and 800 in 1887. Yet Reed maintained his personal contact with the factory people, and not only called most of them by name, but retained a prodigious amount of information about individual peculiarities and family circumstances. Reed insisted upon examining the character and background of each applicant for a job, and Taunton tradition noted the difficulty of obtaining employment at Reed & Barton's. Meticulous selection combined with fair treatment to produce a talented and devoted group of men and women in the factory.

The story of the Reed & Barton working force between 1860 and 1901 has survived both in company books and in the memory of living men. Parts of the record are missing, but many details and most of the general trends can be noted. In respect to the latter, the situation in the Reed & Barton factory does not deviate far from that of industry in general. Company employees experienced rising money wages to 1873 and a sharp decline thereafter, coupled with living costs which rose faster than wages to 1873 and declined more slowly after that time. The working day was shortened, and a vigorous new class of men and women began to be employed in the factory.

The average daily earnings of Reed & Barton employees increased steadily to 1873, when severe depression reversed the trend and instituted a steady decline which terminated only in the late 1880's.

Several comparisons can be drawn between Reed & Barton earnings and earnings in other industries in Massachusetts. These comparisons reveal the fact that the earnings of Reed & Barton employees occupied a middle position, substantially exceeding those in low-wage industries, but not equaling the average earnings in the highly paid metal trades.

An examination of living expenses over this period (1860–83) reveals the fact that the Reed & Barton wage increases up to 1873

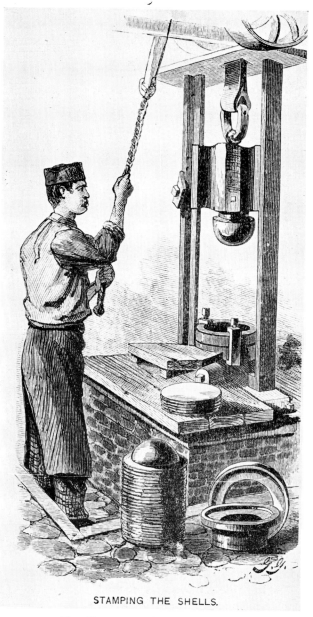

STAMPING THE SHELLS.

The Factory in Operation, 1878

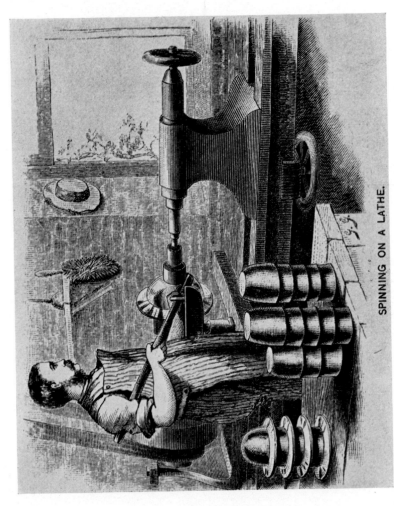

SPINNING ON A LATHE.

THE FACTORY IN OPERATION, 1878

were probably more than absorbed, and that employees were actually able to buy less with their money in the early 1870's than they had been able to buy with much less money in 1860. After

TABLE 13

AVERAGE DAILY EARNINGS, ALL REED & BARTON EMPLOYEES, 1860–1883

Year	Earnings
1860	$1.12
1867	1.46
1870	2.09
1875	1.82
1883	1.37

Source: Reed & Barton Mss., Total payroll divided by number of employees.

1873, moreover, money wages declined faster than living costs, rendering these years of deep depression doubly difficult. By 1883, however, a much more favorable ratio between money wages and cost of living prevailed.

TABLE 14

GENERAL AVERAGE WEEKLY WAGES IN MASSACHUSETTS, 1860–1883

Industry or Company	1860	1875	1883
Reed & Barton	$6.72	$10.92	$8.22
Metals and Metallic Goods	9.07	13.16	11.25
Clocks and Watches	....	14.38	11.28
Electroplating	....	14.35	....
Cotton Goods	6.50	7.01	6.45
Woolen Goods	5.38	7.76	6.90

Source: Reed & Barton figures from company Mss., Payroll records; other figures, Massachusetts Bureau of Statistics of Labor, *Sixteenth Annual Report*, 1885, part 3, pp. 128–133.

It can be seen from Tables 14 and 15 that, although money wages of Reed & Barton employees were lower than in the metals and metallic goods industries, real wages increased from 1860 to 1883 by nearly the same percentage in both cases.

Little evidence exists by which a comparison can be drawn between Reed & Barton wages and those in other factories in the industry. Table 16 presents one series of comparisons, but the information is so limited in scope that the results should be considered as suggestive rather than conclusive.

The Reed & Barton average daily wage rates compare favor-

TABLE 15

PERCENTAGE CHANGES IN WAGES — REED & BARTON AND A MASSACHUSETTS AVERAGE — AND CERTAIN ITEMS OF LIVING EXPENSES, 1860–1883

	Percentage Change 1860–1872[a]	Percentage Change 1872–1883[b]	Percentage Change 1860–1883
Average weekly earnings, Reed & Barton employees	+86.61	−34.45	+22.32
Average weekly wage, metals and metallic goods industry[c]	+71.10	−27.52	+24.04
Prices of Groceries	+32.24	−16.81	+10.01
Prices of Provisions	+50.60	−10.16	+35.30
Prices of Fuel	+55.12	−29.22	+ 9.79

[a] For Reed & Barton, period ends with 1870.
[b] For Reed & Barton, period begins with 1870.
[c] Computed.

Source: Massachusetts Bureau of Statistics of Labor, *Sixteenth Annual Report,* 1885, part 3, pp. 130–131, 146; Reed & Barton figures from Reed & Barton Mss., Payroll records.

ably with those in other industries, indicating that when Reed & Barton men and women were employed full time their earnings tended to approximate those in the highly paid industries. The contrast between rates (Table 17) and earnings (Table 13) should be carefully noted. Actually, the Reed & Barton average earnings figures in Tables 13, 14, and 16 are conservative, for they are lowered by the inclusion of apprentice and part-time earnings. This downward bias is not corrected by the fact that overtime earnings are also included, for in this period of frequent depression overtime pay was much less common than

CASTING THE HANDLES.

The Factory in Operation, 1878

SOLDERING ON THE TRIMMINGS.

THE FACTORY IN OPERATION, 1878

part-time pay. The averages given for earnings were substantially exceeded by regular, full-time employees. It is, therefore, desirable to consider wage rates in addition to earnings. Average

TABLE 16

Comparison of Average Weekly Wages by Occupations, Reed & Barton Employees and Silverware Workers in Rhode Island, 1869

	Reed & Barton	R. I. Silverware Workers
Burnishers	$14.94	$16.50
Polishers	15.90	13.25
Spoon & Fork Makers	16.80	18.00
Rollers	12.24	13.50
Diesinkers	24.66	26.00
Foremen	41.10	31.75

Source: Edward Young, *Cost of Labor and Subsistence in the United States for the Year 1869, as Compared with Previous Years* (Washington, 1870), p. 37; Reed & Barton figures from Employee pay accounts.

TABLE 17

Average Daily Rates, Reed & Barton Employees and Certain Other Workers, 1860–1888

Company or Trade	1860	1870	1880	1883	1888
Reed & Barton Factory Average	$1.86	$2.41	$1.67	$2.13	$2.22
Machinists in Massachusetts	1.65	2.66	2.16	2.22	2.24
Iron Molders in Massachusetts	1.59	2.63	2.08	2.43	2.10

Source: U. S. Bureau of Labor Statistics, Bulletin No. 604, *History of Wages in the United States from Colonial Times to 1928* (Washington, 1934), pp. 299–302, 311–314; Reed & Barton figures from Reed & Barton Mss., Payroll records.

rates usually differed from average earnings because the rates represented only what the company promised to pay for a day's work. Wage-rate figures do not reflect the number of days or the number of hours per day actually worked, as do earnings figures. Considered in conjunction with one another, rates and earnings present a reasonably complete picture of wages in the Reed & Barton factory.

In considering Table 17 we should note that the Reed &
Barton average wage rate is composed of all trades in the factory and encompasses many low-wage groups such as watchmen
and maintenance crews. Even with this handicap, however, the
Reed & Barton average daily wage rate compares favorably with
those of the highly paid machinists' and molders' trades.

Throughout several protracted periods of depression between
1860 and 1895 many Reed & Barton employees worked only
on a part-time basis. Layoff policies, however, were relatively
mild. The company philosophy appeared to be that it was better
to retain a large number of workers on part time than a small
number full time. Only during the early years of the Civil War
was employment at Reed & Barton's sharply curtailed. The
number of employees declined from 138 in April, 1860, to 40 in
July, 1861, but this decline appears to have been the result of
enlistments rather than of layoffs resulting from depressed business. E. W. Porter tells of men who reported for work as usual
at seven o'clock in the morning and who, at eleven o'clock that
same morning, were on board flatcars with Captain Gordon's
company en route to Washington, "so sudden had been the call,
and so prompt the response." [2] With this exception, however,
employment was surprisingly stable for such difficult years as
followed, and the number of workers appears to have varied
much less than did the volume of sales. The comparison between employment and sales (as shown in Chart VII) is particularly illuminating for the 1871–75 period, which included
years of prosperity, panic, and depression.

As in the case of the 1837–1860 period, considerable information about company wage policies can be gained by studying
certain departments which furnish data not available for the
company as a whole. In the 1860–1900 period, moreover, certain
individual pay records can be followed with profit.

Earnings in the polishing department illustrate the sharp upward climb in wages to 1873 and the subsequent decline. The

ENGINE-TURNING.

THE FACTORY IN OPERATION, 1878

THE BURNISHER.

The Factory in Operation, 1878

figures in Table 18 also reveal the greatly increased earning power of women employees after 1860.

Because averages, in spite of statistical precautions, reflect the

CHART VII

VOLUME OF SALES AND NUMBER OF EMPLOYEES, BY MONTHS,
1871–1875, REED & BARTON

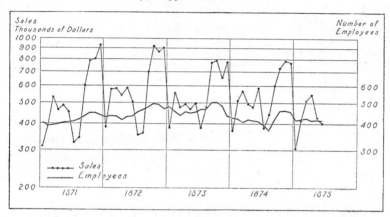

large number of part-time employees in the frequent depressions which occurred between 1865 and 1900, it is of interest and value to trace the wage records of certain regular, full-time workers. For this purpose, the average daily wages of three

TABLE 18

AVERAGE DAILY EARNINGS, REED & BARTON POLISHING-ROOM, 1858–1875

	1858	1865	1870	1875
Men	$1.02	$1.89	$2.59	$2.04
Women	.65	1.25	....	1.00

Source: Reed & Barton Mss., Payroll records.

employees, Harriet Johnson and David Buffington, polishers, and Orin F. Bacon, lathe-burnishing boss, have been selected as representative.

TABLE 19

AVERAGE DAILY EARNINGS OF THREE REED & BARTON EMPLOYEES, 1858–1888

Date[a]	Harriet Johnson	David B. Buffington	Orin F. Bacon[b]
1858	$ .87	$ .77	....
1859	1.33	1.53	....
1860	1.34	.83	....
1861	.68	Laid off	....
1862	1.50	.78	....
1863	1.62	Laid off or left	....
1864	1.61	1.40	....
1865	1.98	2.76	....
1866	1.59	3.35	....
1867[c]	1.12	2.68	$2.42
1868[c]	1.34	2.92	2.44
1869[c]	1.59	3.68	3.23
1870	1.23	3.43	2.60
1871	1.46	2.69	2.90
1872	1.32	3.19	2.94
1873	1.80	3.40	3.39
1874	1.51	2.83	3.47
1875	1.42	2.01	4.62
1876	....	....	4.86
1877	....	....	4.58
1878	....	....	5.11
1879	....	....	4.74
1880	....	....	4.67
1881	....	....	5.25
1882	....	....	4.88
1883	....	....	4.74
1884	....	....	4.86
1885	....	....	4.86
1886	....	....	4.60
1887	....	....	4.60
1888	....	....	4.98

[a] For September of given years.
[b] Bacon's rise to the position of foreman in his department more than offset the tendency of wages to decline after 1873.
[c] June.
Source: Reed & Barton Mss., Payrolls and Employees' Pay Accounts.

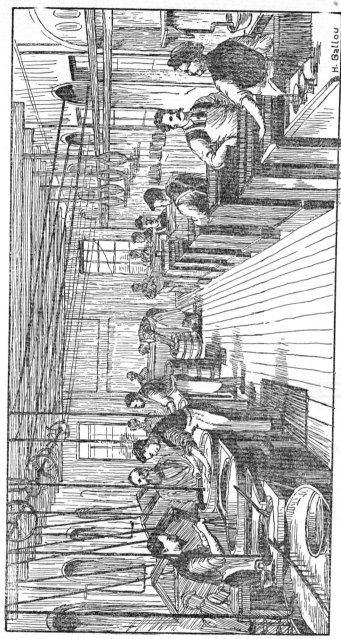

H. Ballou

The Reed & Barton Plating Room in 1879

In the burnishing department women employees continued to receive high pay, many of them exceeding the earnings of men in other departments. A sample week's work, chosen at random from the burnishing records, reveals rates, output, and earnings.

Foremen's pay increased rapidly after 1860. In 1875, in spite

TABLE 20

SAMPLE WEEK'S RECORD, REED & BARTON HAND-BURNISHER
(EMELINE BURBANK), JUNE 3–9, 1865

June 3	1	Basket, #1219	$1.00
	1	Frame	.75
June 6	1	Coffee, #1254	1.12
	1	Tea, #1254	1.00
	2	Waiters, #1836	.75
June 7	1	Waiter	.75
	1	Waiter, #1796	4.00
June 9	1	Shaped Dish & Lining	1.75
		Total Earnings for Week	$11.12

Source: Reed & Barton Mss., Burnishing Pay Records, 1864–65.

of severe depression, Reed & Barton foremen were receiving two and three times as much as in 1858 (see Chapter VII, p. 142).

Partners' salaries also increased sharply after 1860. In contrast to the $3.00 per day received by Henry Reed and Charles Barton in 1858, Reed, Brabrook, and Fish were receiving $500 per month by 1865. In 1888 Reed, Brabrook, and the Fish estate were each paid $1,000 per month, which continued until late in 1898, when Reed began to receive $1,500, Brabrook $1,250, and the Fish estate $995.[3]

Apprentices' wages experienced a sharp rise in the 1860–1901 period, although the practice of paying the apprentices' board was discontinued by the company. In 1870 one solderer's apprentice agreed to learn the trade in three years, wages being $1.25 per day for the first two years and $1.50 for the third. Full-time employment was guaranteed for the first two years, but in the third the boy agreed, "In case of poor trade to share with others in being out of work. . . ." [4] This rate of pay, however, was unusually high. In the 1880's many apprentices worked for three years at $0.75, $1.00, and $1.25 per day, respectively, employment not guaranteed. One apprentice agreement in 1892 called for a four-year term, the daily rate to be $0.50, $0.75, $0.87½, and $1.00. [5] Most of the apprentices appear to have been

TABLE 21
Reed & Barton Foremen's Average Daily Earnings
January, 1875

Wm. Parkin, boss diesinker	$6.20
W. C. Beattie, head designer	7.67
Nathan Lawrence, boss of teaware department	9.26
Burt Cady, boss hand-burnisher	6.59
W. A. Weeden, boss engraver	8.18
Orin F. Bacon, boss lathe-burnisher	3.86
Charles Minchew, boss plater	5.77
Elijah Tolman, boss of flatware department	6.96

Source: Reed & Barton Mss., Payroll, 1867–75.

sixteen or seventeen years of age, although some were only fifteen. The number of boys taken in to learn a trade varied considerably and depended more or less upon the prosperity of the business. Between 1870 and 1873, a period of good trade, thirty-five apprentices' names are recorded on the company books. During the 1874–78 depression, however, only one new apprentice's name appears. From 1880 to 1883, when trade was brisk, forty-nine apprentices were employed. In the succeeding two years, when business fell off, only two new apprentices appear to have been employed. [6]

In hours worked, Reed & Barton employees were better off than their fathers. In September, 1865, the working day was changed from eleven to ten hours. By this time the ten-hour day had become fairly general in industry, although exceptions were numerous and, particularly in Taunton, many companies did not discontinue the eleven- and twelve-hour day until several years later.[7] Times had changed in respect to holidays, as well. Reed & Barton employees appear to have worked on Christmas day in the early 1870's, but by 1880 the custom of closing shop on Fast Day (in April), July Fourth, Labor Day, Thanksgiving, and Christmas seems to have been observed.

Methods of wage payment and computation underwent few changes. In 1887 wages were paid weekly, in compliance with a Massachusetts law passed the preceding year. Overtime pay was computed at regular rates, but accident compensation and continuing pay while employees were disabled still remained the rule. Even in 1870 disability payments were by no means universal, and Reed & Barton workmen counted themselves particularly fortunate in this respect.[8] As in the past, no employee was discharged by reason of old age. Pensions were freely granted, and those who wished to remain active were given small tasks to do about the factory. Harriet Johnson, mentioned earlier in the chapter, was typical of this group. Altogether, she was in Reed & Barton's employ for sixty-two years. In her later days she was repeatedly offered a pension, and just as often she declined it. When she was unable to do even a semblance of a day's work, Mrs. Johnson selected and was granted a room on the third floor of one of the factory buildings. In it were placed a couch, two rocking chairs, a table, and two or three pictures. Each morning she was driven to work about nine-thirty, and escorted to her room by the office boy. There she insisted on rendering some service for her compensation, usually hemming the towels used in the factory washrooms. The owners of the business were "Henry" and "George" to her, and she never hesitated to volunteer her views regarding changes in the plant, regardless of whether or not those views were in accord with the management's own attitude. To the kindly meant suggestions that she retire, Mrs. Johnson would simply say, "I brought this firm up and I propose to stay with it until I die." She did.[9]

CLEANSING THE WARE

THE FACTORY IN OPERATION, 1878

Rules and Regulations.

1. Until further notice, the working time will be from 7 o'clock A. M. to 12 M., and from 1 to 6 o'clock P. M., making ten hours each day.

The whistle will blow at 6 o'clock A.M., at 15 minutes before 7 o'clock A. M., 5 minutes before 7, and 7 A. M., 15 minutes before 1 o'clock P.M.; also 5 minutes before 1 P.M. and at 1 P.M.

2. No time will be allowed for washing before 12 M., or before 6 P.M.

It is expected that all will be at their places in the mill promptly at 7 A.M. and at 1 P.M. and work the ten hours honestly and faithfully.

3 Each overseer is expected to be punctual himself, and to see that all employed in his room are in their places in proper season.

4. Overseers will see that all neglect of work, or damage to work, machinery, or building, that is the result of neglect, is reported at the Office.

5. Any one wishing to be absent will report to the Overseer.

6. No visiting of other rooms in working hours, except on necessary business, is allowed.

7. Pay-day will be on the 15th of each month, or the 14th if Sunday comes the 15th.

8. All peddling, smoking, and snow-balling upon the premises are strictly forbidden.

REED & BARTON.

C. A. Hack & Son, Printers, Taunton.

FACTORY RULES AND REGULATIONS, ABOUT 1880

Many practices of earlier days survived in the factory after 1860. Among them was that of the employees' keeping their own time records. William Morris, the gateman, reported workers who were late and his book was checked against that of Elijah Tolman, Jr., who went through the plant each day and recorded the time each workman reported he had worked the preceding day. During the great Taunton flood of 1887 the maintenance crew worked night and day reinforcing the factory buildings and repairing damage. As one of this group, Maurice McCarthy become involved in a considerable argument with Tolman over his previous day's work. In giving his time Maurice reported that he had worked "thwenty-five hours" the previous day. When the startled Elijah told him that this was impossible because there were only twenty-four hours in a day, McCarthy answered, "Sure, I know that, but I worked me noon hour, too." [10]

Except for the apprentices no definite wage scales were established in the factory. Wages were a matter of individual bargaining, and the primary determinant of a man's pay was his length of service. A young man turning out ten pieces a day, as compared with one of his older associates who produced eight, could not offer the additional production as reason for an increase to the older man's level of wages.[11] Productive ability was not ignored, but had to be coupled with experience. The element of cost was not defined to a point where mere extra production was a vital consideration. This attitude on the part of management tended to encourage careful, painstaking work rather than speed. In justice to Henry Reed it should be pointed out that never was he accused of unfairness, and few inequitable situations in the factory wage system remained long. His strictness in granting increases to young men became progressively less as they grew older and proved their worth beyond all doubt.

Key to the management of labor were the foremen — outstanding figures in the factory and absolute rulers of their departments. This era of foreman rule was one of the most remarkable in the managerial history of Reed & Barton, persisting from post-Civil-War years until well into the twentieth century. In the first place, the foreman was a master of his trade. Not only was he the head of the department, but usually he was the best workman in it. That, indeed, constituted the main reason why he had been chosen boss, for one of his most vital responsibilities was the quality of the work performed. Second, and most important in the development of the foreman's high position in the factory, his initiative and independence were strongly encouraged by the owners. The foremen directed production, scheduled orders, dictated methods, hired and fired employees (with Reed's approval), made wage changes, ordered tools, equipment, and materials, decided how much ware to produce for stock, and passed judgment upon new designs. One of the functions of Reed and Brabrook was to ensure coöperation between foremen. In many cases this was no easy task, for these czars of production exhibited highly individualistic tendencies and brooked little interference from anyone. On one occasion superintendent Nathan Lawrence objected to some process which Charles Minchew, boss plater, was using. One word borrowed another. Finally Minchew ordered Lawrence out, and told him he would kick him out if he came into the department again that month. Lawrence immediately reported the incident to George Brabrook. Thinking it over a moment Brabrook replied, "Well, Mr. Lawrence, the foreman of the plating-room has the reputation of carrying through with his word. If I were you, I think I should keep out of that department for the rest of the month." [12]

Authority was not a casual matter with the foremen, and their sense of responsibility and importance in many cases bordered almost on the pompous. On all occasions they deported themselves with great dignity, and the foremen customarily reported for work attired in silk hats, cutaway coats, and attendant

Maurice McCarthy: a Company Tradition

THE REED & BARTON FIRE BRIGADE, ABOUT 1890

accessories. Men in the departments always were careful to address their bosses with a respectful "Mr." Because the foremen were chosen for ability and experience rather than for their qualities of leadership, a certain amount of friction occurred both in and between departments. Only once in the entire history of Reed & Barton did a serious labor dispute occur, and this dispute arose over the dictatorial attitude of one of the foremen. One Saturday morning in June, 1895, fourteen men from the hollow-ware burnishing department marched in a body to the front office to complain of ill usage and low pay. Henry Reed confronted them. "Is this a strike?"

"No, Mr. Reed."

"Then go back to work and we'll see about this." [13]

Two days later the foreman was a sadder but wiser man. The burnishers were materially richer, and the Taunton *Gazette* commented that "The firm, always liberal and just, have even outdone themselves in arranging . . . the difficulty." [14] With such infrequent exceptions the foremen commanded the whole-hearted respect, and even affection, of their men. They were as fine a group as could be found in any factory, and they constituted the backbone of the factory organization.

The system of foreman supremacy at its worst produced a few petty feuds and misunderstandings, and in occasional non-co-operative moments friction between department heads slowed production. The feuds in question were considered the inevitable accompaniment to artistic temperaments; the slowing-down was not deemed important in an age when speed was subservient to quality. At its best the system produced work of superb quality and provided the growing number of new employees with a rigorous schooling in the Reed & Barton traditions.

The retirement of Charles Minchew, one of the last of the old bosses, symbolized the passing of a colorful era in company management. By arrangement, the day he finished his work a coach was ordered to meet him at the factory gate. The employees lined up from the door of the plating-room to the gate. About five minutes past six, Minchew, an impressive figure with his flowing white beard and aristocratic bearing, stepped out on the arm of his son, Percy. As he wended his way to the gate the workmen applauded. When he reached the coach Minchew turned, doffed his top hat, and bowed low to the company he had served so well.[15]

By 1885 it must have appeared that the "Old Guard" was passing as great expansion brought new faces and age emptied long-occupied benches. Only Henry Reed, Deacon Burbank, Luther Babbitt, N. B. Leonard, William Thayer, and Alfred Brabrook could recall the uncertain beginning of the firm of Leonard, Reed & Barton in 1837. Native residents viewed with some uneasiness an influx of fresh, vigorous blood from England, Ireland, Scotland, and Canada. This influx had begun to be felt in force in Taunton as early as 1855 and in the Reed & Barton factory soon thereafter. In 1855, of a total Taunton population of 13,477, foreign-born residents numbered 3,381.[16] By 1870 the textile mills were employing a far higher percentage of foreign-born than of native help.[17] Many of Irish and Canadian extraction found a place in the Reed & Barton factory in the 1880's and 1890's. Most of the first arrivals assumed common laboring jobs, but energy, initiative, and a disposition to work long and hard brought prompt rewards. Henry Reed showed no prejudice in favor of his native Taunton families, and the factory soon lost its almost exclusively native-stock character. To those who doubted, it was indeed proved, however, that the old customs were not passing. Just as the handful of men and women who witnessed the founding of the enterprise had worked long and faithfully to establish traditions, so the new workmen of all nationalities stayed on and worked just as faithfully, until they themselves were referred to by a subsequent generation as the "Old Guard."

Changes in Ownership and Management, 1860–1900

While the character and personnel of the factory were undergoing many alterations, so too did the nature and constituent interests of the Reed & Barton partnership change, although to a lesser degree. On September 13, 1867, Charles Barton was stricken while on his way home from the factory, and died shortly afterward with Henry Reed at his bedside. Barton's place in the partnership is difficult to appraise, for he was a shadowy figure whose participation in the affairs of the concern was limited by ill health. His contribution is easy to underestimate, for it was not manifest in the direction of any important phase of the business. Barton appears, however, to have exerted a profound influence over Henry Reed, and this friendship cemented the partnership in the precarious early years. Barton was the conciliator, and held a high place in the esteem of the men. It seems probable that he was at least as close to the factory workers as was Reed himself. Much of the harmony that prevailed in the factory must be ascribed to Barton's presence there, and the beneficial results of his quiet existence lived long after the man.

Barton's death terminated the partnership as then constituted, and Reed, Brabrook, and Fish negotiated with Barton's widow, Amanda, for the purchase of the Barton interest. Eventual settlement of all claims was effected by the payment of $102,081.25 to the Barton heirs.[18] After some further negotiations, permission was obtained to continue the Barton name in the firm title.[19] The surviving members of the partnership considered incorporation, and in 1868 even went so far as to have a set of bylaws and a charter framed.[20] For some reason this plan was abandoned, and in the same year a new partnership was formed. Henry Reed, Henry Fish, and George Brabrook each assumed a third-interest, and profits and losses were to be shared equally. The name of the firm was continued unchanged.

Shortly after this time Henry Fish gave up most of his Fall River banking and mercantile activities and moved to Taunton, assuming the duties of treasurer in the Reed & Barton organization until his death in 1882.

In the affairs of many concerns the transition from control by the founders to their sons and heirs has had profound repercussions, often presenting a managerial crisis of important dimensions. In the Reed & Barton firm there seemed to be no lack of candidates for their fathers' interests. George and Frank Fish, sons of Henry; Carleton and Hale Brabrook, sons of George; H. F. Reed, son of Henry; and Edward Barton, son of Charles — all were employed by the company at one time or another. H. F. Reed's premature death blasted any plans his father may have had for him, and Ed Barton's interest in the firm was disposed of long before he entered the company's employ. The Fish and Brabrook boys all served Reed & Barton in varying capacities and, in some cases, with moderate success. None, however, played a vital part in company affairs, and none showed a disposition to work together in such complete harmony as did their fathers. The large number of potential and actual heirs, moreover, threatened to split partnership interests into so many segments as to make effective administration difficult. Perhaps it was this factor which finally prompted the incorporation of the company in February, 1888. The capital of the Reed & Barton Corporation was fixed at $600,000, and the shares, of $100 each, subscribed to in the following amounts: [21]

Henry Reed ......2,000 shares	Jane Brackett ....200 shares	
George Brabrook ..2,000 "	Caroline Fish ....200 "	
Eliza A. Fish ....1,000 "	Frank L. Fish ....200 "	
George Fish ...... 200 "	James Eddy ⎱ Trustees 200 " Frank Fish ⎰	

The first meeting of the board of directors, composed of Frank Fish, George Brabrook, and Henry Reed, voted Henry Reed president of the corporation; George Brabrook, treasurer; and

Frank Fish, clerk. With incorporation were concluded all ownership and organizational changes until Henry Reed's death thirteen years later.

The Management of Finance, 1860–1901

From 1860 on, the management of financial affairs presented a series of difficult and often critical problems. Surprisingly enough, this struggle was less the outgrowth of the great uncertainties of general business than of internal company policies. A heavy strain was placed upon the resources of Reed & Barton by three major developments: the assumption of the Barton interest, real-estate and product expansion, and inventory speculation.

The period started inauspiciously with heavy losses in the early Civil War years, notably 1862. A favorable balance of cash was maintained, however, and the company's financial position remained strong. In 1863 and 1864 moderate profits appear to have been realized, and the company had practically no debts. A large building program was financed out of current earnings. In 1863 a three-story brick office building was constructed on the east bank of the river. Shortly afterwards a burnishing building was appended to the rear of the new offices, and a plating mill erected. Expansion continued through 1864 with the construction of a three-story brick building for a spoon and fork mill at the rear of the 1830 brick building on the west bank of the river. Several smaller structures were erected for various purposes, and the company purchased a large amount of land in Britanniaville upon which to build houses for the employees. By the end of the year, six cottages had been erected and rented. Subsequent construction assumed such dimensions as practically to eliminate a local housing shortage.

The 1863–64 expansion depleted company cash reserves, but the immensely profitable year of 1865 remedied the situation. Henry Reed's personal income tax returns for this year show, in addition to a $6,000 salary, undistributed profits from his share in the partnership to the amount of $32,405.[22] From 1864 to 1867 the partners' investment in the business was increased by undistributed earnings from $157,828.64 to $420,648.42.[23] Plant facilities continued to increase. The value of tools and equipment grew from $10,000.00 in 1864 to $36,000.00 in 1867, while over that same period the value of real estate increased $49,-637.84.[24]

In 1867 the purchase of Charles Barton's interest created a heavy liability, but in the three profitable years which followed, notes payable were whittled down to a normal amount. Few records have survived the 1870–88 period, but it is evident that tools, equipment, and real estate continued to expand even through the severe depression which followed 1873. By 1888 the partners' interest in the business exceeded half a million

TABLE 22

Recorded Loans to Reed & Barton for Selected Years, 1872–1879

Creditor	1872	1873	1874	1879
Taunton Savings Bank	$11,000	$26,000	$11,000	......
Henry G. Reed	39,000	75,000	54,000	$70,000
Bristol County Savings Bank	10,000	10,000	25,000	......
David Burns	10,600	7,000	......	......
Henry H. Fish	......	10,000	10,000	5,000
Total	$70,600	$128,000	$100,000	$75,000

Source: Reed & Barton Mss., Canceled checks.

dollars, a truly remarkable record of growth for the period.

In 1873 a three-story burnishing building was erected, adjoining the 1863 burnishing shop. Eight years later another three-story wing was built into this group to house the designing rooms and other departments.

Virtually no long-term debt had been incurred, although considerable short-term borrowing was resorted to in order to finance current operations and construction. There is no evidence that between 1860 and 1888 any dividends were paid; profits were left in the business to finance expansion.

Short-term loans to Reed & Barton were made either by the partners or by local banks and financiers. The very considerable sums loaned by Henry Reed, however, suggest that the creation of creditors outside the company was being scrupulously avoided.

The death of Henry Fish in 1882 was a genuine loss to the company, for his management of finances had been astute. Brabrook took over the position of treasurer at a time when problems in the field of sales alone were all one man could handle. His career in this office exhibited throughout a greater consciousness of market requirements than of the precepts of financial caution.

Brabrook's first great task in his new capacity was to finance the sterling line in 1889 and 1890. No estimate is possible of the investment required by this undertaking, but the dies, tools, materials, and initial promotion must have involved thousands of dollars. Taunton banks supplied most of this capital with loans which ran from six months to a year. In addition to this considerable investment, Brabrook began to speculate heavily in metal and supplies inventories. His first venture involved the purchase of large amounts of silver just prior to the passage of the Sherman Silver Purchase Act of 1890. Old employees tell of seeing the storage vaults piled to the roof with silver bars. Henry Reed protested vigorously, but in vain. The price of silver mounted rapidly, and Brabrook exultantly remarked to Reed, "Well, Henry, we're now using dollar-twenty silver that only cost us sixty cents!" [25]

Under the impetus of the investment and inventory purchases for the sterling line, notes payable increased from $86,500 in May, 1890, to $202,500 in October. Cash reserves declined from $6,057.01 in December, 1889, to a deficit of $3,372.44 in October,

1890.[26] An analysis of payables in 1890 shows loans made to the company as follows: [27]

Taunton Savings Bank	$62,500
Bristol County Savings Bank	105,000
Taunton National Bank	192,000
Bristol County National Bank	25,000
Machinists National Bank	5,000
Henry Reed	41,500
George Brabrook	28,500

Neither tools nor inventory were charged to their respective accounts on the books of the company, but were charged instead, and for some reason not now apparent, to current operating expense. This practice resulted in startling changes in the Profit and Loss account. For the year ending May 1, 1888, the operating profits amounted to $69,054.90. In the following year the heavy investment in tools and inventory charged to expense resulted in an operating loss of $32,771.81. In 1891 a loss of $121,260.75 was recorded.[28]

In 1891 the heavy indebtedness to local banks was relieved somewhat by loans made by Reed and Brabrook, of $30,000 and $70,000 respectively.[29] By 1892 the sharp increase in sterling sales relieved the company of the necessity of further borrowing to finance the line, but Brabrook continued to speculate heavily in inventory. Perhaps it was unfortunate that his first plunge was so successful, for he was encouraged thereby to continue. The company books were kept in such a way as to conceal any inventory losses that may have been sustained. Throughout the 1890's, however, when Brabrook was known to have been buying heavily, the price of silver steadily declined, and the suspicion therefore exists that heavy inventory losses were sustained. Certain losses are known to have been occasioned by sudden changes in demand which left the company storerooms filled with obsolete wares. When the popularity of castor frames began to wane, for example, it was found that one whole attic room in the factory was stacked with expensive castor glassware, much of it imported, which eventually had to be written off as an almost complete loss.

Heavy borrowing to sustain this costly program continued throughout the 1890's, and losses continued to pile up in the Profit and Loss account. Most of the loans were made by Taunton banks, although Brabrook and Reed took from $15,000 to $50,000 of company notes yearly. Table 23 reveals the condition and progress of the company's finances.

TABLE 23

Condition of Financial Accounts, 1890–1897 [a]

Reed & Barton

	Cash	Payable Notes	Operating Loss	Accumulated Loss
1890	$168.52	$105,000	$32,771.81	
1891	10,447.97 [b]	208,500	121,260.75	$84,993.27
1892	18,719.67 [b]	353,000	71,808.01	156,481.10
1893	31,282.41 [b]	433,000	65,482.98	221,964.08
1894	2,935.93 [b]	489,130	66,558.40	288,522.48
1895	1,566.55 [b]	534.408	60,129.74	348,652.22
1896	1,566.40 [b]	583,908	37,915.06	386,567.28
1897	10,707.40 [b]	620,203	59,597.08	446,164.36

[a] As of April 30.
[b] Deficit.

Source: Reed & Barton Mss., Ledgers, 1888–94, 1894–1902.

The financial situation of the company in the late 'nineties was in marked contrast to more readily apparent conditions. Orders were pouring in, sales increased steadily, more help was being employed, and in the factory a feeling of active prosperity prevailed. Yet the indebtedness incurred by Brabrook was rapidly assuming crisis dimensions.

On April 30, 1898, the inventory and equipment values accumulated over the past few years were at last taken out of the Profit and Loss account and the full extent of Brabrook's purchasing policies stood revealed. Even after the withdrawal of large material requirements for production, Profit and Loss was cleared of, and the inventory account charged with, materials to the amount of $700,503.26.[30] After this time, inventory acquisitions were charged to the Inventory account, and tools and equipment to the Tools and Equipment account. Possibly this change in procedure was made to prepare the Profit and Loss account for the payment of dividends. This account, relieved of its heavy burden, showed an operating loss of only $36.92 in 1899, and a dividend of $3,395.00 was declared. In 1900 Profit and Loss showed a profit of $135,653.07, and another dividend, of $3,555.00, was distributed among the stockholders.[31]

The fundamental cause of the company's difficulties, however, was not remedied, for inventory accumulation and borrowing to finance it continued. Brabrook himself made very heavy loans to the company; in 1898, $150,000 of new capital was paid in, $100,000 by Reed and $50,000 by Brabrook.[32] The unwise scheduling of production in advance of orders made inventory accumulation still more dangerous. Comparatively little of the metal purchased was left in bullion form, which would have insured a high degree of liquidity. Large amounts of goods were manufactured and placed in stock in finished or partly fabricated condition. Departmental foremen with little knowledge of the potential requirements of the trade utilized the spare time of their men and equipment to manufacture for stock. Little effective control was exercised over the amounts of materials in process throughout the various departments in the factory. Foreman psychology naturally held that it was better to have plenty of ware on hand than to be caught short by some sudden demand from the order department. Brabrook, as sales manager, felt that large inventories in the branch offices were necessary to provide quick deliveries and maintain the good-will of company customers. For the year ending April 30, 1900, sales totaled $938,053.68. As of that date, inventory on hand totaled $1,122,600.00. At the same time notes payable totaled $633,999.98.[33]

What the result of Brabrook's financial policies might eventually have been, had they continued longer, is difficult to surmise. His greatest abilities were not financial, nor was he so astute a speculator as he perhaps imagined himself to be. His administration of company finances was unfortunate in more ways than one, for in many eyes it tended to obscure his proven talents. In spite of the financial difficulties which developed at the turn of the century, however, the over-all accomplishments of George Brabrook's administration were great. The years from 1859 to 1900 were difficult, but the company survived, prospered, and spread its name and reputation throughout much of the world. Brabrook's mistakes were unfortunate, but his lasting contributions to Reed & Barton's well-being can truly be considered as second only to those of Henry G. Reed in the fields of sales and design.

The event which terminated a great era in Reed & Barton's history was the death of Henry Reed, on March 1, 1901. Reed's last years were little impaired by advancing age, and while he left the active management of selling and finance to Brabrook, he was still deeply interested in factory affairs. Gradually his active experimentation with products and processes became less, but Reed sat in his small office overlooking the factory yard until a short time before his death, grimly intent that nothing should escape his notice. Very little did. When he closed and locked his desk and was driven home from the factory for the last time, he concluded the longest term of service in the company history. Seventy-three years of the hardest kind of work, and, in his own words, "just putting one dollar on top of another" enabled Henry Reed to build his own monument. His career was not spectacular, and yet, in everlasting insistence upon making the best that could be made and in treating his men with fairness and consideration, Reed's life was inspirational in the highest degree.

PART IV

FINANCIAL CONSOLIDATION UNDER
WILLIAM B. H. DOWSE
1901–1923

CHAPTER XIV

A DECADE OF TRANSITION, 1901–1910

THE DEATH of Henry Reed in 1901 abruptly terminated the old era of rule-of-thumb management and introduced many modern concepts of business to the Reed & Barton factory. The change was necessary for survival in a rapidly evolving business society, but the necessity, though recognized by all, was nevertheless resented by some. A new and untried management super-imposed itself upon the active remnants of a popular and long-established management, and the inevitable consequence was friction. The rapidity, however, with which initial, petty resentments in the factory resolved themselves into wholehearted coöperation indicates both the flexibility of the old organization and the caliber of the new men who came to Taunton. Had there not been a most unfortunate struggle for control of the company, the complete transition from old to new would have been much less difficult and the transition period shorter by several years.

Reed's death left Reed & Barton without a president and created momentary uncertainty as to the disposition of the largest single proprietary interest in the company. Reed be-queathed his stock in equal shares to his daughters, Fanny Dowse and Clara Hubbard, and his will designated son-in-law William B. H. Dowse as trustee of the estate.[1] Dowse's action was prompt and vigorous. A meeting of the board of directors was called just one week after Reed's death, and four motions were presented and passed. The first elected William Dowse a member of the board of directors; the second elected William Dowse president pro tem of the company; the third elected William Dowse president of the company for the ensuing year;

the fourth directed that the whole established system of time-keeping in the factory be abolished and a new system installed immediately. Clearly, a dynamic force had injected itself into company affairs. An examination of Dowse's career and background reveals at once a man with an immense capacity for powerful action.

EARLY CAREER OF DOWSE

In his youth William Bradford Homer Dowse enjoyed far greater educational advantages than had Henry Reed. Yet, like Reed, Dowse was of that group which a career-conscious generation referred to as self-made men. William Dowse was born in Sherborn, Massachusetts, February 29, 1852, the son of the Reverend Edmund (and Elizabeth Bowditch) Dowse and a descendant through sturdy New England ancestry of Lawrence Dowse, who came to Charlestown from Lincolnshire, England, in 1639. The Reverend Edmund Dowse was a distinguished Congregational cleric, who served as pastor of the Sherborn parish for sixty years and as chaplain of the Massachusetts Senate for a long and noteworthy term. William Dowse's boyhood environment was, therefore, both pleasant and cultured, but no rods were spared in his upbringing. The Reverend Edmund, in his capacity of domestic disciplinarian, seldom resorted to sermons. The eleventh commandment in the Sherborn household was that any undertaking worth commencing was worth finishing. Painstaking thoroughness was the best-learned lesson of Dowse's boyhood. It is not surprising that this early training had a profound effect upon William Dowse and that he should have become a firm believer in the value of stern discipline, not only in dealing with others but in ordering his own life as well. At Harvard he attacked his studies with characteristic vigor and thoroughness, graduating high in the class of 1873. Two years later he had his LL.B. degree from Harvard Law School, and by 1878 he had been admitted to the

Massachusetts bar, the United States Circuit Court, and the United States Supreme Court. A fondness for mechanical sciences, developed in early boyhood, attracted Dowse to the patent field and he quickly gained distinction as a successful patent attorney, with offices in Boston and New York. William Dowse's greatest talents, however, lay along financial lines, and the times were propitious for men of his caliber and ability. The difficult 1870's and 1880's placed many manufacturing enterprises in a precarious position. The conditions of a larger trade, keener competition, and more intricate business procedures called less for the mechanical ability which old-school manufacturers possessed than for the financial ability which many of them lacked. Financial genius coupled with a talent for organization found, therefore, an unparalleled opportunity for profitable employment.

William Dowse became interested, through his patent work, in manufacturing enterprises and this interest focused upon development of a snap fastener based upon the ball and socket principle, to be used in place of the button and hole. Several small companies were producing fasteners, and Dowse succeeded to the position of treasurer of one of them, the Consolidated Fastener Company, of Boston. Early profits in this field do not appear to have been large, for competition and a maze of conflicting patents retarded development. Dowse, however, acquired sufficient capital to obtain control of the Consolidated Fastener Company. His next move was directed against the chaotic condition of that industry, and by 1902 he had effected a merger of the several interested companies into the United States Fastener Company, of which he in conjunction with one stockholder held the controlling interest. This company proved immediately lucrative,[2] and the company became an important unit in the field.

William Dowse's attention turned almost immediately from the United States Fastener Company to the affairs of Reed &

Barton, which were not unfamiliar to him at the time of Henry Reed's death. In 1883 Dowse had married Reed's daughter, Fanny Lee, and about five years later he apparently had begun to handle the firm's legal matters through his Boston office. What plans Henry Reed had for his son-in-law cannot now be ascertained, but undoubtedly they would have included a much more prominent position for Dowse in the management of Reed & Barton prior to 1900 if Dowse had been able to devote the necessary time. The two men had a profound respect for each other — Dowse for Reed's mechanical talent, and Reed for Dowse's financial ability. In so far as company finances were concerned, it may be considered unfortunate that circumstance kept Dowse from Taunton until after Reed's death.

First Impact of Dowse's Control

No easy task awaited Dowse in his capacity as trustee of the Reed estate. Few persons had questioned the inherent soundness of the company so long as Henry Reed continued to sit at his desk in the front office. His death abruptly lifted the veil of complacency, and many weaknesses, which had been developing almost unnoticed, stood revealed. It became forcibly apparent to those who had access to the records that the company was suffering from bad financial management. Advancing age had prevented Henry Reed and George Brabrook from exercising the initiative which had characterized their younger years. The ensuing delegation of administrative authority could not be adequately controlled by the owners of the business. Seventy years of sporadic growth had produced a sprawling factory designed more to fit the contours of company-owned land than to meet the requirements of modern low-cost production. Plant equipment in general had deteriorated, and much that was obsolete had been allowed to remain. The superb skill of the Reed & Barton craftsmen had maintained the quality of company wares, but at a premium of excessively high manufac-

WILLIAM BRADFORD HOMER DOWSE, 1852–1928

turing costs. Bookkeeping methods were considered adequate for the needs of the business, but methods of timekeeping and certain costing procedures in the factory were reminiscent of the days of the Taunton Britannia Manufacturing Company. Many a useless cobweb from other years persisted, simply through lack of managerial enterprise. Over all hung a heavy atmosphere of tradition which almost seemed to defy cleavage.

Auguring well for the future of Reed & Barton, however, was the deep suspicion and even open antagonism which greeted Dowse when he assumed Henry Reed's position as president of the concern. Only employees with a real and active loyalty to their company would have expressed such decided opinions and exhibited such anxiety over the abilities of the new management. William Dowse came to Taunton a confident and brilliantly successful man, justly determined to put the whole Reed & Barton organization on trial. Somewhat to his discomfort, Dowse found that it was he, himself, who was being cross-examined. That examination was a subtle one, but it was devastatingly thorough. The Reed & Barton employees were suspicious of William Dowse on several counts. In the first place, he was a lawyer. As such, the burden of proof was upon him so far as a community such as Taunton was concerned. His manufacturing experience, moreover, had been confined to snap fasteners, than which, in the minds of the Taunton craftsmen, nothing was further removed from the art of silversmithing. His personal appearance tended to place people in awe of the man, rather than to inspire spontaneous friendship. Dowse carried himself with almost haughty dignity, a bearing which imparted to his rugged frame an appearance of even more imposing size. A fierce mustache and an impressive goatee heightened the impression of formidability. William Dowse was neither unaware of nor disturbed by the impression his physical appearance created, and the impression was reinforced by both his disposition and his manner of speaking. Neither tactful nor even-tempered in his business life, Dowse could overwhelm opposition by the sheer force of his personality. On appropriate occasions his voice would rise in a spectacular courtroom crescendo to blast the offender of the moment. Contrary opinions were tolerated with scant patience, and often not tolerated at all. These qualities, thrust suddenly upon men accustomed to the quiet ways of Reed and Brabrook, caused open bitterness and frequent resignations during the first weeks of the Dowse régime; and yet, in a surprisingly short space of time, Dowse had been weighed and not found wanting by the factory people. The qualities which they uncovered in the period of trial and which did much to change resentment into coöperative approval were complete frankness and religious adherence to a promise. No man stood long in doubt as to William Dowse's intentions and no man ever complained that those intentions, once announced, were not carried out. Even his brusqueness came, in time, to inspire less fear among those who discovered that it concealed a keenly sensitive and sympathetic nature.

Dowse moved quickly and with the sure confidence which a successful career had instilled in him. In effect, the vigor of Dowse's actions startled Reed & Barton out of the lethargy induced by age and past success. Once the awakening had been achieved, a delicate balance of forces was effected. In one direction Dowse's confidence was contagious, and swayed the company to his support; in the opposite direction, the experienced administrative personnel of the organization recognized Dowse's inexperience and endeavored to exercise a corrective, restraining influence. Both confidence and restraint were necessary: confidence, because drastic measures had to be taken to save the business; restraint, because certain of the proposed reforms were by no means appropriate to the requirements of the trade.

New Policies, Equipment, and Procedures

William Dowse's concepts of business were typically modern, and clashed, therefore, with prevailing attitudes in the Reed & Barton factory. Spend money on modern equipment; increase the volume of business and lower the unit costs; emphasize finance and promote sales vigorously; above all, call in specialists when in doubt — these were the principles which were making America industrially great, and these were the principles which William Dowse sought to apply in Taunton.

Immediately in Dowse's wake arrived the professional consulting experts. Accountants overhauled company costing methods, a civil engineer made a detailed study of the power system, and industrial engineers installed a new system of timekeeping. The more farsighted employees approved of these measures, many others in the factory were indifferent, and some grumbled and took offense at the "intrusion." Dowse forged ahead over all objections, determined in his efforts to act on the basis of expert knowledge. Fresh administrative talent was brought in, for the breadth of Dowse's business interests allowed him to spend only two or three days each week in Taunton. From a large competing firm came Mr. Mark Anthony to assume the position of general manager of the company. From the Merchants National Bank of Boston several years later came William R. Mitchell to supervise company sales and finances. Both men possessed the courage and initiative necessary for the great task which faced them, and Dowse lent strong and consistent support to the management he set up. Mr. Anthony's position, particularly, was far from an enviable one, for he was placed in charge of a proud and sensitive group of foremen, more than one of whom had aspired to the post which they now saw awarded to an outsider. The new general manager, however, exercised his authority with rare tact and soon inspired the remark from one old workman, "Well sir, he's a good man, he don't allow no mischief, and he knows the business well." [3]

The first and most heartily welcomed of Dowse's reforms was factory modernization and improvement. Electric lights and modern plumbing met with approbation from all. The only dissenting voice was that of George Brabrook, who was heard to grumble that the company had done fairly well for seventy years without such frills. New machinery was installed where, in the opinion of the general manager and the foremen, it was most vitally needed. In November, 1901, a competent civil engineer reported to Dowse, after a detailed examination of the plant: [4]

> This manufacturing plant has reached its present size by a gradual growth, and additions of floor space, machinery, and departments have been made from time to time with the result of throwing some parts of the plant out of balance. The use of the power generated is wasteful; the systems of shafting for transmitting the power are in some cases unnecessarily complicated and considerable power is lost in connecting the several lines of shafting; the location of some departments in relation to others is inconvenient; . . . and the programme of work is not in many respects favorable to economical production.

New turbines were promptly installed in the factory to replace the old vertical water wheels which had hitherto supplied a part of the factory power. It is of interest to note, in passing, that the smaller of these two wheels was the one installed by the Taunton Britannia Manufacturing Company in 1830 and used more or less continuously until a short time before Henry Reed's death. The dam property and water rights of the Hopewell Manufacturing Company, located down river from Reed & Barton, were acquired to insure proper flowage, and repairs were made in the Reed & Barton dam and mill race. By these various improvements it was hoped that water alone could be made to furnish 250 horsepower per day for seven months of the year, and the more expensive steam power resorted to only during the five months when the Mill River flowage was inadequate. Extensive changes were also made in the power transmission system, and a coupling arranged by which either water or steam power could be used independently of the other. An effort was made to rearrange the rolls, hammers, presses, and other heavy machines to utilize steam and water power with a minimum of waste. Some attempt was also made to schedule work on these machines in regular installments and at regular periods which allowed the power to be expended on a continuous run, without interference with the use of power in other departments and without waste of energy in the steam engine. At the same time many improvements were made in the factory buildings themselves. Four separate machine shops scattered throughout the plant were combined in one new building. A new "case shop" and a bronze foundry were also erected.[5]

The primary purpose contemplated by the various factory improvements was the lowering of unit costs of production, and Dowse took immediate steps to ascertain what those costs actually were. Outside accountants studied Brabrook's costing methods and apparently advocated a more realistic treatment of certain of the elements involved. In many respects, however, the old system was vindicated of the suspicion with which it was regarded by the new management. A prolonged and minute study of factory overhead was made which resulted (to the intense amusement of Brabrook's bookkeeper) in a figure only 2 per cent removed from the old rule-of-thumb estimate hitherto employed. Manufacturing, selling, and administrative expenses were broken down into greater and more useful detail, and for the first time an annual charge for depreciation began to be made. Manufacturing costs of the various classes of products were computed monthly, and a careful check was maintained on selling prices and profits for each class. The charging of metal into production at inflated prices was abandoned; instead, metal was charged in at what appears to have been an average cost figure. In general, the cost-accounting changes effected by Dowse were not drastic, and much of the old system was allowed to remain. His improvements were directed principally at making the cost-gathering process more rapid, and hence more useful, rather than at altering the fundamental nature of that process.

The manufacturing improvements made by the new management were shortly followed by sweeping innovations in finance and in sales, but the study of William Dowse's efforts in these fields must yield precedence to an examination of even more vital events. The struggle for control of the company, growing out of the vigorous action taken by Dowse immediately following the death of Henry Reed, overshadows all else in the 1900–10 transition period; it even threatened, for a time, the independent existence of Reed & Barton.

The Struggle for Company Control

The actual struggle for company control did not materialize until 1907, but the background was laid as soon as the new company president assumed office. William Dowse represented one school of thought, one line of action, one type of personality; George Brabrook was the unalterable opposite in all three particulars. This fact is important, though it was somewhat obscured by the initial behavior of the two men toward each other.

Brabrook had grown old in the service of the company by the time Dowse came to Taunton. His contributions had been great throughout his career, and his control over company policies had been almost absolute for the better part of twenty years. In the space of time encompassed by one meeting of the board of directors, Dowse reduced Brabrook to the position of a figurehead in company affairs. There is no question but that the best interests of the company called for such a move; had it been executed with less bluntness, however, a later crisis might conceivably have been averted. Brabrook relinquished his powers in finance, sales, and manufacturing with little outward struggle. Nominally retaining the office of treasurer, he contented himself with his purely advisory capacity and devoted much attention to the designing-room when his services seemed little in demand elsewhere.

William Dowse and George Brabrook did not clash openly, to the immense relief of those who understood the overwhelming abruptness of the change in management. Brabrook's personal flexibility was, in spite of his age, sufficient at first to acclimate him to the new conditions he saw around him. The two men found that much common ground existed between them. Both were keen patrons of the fine arts and both exhibited a feeling for clear, straightforward design. Each cultivated the stimulus of wide social acquaintances, although Dowse moved in the broader orbit of his Boston environment, while Brabrook seldom left Taunton. Each man was unusually sensitive; Brabrook, however, was inclined to brood over his hurts, while Dowse relieved his feelings by spontaneous word and action. Actually the two men were of that delicate personal composition which the force of external events could easily weld into a great friendship, or just as easily turn into bitter mutual animosity.

Before many months had elapsed it became apparent that the harmony which existed between Dowse and Brabrook was not destined to continue. The measures of reform undertaken by the new management necessarily emphasized the points of dissimilarity between the two men, and the elements of disunity inherent in those measures were cumulative in their effect. William Dowse was, above all else, a keen realist, and his intensely practical nature clashed with Brabrook's primarily artistic disposition. They took a diametrically opposite viewpoint of the general aims of the company. Brabrook was thoroughly imbued with the idea of a restricted output sold at a high price. This obsession reached a point where he automatically regarded any fast-selling item in the company line as being priced too low. Dowse could countenance no such attitude and rightly felt that such a program meant certain failure for a company of Reed & Barton's size. Indeed, Dowse was at this time as extreme a proponent of mass production as Brabrook was of restricted output, and his initial attitude was to sell everything possible to as wide a market as possible. A compromise between the two opposing aims was clearly called for, but Dowse made no retreat until experience proved it to be necessary. Brabrook, therefore, saw the whole basis of his managerial policies reversed, and this reversal was not the last to which he was forced to bow. Implicit in the financial reform undertaken by Dowse (Chapter xvi) was a condemnation of the methods employed by the administration which preceded him. Brabrook, the proponent of those measures, could scarcely have been untouched by this criticism of his financial management.

Other factors, not in themselves important enough to cause a break, added to the increasingly restive undertone of the Reed & Barton management. George Brabrook enjoyed good living and was not disposed to spare the financial means of attaining it. His private investment activities, moreover, required generous backing. Company operations were most profitable, yet no dividends were declared and the salaries of both Dowse and Brabrook were conservative. These factors apparently combined to produce in Brabrook the attitude that his services deserved a greater reward than they were getting. Combined with this was a feeling of uneasiness in Brabrook and the heirs of the Henry Fish estate as they watched Dowse forge vigorously ahead to acquire a majority interest in the company stock outstanding.

William Dowse's appraisal of the company's condition in 1901 apparently convinced him that only by acquiring absolute control could he carry out complete reform. He saw in the dispersal of the Fish holdings, moreover, an unparalleled opportunity to achieve that control, and proceeded with expedition to do so.

Stock ownership at the time of Henry Reed's death in 1901 was divided between Henry Reed (3,000 shares), George Brabrook (2,500 shares), and five heirs of Henry Fish (2,000 shares). No one family controlled the company, but a merger of the Fish and Brabrook interests could easily have done so. Reed's shares, though temporarily consolidated in a trust by the terms of his will, threatened eventually to become dispersed by inheritance or sale. Dowse turned his attention toward the holders of the smaller blocks of stock. Apparently Frank Fish, and possibly some others, were induced to part with their individually unimportant holdings, with the result that in 1906 William Dowse suddenly revealed the fact that he then owned 3,753 shares, a clear majority.

From this time on, events moved rapidly. Dowse left no doubt as to who owned the company, and sources of petty irritation multiplied. The tension which had been accumulating over the past five years caused a rupture at last, and although the precipitating events remain obscure, open conflict flared. On December 31, 1906, Brabrook offered his stock to Reed & Barton for $535,000.[6] This offer was in accordance with a provision in the bylaws which stated that any holder of company stock was required to offer his holdings to the company before offering them for sale elsewhere. For some reason William Dowse never learned of the Brabrook offer, and no company bid was made for the stock. The waiting period expired and on January 10, 1907, George Brabrook and the Fish heirs sold their interests in Reed & Barton to the Silverware Stocks Company, controlled by Edward Holbrook, of Providence.

Reed & Barton was little prepared for such a move, and it shocked even Brabrook's most intimate friends. Many persons felt that he had received a minimum of consideration from the new management, but few condoned what was popularly felt to be treachery toward the company. Rumors multiplied in the atmosphere of crisis which prevailed, and speculation over the "sell-out" was rampant in the factory. The flurry was short-lived, however, for little additional information surmounted the barrier of secrecy erected by the principals involved. From this time on, few employees realized the true significance or extent of the events which followed. William Dowse knew, however, and prepared to fight for the independent existence of Reed & Barton.

On the morning of May 29, 1907, a crucial meeting of the board of directors was held.[7] William Dowse and his party seated themselves on one side of the directors' table; George Brabrook and representatives of the Silverware Stocks Company aligned themselves on the opposite side. The Dowse contingent nominated William Dowse treasurer, Mark Anthony clerk, and Dowse, Anthony, and George A. Holmes directors. The test of power had come, and it was William Dowse who mustered the majority of votes. George Brabrook returned to his office, gathered his papers and personal belongings, and left the company never to return. In the afternoon his sons, Hale and Carleton, did likewise. This was the beginning of the real struggle for control of the company.

The aims and purposes of the Silverware Stocks Company are difficult to determine from available data. Contemporary trade opinion held that an attempt was being made to obtain control of all important sterling silverware producers in the country. This may or may not have been the ambition of John Holbrook, vice-president and manager of the Silverware Stocks Company, but by 1907 he had built a formidable organization. The company at this time appears to have held controlling interests in the Gorham Manufacturing Company, W. B. Durgin Company, William B. Kerr Company, and the Whiting Manufacturing Company. William Dowse looked with some anxiety and no little suspicion at the new Reed & Barton stockholder. Dowse's margin of control was not a large one, for the Silverware Stocks Company held 3,530 shares of stock against the

3,960 shares controlled by Dowse. In 1,500 shares of unissued treasury stock lay the balance of power.

A campaign of non-coöperation commenced almost immediately. The Silverware Stocks Company encountered stonewall resistance in its efforts to obtain information upon the current operations of Reed & Barton. Dividends were paid, but in trifling amounts. Dowse flatly refused to see the representative sent to him. When the Silverware Stocks Company was taken over by the Silversmiths Company, a newly organized holding company, Reed & Barton issued a new stock certificate only when ordered to do so by the Supreme Judicial Court of Massachusetts, and after a maximum of delay.[8] Finding that its Reed & Barton stock afforded no dividends, no representation on the board of directors, no access to company records, the Silversmiths Company decided to take the issue to court, an eventuality for which Dowse appears to have been carefully preparing.

Late in 1908 suit was brought by the Silversmiths Company against Reed & Barton and William Dowse to force the defendants to grant access to company records. The implications of the case went much deeper than this. There is some indication that the Silversmiths Company suit was a preliminary step in a carefully laid plan to force Reed & Barton treasury stock upon the market. To do this it was first necessary to establish the fact of Reed & Barton's need for new capital. The information believed necessary to prove this need could be found only in the Reed & Barton records, and William Dowse stood squarely and capably in the way of any audit of the books. A multiplicity of charges and countercharges grew out of the suit. The central issue involved was a claim that Reed & Barton's retail operations in New York were being carried on "at a heavy loss amounting to many thousands of dollars."[9] Dowse's answer to the charges was thoroughly characteristic, and in the end it was he who struck the hardest blow. Contenting himself with a brief denial of all claims brought against Reed & Barton and himself, Dowse launched a vehement charge of monopoly against the Silversmiths Company. Whether this could have been decisively proved is doubtful, but coming at a time when antitrust sentiments were strong in the minds of the public and the judiciary, the charge was effective. On February 8, 1910, the case against Reed & Barton was dismissed.

The Silversmiths Company now found itself in possession of a block of stock rendered useless by court order and unprofitable by Dowse's avowed refusal to distribute earnings. The only recourse left was to sell, and negotiations were immediately commenced through the medium of the Hopewell Manufacturing Company, a holding company organized in February, 1910, by Dowse for the purpose. An eventual settlement was made for $796,750, upon the fulfillment of which terms William Dowse became virtually sole master of Reed & Barton. With this event the transition from the Brabrook to the Dowse administration can be said to have been completed.

To criticize Dowse for his lack of tact in dealing with Henry Reed's associates would be to ignore the times, the condition of the company, and the abilities of the men involved. George Brabrook's departure from Reed & Barton was an unhappy termination of a fine and devoted career, but the time is past for a judgment on the motives involved in the dispute. The one statement of circumstance must suffice: William Dowse acted in the manner dictated by current practice and by his own vigorous training. The important fact to remember is that he acted, and by so doing saved Reed & Barton. A weaker man might have avoided personal animosities — and failed in the main task which confronted him.

CHAPTER XV

DISTRIBUTION AND PRODUCT POLICY UNDER
WILLIAM DOWSE, 1901–1923

COMMENCING with the prosperity of the late 1890's, the pace of competition in the silverware industry noticeably quickened. Promotional effort aspired to, and quite frequently began to achieve, an air of dignity and smartness appropriate to the nature of the product. The art of merchandising was being born, and sales campaigns were launched with verve and imagination and with keen insight into the whims of consumer demand. The industry explored with enthusiasm the meaning of the new phrases "market appeal," "buying motives," "brand policy." New products, new designs, and new advertising followed one another in rapid succession. Even the casual observer could sense the fresh spirit which centered in the elbow of New York's Maiden Lane and spread from there throughout the silverware marts of the country.

The new world of marketing, regarded with particular favor by the silverware industry, was reviewed with suspicion by the Reed & Barton home office. George Brabrook, the great competitive leader of other years, saw no challenge, and the stagnation which gripped the internal affairs of the company seemed on the verge of affecting the market position of Reed & Barton. This very imminent threat, however, never really eventuated, principally because of the efforts of a brilliant salesforce. Mr. E. H. Adams, the two Lanes, Mr. J. F. Dean, and "Easy" Reed were close to the market and did sense the challenge. In the field they fought it to the point of earning the admiration of every competitor in the trade. In Taunton they fought it until the home office became exasperated with the insistence of their demands for new promotion and modern advertising. It was at this point, in 1901, that the management of Reed & Barton was taken over by William Dowse.

The control of sales policies which, in the absence of a strong central sales management, had come to rest largely in the hands of the salesmen, passed quickly and without friction to the new Reed & Barton president. Dowse was immediately impressed by the abilities of the salesmen and devoted considerable attention to the matter of securing their coöperation. In this he was successful, for the salesmen sensed in William Dowse a warm personal friend and a man who would be both willing and eager to make changes. The interest which Dowse began to show in the details of marketing was by no means usual in a man with such pronounced financial and technical leanings. That interest, moreover, was far from a passive one; it came to constitute the driving force behind significant alterations in company policy — first in distribution, then in the character and design of Reed & Barton products.

The Marketing Organization

Dowse's initial attitude upon assuming control of the company was that vigorous, modern promotional methods were called for, that a greater variety of products could be sold and a wider market reached, and that the art of sales management could be vastly improved by conscientious financial regulation. Almost at once, he proceeded to apply his ideas in a selling campaign which centered in New York, the elements of which had long been contemplated but never carried out by Reed & Barton.

Plans for a company-operated retail store had been drawn up in some detail by Henry Reed and George Brabrook in 1894,[1] but caution prevailed and the scheme was abandoned when business conditions showed signs of deterioration. William Dowse lost little time in retrieving these plans and putting them

into execution. Early in 1902 a New York subsidiary corporation was established. The charter of this corporation permitted
retail selling and the handling of jewelry and precious stones.
At the same time, important tax benefits were realized by the
creation of a company which was legally resident at the scene
of operations. Reed & Barton Company, of New York, took
over the leases of the Maiden Lane and Union Square wholesale
offices, and assumed nominal responsibility for the direction of
New York sales. Actually, the creation of the new company,
with Dowse as president, Brabrook as treasurer, and Calvin
Harris as assistant treasurer and resident agent, caused little
change in the management of New York wholesale operations.
The purpose for which the company had been organized was
finally effected in 1905, when its large and luxuriously appointed
retail store was opened on the corner of Fifth Avenue and 32d
Street.

The opening of a retail store might well have been regarded
as the natural consummation of Reed & Barton's long marketing
development and of the very apparent trend toward first-hand
contact with the final purchaser of the company's products. In
retrospect, the evolution of distributive methods exhibits an
orderly, natural sequence of movement toward simplicity.
Gradually the cumbersome system of agency selling had been
succeeded by the wholesale market, which yielded in the years
following the Civil War to the manufacturers' desire to reach
retail stores directly. But it was only in 1905 that Reed &
Barton was ready to experiment with the ultimate contemplated
goal. As in the past, the company had hung behind the industry.
Most of the important silverware manufacturers had by this
time established stores of their own in New York, and the results
seemed good. The glittering brilliance of a retail store on Fifth
Avenue was rapidly entrancing the few factory men who, so far,
had withstood temptation. There were, moreover, many successful precedents in other industries, and the contemporary

fashion of American business management was to view "middle-man's profit" with distaste. The silverware industry in general, however, did not follow up its initial New York retail ventures with further efforts on a comparable scale, possibly because of the strongly entrenched opposition of the retail jewelry trade to any serious extension of the practice. Few manufacturers of silverware progressed beyond the experimental stage of retailing, and all continued, as they do today, to distribute their products through independent retailers. Reed & Barton, though operating the large retail store on Fifth Avenue, continued to do the bulk of its selling in the New York area at wholesale through the Maiden Lane office. Like Reed & Barton, most of the other manufacturers confined their retail efforts to New York and came to regard their stores there as valuable chiefly from an advertising viewpoint. Reed & Barton's experience is an illuminating commentary on the validity of this justification.

In general attractiveness and quality of merchandise, Reed & Barton's store at 320 Fifth Avenue rivaled the best jewelry and silverware shops in the city. The investment involved was a large one. The initial cost of store fixtures exceeded $33,000, and in the second year of operations further expensive improvements were undertaken.[2] Lease of the property virtually doubled the financial commitment, and inventory requirements were large, for it was deemed necessary to stock not only company-manufactured ware but a substantial line of jewelry, watches, precious stones, lamps, leather goods, and cut glass.[3]

There is no question that, in the field of luxurious merchandising, Reed & Barton's store made its mark. Operating results, however, were far from satisfactory. Sales for the first year achieved the creditable total of $102,408, but expenses for the same period amounted to $121,320.[4] It became apparent almost immediately that the store represented a serious geographical mistake. Potential patrons from wealthy uptown quarters had to pass by every other jewelry shop on the Avenue

Interior of Reed & Barton's Fifth Avenue Store
Corner of Fifth Avenue and 32d Street, New York, 1905–1918

before reaching Reed & Barton's! The garment-making district nearby, moreover, contributed scores of window shoppers whose admiration for fine silverware was more enthusiastic than profitable and who totally obscured the front of the store and blocked the main entrance every noon hour.[5]

Operations in succeeding years showed little improvement. Profit and loss figures for the New York company were merged with those of the Taunton company, so that no separate financial statements can now be drawn up. From what information is available, however, it appears that losses were heavy in relation to the capital invested.[6] Several factors, aside from location, contributed to this unsatisfactory situation. High rent was a perennial drain on operations, and heavy operating expenses appear to have been incurred. Lack of experience in the handling of a costly inventory of jewelry and precious stones may also have played a part. In 1911, executive salaries were drastically increased. William Dowse, as president and treasurer of the New York corporation, received not less than $30,000 annually,[7] an amount so disproportionate to the profitability of the business as to suggest the gradual withdrawal of capital and liquidation of the enterprise. Perhaps the most important of all factors contributing to the indifferent success of the store was a general lack of understanding by the Taunton management of the problems faced by the men immediately in charge of New York retail operations. The experience and particular abilities necessary to make such a venture successful did not reside in the home office; none the less, it was in Taunton that New York operational policies were formulated.

One major attempt was made to reorganize the company store and place it upon a profitable basis. In 1918 Reed & Barton purchased control of the well-known jewelry store of Theodore B. Starr, Inc., at 576 Fifth Avenue, and placed the company line on sale there.[8] Reed & Barton Company, of New York, was merged with the Starr organization and all business in New

York was carried on under the name of Theodore B. Starr, Inc.[9] Actually only the management of the retail store was affected by this move, the Maiden Lane office continuing as before to handle wholesale distribution in the area. The personnel of the Starr organization handled well the retail distribution of both the jewelry and the silverware lines, but the store's fine reputation, founded primarily upon precious stones and jewelry, does not appear to have attracted silverware purchasers in large numbers.[10] In 1924, after only indifferent success in the new location, the retailing experiment was abandoned completely by Reed & Barton, and the assets of Theodore B. Starr, Inc., were disposed of at sale and auction.

In the last analysis, the retail store failed in its primary purposes of providing effective advertising and of building good-will in the largest silverware market in the country. Unfortunately, the number of potential customers reached was not large in relation to the investment made. Moreover, the good-will value of the store was dubious. The retail jewelry trade did not look with great favor upon competing manufacturer-operated stores.[11] Reed & Barton's experience in the field of retailing can scarcely be considered as conclusive evidence concerning the new policy, inasmuch as occasional faulty management played a part. It suggests, however, that the considerable difference in business viewpoints involved in manufacturing and in retailing represented too wide a gap for Reed & Barton, as for many other organizations of comparable resources, to bridge successfully.

The fate of the New York experiment was not shared by Reed & Barton's regular marketing organization, though marketing efforts throughout the country may have suffered somewhat from Dowse's preoccupation with the New York store. The distributing system outside New York remained relatively stable in form. As in the past, the branch offices served as warehouses, salesrooms, and general headquarters for com-

pany promotion in their respective districts. In addition, a large
and active group of travelers operated out of Taunton and from
the various offices. The marketing organization was simple,
yet it continued to be effective, principally because of the great
ability of the salesmen.

A few developments in the field are to be noted. The Philadelphia branch office was discontinued shortly after Dowse had
assumed control of the company, but this was because of its
proximity to the New York distribution center. Reed & Barton's
Chicago office, however, grew in size and importance. For a
short time a branch office was also maintained in St. Louis,
while in Dallas, Texas, the Storm-Cummings Company took
over the distribution of Reed & Barton's line. On the West
Coast Mr. E. H. Adams developed company markets so successfully that in 1905 a branch office was opened in San
Francisco. Earthquake and fire promptly challenged the permanence of this venture. At the peak of the San Francisco con-
flagration the necessity arose for dynamiting that section of the
city in which the Reed & Barton office was located. The samples
in the showrooms at the time were valued at approximately
$35,000. Disregarding orders from military and civil authorities,
and with the aid of a mysteriously acquired policeman's badge,
"E. H." made a daring trip through police lines and loaded
thousands of dollars' worth of company stock into an old wagon.
Never before or since, it is said, was a load of silverware packed
like that one! [12] The spectacular salvage operation, however,
made possible the prompt reopening of the office and saved a
substantial part of Reed & Barton's West Coast investment.

The marketing organization under William Dowse was never
a carefully planned and integrated unit. It was, perhaps, the one
field of company activity where Dowse failed to remedy a
fundamental defect surviving from the preceding administration. The offices of treasurer and sales manager were immediately vested in one man, William Mitchell. In many

respects the result was the same as in the late 1890's, when George Brabrook attempted to perform both functions. Mitchell inclined toward the financial viewpoint, and the selling effort suffered somewhat from lack of guidance. No strong central control over sales was exercised, nor were marketing policies clearly defined. In matters of detail the financial emphasis proved mildly annoying to customers and salesmen alike. Accounts were always promptly called for settlement, and the privilege of extended credit was, for a time, denied even the most reliable customers. Good-will suffered from perfunctory efficiency in the home office.

Throughout the major part of Dowse's administration the company, for all practical purposes, had no sales manager. Mitchell found, as had Brabrook in his later years, that the multiplicity of duties in the treasurer's office precluded all but a passing attention to the administration of sales. This structural weakness might have assumed serious dimensions, had it not been for the general prosperity of the times, the skillful work of the salesforce, and the market reputation of the company.

Products and the Course of Sales

In only one respect did Dowse and his sales organization break with each other, and this was on the sacred ground of product policy. Dowse saw endless opportunities for doing business and exploited them over the frequent opposition of more conservative forces in the company. His first experiment was with the volume market for moderately low-priced lines — the field from which George Brabrook had shrunk thirty years before. In 1911 the manufacture of a small selection of inexpensive plated hollow ware was commenced. One of the primary objects of the undertaking was to utilize idle tools, space, and equipment in the factory. Few new designs were created, and many obsolete or inactive dies were reëmployed. The new line of ware was marked "Reed Silver Company," and distribution was contemplated through stores to which the regular Reed & Barton line had been denied. This experiment was typical of contemporary trade practice, and appears to have been an attempt on the part of William Dowse to duplicate the success with which certain competitors had tapped the volume market with price-appeal brands.

Fortunately for Reed & Barton, the investment in the new line was not large nor were the wares ever widely distributed. This venture was a failure from nearly every point of view. Almost immediately it became apparent that Reed & Barton possessed neither the experience nor the inclination to produce the wares of the required low quality. Efforts to reduce manufacturing costs to a competitive level in this low-price field were unsuccessful because they involved a concept of manufacturing technique still unfamiliar in the factory. Nowhere in the history of Reed & Barton has the tangible force of tradition been more clearly demonstrated than in this instance, where the factory personnel concerned was asked to place low costs ahead of high quality. Foremen trained under Henry Reed and George Brabrook listened with gentle tolerance to explanations that this class of goods was "different," then proceeded, as before, to improve the ware far beyond the point where profits could be realized.[13] Contributing still further to the failure of the Reed Silver Company venture was the market's reception of the ware. The stores handling lines of this quality proved to be as discriminating buyers as were the regular Reed & Barton customers and scorned most of the outdated patterns presented. Moreover, none-too-scrupulous dealers took ready advantage of the opportunity to trade upon the Reed & Barton name. In the face of increasing opposition from the factory and as the evidence of failure accumulated in the market, William Dowse's faith in the venture became severely shaken. It remained for a buyer from a prominent Philadelphia house to pronounce final sentence upon the experiment. Examining the Reed ware displayed in one corner of the Taunton showroom, the visitor remarked quietly, "When we want things like this, we do not expect to find them at Reed & Barton's." [14] Never before had company policy presented the occasion for such a comment, nor has it ever done so since. In 1913 the Reed Silver Company passed out of active existence, a testimonial to inexperience in the guarding of that most delicate and valuable asset — company reputation. From that time on, the staunchest supporter of Reed & Barton's name and traditions was William Dowse; for this reason the 1911 experiment may be considered as one of the significant incidents in his administration.

The new lines and products brought out by Reed & Barton after 1913 experienced varying degrees of success, but the general product policy of the company behind each remained inalterable. Only ware of the high quality which customers had come to expect from the company was produced. A basic change in William Dowse's attitude toward company operations appears to have taken place. In part, this change was prompted by Dowse's realization that his ideas were not conducive to the achievement of maximum profits. Beyond this strictly practical conclusion lay another explanation. Reform had run its course and served its essential purposes; as it did so, Dowse's pride in his organization grew. Chastened by his early experiments and with more than passing sentiment, Dowse embraced the philosophy of the men who had come before him. Concepts of volume markets faded, and his determination to produce only the best that could be produced increased as his association with the company lengthened.

Shortly after the Reed Silver Company line had been abandoned, two new experiments were launched. As might be expected, the later efforts differed in nearly every detail from the earlier one; Dowse was not slow to learn. Under the name and stamp of "Hopewell Silver Company" a line of high-quality, sterling vanity cases, eyeglass cases, thimbles, jewel cases, and

PUNCH BOWL FROM THE REED & BARTON SERVICE FOR THE
U.S.S. MINNESOTA
In the second decade of the twentieth century

A Plate from the Reed & Barton Service for the U.S.S. Arizona
In the second decade of the twentieth century

novelties was brought out. About the same time Reed & Barton began to manufacture an expensive line of china deposit ware. This consisted of Lenox china, handsomely decorated with sterling and gold deposit. Both lines compared most favorably with competing products in the market, but sales were too limited to be profitable. Manufacturing costs were high, and distribution of the Hopewell wares involved entry into a highly competitive market characterized by rapid style changes.[15] Both lines appear to have been abandoned by 1918.

The second experiment was the introduction of a type of product which deserves particular notice in this period, though its benefits to the company cannot be measured directly in terms of sales and profits. This was the trophy line. Reed & Barton, as well as competing firms, had manufactured elaborate vases, cups, and statuettes for many years. Dowse, realizing the advertising value of such special orders, enthusiastically encouraged the further development of this market. Although all companies in the industry at one time or another received public acclaim for particular trophies produced, the bulk of this trade fell to Reed & Barton, the Gorham Manufacturing Company, and Tiffany. Competition was keen and reminiscent of the rivalry which had existed years before at the many exhibitions and fairs throughout the country. The Wrigley trophy, the Victor Herbert cup, the Roosevelt cup, and many other Reed & Barton creations were as famous in the first two decades of the twentieth century as the Progress Vase had been in the 1870's. It remained for William Dowse, however, to capitalize on the reputation of the company and to turn the intangible publicity value of the famous trophy orders into measurable profit. About 1910 a commercial line of ready-made sterling cups was introduced and met with great success. By placing silver trophies within the means of the smaller clubs and associations a substantial volume of business was built up. The practice of soliciting orders for widely publicized contests was continued, nevertheless, since this special-order trade increased not only the sale of the commercial trophy line but of all Reed & Barton products.

From 1912 to 1920 a substantial business was done in bronze memorial plaques; enough, in fact, to justify issuing a special catalogue of bronzes in 1919.[16] During this same period Reed & Barton also executed orders for large sterling services to be placed on the battleships *California, South Dakota, Montana, Arizona,* and *Utah*.[17] These services, the money for which was generously donated by the people of the respective States, provided the Reed & Barton designers and craftsmen with an unparalleled opportunity to exercise their skill. In each case the result was outstanding and a tribute to the great ability of George Parker and the others who so painstakingly labored on the creations. Henry Reed's policy of having one or more masterpieces in production in the factory at all times was echoed in the special orders performed by the company under William Dowse.

Perhaps the most spectacular of these orders and the most elaborate service ever produced by Reed & Barton was that turned out in 1924 for the Maharajah of Barwani. This East Indian potentate called upon the leading silversmiths of the world to submit designs on a sterling silver dinner service, the cost of which was to be approximately $100,000. Learning of this opportunity, Reed & Barton submitted the designs of their Francis First pattern and received the award. When completed, the Barwani order was carefully packed in small boxes and shipped out of Taunton to New York, thence to Liverpool and Bombay. From Bombay the order traveled eight hundred miles inland by train, four hundred miles farther by mules, and a final hundred miles on the backs of the Maharajah's native carriers.[18] Not since the days of Tom Raddin and the Java trade of the 1870's had Reed & Barton ware been sent by such devious ways to so distant a point. This order might indeed be con-

The Roosevelt Cup: Shown in a Trophy Catalogue about 1910

Pewter Reproductions, Reed & Barton, between 1910 and 1930

sidered as a testimonial, not just to a new generation of craftsmen, but to the old generation of salesmen as well. Reed & Barton's foreign travelers had established a prestige in markets of the East which even time and neglect failed to obliterate.

It cannot be denied that certain of William Dowse's ventures into the field of product policy were unsuccessful and that others returned only small gains to the company. The efforts of other manufactures followed a similar course, for this was an adventurous, experimental period in product management. Dowse was too astute a business man, however, not to have achieved at least one major triumph in this field. As early as 1903 Reed & Barton began to reproduce colonial pewter ware, and for over thirty years this line enjoyed popularity and financial success. The company anticipated not only the efforts of competitors but even the trend of public demand. As a consequence, when the American passion for things American grew to important dimensions in the 1920's, Reed & Barton's pewter wares fared well. In this instance Dowse's fondness for simplicity of design, coupled apparently with a nostalgic interest in the "good old days" of the company and of the community, resulted in the creation of one of the most successful of Reed & Barton's secondary product lines.

The promotion of new product ideas, good, bad, and indifferent, was certainly the most spectacular phase of marketing in William Dowse's day, but it was by no means the most significant. The real measure of interest in Dowse's management lay, not in the course of relatively inconsequential pewter, bronze, and trophy sales, but in the trend of total sales and in the performance of the main product lines. Effects of the minor mishaps of distribution were not lasting, for they were swallowed up by a broad upward surge in demand for the company's products.

Sterling flat and hollow ware replaced plated ware in more and more homes, and by 1904 sterling had become the largest

CHART VIII
Sterling, White-metal, and Nickel-silver Sales, Percentage Change from Preceding Year, 1904–1924, Reed & Barton

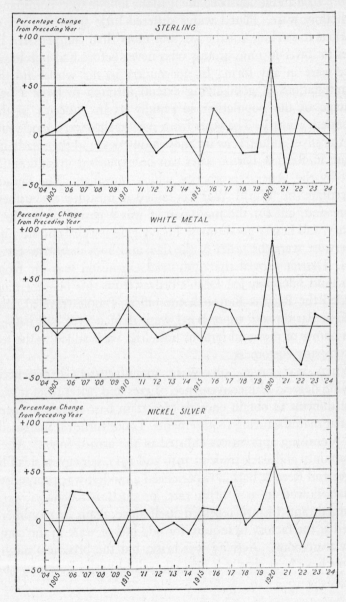

selling line produced. Flatware confirmed a trend established before 1900 and seriously challenged the long market dominance of hollow ware. Plated wares suffered little from the loss of markets to sterling, for the loss was more than compensated by sales to lower-income groups who never before had purchased silverware in any form. In no country in the world did the manifestations of good living extend through so large a percentage of the population so rapidly as in America in the twentieth century. The years from 1900 to 1929 were good years for the silver industry, as for most industries, and the steady increase in Reed & Barton sales can be explained in substantial part by the general prosperity which prevailed. The decade preceding the World War contained a measure of business depression, but for the most part it was a period of comfort, luxury, and hearty good times. Heavy gold jewelry and sterling silverware were the order of the day, and both industries fared well. Detroit proved that industrial expansion was far from over, and salesman Joe Dean's orders from this boom region startled the Reed & Barton home office. People traveled, and Reed & Barton sold more hotel ware than it ever had before. The names of new and famous hostelries were added to the list of company customers.

When war came, silverware manufacturers experienced varying degrees of inconvenience. Taxes and prices rose; it was even difficult to obtain enough of certain base metals to meet regular manufacturing requirements. Labor turnover increased, and promising apprentices enlisted in the armed forces. After uncertainty and slack trade in 1916 and 1917, sales grew steadily larger and Reed & Barton experienced a modest war prosperity. Orders flowed in at a brisk rate, production schedules were enlarged, and history repeated itself once again as customers called at the factory to inquire for odd lots of ware in the company storerooms. Activity was brisk, but the briskness might almost have been that of a normal cyclical peak. Foremen carried with them small notebooks to record Liberty Bond subscriptions in their departments, but aside from this and the noticeable lack of young men at the bench, few changes betokening war were apparent in the factory. Reed & Barton's war expansion was conservative in comparison to that in many industries, but the company also avoided the destructive extremes of postwar deflation. The comparative stability of silverware sales throughout the war and succeeding years gave emphasis to the conclusion that the buying public regarded this class of product more as a necessity than as the luxury it once had been considered. Reed & Barton recovered quickly from the 1921 recession, and by 1923, when William Dowse retired, company sales were once again increasing at a conservative but steady pace. War introduced few fundamental changes to the factory and left few scars (except for losses arising through overoptimistic credit sales in the South American market).

THE PROMOTION OF SALES

The growth of sales after 1902 was not exclusively a product of the trend of general business. That Reed & Barton was able to maintain its relative position in the industry is attributable to alert sales-promotion policies. Dowse and the men who worked under him realized the value of carefully conceived and well-placed advertising. Apparently they also appreciated the difficulties involved in planning an adequate program, for outside assistance was sought in planning a campaign. It was also felt by William Dowse that the time had come for the company to have a trained advertising manager. Accordingly, soon after Dowse came to Taunton, William Montgomery Flagg was hired and an advertising department created under his supervision.

Reed & Barton's modern advertising commenced in 1905, when the New York retail store was opened. Much of this advertising was for the benefit of the store, but it was hoped that sales throughout the country would also be stimulated. In 1909 the services of the Morse International Agency, of New York, were engaged, and the program which was drawn up was on a somewhat more extensive scale than any previous to that time.[19] The resulting advertising was directed primarily at New York sales, but provision was also made for nationwide promotion. Individual pamphlets which described the various company wares were extensively used, a system which had been previously tried by Reed & Barton and found successful. Advertising appropriations were expanded to cover the publication costs involved, and a long series of well-designed folders were distributed to customers. Each new sterling flatware pattern was accompanied by its own descriptive booklet, which featured cuts of the ware and a brief discussion of the historical precedents of the particular pattern.

The pamphlet system of promotion was effective for particular items or patterns, but the dealers' great need was for an up-to-date general catalogue of all the company's products. This need was met in 1914 by the issue of a catalogue in several volumes, each devoted to a main product line. Additional issues of folders and pamphlets were also made from time to time, and these publications served to keep customers informed about current product developments. Pamphlet and catalogue advertising was augmented by national advertising in certain of the leading monthly periodicals. In addition, prepared cuts and copy were furnished to dealers for use in local newspaper advertising.

Expenditures from 1906 through 1915 reflect the strong attempt made to help the New York store. The War and ensuing depression curtailed the advertising appropriation sharply, but in 1922 and 1923 greater efforts were again made, directed principally at promoting the sterling flatware line. The centennial anniversary of the company, in 1924, was the occasion for the most extensive advertising ever done. In addition to dramatizing the event through printed media, the company manufactured thousands of pewter cream pitchers, presumed to be replicas of the first pitcher produced by the house. These were distributed with the compliments of Reed & Barton to the trade.

Although expenditures fluctuated widely from year to year, Dowse's advertising was on a scale larger than any previous

CHART IX

ADVERTISING EXPENDITURES AND TOTAL SALES, PERCENTAGE CHANGE FROM PRECEDING YEAR, 1904–1924, REED & BARTON

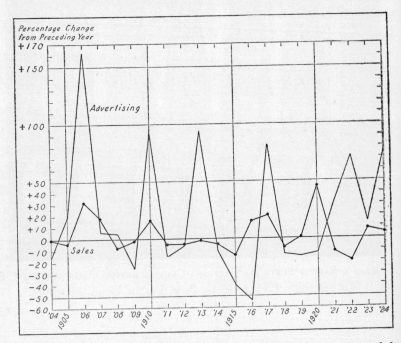

effort made by the company. There is much evidence of careful planning in the campaigns which were put into effect after 1909, and great progress was made in the skill with which pamphlets were designed and catalogues assembled. Compared with the efforts of competitors, Reed & Barton advertising was normally on an extremely modest scale. Its principal effective-

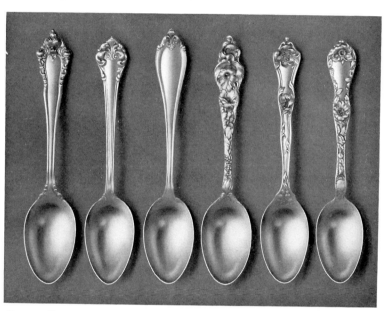

REED & BARTON FLATWARE PATTERNS CREATED BETWEEN 1901 AND 1907
La Splendide, L'Elegante, La Perle, Les Six Fleurs, Intaglio,
Les Cinq Fleurs

ness appears to have rested in the coupling of the company's long reputation for quality with an emphasis on smartness and modernity. This objective was a wise one and probably represented the best possible utilization of the funds and efforts available for promotion. The market showed an unmistakable disposition to purchase on the basis of modern styling, and Reed & Barton advertising shifted rather skillfully in emphasis from past tradition to present performance.

THE TREND OF DESIGN

The Dowse administration achieved conspicuous success in the field of design. This success was the joint result of William Dowse's personal interest and the abilities of an exceptionally gifted group of designers. After William Beattie and Austin Jackson, the last of the old-school English designers, had retired, the designing department under William Dowse functioned without a supervisor. The change appears to have been for the better, however, for the supervisor's place was taken by a joint committee which examined all designs of importance. From 1902 to 1905 this committee consisted of George Brabrook and Mr. Anthony, representing the factory; Luther Hyde, representing the New York office; and William Dowse as final arbiter.[20] Later, when Brabrook had left the company, the responsibility for supervision fell largely upon the general manager. William Dowse, however, continued to exhibit great interest in the work of the department. Showing scant sympathy for company traditions which were conducive to obsolete practice and inefficiency, Dowse nevertheless became sentimentally attached to the best and most constructive in the company's history. He shared the conviction of Henry Reed and George Brabrook that the heart of the enterprise was the designing-room, and, particularly in the early and middle years of his administration, he devoted much thought and active effort to sustaining Reed & Barton's reputation in design. There was little break between the Brabrook and the Dowse administrations in this department, for the tastes of the two men were much alike and the personnel of the designing-room underwent only gradual change.

In design, the French Renaissance influence remained strong for several years following 1900. This influence was expressed in Reed & Barton products by several notable flatware patterns, all of them creations calling forth great skill in designing and die-cutting. La Splendide, Intaglio, and Les Cinq Fleurs all were produced between 1901 and 1904, and all were well received in the market. This success led to plans for a consummate effort in the field of ornate sterling. Ernest Meyers, a French artist and authority on the Renaissance period, was engaged to create the designs for a flatware pattern, and Max Boewe, a German, was entrusted with the die-cutting. Temperamentally the two men were quite unsuited for working together, and progress was slow. As time went on, however, each came to have a high regard for the ability of the other, and as the realization came to both that a masterpiece was in the process of creation, difficulties, both personal and technical, speedily dissolved. The joint result of their work, completed in 1908, was the Francis First pattern. This pattern, so finely wrought and so costly in production, was not so well received at first as had been hoped, for it came at a time when public attention was beginning to turn in a new direction. Sales, however, persisted long after other ornate styles had been discarded, and today the pattern ranks among the foremost in the industry in the length and extent of its market appeal.

The majority of the Reed & Barton flatware patterns prior to 1910 were the products of foreign-born and foreign-trained designers. Apprentices and the younger designers, however, were American — the product of American art schools. As these young men, both at Reed & Barton's and in the designing-rooms of other silverware manufacturers, began to mature, the influence of their training began to make itself felt. It is perhaps

FRANCIS FIRST FLATWARE, REED & BARTON
First made in 1908

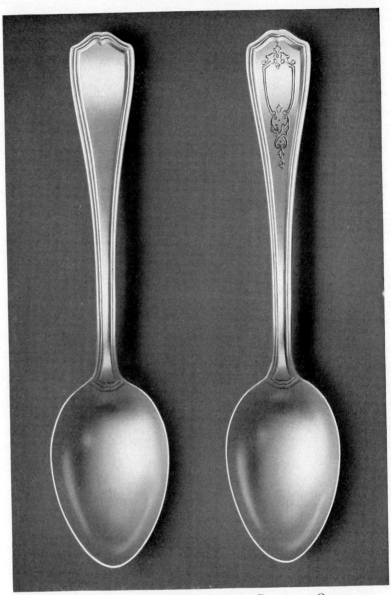

SPOONS IN THE HEPPLEWHITE PATTERN, PLAIN AND CHASED,
REED & BARTON
First made in 1905

more than coincidence that about this time commenced a rever-
sion from European heaviness and reawakening interest in
English Georgian art and its American derivatives. In 1905,
while other silverware manufacturers were riding the peak of
the Renaissance cycle and plans for the Francis First service
were still in a tentative stage in Taunton, Reed & Barton released
to the trade a pattern revolutionary in its implications. Never
deliberately a leader in the conception of new trends, the company caught the industry by surprise, and the success of the
new offering was spectacular. The Hepplewhite service appears
to have been George Brabrook's inspiration, but the idea was
heartily approved by Dowse and cleverly converted to reality by
the designing-room. Reed & Barton's Hepplewhite proved that
the dignity, grace, and refinement of the late eighteenth century
once again held a spontaneous appeal for the American public,
and the pattern may well be considered one of Reed & Barton's
greatest and most significant achievements in the field of
sterling flatware.

After 1910, patterns in silver reflecting the simplicity of
colonial and early nineteenth century times were turned out
with increasing frequency, and the fashion reached a great
climax of popular enthusiasm in the 1920's. Dowse did everything in his power to encourage the trend. Mr. George Turner,
an honor student from the Rhode Island School of Design, who
had created the designs for the Francis First hollow ware, together with George Parker, Wilkes, Bennett, Chesterman,
Uhlman, and Mr. August Miller all made substantial contributions to the new epoch of fashion. Most of these men had served
their apprenticeship under exponents of continental European
design, yet all were young enough, vigorous enough, and amply
gifted to progress beyond the scope of their early experience.
They returned at last to that concept of beauty through line and
surface which had been espoused with so much promise in the
almost forgotten days of Crossman, West & Leonard and the

Taunton Britannia Manufacturing Company. Thus the grand cycle of fashion consumed the better part of a century in running its course. The conclusion of that cycle found a vastly more sophisticated public taste and a greater versatility among designers than had been in evidence at the beginning. The early stages of the evolution, from 1850 to 1890, were degenerative, but the two final phases held much promise for the future. The Renaissance revival from about 1890 to 1910 and the "Colonial" revival which followed produced equally fine work. The future course of American taste could not be predicted, but there was every reason to believe that American designers were at last capable of interpreting and satisfying that taste, whatever it might be, in a thoroughly sincere and wholesome manner.

CHAPTER XVI

PROFITS IN THE MAKING, 1902–1923

THE PERIOD of William Dowse's management of Reed & Barton was one of considerable prosperity for the company. In every year from 1902 to 1923 profits were made. After 1906, increasingly liberal dividends were paid and large amounts of earnings were turned into surplus. In these two decades the company repaid its owners with fair interest for the small returns of immediately preceding years. Acting with decisive confidence born of long experience, William Dowse instituted wise financial reforms, and for many years growing profitability went hand in hand with growing soundness. Great effort and a keen attention to details in Taunton characterized Dowse's administration of company affairs up to the time when the company was once again on firm financial footing and undisputed ownership and control was his. After this came a period of partial relaxation during which Dowse gradually relinquished many of his supervisory functions and permitted increasing freedom in the local management of the company. Dowse's interest in Reed & Barton never flagged, but rather shifted in his later days from the office to the designing-room and from detailed management to general policy. Dowse trained no successor, delegated to no one person the necessary autonomy of control to carry on effectively, and created no institution capable of so doing. As a result, inefficiencies crept into the organization, and by 1923 many of the financial conditions which Dowse had sought to eradicate in 1902 were once again present, though scarcely to a dangerous degree.

GENERAL ASPECTS OF FINANCIAL MANAGEMENT

In the midst of booming prosperity, Dowse found himself in 1902 with an immensely profitable business stifled by heavy outstanding loans and an acute shortage of working capital. Demand for the company's products had never been better, but cash was practically non-existent and the prospects of obtaining further credit to finance daily operations were far from hopeful. Remedial measures adopted by the new administration were direct, simple, and effective. The large profits of 1902 and 1903 were parsimoniously guarded; no dividends were declared; and some of the large store of metal inventory appears to have been liquidated. By stringent, and not always popular, economy Dowse reduced the outstanding notes payable from $583,000 in 1902 to $195,000 in 1905 and at the same time preserved a small though adequate balance of cash.[1] From 1902 on, the current position of the company steadily improved and in 1906 dividends began to be paid. The loans outstanding among dozens of small country banks and private individuals were gradually liquidated or refunded, and the bulk of Reed & Barton's large current working capital was supplied at lower rates of interest through several of the larger Boston banks. The borrowing mechanism was further simplified and even lower interest rates were obtained after 1916, when Dowse entrusted one institution, the National City Bank of New York, with most of Reed & Barton's current financing.[2] Never again was the company faced, as it often had been in Brabrook's day, with the necessity of bargaining with a large and scattered group of creditors, each imposing different terms and conditions on their loans. The process of meeting the highly seasonal cash needs of the business was reduced to a well-ordered routine — but a routine which appeared to function best when Dowse's confident direction indicated the pitfalls to be avoided. After 1905 the indebtedness of the company began once more to increase. This was made inevitable by the expansion of sales and the extensive capital requirements of New York market operations. While Dowse supervised company borrowing, the loans outstanding do not appear to have been disproportionate to the size and nature of the business. Later, when Dowse had begun to withdraw from active management and the detail work of financing fell to Mitchell, the treasurer, the burden of notes payable became increasingly awkward. The solid financial strength built by Dowse in the first ten years of his administration, however, proved to be an adequate cushion against the effects of weakening central control in subsequent years.

The general prosperity of the company, measured in terms of earning power, increased considerably during the Dowse administration, but actual physical growth was not large. The investment in tools and equipment did not increase greatly between 1902 and 1925, nor were substantial additions made to the working force, yet the amount of wares manufactured annually and the manufacturing profit on those wares showed a steady upward trend. General Manager Mark Anthony labored effectively to combine men, machines, and materials in new and more efficient proportions, and internal improvement supplanted expansion as a source of new profits.

Financial management in this period functioned not without its obscurities. Large corporations, fearing antitrust legislation, showed a sigular disposition to present to the public financial statements which, if not actually misleading, gave only an insignificant minimum of information. Duplicate and even triplicate sets of books were often maintained. At the same time industrial combinations grew complex beyond comprehension, and subsidiary companies became a necessary vehicle of control in the larger networks of companies and industries. These trends in corporate management spread inevitably to many smaller companies, and the mimicry was often faintly ludicrous. Even the most confidential Reed & Barton records became progressively less meaningful after 1902. The assets accounts during Dowse's administration were approximations only, and often not even close ones. Reasons for this obscurity are difficult to perceive, beyond the popular disinclination of owners to allow anyone, even the bookkeepers, to see what the concern was worth. Dowse, possibly influenced by his outside associations with big business, not only developed a sympathy for financial secrecy, but adopted with much success the useful legal fiction of the subsidiary company. During his administration there appear to have been at least six subsidiary companies formed and there may have been more. Three of these were incorporated for manufacturing purposes, one was for selling, and the remainder were instruments in the transfer of company stock. Only the New York subsidiary, however, assumed any measure of importance in the Reed & Barton history. The others were for the most part paper corporations, formed for the purpose of affording legal protection to Reed & Barton and to Dowse and the Reed estate. William Dowse sought to eliminate the possibility of claims against his own or the company's assets by conducting his important financial transactions under other corporate names than Reed & Barton. His legal background strongly influenced his methods, and there is much justification for believing that this aspect of his financial policy from 1902 to 1923 was dictated as much by custom as by business necessity.

The Trend of Profits

Reed & Barton profits from 1902 to 1923 exhibited a far greater amount of variation than did either sales or manufacturing costs. Yearly operating results usually returned a substantial gain, but the practice of charging certain large adjustments directly to the current year's operations imparted a highly erratic movement to the trend of profits. Table 24 presents a general picture of net profits as they appear on the company records.

Rarely in the Reed & Barton history does the opportunity present itself for analyzing the making of profits. For all too many years even the total profit figures are lacking. Behind the income

TABLE 24

NET PROFIT, 1903–1924

REED & BARTON

Year	Net Profit	Percentage of Sales	Year	Net Profit	Percentage Of Sales
1903	$128,239	10.6	1914	$17,862	1.1
1904	88,470	7.3	1915	19,109	1.4
1905	86,400	7.4	1916	28,954	1.8
1906	87,129	5.7	1917	51,611	2.7
1907	27,524	1.5	1918	55,814	3.2
1908	23,630	1.4	1919	59,143	3.4
1909	87,068	5.3	1920	93,155	3.7
1910	147,716	7.8	1921	95,370	4.3
1911	21,284	1.2	1922	90,174	5.1
1912	50,177	2.9	1923	116,011	6.0
1913	51,243	3.0	1924	149,879	7.5

Source: Reed & Barton Mss., Ledgers, 1902–24.

statement lies an important part of the picture of management, and it is particularly enlightening to note the interplay of forces which produced the wide profit fluctuations throughout the administration of William Dowse.[3]

Three clear trends are apparent from a study of Reed & Barton profits expressed in terms of percentage of sales. From 1903 to 1908, profits declined markedly as Dowse labored to institute changes in factory and market organization. Expenses and losses incurred in the New York retail store imposed a heavy burden on current operations. The period from 1909 to 1913 exhibits no decisive movement of prolonged dimensions. New York losses, depreciation of assets, and general prosperity were the principal elements which pushed profits first in one direction and then in another. From 1914 on, the profit trend was slowly upward. Marketing experimentation yielded to conservatism, and the factory reforms of prior years began literally to pay dividends. Within these general trends a wide margin of fluctuation occurred.

The year 1903 was an exceptionally prosperous one for Reed & Barton, with sales at a high level and manufacturing costs cut drastically by the new management. Profits were inflated, however, by a $23,799 mark-up in the value of company-owned patents. In 1904 sales declined somewhat, and an increase in the cost of metals was primarily responsible for the increase in manufacturing costs which dropped profits sharply from the 1903 mark. The profit level of 1904 held through 1905, when a sharp increase in selling expense was compensated by a decline in factory labor costs. The upward trend in selling costs continued through 1906, together with an increase in labor costs, but larger sales and greater manufacturing efficiency combined to maintain the profit level.

The effects of the Panic of 1907 were not immediately felt by Reed & Barton. Profits declined sharply in 1907; this result must be ascribed to an increase in the amount of wages paid, a rise in the cost of metals used, and a further increase in selling expense resulting from large expenditures on the New York retail store. In the following year of depression Reed & Barton reduced selling expenses appreciably, but profits fell to a six-year low when sales declined approximately $145,000. Despite the loss of business and general sluggishness of trade, however, the factory wage level of the preceding year was maintained — a fine tribute to company labor policies in a period of uncertainty, and a point of particular pride to William Dowse.

General prosperity was the rule in 1909, and Reed & Barton was no exception. Sales increased only slightly, but selling costs decreased somewhat, and the cost of metals used in manufacturing was much less per dollar of sales than in the preceding year. Recovery from depression continued through 1910. Sales increased sharply, and manufacturing costs were so successfully kept down that the profit showing in this year was the second best in the entire 1903–24 period.

Profits for 1911 were in marked contrast to the preceding year, in spite of the fact that sales decreased only slightly. Several factors contributed to the abrupt decline. Wages paid in 1911 were $112,282 higher than in 1910, and the cost of metals used also increased substantially. The principal cause of the poor profit showing, however, was a wholesale write-down of certain company assets which William Dowse justly considered as either overvalued or worthless. Fittings and fixtures in the Maiden Lane, Fifth Avenue, Chicago, and San Francisco offices were depreciated $25,171. At the same time approximately $65,000 of company-held hotel bonds, accepted by Brabrook some years before in settlement of outstanding accounts, were written off the books. The impact of these losses more than offset the generally prosperous state of current operations, making 1911 the second poorest year in the Dowse administration from a profit standpoint.

Despite a slight decline in sales through 1912 and 1913, profits for these two years regained a normal level. The factory management of Reed & Barton proved itself capable on many occasions of applying strong pressure on manufacturing costs. Slackening of sales activity appeared to stimulate manufacturing economy so successfully that often the years of indifferent market performance were years of better-than-average profits. Efficiency in the factory was not altogether a matter of machines and studied operations. William Dowse proved to be a good judge of men, and his appreciation of conscientious workmanship was keen. Certain employees in particular were highly regarded by Dowse, and his faith in them proved to be well founded. For many years M. J. Duffy was entrusted with the general maintenance of factory machines and equipment. Although he lacked the benefits of a formal technical education, Duffy's skill in his chosen profession became proverbial. When "M. J." laid a granite base under an automatic hammer he did it for eternity. With a straight eye he could measure a length of shafting and with inherent knowledge prescribe accurately what was needed in the way of supports to sustain it. Almost by hearing he could detect the slightest difficulties in the engines, take them apart, repair the breakdowns, and have them operating again in the morning. On one occasion Dowse was showing a friend through the factory, and in the course of the inspection "M. J." was encountered and introduced. Later the friend remarked that he would have expected to find a skilled graduate of a technical school in such a responsible position. This was William Dowse's reply, and it encompassed his whole philosophy of factory management: [4]

> We have never had to close this plant one hour because of a breakdown in our engines or our machinery. No foreman has ever complained because of undue delay in remedying some mechanical condition that contributed to his production. When we have had a fire here, every hydrant and every pump has worked perfectly. Now, when I have to close up because the machinery doesn't work, or when production is retarded because the master mechanic doesn't know how to remedy the condition, or when a fire gets a good start here because the pumps and hydrants don't work, then I'll get rid of Mr. Duffy and put a technical expert in his place — but until then he stays on the job.

The new equipment and the improved manufacturing techniques instituted by Dowse in his reorganizing years followed the usual pattern of great initial success and subsequent gradual obsolescence, but the ability of the key men in the factory did not depreciate with use and age.

Precisely where the points of greatest cost flexibility in the company occurred is difficult to judge in the absence of detailed manufacturing records. Supposedly the factory payroll was one of the most variable and easily controlled of cost factors. Wage cuts were rare, however, and wholesale layoffs were not looked upon with favor. Dowse endeavored to preserve his working force intact and to effect the occasionally necessary payroll reductions by allocating available work on a part-time basis among as many employees as possible. Selling expense, which was also regulated in accordance with the urgency for economy, on several occasions was drastically reduced in the interests of current profits. The manipulation of labor and selling costs accounts for some of the total flexibility exhibited by Reed & Barton factory operations. The full potentialities for economy latent in these two cost factors were seldom realized, however. In the one case, Dowse refused to cut working hours except as a last resort, and in the other case, he refused to abandon his various selling experiments until they had run their course. This disinclination to utilize completely all the available means for economy explains, in part, why occasional large fluctuations in profits occurred. Frequent and, in many instances, large write-downs of assets, charged to current operations, complete the general explanation.

In 1914, despite a continued decline in sales, labor costs were not reduced. Selling expense and cost of metals used declined considerably, but a $44,482 charge to depreciation offset minor operating economies, and profits declined to a new low. In the following year further large reductions in selling expense and a substantial cut in manufacturing costs were insufficient to compensate for general business uncertainty and a $237,991 drop in sales. Profits were again small, though larger than in the preceding year.

After 1915 the trend of profits was steadily upward. Occasional heavy charges to current operations in the 1916–24 period, however, had the effect of understating the general prosperity of the company as measured by the operating statement. The first of these charges occurred in 1916. In this year sales increased and manufacturing costs decreased, but the resulting increase in profits was partially offset by Dowse's action in writing down the value of the Reed & Barton Company, of New York, by $25,170. In 1917 the books reflected more accurately the true earning potentialities of the company, although even then the operating statement could hardly be considered to reflect normal cost conditions. Once again Dowse chose to take advantage of current prosperity to write down the value of company assets, and a large depreciation charge was made. A pay bonus of $12,443 was also distributed to employees. Under the impetus of general prosperity, however, Reed & Barton sales increased over $300,000, and profits virtually doubled.

War activity in business continued throughout 1918, but the latter half of the year brought recession in many industries. This temporary reaction from feverish war buying caused Reed & Barton sales to decline somewhat, though the volume of sales still remained at a high level in comparison with prewar years. Once again, however, the trend of gain opposed that of sales, and the profit showing for 1918 was slightly better than that of 1917. The means through which this result was achieved appears to have been a substantial reduction in administrative expense and strict economy in the factory.

The period from 1919 to 1924 is of particular interest, for in the course of those years the country's business went through virtually every phase of the business cycle. Reed & Barton was not immune to the effects of general financial stringency and a rapidly deflating prosperity in 1920 and 1921, but the trend of profits through this period of stress remained significantly upward. Unfortunately, detailed cost information for these years is lacking, and only a tentative explanation can be given for the excellent profit showing of the company.

Through 1919 and early 1920, sales reached the highest peak in the company's history to that time. Unparalleled activity in the silverware markets, however, hardly justified unqualified optimism as to the future. Buying was at a feverish rate, but manufacturing costs were the highest yet experienced by the company. The increase in dollar profits was substantial, but a narrowing margin between sales and costs was clearly in evidence. Company operations reflected a curious combination of good management and poor, an inconsistency directly attributable to Dowse's gradual withdrawal from close supervision of the business. During 1919 and 1920, when sales increased over $786,000, conservative financial policy prevailed and annual dividends were raised only $3,000. Factory operations were probably as economical as the equipment in use would allow, and marketing efforts were extended rather than curtailed. Inventories of metal and ware, however, were excessive, and the outstanding debt of the company passed $500,000. In spite of these weaknesses in the capital structure, recession and depression found Reed & Barton far from unprepared. Sales fell off through the last half of 1920 and the decline continued through 1921 and part of 1922. Profits, however, held steady during the worst of the depression. Chiefly compensating for the decline in sales was a sharp cut in general administrative expense. Depreciation charges were also reduced considerably, an economy which seems to have been made possible by the heavy charges in previous and more prosperous years. Late in 1922 the pressure of trade conditions began to lighten, and sales once again climbed upward. In a rising market Reed & Barton reaped the benefits of economies forced by the months of depression, and profits mounted rapidly. There was much to criticize in the company when William Dowse retired in 1923, but the trend of current operations held more than usual promise for the future.

Reed & Barton's financial history from 1902 to 1924 forcefully illustrates the importance of careful management at every level from owner to foreman. In this generally prosperous period marketing skill was less vital to success than the ability to so organize the factors of production that the comfortable volume of demand could be supplied at a profit. Only in 1908, 1915, 1917, and 1920 did large increases or declines in Reed & Barton's sales constitute the primary factor in the making of profits. Much more important in other years was the skill with which material, labor, and administrative costs were manipulated. Adaptability to changing conditions was a feature of the Dowse administration. This was achieved by the flexible policy of taking losses in years when the company could best afford to do so. Relatively few capital expenditures and write-downs of asset values appear to have been amortized over a period of years. Heavy charges in good years resulted, on numerous occasions, in a remarkably excellent profit performance in succeeding years of lesser prosperity. This period in business history placed a premium on the ability to organize, control, and manipulate, and William Dowse was more than ordinarily qualified to operate in harmony with the requirements of the times.

THE DISTRIBUTION OF EARNINGS

In general, conservative practice dominated the distribution of earnings, and in the twenty-four years of Dowse's administration approximately $938,000 was contributed to the Earned Surplus account.[5] Over the same period $876,500 in cash dividends was distributed.[6] The Earned Surplus account grew from $377,005 in 1901 to $1,023,063 in 1910. In this latter year a stock dividend of $250,000 was declared, and in 1919 a further stock dividend of $200,000 was distributed.[7] Even after these divisions the Surplus account stood (in 1924) at $617,141.

The return on capital invested in the company was much larger from 1902 to 1923 than it had been in the 1890's, when all that Reed and Brabrook appear to have been receiving was a $6,000 annual salary. Even so, the investment return was conservative in view of the general prosperity prevailing. The annual average dividend, cash and stock, from 1902 to 1924, was $57,674, or only 6.09 per cent of the average capital invested over these years. William Dowse received, in addition to the dividends to which his share in the Reed estate entitled him, substantial sums as salary for the various offices he held. From 1902 to 1910 the customary $6,000 annual salary was paid him

CHART X

Net Profits and Cash Dividends, 1903–1924, Reed & Barton

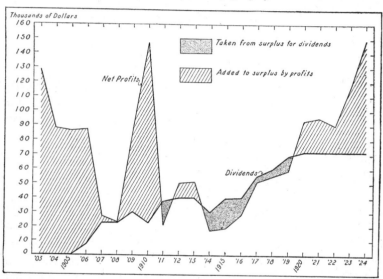

as president of the company. In 1910 this was raised to $25,000.[8] Throughout most of his administration Dowse also held the office of treasurer, with a salary of $6,000 additional to that received as president. It should be noted, however, that although individual executive salaries were smaller prior to 1902, there were then more executives. Dowse simply combined in himself the offices held by Reed, the Brabrooks, and the Fishes. Actually, regular executive salaries during Dowse's administration did not exceed those paid under Reed and Brabrook by any more than the enlarged extent of the company business in the later period justified. The large salaries paid to William Dowse by Reed & Barton, of New York, however, made this period of ownership the most lucrative in the company's history.

CHANGING ASPECTS OF CONTROL AND MANAGEMENT

The making of profits constitutes a matter of primary interest in the 1902-23 period of Reed & Barton's history, but scarcely less important than the fact of great managerial accomplishments is the constituent nature of management and ownership under which those accomplishments were effected.

With the purchase of the Brabrook and Fish stock from the Silversmiths Company in 1910, Reed & Barton became for the first time in its history a one-family concern. Ownership was vested in the Reed estate, but control rested with William Dowse in his capacity of administrator of that estate. This centralization of authority was essential to the company's well-being, for William Dowse, if he was to work at all, had to work alone. His great ability in the precise fields where Reed & Barton lacked strength justified completely his demands for supreme and unrestricted authority. The final step in concentrating control to the utmost was taken in 1927, when Dowse effected a consolidation of interests within the Reed estate itself by purchasing the shares of stock held by Reed's daughter, Clara Hubbard.

Even more significant than the unification of control was the changing relation between ownership and management. Not since the days of the joint-stock company of 1830 had the slightest breach appeared between these two functions. Most of the Reed & Barton partners and stockholders prior to 1902 had lived in Taunton and given the affairs of the company their undivided attention. Henry Reed, Charles Barton, and most of their predecessors had actually managed the company from the workbench. Reed & Barton under William Dowse functioned in a markedly different manner, a manner which was to some extent characteristic of the times. A changing order of business found financiers and financial institutions reaching out to control, from a central office, the affairs of many different companies in many different places. This was in many cases a precise, machine-like control, in which traditions and personalities played a subservient part to the demands of efficiency. Reed & Barton, with its unfortunate period of financial mismanagement under Brabrook, created just that necessity for outside assistance which, in many companies, had meant a loss of independence.

Absentee ownership under William Dowse was a far step from the circumstances which prevailed when Henry Reed was alive, and yet Dowse never allowed the gap between ownership and management to become so wide as contemporary examples indicated it could be. Dowse's rapidly quickening interest in the company eliminated much of the impersonal element from his administration and kept him close to Taunton. Some adjustments, nevertheless, had to be made. Into the hands of the factory manager came greater responsibilities. Routine matters which Henry Reed would certainly have handled personally were scarcely brought to William Dowse's attention, nor was there any need for so doing. Dowse passed on all matters of general policy, negotiated most of the financial details of the business, and looked into such questions of manufacturing, product creation, and selling as interested him. In general it may be said of Dowse's first years at Reed & Barton's that his participation in management, though naturally less active than that of Henry Reed, extended well beyond the requirements of his position in the company and probably far beyond the point indicated by contemporary practice. It was this fact which, more than any other, commanded the continued loyalty of men who had worked shoulder to shoulder with Henry Reed.

The change from local to "outside" ownership was a particularly delicate one for Reed & Barton to make, and acceptance of the new régime in the factory came by degrees. Dowse, working under many handicaps, first gained support and respect from his men by fighting for the company with every ounce of his abundant energy. This initial advantage was reinforced by the obvious sincerity which characterized his relations with company employees. Dowse knew he could never fill the unique position in the factory vacated by Henry Reed, and he made no pretense of doing so. His was a new era in ownership, and he knew it. What is more important, Dowse realized that the factory knew it, and he wisely and naturally abstained from the superficial fraternizing which in so many companies was substituted for genuine interest.

Only a few people in the factory came to know Dowse well. This fact constituted no obstacle for Dowse in administering company affairs, but it did conceal from many the extent of his interest in and respect for the Reed & Barton employees. Reticence in the public expression of his kindly, more intimate side fostered the growth of Dowse's reputation for fierceness. It must be admitted that the incidents upon which this reputation was founded were not diminished in the telling, but the impression became established, none the less, and Dowse himself never denied it. His concern over personnel problems was confided to immediate associates — rarely to the employees themselves — and it usually took an emergency to elicit a statement of his feelings in such matters. One such occasion is well remembered by those few who were close to Dowse. During one winter of depression orders fell off so abruptly that a sharp curtailment of factory operations, with attendant dismissals, appeared inevitable. Dowse's orders were quick, blunt, and thoroughly characteristic: "Keep things going. A lot of people around here have to eat." [9] No person in the factory ever heard those words, and William Dowse would have been acutely uncomfortable had they been revealed. There were those who never saw beyond the stern exterior nor forgave Dowse his gruff tone, but in time his true nature became widely felt. Dowse was too intensely proud of his company to be considered always as an outsider. No person could question the sincerity of his interest in Reed & Barton's accomplishments, and that interest operated to assure William Dowse of an esteemed place in the memory of his times.

Then, too, there were many ties with the past — ties which still further eased the transition from one system of ownership to another. There existed a continuity of product which strongly linked past with present. The tradition of painstaking craftsmanship, moreover, persisted as the dominant force in the factory. These were intangible links, but there were others of a physical, readily felt nature. Sons, fathers, and grandfathers were Reed & Barton men, often practising in succession down through the years the same skilled trades. The automobile destroyed some of the feeling of community which had existed for so long in Britanniaville, but the tradition of family trade inheritance persisted nevertheless, and to a remarkable degree. The link with the past was strengthened by the impressive number of men whose service in the company's employ was counted in more years than twenty or thirty, and these records in the skilled trades exerted an important influence on the more transient, unskilled occupations. Britanniaville had its tenements, but the number of permanent homes was impressive. Pensioned employees passed their days within sight of the factory and kept alive the memory of old names and old events. In these essential respects the Reed & Barton of William Dowse's time was the Reed & Barton of Henry Reed's. Changing operational tactics actually changed few of the vital, fundamental company characteristics and traditions.

The over-all impression of William Dowse's administration is one of great material success. He brought scientific organization and clear financial guidance to the company at the precise moment when it was most needed. In spite of certain weaknesses which had been allowed to develop, it was a compact, profitable company which Dowse turned over to younger hands in 1923, when he retired from active participation in the business affairs of Reed & Barton. The passing of time since Dowse's death in 1928, moreover, imparts a clearing perspective to the affairs of his day in other than financial fields. It may well be that his greatest contribution to Reed & Barton was in perpetuating, under the handicap of a brusque and often misunderstood personality, that community of interest which Henry Reed and Charles Barton had first established in their days at the workbench with their men.

PART V

THE RECENT PERIOD
1923–1943

CHAPTER XVII

MODERNIZATION AND THE PRESERVATION OF OLD IDEALS, 1923–1943

OF PRIMARY IMPORTANCE to William Dowse in his later years was succession to the control over the estate which he had labored so effectively to create and preserve. Involved in the inheritance was the task of operating both Reed & Barton and the United States Fastener Company and of administering the family trust. The task fell to a not completely acquiescent son-in-law, Mr. Sinclair Weeks.

THE THIRD GENERATION IN COMMAND

In 1923, when Dowse turned over the management of Reed & Barton to Mr. Weeks, the latter was engrossed in a different career, and Dowse's demands upon his services called for a sharp change in plans. To be sure, the call to participate in the affairs of Reed & Barton was a strong one, backed as it was by nearly one hundred years of Reed and Dowse family ownership; but John Wingate Weeks, Sinclair's father, had established precedents in his own right which the son found attractive. The precedents set by John Weeks were enviable ones, including not only a distinguished banking career as co-founder and partner in Boston's brokerage house of Hornblower & Weeks and as a dominant personality in the affairs of the First National Bank of Boston, but also noteworthy public service as staunch Republican mayor of Newton, member of the United States House of Representatives, United States Senator, and Secretary of War under President Harding and President Coolidge.

After graduation from Harvard in 1914, Sinclair Weeks entered the employ of the First National Bank of Boston. Mar-

riage to Miss Beatrice Dowse followed a year later. Two years
of war service on the Mexican border and in France interrupted
the banking career, and Mr. Weeks returned to face the fact of
William Dowse's declining health and increasingly positive desire to have his son-in-law take over the Dowse business interests. On May 26, 1920, a vote by the board of directors elected
Mr. Weeks vice-president of Reed & Barton. Three years later
the decision was made, and formal connections with the First
National were reluctantly severed. Mr. Weeks, after securing
Dowse's promise of a free hand and with some misgivings as
to the task before him, assumed control of Reed & Barton in
1923. The change was formalized in October, 1925, when Dowse
resigned the presidency and his son-in-law was elected to that
position of responsibility.

The transition from the Dowse to the Weeks administration
was not a painless one. Neither was it beset by the difficulties,
immediate and potential, which had faced Dowse in 1901.
Diversity of stockholding interests in 1923 was not the problem
it had been in 1901, for control of the company had been assured
the new president by the consolidation of ownership effected by
Dowse in 1910. Most important of all, perhaps, was the fact
that personal friction between the new administration and
the remnants of the old was at a minimum. The 1923 change
was carried through with infinitely more tact and consideration
than had been the case in 1901.

To Taunton, the assumption of control by Mr. Weeks appeared far less revolutionary than had the the coming of William Dowse twenty-two years before, and the dramatic, dis-
concerting upheavals of 1901 were not repeated. Mr. Weeks
brought, not a radically new system of administration, but an
improved continuation of many of William Dowse's own
policies. Local management was to play a major part in the
control of company operations. Mr. Weeks, residing in Newton,
drove to Taunton whenever affairs required his attention: at

MR. SINCLAIR WEEKS

Bachrach

first, almost daily, less frequently after the business was running smoothly. A basic requirement for success, then, was a group of capable factory men who could operate on their own initiative. For best results, it was obvious that such men should be of Mr. Weeks' own choosing. Conditions at the factory indicated, moreover, that the time had come for younger talent to try itself.

On the surface Reed & Barton in 1924 was enjoying great prosperity. Sales were substantial and current operations were yielding the largest profits in many years. The Earned Surplus account stood at $629,986. Standards of measurement imposed by the new administration, however, were strict. Judged by those standards, company performance was unsatisfactory in many important particulars. Notes outstanding against the company were higher than either cautious policy or contemporary prosperity justified. Heavy stocks of white metal, carried at a high valuation, filled the storerooms, and outmoded finished wares gathered dust in the attics. Factory machinery was not universally inefficient or obsolete, but prolific opportunities existed for lowering production costs. Managerial personnel at the foreman level presented a difficult obstacle in the path of modernization. A group of men more devoted to their company could not have been found than the various foremen of William Dowse's day. Their ability to turn out quality wares was as unquestionable as their integrity. But greater than either was their independence. Dowse had encouraged independence among his foremen and then neglected to introduce subordination to the end in view, namely, a smooth-flowing production line.

At the moment of transition these problems were not crucial. With great foresight, however, the new administration treated them as though they were. Mr. Weeks acted with vigor, and, like Dowse before him, upon the advice of seasoned experts. A firm of management consultants was called in to appraise the situation of the company. Its advice, coupled with Mr. Weeks' personal analysis, produced major changes in Taunton. The first of these changes was in factory personnel. Those whose inefficiency could be established beyond doubt were released. Not so easy, however, was the task of retiring faithful and often still capable men to make room for a young and energetic new management. Treasurer Mitchell was retired on pension; General Manager Anthony concluded a long, capable, and far from easy term of service and followed Mitchell into retirement.

Technical modernization at Reed & Barton was, or would soon become, a necessity. This fact was clearly recognized by the new company president; but the need for technical ability, though great, was not so great as the need for organizing ability. To handle the men who were to handle the machines, Mr. Weeks brought Mr. Arthur Ashworth to Reed & Barton's. A varied business background of retailing and investment banking was a lesser qualification for the general manager than his military experience. In the end it was his ability to handle men, coupled with military efficiency, orderliness, discipline, and precision which proved to be of the greatest value to Reed & Barton. Entering the service of the company in 1924, Mr. Ashworth became general manager a few years later and finally vice-president.

One year and a half after Mr. Ashworth had been brought to Taunton, Mr. Weeks assigned to Mr. Russell G. Scott the task of rearranging Reed & Barton's manufacturing controls. This selection, too, was a significant one and indicated the trend of the new administration's thinking. Mr. Scott's previous experience in the Franklin Automobile Company with scientific management and the development of visual controls of production benefited Reed & Barton materially in the reorganizing years which followed. His initial appointment outlived its temporary nature, and Mr. Scott stayed on to become treasurer of the company.

As had Dowse before him, Mr. Weeks brought in several men from outside the company to fill key managerial positions. There was a notable exception made to this general policy, however, which had wide repercussions in the factory. In 1925 the office boy who had run errands for George Brabrook twenty years before was made sales manager, and in 1938 vice-president in charge of sales. Mr. Joseph H. Martin brought to this position the knowledge imparted by laborious apprenticeship, and to the new management a voice which could speak with authority on Reed & Barton traditions and experiences. His career commenced as errand boy at $3.00 a week and extended through the stamping- and burnishing-rooms to the office; later, through the shipping-room and cost department to a position as salesman. Under Mitchell, Mr. Martin had returned to the factory and was rewarded for his work on the road by a supervisory position in the sales department as it was then constituted. His appointment as sales manager imparted to the new administration a balance between experience in the company's service and experience in other fields of enterprise which could not but be beneficial. In the factory the appointment was regarded with deep satisfaction, and gave evidence of the fact that positions of responsibility were to be open to local as well as imported ability.

With key men chosen, and the limits of their duties and responsibilities outlined in general, the next step in reform was isolation of the trouble spots in company operations. The more serious of these were well known to Mr. Weeks; others appeared after a careful examination. To Mr. Ashworth fell the difficult task of gaining the complete confidence and coöperation of the foremen, without which no detailed knowledge could be gained and no permanent improvements effected. His success in this mission has been the foundation for the new program and a major explanation for its successful accomplishment.

Working Out the Program in the Factory

Mr. Ashworth did not pause long in the office provided for him. Every room in the factory came to know him as he examined, questioned, appraised, and planned. Out of his quickly gained intimacy with actual working conditions and techniques, emerged system, organization, and cleanliness. Of these the last-named was by no means the least important, and it probably was the most revolutionary. Storage bins were emptied, scrap was burned or melted, floors were scoured, walls painted, and machinery cleaned. Obscure corners inside the factory were painted spotless white, a subtle hint to the tobacco-chewing fraternity which did not pass unheeded. "The Colonel," as Mr. Ashworth is commonly called, warned that he would not be satisfied until he could eat his dinner off the engine-room floor; and when the clean-up had been completed, he could have done so.

A beginning and considerable progress in scientific plant lay-out and production planning had been made under William Dowse, but early efforts had not been sustained in many departments. The prevailing condition appeared to lie somewhere between moderate efficiency and moderate inefficiency. Just as there were particularly well-ordered departments, there were others where waste of time and material was at a maximum. Most noticeably lacking was a centralized, coördinated control over operations. The efforts of Mr. Ashworth and Mr. Scott to improve the work-flow ran immediately into the same obstacle which Mr. Anthony had faced twenty years before. The sprawling collection of buildings which comprised the plant almost seemed to defy order and logical arrangement of work. Limitations imposed by brick and mortar notwithstanding, however, great progress was made by the new management in simplifying the routing of materials.

Making every effort to utilize existing floor space, departments

The Reed & Barton Factory, 1940

THE MODERNIZED EAST WING AT THE FACTORY, 1943
This wing houses new offices and showrooms

were rearranged and even moved bodily from one section of the plant to another. New construction was used only as a last resort, but new equipment soon made its appearance. In eleven years $174,000 of old machinery was written off the books, to be replaced by $294,000 of efficient new tools![1] In a move symbolical of the readjustments taking place and of the "clean-up" period, the dingy offices in the West Britannia Street building were removed to the three-story east wing, which ungainly Victorian structure then had its face lifted. The red-brick front yielded to silver-and-black trim, and a smart foyer distinguished each floor. The new offices occupied all three floors, and two spacious showrooms were installed and fitted out. It may be significant that increased trade followed these improvements. Set amid century-old buildings, the modern smartness of the remodeled east wing presented a unique appearance to the casual observer. To those familiar with events within, this close proximity of venerable age and new efficiency was not inappropriate.

The problem of production control was faced early in the adjustment period, and in a company of many departments, many processes, and many products it was not easy of solution. Some of the devices employed to trace the progress of wares from metal stock to customers' shelves were the usual ones, but others were ingenious and original. Of particular pride to Mr. Ashworth was his production-control board: colored tabs, moving across the board in accordance with the departmental job tags which were turned in at the central office, revealed the progress of work orders throughout the plant. With this device "production chasing" was confined to a minimum, and job routing became quicker and vastly more efficient than it had been before. Closely correlated with the stock control system were the sales charts, set up to show at a glance the trend of demand for individual products. Accurate inventory records were installed with a view to eliminating once and for all the old complaint of garrets filled with obsolete wares. In the die-storage rooms a revolution took place, and from the upheaval emerged orderly shelves of carefully labeled and immediately accessible tools. At the same time improvements were effected in the accounting system which resulted in more accurate costing and in the compilation of comprehensive statistical data on company operations.

Departments and functions were clearly defined and new men were brought in to carry out the details of orderly control. In 1927 Mr. Arthur Schutzmeister, who had been engaged in making time studies, was taken from the management consultants and later made plant superintendent and given general control over the details of machinery and workmen. The purchasing department was put under the supervision of Mr. Earl Watson. To translate new ideas into production Reed & Barton claimed one of its own, and brought Mr. Charles A. Rivard to Taunton. Son of a famed member of Reed & Barton's old burnishing-room aristocracy, Mr. Rivard was not new to silversmithing tradition or practice. Under his direction the objectives of designing room and factory became more closely reconciled than at any time since the days when the two were one in fact.

In any such clearly defined organization as was set up in the Reed & Barton factory after 1923 the problem of insuring co-operative action at the top levels of management is not an insignificant one. To prevent departmental lines of authority from becoming barriers to mutual understanding of general problems, Reed & Barton instituted the usual remedy of conferences between the top executives in every branch of the business. A less formal method of bringing these men together grew out of a scarcity of dining facilities in Britanniaville. In 1928 a well-appointed luncheon room was opened in the factory to serve the management and its guests, who otherwise would probably have had difficulty in finding accommodations. The social and gastronomic advantages of this institution proved great — but even more significant was the opportunity provided to discuss, informally and at will, the shop problems of the day. The dining table has not superseded the conference table at Reed & Barton's, but the intangible benefits of daily assembling company executives in a pleasant atmosphere are not likely to be exaggerated when we remember the advantages of the exchange of information and points of view, which helps to prevent even the beginning of misunderstanding. Two-way information to and from the chief executive is vital, but so is cross-information between departmental heads.

The new administration's factory reforms have not been confined to machinery, departmental organization, and production controls. In the management of labor much that was new has been introduced. Here, however, more of the old system has been retained than in most spheres of company activity. Institutions and customs, a century old, have been carefully perpetuated. The company's pension system, operated on the informal basis of payments according to need and financed entirely by the company, was continued with few changes. Informality, indeed, has characterized all possible relationships between workmen and management, and to a degree unusual in any such system of precise modern efficiency. In a company where such a relationship was traditional, the refusal to substitute a different condition has been farsighted and has assured a maximum of efficiency and mutual satisfaction.

Several policies and institutions helped to preserve vestiges of that community interest which once had operated so strongly in Britanniaville. Reed & Barton disposed of most of its local real-estate holdings to workmen, and in many cases advanced the money necessary to finance these purchases. To a large extent the neighborhood surrounding the factory remained identified with Reed & Barton — a majority of the dwellings were, and are now, homes of workmen, pensioners, or families of old employees, and almost every house has some personal tie, past or present, with the company. In one small cottage beside the factory lived a ninety-year-old Reed & Barton workman, who, in accord with an arrangement made by Mr. Ashworth, was cared for by a family now active in the company's employ. The Taunton Silversmiths Mutual Society, formed in 1893, functioned from the start as an independent organization, but it is Reed & Barton none the less. The aims of the society, accident and sickness benefits, augment the company's long-continued policy of assistance in time of need. The Mechanics Co-operative Bank, in Britanniaville, was also founded as an independent organization, but, from the first, many of its officers and directors have been Reed & Barton employees. In the factory itself the practice of bringing sons into the business to follow the trade of their fathers has broken down somewhat under the impetus of a more mobile population, but long performance in the company's service has remained a characteristic of the skilled trades. The entire factory has been proud of these careers, and this pride found expression in the formation of a Half-Century Club, composed of men whose term of employment exceeded fifty years. Not exceptional was the case of old Mr. Wilbur, a white-metal spinner, who served the company for sixty-four years and whose proudest boast was that he wore out three floors beneath him. Through such institutions and personalities, as through company tradition itself, a strong local independence has persisted, the more remarkable for the fact that Reed & Barton can scarcely any longer be considered as a local organization. Unionization, twice proposed (January, 1941, and April, 1942) by interests outside the factory, was twice rejected by vote of the employees.

Such changes in the company's labor policies as were instituted in the years immediately following 1923 were not revolutionary, but many of them were important. Standardized rates were substituted for the ritual of bargaining between workman and foreman which formerly preceded each employment

Reed & Barton's Half-Century Club, December 18, 1941

A Craftsman at Work
Mr. Arthur E. Pepper, Engraver

contract. The task of hiring was taken out of the foreman's hands and centered in a newly created personnel department. Wage incentives for above-average production were introduced, while the practice of paying for improvements in techniques suggested by the employees was adopted. Most important of all, perhaps, was the new policy of explaining to the men and women in the factory the changes which affected them and the managerial objectives behind those changes. This was a long step from the régime of the "czars," when department foremen managed in stern autocracy. In general, an atmosphere of greater freedom pervaded the factory after the first World War, and the distinction which formerly separated foremen from workmen gradually diminished. The advent of the automobile and subsequent ease of commuting, better education on the part of young applicants for jobs, and the socializing influence of the war experience itself were three factors which helped change the trend of thought.[2] These established tendencies were strengthened by company policy after 1924. Men and women working at less skilled jobs came to have a greater respect for their own talents and position. Respect for the guidance of management and the authority of the foremen has perhaps increased, while at the same time the heavy consciousness of both, which prevailed for a period, has largely disappeared from the factory.

REBUILDING THE SALES DEPARTMENT

Reed & Barton's marketing organization was characterized, in 1923, by a curious combination of weakness and strength. No company in the field possessed a finer group of salesmen, but it is doubtful if any other company had lacked for so many years a firm hand to guide the selling effort. Under Mr. J. H. Martin, a program in the sales department parallel to that in the factory was worked out. Intra-departmental organization lines were clarified, salesmen's compensation was uniformly fixed on a salary-plus-commission basis, and great effort was exerted to analyze market demand scientifically. For the first time in well over two generations of management, a department was created which possessed the authority not only to establish definite marketing policies but to insure that such policies, once established, would be uniformly adhered to. And for the first time since George Brabrook's day, the salesforce had a leader whose personal experience in the factory and in the field qualified him to lead.

As in the past, salesmen were allowed a considerable degree of independence, but the extent of their independence was varied according to performance. In the home office careful checks were instituted on the long-term results of men in the field, and their action in respect to credit standings, exclusive arrangements, and market conditions was made subject to more regular review than had previously been the case. Ties between office and salesmen were greatly strengthened by regular correspondence and scheduled meetings, and the headquarters of operations came, in fact as well as in theory, to reside in Taunton.

An immediate problem facing the new sales manager was that of staffing the department with new personnel. The crack salesforce of William Dowse's day had grown old in the company's service; to replace men of their caliber was not an easy task, nor one which could be accomplished in a short space of time. New men were brought in, trained in the field under experienced eyes, and tried on their merits. Slowly there was created, even as the famous old organization stepped aside, a new group of field representatives whose performance came, in time, to equal that of other days. Foresight in the training of replacements thus assured a continuity of ability, undiminished selling efforts, and maintenance in the market of the reputation of Reed & Barton's salesforce.

Advertising efforts of the new sales administration were both more consistent and more skillful than those of the old. A

A Craftsman at Work
Mr. Samuel J. Fowler. Spinner

A CRAFTSMAN AT WORK
Mr. Joseph Rudolph, Diesinker

keener understanding of the place of advertising in modern business contributed to the improvement. So, too, did the new techniques of demand analysis developed by advertising agencies, industrial advertisers, and independent students of marketing method. In general, however, Reed & Barton's policy remained conservative and embodied many of the ideas developed under William Dowse. Copy continued to be placed in a few carefully selected periodicals, and considerable emphasis was placed as before upon the use of pamphlets. Advertising Manager William T. Hurley, Jr., in Mr. Martin's department, advanced a revolutionary solution to the catalogue problem by dispensing with catalogues altogether. In their place was substituted a card index of company products. The cards, measuring six inches long and four inches wide, carried a picture of the product, description, itemization of pieces, prices, and a brief exposition upon the character of the design. Approximately a thousand cards, contained in an attractive roll-top box, were distributed to each dealer, and new cards have been added from time to time. This system, unique in the industry, has proved its merits in actual practice. Responsibility necessarily has been placed upon the dealer to maintain his files in order, but the advantages over the bound catalogue in flexibility and ease of use have proved great.

Product Policy — Methods and Results

Fundamental methods of adapting company products to variable market demands have not been greatly altered by the new administration, but improvements in the details have been effected. The highly satisfactory procedure of previous years has been continued, and determination of what should be produced has remained a joint function of the sales, cost, designing, and manufacturing departments of the business. This program has been administered by a New Goods Committee which has met weekly. Mr. Ashworth has presided over the committee meetings; associated with him have been the head designer and members of the designing staff, the general superintendent, the head of the cost department, the supervisor of sales charts and production schedules, and Mr. Martin, sales manager. A fair analysis of new competitive goods and frequent reports on marketing trends have kept the New Goods Committee abreast with current needs. The result has been a constant flow of new ideas emanating from the designing staff to meet these needs. This procedure has been supplemented by recommendations presented at sales conventions by the men in the field. At these conferences both the offerings of the New Goods Committee and the recommendations of the salesmen have been individually considered. Invariably when the reaction has been favorable, the item has been placed in the line of sales goods. If after mature deliberation a sample was vetoed, then it was either changed to meet the objections or eliminated entirely.

The personnel of the committee has been well chosen, and the many-sided analyses of product problems have done much to perfect the company lines. A greater consciousness of over-all operations has been engendered among those participating in the discussions. Designers have become familiar with the salesmen's point of view and the sales department has come to appreciate manufacturing problems. All concerned have become better acquainted with costs, and the charting department has been able to plan its work with greater accuracy. Action upon the committee's recommendation has not been left to chance. At each meeting, careful notes have been made of the plans adopted, and each person concerned has received a copy of the proceedings checked to indicate the specific responsibility that was his to carry through.[3] War and ensuing operational changes terminated the activity of the committee in 1942, but the proven worth of the system in the past indicates its future potentialities.

In January, 1928, an effort was made by the company to in-

crease the relative volume of sterling sales by the purchase of a
company which dealt in parallel lines, Dominick & Haff, of
Newark, New Jersey. Founded in 1821, this firm possessed an
old and respected name in the industry. Its products were confined to sterling hollow ware and flatware, many of which in
design and in craftsmanship were among the finest of the industry. Its distribution, like Reed & Barton's, was confined to
the finer retail jewelry and silverware outlets. Therefore, when
it was decided to abandon the operation of Dominick & Haff as
a separate entity, the merging of the two lines of products was
a natural fusion and one that was readily accepted by retailers.
To Taunton were brought certain key executives of Dominick
& Haff, some equipment, good personnel, and the company's
established line of patterns. Regardless of the continued success
of some of these patterns, such as Pointed Antique, the Newark
purchase was not so prolific in results as had been anticipated.
Reed & Barton found that it was maintaining two designing
staffs. These were shortly united, and one designing room
worked thereafter on both Reed & Barton and Dominick &
Haff lines. Eventually the two lines were merged, certain patterns discarded, and the best of the Newark designs retained.

Certain significant changes in Reed & Barton product policy
were required by market conditions beyond the company's control. Identical conditions were encountered by other companies
in the industry, and the solutions adopted were necessarily
similar throughout. In the hotel trade a downward trend became apparent in the quality of wares demanded. Loss from
theft and competition from less pretentious eating places were
two factors which tended to discourage the use of heavy plate.
Inexpensive services with more frequent reorders characterized
business from all but the proudly old-fashioned hotels, and
silverware manufacturers' lines were adjusted accordingly.

After 1930, depression produced drastic alterations in demand,
and, in order to stay in business, silverware manufacturers were

forced to follow the market downward. Quality lines were not sacrificed in the readjustment. Instead, the general policy followed was to bring out new lines, new brand names, and new patterns. The repercussions of the less expensive offerings upon old-established reputations are difficult to appraise without the perspective of time. Certainly the downward movement was not without danger, but it may be that individual risk was minimized by universal participation. To meet increasing price competition Reed & Barton brought out certain lower-priced wares which could be sold in volume. In the hotel field these lower-priced items were confined particularly to the essential pieces in flatware and such standard items in hollow ware as coffee- and teapots, sugar bowls, cream pitchers, small meat dishes, and a few kindred pieces. The Viking brand of plated hollow ware was inaugurated during the 1930 depression. It was brought out to meet the new needs of the finer jewelers and silverware distributors for silver-plated hollow ware that would be lower in price than established standard brands. Again, in the retail field this new line was confined to essential and commonly used items. With the reviving demand for quality wares after the depression and the shortages in metal occasioned by the War, the Viking brand was eventually terminated in 1941. In the field of sterling flatware the Marlborough pattern was reinstated with the express purpose of meeting price competition, particularly in big cities. This pattern, which offered excellent quality at a lower cost, proved particularly adaptable to a depression market. Implicit in the company's promotion of this number, however, was an awareness not only of curtailed consumer budgets but of a fundamental and steadily increasing demand for sterling flatware from lower-income groups of people. This movement did not lose its strength, even in the depths of the depression, and it maintained itself afterwards as an important market factor. Like Britannia ware, and electroplated ware after it, sterling silver products had become a

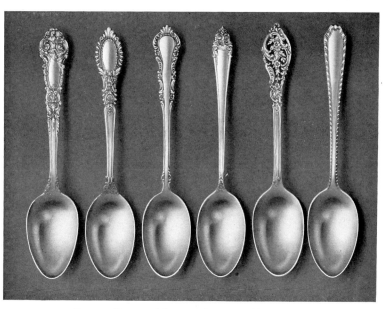

REED & BARTON MODERN STERLING FLATWARE
French Renaissance, Guildhall, Georgian Rose, Fragrance,
Trianon Pierced, Hawthorn

REED & BARTON MODERN PLATED TEA SERVICE
Renaissance Pattern, No. 6000

coveted and almost attainable possession to those who hitherto
had found it far beyond their grasp. On this occasion Reed &
Barton did not wait, as it had done in other days, for the new
demand to rise to the price level of the regular company lines.

Design — Experiments and Revivals

If American silverware design after 1923 exhibited any one
distinguishing feature it was independence — a complete lack
of subservience to the dictates of any one school of thought.
Designers drew their inspiration from many sources, but were
bound by none of them. Definite waves of fashion continued to
be apparent, but none dominated to the exclusion of all others.
Existing side by side at one time or another were to be found the
patterns of almost every period of art the civilized world has
ever known. At the same time an original "Modern" movement flourished briefly, and streamlined silverware made a
somewhat awkward bow to the public. Eclecticism reigned, and
designers, often with great skill, combined the best features of
several periods. In general, the diversity was a tribute to the
knowledge of the American public and to the interpretive skill
of American artists.

Reed & Barton's designing, under the more than able supervision of Mr. George Turner, cautiously explored first one and
then another of the infinite variety of promising trends. The
quality of the work performed was in the best company tradition; it was practical work, directed not at improving American culture but to the end that company wares should find a
ready acceptance in an intelligent market. The expensive luxury
of pioneering was not indulged in as a company policy, but
occasional opportunities of assuming leadership were not
ignored. In general, Reed & Barton stood by its many times
proven conviction that conservative practice paid the most consistent dividends.

The market movements to which Reed & Barton's designers

have responded in the years following 1923 are too numerous to discuss in detail. Certain trends and designs, however, stand out, and will be remembered as characteristic of the period. Reed & Barton's Contempora design illustrates in flatware the height of the modern art movement. Sleek smartness held a strong appeal through the decade of the 1920's, but, as in so many other experiments in originality, the public grew weary and sought once again the proven and the familiar. The modern movement, however, did not die. Clever artisans disguised the new with subtle touches of the old, and the results were both good and popular, and so remain. Reed & Barton's Fragrance pattern is characteristic of the union.

Americans were not to be distracted by any means from what was, and is, popularly felt to be the American tradition in design. Of fundamental, and probably lasting, appeal have been those patterns which reproduced authentically or in spirit the work of Colonial silversmiths. The Pointed Antique pattern illustrates the strength and consistency of this demand in flatware, as does the Sierra service in hollow ware. A closely allied movement which gathered strength after 1930 was the popularity of chaste decorations, imposed on a background of simplicity. English Georgian patterns, of varying degrees of authenticity, answered the demand. Flowery, ornate design also sprang once again into the foreground after a period of subservience to Colonial restraint. Reed & Barton was admirably situated to cater to the revival; and the lavish expenditure on the Francis First dies proved not to have been in vain. •

In the work of the silversmith manufacturers appears no disaffection for originality. Now, however, to a greater degree than ever before, exists an appreciation of the basic appeal which authentic period design holds for the American market. Freedom in varying details has been established by designers and endorsed by the public, but it is clear that independence of the basic, tested designs of the past can never be tolerated for long.

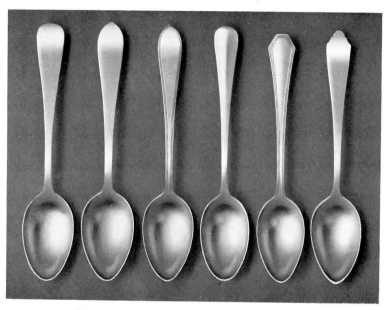

REED & BARTON MODERN STERLING FLATWARE
Old English Antique, Pointed Antique, Mayflower, Seventeenth
Century, Queen Anne, Yorktown

REED & BARTON MODERN PLATED TEA SERVICE
Winthrop Pattern, No. 1795

Operating Results through Prosperity and Crisis

The over-all progress of the new administration was steady and, until 1929, not beset by external problems of a serious nature. The debt burden was reduced in a period of three years to considerably less than half what it had been in the last years of William Dowse's control. Average yearly sales from 1925 to 1929 were higher than for any other period of comparable length in the company's history. Profits turned into surplus approximated 5 per cent of sales, and the average annual dividend for the period moderately exceeded the highest level reached in the Dowse administration.

The abrupt beginning of depression caught Reed & Barton with a heavier-than-average burden of notes payable and a large inventory of goods. Sales declined too quickly in 1930 to allow a corresponding adjustment in manufacturing costs to be made. The net loss for the year was considerably greater in amount than had been the large net profit of the preceding year. Through the year 1930, metal inventories were written down in value approximately $200,000 and the company's debt decreased to less than $400,000. The conditions of trade deteriorated further in 1931, but for Reed & Barton the worst was over. While sales declined even more than in the preceding year, a program of economy in the factory was instituted and vigorously followed through. At the same time selling expenses were curtailed sharply (and the dividend rate cut); as a result, operations for the year showed a net profit. By 1932 the company was out of debt, though sales declined further and a net loss for the year was reported. After this, conditions improved steadily. The recession of 1937 proved only a minor check to progress, and Reed & Barton, like other companies in the industry, moved into the crisis of war in a highly prosperous condition.

Financial policies of the Weeks administration departed, in many respects, from the precedents set by William Dowse. The great reservoir of earned surplus which had existed since 1890 had been almost liquidated by 1933, largely by writing off accounts receivable (including a number arising from South American trade) which were of little value and an excess of inventory of obsolete finished goods. Thereafter, the surplus account was steadily built up again until by 1942 it amounted, roughly, to half the average figure carried on the books by Dowse. Accompanying the shrinkage of this account, however, was a decisive reversal in borrowing policy.

At no time after 1929 did the outstanding debt approach the figure considered as normal by the previous administration. For a great majority of the years between 1929 and 1943 no notes payable whatsoever were outstanding. Dividend policy likewise was reversed, and since 1923, in contrast to the inflexible practice of preceding years, the dividend rate has been closely tied to the current condition of the company. Mr. Weeks has, of course, received a salary, but no share in the bonuses which were distributed to management and employees in 1941 and 1942. Extreme conservatism characterized the valuation of physical assets. In 1943 the depreciation allowance, accumulated over a period of years, was equal to approximately 57 per cent of the gross value of land, buildings, and equipment. The total value of plant carried on the books was stated to be equal to one-third the current cost of replacement. These were the changes effected by a one-time banker's administration of the affairs of Reed & Barton after 1923. In so far as financial policy was concerned, the break with the past was complete; the events of subsequent years, particularly the years of depression, indicate that the change did not come too soon.

REED & BARTON GOES TO WAR

War provided one of the greatest tests of managerial ability in Reed & Barton's entire history. It is doubtful if such drastic readjustments have ever before been demanded in so short a space of time as those which were made in factory and office in 1940 and 1941. The first World War provided no precedents to follow. In a period of something less than two years Reed & Barton virtually abandoned its commercial line of wares, sold its samples, and embraced an entirely new concept of manufacturing. Operations expanded rapidly, and the number of employees grew to 600 men and 300 women, with many departments working three shifts a day. Confusion was inevitable and mistakes were not avoided; yet out of the tangle of paperwork, material shortages, labor scarcity, and hasty experiments with new techniques came a new line of products. The new requirements were trying, for manufacture was on a mass scale never before attempted by the company. Products and materials, too, were frequently new. Tableware for the Army and Navy presented quantitative problems, and the fabrication of steel surgical instruments had to be learned by experience. The tremendous conversion process still goes on, and the history of this period cannot properly be recorded in detail for many years.

Almost as soon as Reed & Barton turned from peace to war, however, a factor deeply rooted in company history and tradition emerged as a dominant feature of the war production program. Craftsmanship and high standards of performance, developed to satisfy fastidious luxury demand, have proved indispensable to a grimmer necessity. Turning all resources and abilities to the filling of war contracts, Reed & Barton was soon producing instruments of a quality equal to that of the old specialized surgical houses. Changes in technique suggested by the company have been adopted elsewhere, and other silverware manufacturers have come to Taunton to observe procedures and results. Whatever permanent alterations war may effect in organization, product, or technique, that pride in workmanship which has survived all trials through the hundred and twenty years of Reed & Barton's existence promises to survive what may prove to be the greatest trial of all.

Better Metal, 1824–1943

Reed & Barton's history exhibits all the usual characteristics of American industrial development — the years of great profits, the periods of desperate uncertainty, the triumphs and the failures in all branches of the business. Although the company is typical, yet the very fact of its long existence indicates the presence of unique and distinguishing features.

Thoroughly American, or perhaps thoroughly Yankee, were the origins. Raw, untutored ingenuity founded the firm. Crusty New England stubbornness and thrift carried it through the crucial beginning years. Success has been the product of occasional inspiration coupled with unceasing manual labor. These factors do not constitute an unusual story, but the results of conservative, consistent business policy are startling when viewed over the long period of time which Reed & Barton's life encompasses. From 1824 to 1943 the net worth of Reed & Barton increased from $2,000 to $1,549,012. Of the increase, 14 per cent represents contributions of capital by owners; 86 per cent has come from reinvested earnings — in Henry Reed's words from "just putting one dollar on top of another." The sums distributed to owners and employees over the period can only be surmised.

Long-continued and remarkably stable prosperity has been a fundamental characteristic of Reed & Barton. The factors responsible for that state of affairs are neither subtle nor numerous. Caution in all business affairs constitutes a primary explanation. From one generation to another the precedent of conservative policy has been passed down, and seldom in the course of years has precedent been ignored. The refusal to experiment heavily in untried fields or to expand operations on other than the basis of reinvested earnings cost the company its early position of leadership in size and scope of productive facilities, but the reward has been a stability of organization and a permanence unique in the industry.

REED & BARTON MODERN STERLING TEA SERVICE
Francis First Pattern, No. 570 A.

REED & BARTON MODERN STERLING TEA SERVICE
Plain Antique Pattern, No. 87

Reed & Barton has been particularly endowed with managerial ability. With fortunate consistency, the right man has appeared at the right time, and special talents have been available to meet special needs. Long-continued family control has been as unusual in its flexibility as in the consistency of its

TABLE 25

Statement of Paid-In and Accumulated Capital
1824 — January 31, 1943

Capital Contributed By	Date	Capital Paid In	Total Net Worth of the Business, Cumulative	
I. Babbitt & W. Crossman	1824	$ 2,000 [a]	1824	$ 2,000 [a]
W. A. West	1826	2,000 [a]	1826	4,000 [a]
Zephaniah Leonard	May 23, 1829	5,000		
Horatio Leonard	July 27, 1829	5,000	1829	9,000 [a]
Assessment on Shares	Dec. 31, 1831	7,200	1831	21,200
Assessment on Shares	Jan. 8, 1832	4,000	1832	25,200
Gustavus Leonard	Feb. 20, 1837	3,719		
Henry G. Reed	1837	3,500		
Charles E. Barton	1837	3,500	1837	(no data)
Henry H. Fish	Mar. 9, 1858	5,000		
George Brabrook	Mar. 20, 1858	5,000	1858	107,597
George Brabrook	Apr. 9, 1867	27,000	1867	(no data)
Henry Reed	Nov. 11, 1898	100,000		
George Brabrook	Nov. 11, 1898	50,000	1898	900,408 [b]
Total to Jan. 31, 1943		$ 222,919	1943	$1,549,012
Total Paid-In Capital	1824–1943	222,919		
From Earnings	1824–1943	1,326,093		
Net Worth, Jan. 31, 1943		$1,549,012		

[a] Estimate.
[b] Approximate figure.
Sources: Statement of Paid-In and Accumulated Capital in the Business, author's compilation, Reed & Barton Mss.
       Statement of Condition, Reed & Barton Corporation, Jan. 31, 1943, Ernst & Ernst.

quality. A willingness to disregard blood ties in awarding positions of responsibility in the company has contributed substantially to the caliber of management, particularly in those years when increasing age restricted the activities of owners. One hundred and ten years of Reed's, Dowse's, and Weeks' control have resulted in stability without stagnation and have provided, both from and beyond the family line, an unbroken succession of capable administrators.

Caution, alertness, and the steadying influence of continuous ownership played important rôles in Reed & Barton's development, but one factor stands out above all others in any comprehensive examination of the company's history. "We are now taking all pains to give you your 200 setts better than *any ever* has been sent into market as yet," wrote Gustavus Leonard to a customer in 1838. The words sounded the keynote of company policy for that time and for all succeeding years. Not good metal, but better metal was the tradition established in the founding years, and unswerving fidelity to the quality of product constitutes the dominant reason for continued success. The emphasis of management has changed many times in Reed & Barton's life, but whether the men in control were salesmen, financiers, or technicians, an appreciation of craftsmanship has prevailed. No necessity has been more clearly recognized than that one which dictates painstaking care in design and production. Each new era of management has demanded a rebirth of ideas, but throughout Reed & Barton's existence the value of tradition has been both tangible and great. Occasionally tradition has obstructed progress — more often it has pointed the way to continued prosperity. It is, therefore, neither prosaic nor unduly sentimental to say that amidst the modern atmosphere of the factory today, the memory of Henry G. Reed's example and teachings remains.

The affairs of Reed & Barton, like those of a vast majority of other relatively small companies, have been from the beginning carefully withheld from public view. The cumulative result of this reticence has been unavoidable historical underemphasis of the important part such companies have played in the development of American business society. It seems particularly desirable, therefore, that Reed & Barton's story be revealed. To its owners the company has brought financial success and the satisfaction of achievement; to the factory men and women, homes, security, and a friendly environment; to the public, wares of lasting beauty and use; to industry, valuable technical advance. The precedent set by this company represents a genuine contribution to modern business society. Reed & Barton's foundation has been organization; its cornerstone, integrity; its necessity, caution; its demand, craftsmanship; its inspiration, pride; its reward, the esteem of those whose lives and affairs it has affected.

As this book was going through the press Reed & Barton was given the Army-Navy E award for excellence in war production, on Friday, November 19, 1943.

NOTES AND REFERENCES

CHAPTER I

1. J. B. Kerfoot, *American Pewter* (Boston, 1924; reprinted, Crown Publishers, New York, 1942), p. 15.

2. For the preservation of these records we are indebted to Edmund W. Porter of Taunton, whose spirited efforts have made available much information of inestimable value about the early history of Reed & Barton.

3. *Columbian Reporter, and Old Colony Journal* (Taunton), June 26, 1822.

4. Taunton *Daily Gazette*, Jan. 11, 1939 (Old Colony Historical Society, Scrapbook No. 4); William Bradford Browne, *The Babbitt Family History, 1643-1900* (Taunton, 1912), pp. 153, 441, and 448.

5. Edmund W. Porter, "Metallic Sketches," in Taunton *Daily Gazette*, Mar. 19, 1906, to Sept. 28, 1907, chap. iv.

6. See Browne, *op. cit.*, for interesting information on the mechanical talents of this unusual family.

7. Porter, "Metallic Sketches," chap. iv.

8. *Ibid.*

9. *Ibid.*

10. Crossman family genealogical papers (unpublished), Old Colony Historical Society, Taunton.

11. Porter, "Metallic Sketches," chap. iv.

12. *Ibid.*

13. Taunton *Free Press*, May 7, 1824.

14. *Columbian Reporter, and Old Colony Journal*, June 9, 1824.

15. This mill was situated on Spring Street where the abandoned factory of the A. Field Tack Works now stands.

16. Samuel Hopkins Emery, *History of Taunton, Massachusetts* (Syracuse, N. Y., 1893), part 1, p. 99.

17. Elias Nason, *Gazetteer of the State of Massachusetts* (Boston, 1890), p. 633.

18. See Emery, *op. cit.*, part 1, pp. 675-676; Alanson Borden, compiler, *Our County and Its People, a Descriptive and Biographical Record of Bristol County, Massachusetts* (Boston, 1899), p. 270; Frank Walcott Hutt, *History of Bristol County* (New York, 1924), pp. 278-279.

19. *Columbian Reporter, and Old Colony Journal*, 1823-24, stage notices.

20. Emery, *op. cit.*, part 1, p. 617, quoting from *Baylies' Historical Memories of New Plymouth*.

21. D. Hamilton Hurd, compiler, *History of Bristol County, Massachusetts, with Biographical Sketches of Many of Its Pioneers and Prominent Men* (Philadelphia, 1883), pp. 729, 822 ff.

22. Borden, *op. cit.*, pp. 272-273.

23. Victor S. Clark, *History of Manufactures in the United States* (New York, 1929; copyrighted by Carnegie Institute of Washington), vol. i, p. 464.

24. Porter, "Metallic Sketches," chap. x.

CHAPTER II

1. J. B. Kerfoot, *American Pewter*, pp. 18–19.

2. *Ibid.*, p. 17.

3. *Ibid.*, p. 19.

4. Ledlie Irwin Laughlin, *Pewter in America* (Boston, 1940), vol. ii, p. 92; Kerfoot, *op. cit.*, p. 18.

5. *Ibid.*, pp. 18, 36–37.

6. Laughlin, *op. cit.*, vol. ii, p. 92.

7. *Ibid.*

8. Frederick Bradbury, *History of Old Sheffield Plate* (London: Macmillan & Co., Ltd., copyrighted by Pawson & Brailsford, Sheffield, England, 1912), p. 495 (quoting Charles Dixon's notes).

9. *Ibid.*, p. 494.

10. Matthew Boulton's establishment at Soho should be mentioned, and its influence noted, as the earliest and most outstanding example of large-scale production in a trade closely allied to the Britannia industry. In 1764 Boulton, engaged in the manufacture of buttons, watch chains, buckles, and many other products, finished the construction of what at that time must have seemed a huge factory. The cost has been estimated at from £9,000 to £20,000, and the buildings were capable of holding 1,000 workmen. For accounts of this enterprise see Bradbury, *op. cit.*, pp. 47–50; N. S. B. Gras and Henrietta M. Larson, *Casebook in American Business History* (New York, 1939), pp. 191 ff.; and Samuel Timmins, editor, *Resources, Products, and Industrial History of Birmingham and the Midland Hardware District: a Series of Reports, Collected by the Local Industries Committee of the British Association at Birmingham, in 1865* (London, 1866), pp. 217–221.

11. Laughlin, in *Pewter in America* (vol. ii, pp. 95–118), has compiled a splendid list of Britannia ware manufacturers, among whom are found several who were working before 1810.

While men like Ashbil Griswold of Meriden, who began work in 1808, made clearly recognizable Britannia ware and were listed as Britannia workers at a somewhat later date, there is some question as to whether or not the classification would have applied equally well before 1810. There is no evidence to prove that Griswold regarded himself as a Britannia worker at that early date, and it is practically impossible in his case, as in others, to say when the manufacture of Britannia ware commenced. (Letter from Mr. W. G. Snow, International Silver Company, to the author, Aug. 21, 1941.)

Another source says that before 1806 those who wished to manufacture Britannia ware were forced to melt up old imported ware, but that in 1806

T. D. Boardman of Hartford discovered how to mix the metal and communicated his knowledge to others. (Edwin T. Freedley, editor, *Leading Pursuits and Leading Men*, Philadelphia, 1856, p. 404.)

12. *The Diary of William Bentley, D.D.* (Salem, Mass., The Essex Institute, 1905-1914), vol. iv, p. 237.

13. Notable exceptions were the Boardmans of Hartford, Gleason of Dorchester, H. Yale & Company of Wallingford, Israel Trask and Eben Smith of Beverly, Morey & Smith of Boston, Rufus Dunham of Portland, and B. Putnam of Malden. (Letter of Aug. 28, 1941, Mr. L. I. Laughlin to the author.)

Ashbil Griswold, though employing possibly only six or eight men in his shop, "had people outside casting spoons, or finishing them up so that his output may have been the result of eighteen or twenty people." (Letter from Mr. W. G. Snow to the author, Aug. 21, 1941.)

14. U. S. Bureau of the Census, *Digest of Accounts of Manufacturing Establishments in the United States and of Their Manufactures, 1820* (Washington, 1823).

15. Robert G. Proctor, compiler, *Tariff Acts Passed by the Congress of the United States from 1789 to 1897, Including All Acts, Resolutions, and Proclamations Modifying or Changing Those Acts* (Washington, 1898).

16. Actually the 1824 tariff affected imports very little. For the year ending Sept. 30, 1823, total imports were $72,481,371; in 1824, $72,169,172; in 1825, $90,189,310. (Worthington C. Ford, "Imports and Exports," in *One Hundred Years of American Commerce, Consisting of One Hundred Original Articles on Commercial Topics* . . . , Chauncey M. Depew, editor, New York, 1895, p. 23.)

17. See statement of Jefferson, quoted in J. Leander Bishop, *History of American Manufactures from 1608-1860*, . . . (Philadelphia, 1864), vol. ii, p. 221; see also vol. ii, pp. 237-238, 245, 252-253.

18. Clark, *History of Manufactures*, vol. i, p. 372.

19. Bishop, *op. cit.*, vol. ii, pp. 219 ff.; *Niles' Weekly Register*, for the years 1816-24.

20. N. S. B. Gras, *Business and Capitalism: An Introduction to Business History* (New York, 1939), pp. 175 ff.

21. Clark, *op. cit.*, vol. i, p. 528.

22. Laughlin, *op. cit.*, vol. ii, p. 92.

23. Kerfoot, *op. cit.*, p. 36.

24. Talbot Hamlin, *Architecture Through the Ages* (New York, 1940), p. 557.

CHAPTER III

1. *Rhode Island American, Statesman, and Providence Gazette*, Sept. 29, 1829.

2. By placing a flat disc of metal upon a lathe adjacent to a mold and pressing the rapidly revolving metal against and around the mold with a

burnisher, the necessity for laboriously hand hammering depth into hollow ware was largely eliminated. The flat metal could be "spun" into the desired shapes with far greater rapidity and uniformity than had ever been possible before.

3. The 1824–27 period of operations is prehistoric in so far as the Reed & Barton manuscript collection is concerned. No account books, letters, or other documentary materials directly connected with the early companies have survived. The history of these years is traced for us in outline by Edmund W. Porter in his "Metallic Sketches," in scattered periodical references, and in certain recorded deeds.

4. Newspaper articles written about 1875, in Scrapbook No. 4 of the Old Colony Historical Society (Taunton), p. 9. Author and exact dates unknown. The list of products is probably far from complete.

5. Now No. 37 School Street, Taunton. The original main building of the works was only recently demolished. The site at present is a vacant lot opposite the Central Fire Station and next to the school building.

6. Porter, "Metallic Sketches," chap. iv.

7. *Ibid.*

8. *Ibid.*

9. In 1828 an advertisement of a jewelry store at No. 3 Merchants' Row appears under the name of W. W. Earl (*Columbian Reporter, and Old Colony Journal*, Oct. 29, 1828), and no further mention is made of the establishment in any connection with the Britannia works.

10. Register of Deeds, Bristol County, deed of Feb. 23, 1828, vol. 123, p. 219.

11. Newspaper clipping, date and author unknown, Scrapbook No. 4 of the Old Colony Historical Society.

12. Tariff rates on manufactures of pewter, tin, and lead, as well as on plated wares, were unchanged by the 1828 bill. Rates were lowered on tea and coffee, however, which may have indirectly benefited the sale of the company's products by increasing the consumption of these commodities.

13. The fragmentary statistics which are available for the period lend support to this conclusion. Total imports increased from $71,332,938 in 1827 to $81,020,083 in 1828 (Depew, *One Hundred Years of American Commerce*, p. 23). Imports of plated ware for the same period increased from $144,890 to $187,127, and of manufactures of pewter and lead from $20,251 to $30,957 (U. S. Secretary of the Treasury, *Commerce and Navigation of the United States, 1827 and 1828*, Washington, 1828 and 1829).

14. *Rhode Island American, Statesman, and Providence Gazette*, Sept. 29, 1829.

15. The survival of this document, as well as of several other early records, is due to the foresight and care of the late Frank W. Knox, who preserved them, almost forgotten for many years, in a trunk in the attic of the old office building of Reed & Barton, where they were found in a good state of preservation by the author.

16. It is doubtful whether this book represents the complete labor record of the employees. At a slightly later date it was found that in addition to the hours shown on the time books, many employees were being paid for the performance of specific jobs which do not appear on the time books.

17. *Vital Records of Taunton, Massachusetts, to the Year 1850* (Boston: New England Historic Genealogical Society, 1928–29); *Vital Records of Norton, Massachusetts, to the Year 1850* (Boston: New Eng. Hist. Genealogical Society, 1906).

18. *Rhode Island American, Statesman, and Providence Gazette*, Sept. 29, 1829.

19. Porter, "Metallic Sketches," chap. v.

20. *Ibid.*

21. *Ibid.*

22. See the quotation from the *Rhode Island American, Statesman, and Providence Gazette* above.

23. Trade directories of Boston, Providence, New York, and Philadelphia. Unfortunately the directories, in many cases, reveal little about the business of the companies listed and are disappointingly vague and inconsistent in the descriptions given.

24. Carl Russell Fish, *The Rise of the Common Man, 1830–1850* (New York, 1927), p. 97.

25. Taunton *Advocate*, Oct. 9, 1829.

26. *Niles' Weekly Register*, vol. xxxvii, no. 945 (Oct. 24, 1829), p. 142.

27. *Ibid.*, vol. xxxix, no. 998 (Oct. 30, 1830), pp. 162–163.

28. Quoted in *Columbian Reporter, and Old Colony Journal*, Oct. 20, 1830.

CHAPTER IV

1. Son of Zephaniah Leonard, Horatio was extensively engaged in the iron industry of Taunton with financial interests extending over several local companies.

2. From the Articles of Agreement, Bylaws, and Minutes, Taunton Britannia Manufacturing Company, Reed & Barton Mss., Baker Library, Harvard University. Corrected for obvious omissions of punctuation and errors in spelling.

3. Although the major terms of transfer and reorganization have come down to us, it is quite probable that some of the details were never recorded on the books, or were recorded on books which have not survived.

4. Articles of Agreement . . . , T.B.M. Co. Obvious repetition omitted, some punctuation added.

5. Register of Deeds, Bristol County, vol. 129, p. 459. This deed is of particular interest because on the site designated therein are located the present Reed & Barton factories, including the building erected in 1830, representing an uninterrupted occupation of 112 years.

6. Articles of Agreement . . . , T.B.M. Co.

7. Register of Deeds, Bristol County, vol. 129, p. 459.

8. Porter, "Metallic Sketches," chap. vi; Articles of Agreement . . . , T.B.M. Co.

9. Ibid.

10. Porter, "Metallic Sketches," chap. vi.

11. Articles of Agreement . . . , T.B.M. Co., Record of Meeting, Aug. 17, 1830.

12. Journal of the Franklin Institute, Nov., 1831, p. 326.

13. Ibid., Feb., 1832, p. 84.

14. For comment on Taunton's coasting fleet see Charles R. Atwood, Reminiscences of Taunton (Taunton, 1880), pp. 46, 87, 229–230.

15. Clark, History of Manufactures, vol. i, pp. 365–366.

16. The shilling represented an American valuation of six to a dollar.

17. Vital Records of Taunton to 1850. The time book records a suspicious aftermath to this event. On Friday, October 14, only five employees appear on the payroll, and it is possible either that charity subordinated profits to close the plant in honor of the occasion, or that post-nuptial celebrations impaired the ability of employees to get back to work in the morning.

18. Articles of Agreement . . . , T.B.M. Co.

19. Reed & Barton Mss., Journal, 1831–33, p. 21.

20. Reed & Barton Mss., Miscellaneous Accounts, 1830–36.

21. Ibid.

22. Reed & Barton Mss., Journal, 1831–33, pp. 3, 43, 192, and Order Book, 1831–34.

23. Porter, "Metallic Sketches," chap. viii.

24. Reed & Barton Mss., Waste Book, 1833–36, p. 1.

25. Porter, "Metallic Sketches," chap. viii.

26. Ibid., chap. vii.

27. The patent which Babbitt took out in 1839, and for which he received a $20,000 award from Congress in 1841, covers not the metal itself, but an anti-friction journal box constructed of the metal. Thus, though Babbitt himself made no claim to having invented the metal, popular opinion has so confused the true nature of his patent that he receives credit which is due, in part at least, to William Porter.

28. Journal of the Franklin Institute, Sept., 1834, pp. 198–199.

29. Conflicting claims exist concerning the identity of the first manufacturer in the United States to import from England the process of spinning metal, and it is probable that this question can never be satisfactorily answered. On the basis of present evidence, however, there is very little doubt that the evolution of spinning to its present vital position in the metal trades owes as much to the Britannia men of Taunton — Isaac Babbitt, William Porter, and William Crossman — as to any other group or individual in the country.

30. Articles of Agreement . . . , T.B.M. Co.

31. From Taunton, Babbitt went to the South Boston Iron Works, where he pursued a brilliant and well-rewarded career.

32. Articles of Agreement . . . , T.B.M. Co.

33. *Ibid.*

34. Bishop, *History of American Manufactures,* vol. ii, p. 377.

35. U. S. Secretary of the Treasury, *Documents Relative to the Manufactures in the United States* (Washington, 1833), vol. i, p. 354.

36. Bishop, *op. cit.,* vol. ii, p. 387.

37. Articles of Agreement . . . , T.B.M. Co.

38. *Niles' Weekly Register,* vol. xlvi, no. 1,173 (Mar. 15, 1834), p. 33.

39. *Ibid.,* no. 1,176 (Apr. 5, 1834), p. 84.

40. *Ibid.,* no. 1,173 (Mar. 15, 1834), p. 33.

41. According to Porter ("Metallic Sketches," chap. vi), William Crossman and Benjamin Pratt took over the shop for several months in 1834 and attempted unsuccessfully to sustain the failing business. Records for the period, however, fail to give details of any such change in management or even to mention that the change occurred.

42. Porter, "Metallic Sketches," chap. v.

43. Interview with Mr. N. A. Cushman, Jan. 28, 1941.

44. Letter from Luke Bigelow to John Bigelow, Apr. 22, 1835. Bigelow Manuscript Collection, Baker Library, Harvard University.

45. *Bristol County Democrat, and Independent Gazette* (Taunton), July 29, 1836.

CHAPTER V

1. Reed & Barton Mss., Journal, Jan. and Feb., 1837, p. 14.

2. Porter, "Metallic Sketches," chap. vii.

3. Bishop, *History of American Manufactures,* vol. ii, p. 410.

4. Willard Long Thorp, *Business Annals* (New York, 1926), p. 122.

5. Samuel Reznick, "The Social History of an American Depression," *American Historical Review,* vol. xl, no. 4 (July, 1935), p. 665.

6. *Niles' Weekly Register,* vol. lii, no. 1,334 (Apr. 22, 1837), p. 113.

7. *Bristol County Democrat, and Independent Gazette,* Apr. 14, 1837, p. 58.

8. Reed & Barton Mss., Letters and invoices, 1837–39.

9. *Ibid.*

10. Reed & Barton Mss., Letter Book, 1839–49, letter of Apr. 9, 1842.

11. Reed & Barton Mss., Time Book, 1831–39.

12. Reed & Barton Mss., Account of Stock, 1840–57.

13. *Ibid.*

14. Reed & Barton Mss.

15. *Ibid.*

16. Emery, *History of Taunton,* part 1, p. 677.

17. Hunt's *Merchants' Magazine,* vol. xxii, no. 4 (Apr., 1850), p. 466.

18. Reed & Barton Mss. Estimate compiled from Manufacturing Account, 1854-59.

19. Reed & Barton Mss., Account of Stock, 1840-57.

20. Reed & Barton Mss., Letter Book, 1849-54, letter of Jan. 16, 1855.

21. Reed & Barton Mss., estimated from Manufacturing Account, 1854-59.

22. Edmund W. Porter's Notebook, unpublished notes written and added to over a long period of years.

23. Freedley, *Leading Pursuits and Leading Men,* 1856 edition, p. 405.

24. Porter's Notebook, corrected for obvious errors of punctuation, and abbreviations written out.

25. *Ibid.*

26. Reed & Barton Mss., estimated from Manufacturing Account, 1854-59.

27. Reed & Barton Mss., Trial Balances, 1857-60.

28. Reed & Barton Mss., Day Book, 1839-41, p. 174.

29. Taunton *Whig,* Sept. 2 and 9, 1840.

30. Porter's Notebook.

31. An examination of company wares has established the fact that the Leonard, Reed & Barton stamp was used after the firm had become Reed & Barton in 1840. However, according to the *Official Gazette of the United States Patent Office* (vol. 34, Feb. 9, 1886, p. 564), the company, in application for a renewal of the trade-mark registration, claimed that the trade-mark "Reed & Barton" had been used since August 26, 1840. It is therefore possible that both marks were being used from 1840 to 1847.

32. Porter's Notebook, with abbreviations written in full.

33. Articles of Agreement . . . , T.B.M. Co.

34. Reed & Barton Mss., Trial Balances, 1854-57.

CHAPTER VI

1. Porter, "Metallic Sketches," chap. vii.

2. Helen Gardner, *Art through the Ages: An Introduction to Its History and Significance* (New York, 1936, revised edition), p. 671.

3. *Journal of the American Institute,* vol. iii, no. 11 (Aug., 1838), pp. 609-610.

4. Reed & Barton Mss., Letters and invoices, 1837-39.

5. See *The Second Exhibition and Fair of the Massachusetts Charitable Mechanic Association, at Quincy Hall, in the City of Boston, September 23, 1839,* p. 27.

6. Reed & Barton Mss., Letters and invoices, 1837-39.

7. *Ibid.*

8. Reed & Barton Mss., Letter Book, 1839-49.

9. *Ibid.*

10. *Ibid.,* letter of Apr. 13, 1842.

11. Porter, "Metallic Sketches," chap. viii.

12. Timmins, *Resources, Products and Industrial History of Birmingham*, p. 704.

13. *Ibid.*

14. Porter's Notebook.

15. Porter, "Metallic Sketches," chap. ix.

16. *Ibid.*

17. U. S. Patent Office, *Report of the Commissioner of Patents for the Year 1858* (Washington, 1859), vol. i.

CHAPTER VII

1. Interview with Frank W. Knox, Feb. 7, 1942.

2. Porter's Notebook.

3. *Ibid.*

4. Reed & Barton Mss., Letter Book, 1849–64.

5. Prices paid by the company for tin increased roughly 53% from 1843 to 1859, and the index of wholesale prices in the United States advanced 20% (G. F. Warren and F. A. Pearson, *Wholesale Prices in the United States for 135 Years, 1797–1932*, Ithaca, N. Y., 1932, pp. 8–9). Over the same period, however, the average price charged by Reed & Barton for a 5-half-pint teapot increased from $2.26 to $2.86 or only about 11% (Reed & Barton Mss., Day Books, 1839–41, 1855–57).

6. Reed & Barton Mss., Employees' Pay Accounts, 1857–62.

7. *Ibid.*

8. Reed & Barton Mss., Polishing Pay Record, 1857–65.

9. Reed & Barton Mss., Burnishing Pay Record, 1857–60.

10. Reed & Barton Mss., Payroll, 1858–63.

11. Massachusetts Bureau of Statistics of Labor, *Sixteenth Annual Report, 1885* (Boston, 1885), p. 435.

12. *Ibid.*

13. Porter's Notebook.

14. Other Taunton companies seem to have followed Reed & Barton practices more or less closely in the matter of pay and general employee relationships, but some conditions existed in the vicinity which formed a graphic contrast to the freedom and independence of the Britannia workers under Henry G. Reed. The following account is an example:

"During Mr. Lothrop's ownership of Hopewell [a large textile mill near the Reed & Barton factory], he settled with the operatives about once a year, and in order to prevent any of the wages of the operatives being spent elsewhere than in the factory store, he maintained gates at the head of the lane leading to the factory, and on which the greater part of the factory tenements were located. Woe betide the enterprising grocery man or peddler of farm produce who was caught in the lane. The gates were locked, and he might consider himself a lucky man if he were allowed to depart with his team the next morning and not have to answer to the charge of trespassing." (*American Wool and Cotton Reporter*, vol. xiv, Nov. 29, 1900, p. 1454.)

15. Reed & Barton Mss., Payroll, 1858–63.
16. Reed & Barton Mss., Employees' Pay Accounts, 1857–62.
17. Porter, "Metallic Sketches," chap. vii.
18. Porter's Notebook.
19. Freedley, *Leading Pursuits and Leading Men,* 1856 edition, p. 405.

CHAPTER VIII

1. Gras and Larson, *Casebook in American Business History,* pp. 682 ff.
2. Reed & Barton Mss., Letter Book, 1839–49, letter of Sept. 29, 1841.
3. Reed & Barton Mss., Letter Book, 1839–49.
4. Reed & Barton Mss., Letters and invoices, 1837–39.
5. Reed & Barton Mss., Letter Book, 1839–49.
6. *Ibid.,* letter of Feb. 19, 1840.
7. Clark, *History of Manufactures,* vol. i, pp. 356–357.
8. Reed & Barton Mss., Letters and invoices, 1837–39.
9. Reed & Barton Mss., Letter Book, 1839–49.
10. *Ibid.*
11. Reed & Barton Mss., Letters and invoices, 1837–39.
12. Reed & Barton Mss., Letter Book, 1839–49.
13. Reed & Barton Mss., Letters and invoices, 1837–39.
14. Reed & Barton Mss., Letter Book, 1839–49.
15. *Ibid.*
16. *Ibid.* Corrected for obvious omissions in punctuation.
17. *Ibid.,* letter of Sept. 1, 1841.
18. *Ibid.,* letter of July 9, 1844.
19. Reed & Barton Mss., Letters and invoices, 1837–39.
20. Porter, "Metallic Sketches," chap. vii.
21. See Bishop, *History of American Manufactures,* vol. ii, p. 484.
22. Freedley, *Leading Pursuits and Leading Men,* 1856 edition, pp. 402–403.
23. *The Third Exhibition of the Massachusetts Charitable Mechanic Association, at Quincy Hall, in the City of Boston, September 20, 1841* (Boston, 1841), p. 52.
24. *Journal of the Franklin Institute,* Dec., 1845, p. 380.
25. Imports of Britannia ware into the United States for 12 months ending June 30 amounted to $11,479 in 1848; $17,272 in 1849; and $32,305 in 1850. Thereafter, imports steadily decreased. (U. S. Secretary of the Treasury, *Commerce and Navigation of the United States, 1848,* p. 195; *1849,* p. 201; *1850,* p. 201; and following years.)
26. Letter of Mr. W. G. Snow, historian of International Silver Company, to the author, Aug. 21, 1941.
27. *Ibid.*
28. Reed & Barton Mss., Letter Book, 1849–64, letter of Mar. 4, 1854.

CHAPTER IX

1. Gras & Larson, *Casebook in American Business History,* pp. 708–709.

2. The general index of wholesale prices declined from 174 in 1866 to 68 in 1897. Over the same period the index of prices of metals and metal products fell from 278 to 76. (Warren and Pearson, *Wholesale Prices,* pp. 9 and 98.)

3. Porter's Notebook.

4. Reed & Barton Mss., Letter Book, 1849–64.

5. Reed & Barton Mss. Estimate based on four months' figures.

6. Reed & Barton Mss.

7. Porter, "Metallic Sketches," chap. xii.

8. *Ibid.* The Porter Britannia and Plate Co. was organized in Taunton in 1859 by a group of local business men. E. W. Porter left Reed & Barton soon afterward to become superintendent of the new company. The line of wares manufactured was similar to those of Reed & Barton and was distributed through nearly identical trade channels.

9. Conversation with Mr. N. A. Cushman, June 26, 1942. Mr. Cushman, now retired, came to work for the company in 1877, serving in the shipping office and for many years having charge of all the company office work.

10. Porter, "Metallic Sketches," chap. xii.

11. Reed & Barton Mss., Order Book, 1865–66. Estimates based on sampling of customer accounts.

12. Porter's Notebook.

13. Reed & Barton Mss., Order Book, 1865–66.

14. Porter's Notebook.

15. Reed & Barton Mss., Notes and Bills Receivable, 1863–71.

16. Reed & Barton Mss., Letter Book, 1849–64.

17. *Ibid.*

18. *Ibid.*

19. Clark, *History of Manufactures,* vol. ii, p. 37.

20. Mr. W. G. Snow, conversation with the author, May 26, 1942.

21. Reed & Barton Mss., Order Book, 1865–66.

22. Porter, "Metallic Sketches," chap. xii.

23. Reed & Barton Mss.

24. *Ibid.,* letter of J. H. Rines dated Mar. 26, 1875.

25. Reed & Barton Mss.

26. *Ibid.,* Trial Balances, 1868–70.

27. *Annual Report of the American Institute, of the City of New York, for the Year 1867–68* (Albany, N. Y., 1868), p. 62.

28. *Thirtieth Annual Report of the American Institute, of the City of New York for the Year 1869–70* (Albany, N. Y., 1870), p. 24.

29. Reed & Barton Mss., Catalogue (undated).

30. Reed & Barton Mss., Catalogue of 1885.

31. Reed & Barton Mss., Letters and invoices.
32. Reed & Barton Mss., Notes and Bills Receivable, 1863–71.
33. Gras and Larson, *op. cit.,* p. 716.
34. Porter's Notebook.
35. Reed & Barton Mss.
36. *Jewelers' Circular and Horological Review,* 1876–77.
37. Typical of the more formal and binding efforts to control competition at this time was Rockefeller's Standard Oil Trust, which dated from the early 1870's. Centralized ownership, interlocking directorates, legalized agreements all played a part in building rigidly enforced combinations to control competition. Important trusts were formed in the lead, cotton-oil, sugar, and cattle industries. On a less binding basis trade associations were organized in great numbers throughout the 1870's, including the following: Silk Association of America, 1872; Carriage Builders' National Association, 1872; American Bankers Association, 1875; American Paper and Pulp Association, 1878. (U. S. Dept. of Commerce, *Trade Association Activities,* 1923 ed., Washington, 1923, p. 305.) The American Iron & Steel Association was organized as early as 1864, and many local associations were formed in this industry with the object of establishing uniform prices and rates of wages (Clark, *op. cit.,* vol. ii, pp. 280–283).
38. Reed & Barton Mss., Letter Book, Mar.–June, 1878.
39. In the 12 months ending June 1, 1870, the value of plated wares manufactured by 161 establishments in New England, New York, and Pennsylvania was $7,533,401 (Ninth Census, June 1, 1870, vol. iii, *Statistics of the Wealth and Industry of the United States . . . ,* Washington, 1872, p. 467). Ten years later the value of plated and Britannia wares manufactured by 48 establishments in those States was $8,313,681 (*Report on the Manufactures of the United States at the Tenth Census (June 1, 1880),* Washington, 1883, p. 65).
40. Reed & Barton Mss.
41. *Ibid.,* Scrapbook.
42. Reed & Barton Mss.
43. *Ibid.,* letter from J. H. Rines.

CHAPTER X

1. Burleigh [pseud.], Matthew Hale Smith, *The Old Colony Railroad: Its Connections, Popular Resorts, and Fashionable Watering Places* (Boston, 1874), pp. 3–4.
2. Conversation with Mr. Joseph H. Martin, vice-president in charge of sales, Reed & Barton, June 19, 1942.
3. *Jewelers' Circ. and Horol. Rev.,* Sept., 1883, p. 260.
4. Reed & Barton Mss., Letter Book, 1902–03, letter of Aug. 27, 1902.
5. *Standard & Poor's Trade and Securities: Basic Statistics* [Oct, 1942], p. 147.

6. New York *Herald,* July 29, 1894.

7. *Ibid.*

8. Conversation with Mr. N. A. Cushman, Jan. 28, 1941.

9. Reed & Barton Mss., Letter Book, 1902–03, letter of Apr. 5, 1903.

10. *Ibid.,* letter of Feb. 14, 1903.

11. Conversation with Mr. N. A. Cushman, Jan. 28, 1941.

12. Joseph H. Martin, Reminiscences of the Old Guard and Events of Their Day (unpublished); Porter, "Metallic Sketches," chap. xiii.

13. Reed & Barton Mss., Ledger, 1888–94.

14. *Ibid.*

15. Conversation with Mr. W. G. Snow, May 26, 1942.

16. Reed & Barton Mss., Ledger, 1894–1902.

CHAPTER XI

1. For certain incidents and descriptions in this section the author is indebted to Mr. J. H. Martin.

2. Reed & Barton Mss., Employees' Pay Accounts, 1873–80.

3. *Ibid.*

4. Reed & Barton Mss., Payroll No. 2, 1882–88.

5. Material in this paragraph is taken from Martin's Reminiscences of the Old Guard.

6. *Jewelers' Circ. and Horol. Rev.,* June, 1877.

7. U. S. Treasury Department, Bureau of Statistics, *Monthly Summary of Commerce and Finance of the United States,* April, 1903, pp. 3316–3317.

8. Reed & Barton Mss., Letter Book, 1901–02.

9. Reed & Barton Mss., notes in back of Foreign Orders, 1901–02.

10. U. S. Department of State, Bureau of Foreign Commerce, Special Consular Reports, vol. xxiii, part 2, *Silver and Plated Ware in Foreign Countries* (Washington, 1902).

11. *Ibid.,* p. 335.

12. *Ibid.,* p. 341.

13. *Ibid.,* p. 230.

14. *Ibid.,* p. 338.

15. *Ibid.,* pp. 335, 290, 195, 232.

CHAPTER XII

1. Allan Nevins, *The Emergence of Modern America* (New York, 1927), chap. ix; Gardner, *Art through the Ages,* pp. 673, 683.

2. George Frank Jackson, "Works in the Precious Metals, Electroplate, &c," in *Artisans' Reports upon the Vienna Exposition,* 1873, published by the Society for the Promotion of Scientific Industry (Manchester, England, 1873), p. 46.

3. Albert S. Bolles, *Industrial History of the United States from the Earliest Settlements to the Present Time* (Norwich, Conn., 1879), p. 339.

4. Nevins, *op. cit.,* chap. vii.

5. James Bryce, *The American Commonwealth* (New York, 1927), vol. ii, pp. 826 ff.

6. Jackson, *op. cit.,* p. 46.

7. *Jewelers' Circ. and Horol. Rev.,* Sept., 1885, p. 250.

8. *Annual Report of the Commissioner of Patents for the Year 1869,* and following years.

9. Reed & Barton Mss., Book of miscellaneous payroll records, 1863–95.

10. *Jewelers' Circ. & Horol. Rev.,* July, 1881, p. 133.

11. Substantial proof of the high esteem in which Reed & Barton products were held during these years is provided by periodical and newspaper references to the company which appeared in great numbers throughout the 1870's and '80's (Reed & Barton Mss., Scrapbook). The quality of the company's wares requires no comment; what is most significant about the profuse contemporary praise is that so much of it was directed at the designs of those wares. Clearly, the company's efforts in the comparatively new field of original style creation was bringing immediate and very satisfying returns.

12. Mr. J. H. Martin, conversation with the author, July 12, 1942.

13. Reed & Barton Mss., Payroll and Rates, 1883–97.

14. Newspaper article by Margaret F. Sullivan, Paris, May 11, 1889, copyrighted by the New York Associated Press, found in Reed & Barton Mss., Scrapbook.

15. Reed & Barton Mss., Catalogue.

16. Reed & Barton Mss., Payroll and Rates, 1883–97.

17. *Jewelers' Circ. & Horol. Rev.,* July 3, 1895, p. 5.

18. These were not Mr. Howe's only contributions to the company. He also invented "Argentala," a superior grade of silver polish which enjoyed widespread market popularity.

19. Reed & Barton Mss., letter to Reed & Barton, August 20, 1868.

20. *Jewelers' Circ. & Horol. Rev.,* May, 1885, pp. 114–115.

21. Mr. David Howe, conversation with the author, Jan. 27, 1941.

22. The contrast between burnishing and buffing may be explained in the following terms: "Burnishing is an important operation for electro deposits, which consist of a multitude of small crystals, with intervals between them, and with facets reflecting the light in every direction. The deposited metal is hardened and forced into the pores of the underlying metal, and the durability is thus increased to such an extent that, with the same amount of silver, a burnished article will last twice as long as one which has not been so treated." (*Jewelers' Circ. & Horol. Rev.,* May, 1882, vol. xiii, no. 4). Buffing, on the other hand, removes with a flexible abrasive wheel of hide the outer layer of metal, exposing a shiny undersurface but imparting no additional hardness thereto.

23. Clark, *History of Manufactures,* vol. ii, chap. xxx.
24. *Ibid.,* p. 360.
25. *Ibid.,* pp. 364–365.
26. U. S. Letters Patent, No. 112,077, dated Feb. 21, 1871.
27. U. S. Letters Patent, No. 111,086, dated Jan. 17, 1871.
28. "The American at Work, IV: Among the Silver-Platers," by Randolph T. Percy, *Appleton's Journal,* New Series, no. 30 (Dec., 1878), p. 491.
29. *Annual Report of the Commissioner of Patents . . . 1868,* vol. ii, p. 192.
30. Mr. B. P. Minchew, son of Charles, and retired Reed & Barton plating-room boss, conversation with the author, Jan. 28, 1941.
31. *Jewelers' Circ. & Horol. Rev.,* Apr. 10, 1895.
32. *Scientific American,* vol. vi, no. 26, New Series (June 28, 1862), p. 408.
33. U. S. Letters Patent, Nos. 533,382 and 533,383, dated Jan. 29, 1895.
34. U. S. Patent Office, *Official Gazette,* June 28, 1898, vol. 83, no. 13, p. 1809. Patent No. 606,183.
35. Mr. N. A. Cushman, conversation with the author, July 17, 1942.
36. Reed & Barton Mss., Trial Balances, 1854–57, 1863–64, 1868–70.
37. Reed & Barton Mss., Ledgers, 1888–94, 1894–1902.
38. Martin, Reminiscences of the Old Guard.

CHAPTER XIII

1. Martin, Reminiscences of the Old Guard.
2. Porter, "Metallic Sketches," chap. xi.
3. Reed & Barton Mss., Ledger, 1894–1902.
4. Reed & Barton Mss., Notebook giving wage rates, 1870–71.
5. *Ibid.* and 1871–92.
6. *Ibid.*
7. Mass. Bureau of Statistics of Labor, *Report of the Bureau of Statistics of Labor, Embracing the Account of Its Operations and Inquiries from August 2, 1869, to March 1, 1870, Inclusive, Being the First Seven Months Since Its Organization* (Boston, 1870), pp. 223–234, 287–298.
8. *Ibid.,* pp. 268–270.
9. Martin, *op. cit.*
10. *Ibid.*
11. *Ibid.*
12. *Ibid.*
13. Mr. David Howe, interview with the author, Jan. 28, 1941.
14. Taunton *Daily Gazette,* June 11, 1895. (See also June 7 issue.)
15. Martin, *op. cit.*
16. *Abstract of the Census of the Commonwealth of Massachusetts, Taken with Reference to Facts Existing on the First Day of June, 1855* (Boston, 1857), p. 102.

17. Massachusetts Bureau of Statistics of Labor, *Report . . . Aug. 2, 1869 to Mar. 1, 1870*, pp. 387–388.

18. The principal transfer of funds was effected by means of a five-year mortgage for $90,000, given Amanda Barton by the firm in February, 1868. By March, 1870, the mortgage terms had been fulfilled and the deed discharged (Register of Deeds, Bristol County, Mass., vol. 290, p. 455).

19. Reed & Barton paid Amanda Barton $17,964.86 in return for the two-twelfths interest of Barton's son and daughter in the business, and for the right to use the Barton name (Register of Deeds, Bristol County, Mass., vol. 290, p. 469).

20. Reed & Barton Mss.

21. Record of Reed & Barton Stockholders' Meetings.

22. Reed & Barton Mss.

23. *Ibid.*, Trial Balances, 1863–64 and 1868–70.

24. *Ibid.*

25. Mr. N. A. Cushman, interview with author, Jan. 28, 1941.

26. Reed & Barton Mss., Ledger, 1888–94.

27. *Ibid.*

28. *Ibid.*

29. *Ibid.*

30. Reed & Barton Mss., Ledger, 1894–1902.

31. *Ibid.*

32. *Ibid.*

33. *Ibid.*

CHAPTER XIV

1. The creation of a trust for the purpose of holding the estate together is, in itself, an interesting commentary upon company finances at the time. Throughout the 1890's Reed's endorsement had been necessary upon all notes and outstanding obligations of Reed & Barton. After his death, in order to renew these notes and to discount such paper as was necessary for the continuance of the business, the endorsement of the Reed estate was indispensable. Accordingly, a trust was created through which endorsements could be procured and further financial support assured for the company.

2. Mr. C. E. Almy, conversation with the author, July 10, 1942.

3. Quoted by Frank W. Knox in conversation with the author, Dec., 1941.

4. Report of Percy M. Blake to W. B. H. Dowse, Nov. 26, 1901.

5. Mr. Mark Anthony, general manager under William Dowse, letter to author, Mar. 31, 1943.

6. Reed & Barton Mss., Letter from George Brabrook to the Reed & Barton Corporation.

7. Minutes of Directors' Meetings, Reed & Barton, May 29, 1907.

8. *Northeastern Reporter*, vol. 85, p. 433; 199 *Massachusetts Reports* 371.

9. Records of the Supreme Judicial Court for Suffolk County, Massachusetts, The Silversmiths Company vs. Reed & Barton Corporation and William B. H. Dowse, Petition for Writ of Mandamus.

CHAPTER XV

1. Reed & Barton Mss., Letters from George Carlton Comstock to Henry Reed, 1894.
2. Reed & Barton Mss., Ledger, 1902–09.
3. Reed & Barton Co., Fifth Avenue, New York, catalogue of 1905.
4. Reed & Barton Mss., Ledger, 1902–09.
5. Mr. J. H. Martin, conversation with the author, June 26, 1942.
6. Frank W. Knox, Mr. N. A. Cushman, Mr. J. H. Martin, conversations with the author; Records of the Supreme Judicial Court for Suffolk County, Mass., The Silversmiths Company vs. Reed & Barton Corporation and William B. H. Dowse, Petition for Writ of Mandamus.
7. Minutes of Directors' Meetings, Reed & Barton Co., New York.
8. Mr. C. E. Almy, letter to the author, Oct. 27, 1942.
9. *Ibid.*; Mr. Alex K. Clifford, letter to Mr. J. H. Martin, Oct. 31, 1942.
10. Mr. J. H. Martin, conversation with the author, June 26, 1942.
11. Mr. Mark Anthony, conversation with the author, July 30, 1942.
12. Martin, Reminiscences of the Old Guard.
13. Mr. N. A. Cushman, conversation with the author, June 18, 1942.
14. *Ibid.*
15. Mr. J. H. Martin, letter to the author, Nov. 3, 1942.
16. Reed & Barton Mss., catalogue No. 22.
17. Martin, *op. cit.*
18. Mr. J. H. Martin, letter to the author, Nov. 3, 1942.
19. Letter from Morse International Agency to W. B. H. Dowse, Jan. 18, 1909.
20. Mr. Mark Anthony, letter to the author, Mar. 31, 1943.

CHAPTER XVI

1. Reed & Barton Mss., Ledgers, 1902–1909.
2. Minutes of Directors' Meetings, Reed & Barton, Sept. 25, 1916.
3. Material in the following paragraphs is taken from Reed & Barton Mss., Ledgers, 1902–24.
4. Martin, Reminiscences of the Old Guard.
5. Reed & Barton Mss., Ledgers, 1902–24.
6. *Ibid.*
7. *Ibid.*
8. Minutes of Directors' Meetings, Reed & Barton, Feb. 15, 1910.
9. Mr. Mark Anthony, conversation with the author, July 30, 1942.

CHAPTER XVII

1. From this point onward, many of the facts have been obtained through conversation with the company's executives and from its annual financial statements.

2. Martin, Reminiscences of the Old Guard.

3. Mr. J. H. Martin, Letter to the author, Nov. 3, 1942.

INDEX

INDEX